THE POWER TO BREAK FREE

Surviving Domestic Violence

With a Special Reference to Abuse in Indian Marriages

By Anisha Durve, A.P.
Acupuncture Physician

Jyotsna Auntie,

Thank you for your support & standing up for this cause.

— Anisha

Power Press LLC
Cleveland, Ohio
Copyright © 2012 by Anisha Durve

All rights reserved. No part of this book may be reproduced, scanned, or distributed in any form by any electronic or mechanical means, including information storage and retrieval systems, without permission in writing from the author. Please respect the author's rights and do not participate in piracy of copyrighted material.

Disclaimer: The names of people and places mentioned in this book have been changed to protect the privacy of all individuals involved.

Printed in the U.S.A.
Edited by Marielle Marne.
Cover design by Anisha Durve.
Book layout design by Anisha Durve.

Library of Congress Control Number: 2011944343

ISBN: 978-0-9848923-0-3

For more information on The Power to Break Free Foundation,
visit our website www.Power2BreakFree.com.

A portion of the proceeds from this book are donated
to supporting the work of this foundation.

Other Books by Anisha Durve

MARMA POINTS OF AYURVEDA:
The Energy Pathways for Healing Body, Mind, and Consciousness
with a Comparison to Traditional Chinese Medicine
2008 Co-authored by Dr. Vasant Lad
Available at www.Ayurveda.com

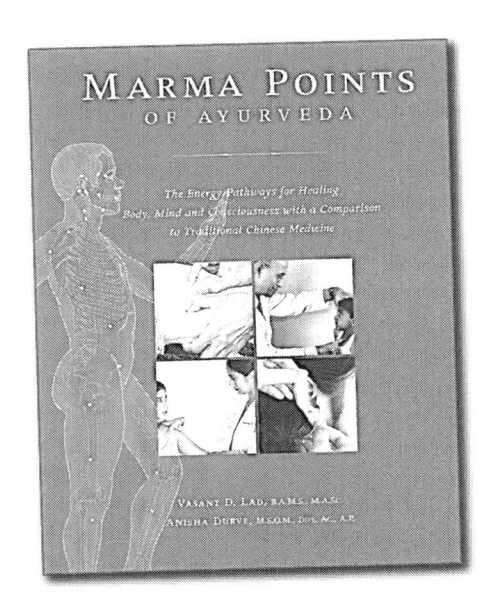

Table of Contents

Prayer for Peace	vi
Mission Statement	vii
Dedication	viii
Gratitude	ix
Foreword	x
Preface	xii
Note to Readers	xiv

PART 1 The Psychology of Abuse

Chapter 1 Shattering the Ideals of Marriage	1
Chapter 2 Shedding Light on Abuse	11
Chapter 3 Recognizing Signs of Abuse	21
Chapter 4 Cycle of Violence	35
Chapter 5 The Creation of an Abuser	47
Chapter 6 The Abuser's Inner World	57
Chapter 7 The Abuser's Outer World	63
Chapter 8 The Creation of a Victim	75
Chapter 9 Layers of a Victim's Wounding	89
Chapter 10 Perpetuation of Abuse	101
Chapter 11 Challenges of Separation	111
Chapter 12 Role & Support of Community	119
Chapter 13 Seven Levels of Community Influence	133
Chapter 14 Community's Call to Action	147
Chapter 15 Stages of Breaking Free	157
Chapter 16 Healing & Recovery	169

Table of Contents

PART 2 My Fight for Freedom

Chapter 17 The Promise of Love	*183*
Chapter 18 Life as Newlyweds	*191*
Chapter 19 Destiny Beckons	*199*
Chapter 20 Endless Battles	*207*
Chapter 21 Keeping the Secret	*215*
Chapter 22 Time Apart	*221*
Chapter 23 Turning Point	*231*
Chapter 24 Dawning of Clarity	*243*
Chapter 25 Waking From a Nightmare	*257*
Chapter 26 Calm Before the Storm	*269*
Chapter 27 Eyes Wide Open	*279*
Chapter 28 At War	*291*
Chapter 29 My Internal Battle	*299*
Chapter 30 My Liberation	*311*
Afterword	*318*

PART 3 Voices of Indian Women

Chapter 31 Devi's Devastation	*323*
Chapter 32 Radha's Redemption	*333*
Chapter 33 Sita's Shackles	*343*
Chapter 34 Lakshmi's Loss	*353*
Chapter 35 Gayatri's Glory	*363*
Chapter 36 The Indian Victim & Karma	*373*

Power to Break Free Companion Workbook	*378*
Appendix 1 Statistics on Domestic Violence	*379*
Appendix 2 Timeline & History of DV Movement	*386*
Appendix 3 South Asian Organizations' Timeline	*388*
Bibliography	*390*
References	*392*

Prayer for Peace

सर्वे भवन्तु सुखिनः
सर्वे सनतु निरामया
सर्वे भद्राणि पश्यन्तु
मा कश्चिद्दुःखभाग्भवेत्
ॐ शान्ति शान्ति शान्तिः

Sarve bhavantu sukhinaha
Sarve santu niramaya
Sarve bhadrani pasyantu
Ma kascit dukha bhag bhavet
Om shanti shanti shanti

Let all beings be happy
Let all beings be free from disease
Let no one suffer from misery
Om peace peace peace

Mission Statement

To inspire, empower, and liberate women

escaping from gender violence

and fuel them with the awareness

they possess the power to break free.

The Power to Break Free Foundation has a visionary approach
and strategy to address and eradicate gender violence.
It strives to provide education and outreach to established
domestic violence organizations and women's groups,
healing workshops and seminars for victims and survivors,
and focus on prevention for young girls worldwide.

Please visit our website at www.Power2BreakFree.com
for more information on how you can make a difference now.

Dedication

To the amazing women who have shaped my life:

Tara Jagannath Durve: my paternal grandmother, for her fearless spirit and determination to not let tradition stand in her way or allow anything to hold her back. She admirably fought for her passion, true love, and education at a time when women were not allowed a voice. She is a role model for women of every generation.

Vijaya Vinayak Gupte: my maternal grandmother, for being the embodiment of grace and compassion. Every moment of her life was a testimony to the purity of love in her heart as she showered us with affection. She taught us true spiritual power comes from love and devotion.

Jayshree Mohan Durve: my devoted mother with a heart of gold, your steadfastness and self-sacrifice in every moment of your life are remarkable. It is your love that guides us, fills us, inspires us, and makes my sisters and me who we are.

Anuja: sister of my soul, your essence is pure; your power knows no bounds; and your beauty touches all who meet you. We are kindred spirits whose thirst and passion for ancient wisdom runs deep within us. You are a beacon of knowledge I strive to follow and emulate.

Namita: sister of my heart, your strength and bravery in the face of life and death has shown me how to be courageous and persevere in my darkest moments. You are such a blessing to our family. Your sweetness knows no bounds and your gracious heart inspires me every day.

❖

And, last but not least, to all the women who have not had a voice or lived to tell your tale, we hear your cries of suffering.

To all the women who have yet to break free... may you choose freedom.

Gratitude

My incredible parents: thank you for being the bright flame of illumination to lead me through the darkest stage of my life and giving me the freedom to make my own choices, standing by me no matter what, and encouraging me to write this book.

My beautiful loving sisters: you are the best gift Mom and Dad ever gave me. It is a blessing and a privilege to have you both in my life. I cherish your unconditional love that has allowed me to heal.

Anita: thank you for being the beacon of inspiration to cross to the other shore, show me it is never too late to make this journey towards freedom, and being there every step of the way.

Sheree: your guiding voice, so pure, clear, and strong, kept me going. Your ability to shift awareness with precision and eloquence offered me my first glimpse of freedom and the knowledge it could be mine.

Lundy Bancroft: it is true that reading one book can change your life. Your brilliant work allowed me to lucidly see my imprisonment for the first time and encourage me to break the destructive pattern in which I was trapped.

All my amazing girlfriends who supported me through this challenging time and helped me discover myself again: you know who you are. Your friendship means the world to me. You have no idea how much every simple act of kindness profoundly touched my heart. A special thanks to my cousin Mayura, Anjali, Devi, Rita, Bhavi, and all those who patiently and enthusiastically assisted in reviewing my manuscript.

Marielle: for going above and beyond the duties of an editor. Your encouragement and belief in the power of this work has truly been inspiring.

Interviewees: To all the women who shared their stories, bared their souls, and exposed their suffering, thank you for breaking your silence.

To the ex: Of course, I feel no gratitude. My heart will never allow me to forgive you for your cruelty when I only showered you with love and kindness. My only wish is that you may finally find the courage to face yourself, look in the mirror, and see the truth of who you are. That is the only way you will begin to heal yourself and learn how to find peace within. May you also find freedom from your suffering.

Foreword

Is it true being born a girl is a curse in many countries around the world? Must a woman always pay the price for being a woman? Will she always be considered a commodity to be passed over, a slave for hire, or property to be possessed, transferred, and owned? Although today more women are marrying when they have established and earned identities of their own, for a significant majority of invisible women around the globe who do not have the resources to fight this evil, life remains the same as it was centuries ago. There is an impression within society, one that women will suffer and not complain due to a sense of shame, a sense of victimization, and social taboos. She will not air her grievances, report the perpetrators who have committed crimes against her, or speak out against these social evils.

How do these concepts perpetuate the bondage of women in abusive relationships? What are the harsh realities of the economics of family violence? The "India crime clock" on women is ticking at an alarming rate: one woman is beaten every minute, one dowry death occurs every 77 minutes, and one act of cruelty against a woman is reported every nine minutes. On an international scale, India stands third on abuse of women, with 45% admitting to suffering. The Protection of Women from Domestic Violence Act passed in India in 2005 is not enough to combat this social injustice. Everyone wants to look the other way but domestic violence will not end until we stare it in the eye, see it for what it is, and take a stand. The time to take action is now.

Respect for women is one of the many nonnegotiable demands of human dignity and should become integral to our whole way of living and thinking. Girls need to be given equal opportunities to grow and be valued for their skills, abilities, and contributions to community development so society can grow as a whole. We can invest in the welfare of humankind by speaking up for the invisible and the voiceless, whatever the injustice. In the end, the true victims of domestic violence are not simply the women who have suffered, but also their children, their families, and their communities who are deprived of their vital contributions.

Anisha Durve's work, *The Power to Break Free*, is a tremendous and timely contribution to dispelling ignorance surrounding domestic violence. It is the first book to address the cultural nuances of abuse within Indian and South Asian communities from the perspective of a survivor. Her own remarkable story to break free along with moving firsthand accounts of other victims demonstrate why leaving a perpetrator is no easy undertaking. From her own experience, Anisha reveals her conflicts over not seeking help and the unexpected responses when she finally did. Now fighting back, she gathers statistics, reports, and accounts of other victims to help those who are ready to stand up to their abusers and reclaim their voices.

The Power to Break Free empowers women to liberate themselves from their abusive environments. It educates, it empathizes, it reminds us that victims should feel no shame. For Indian victims, it offers guidance in overcoming their cultural upbringing to suffer in silence, endure their husband's mistreatment, and avoid divorce to preserve the family unit. There is excellent advice and inspiration for victims of any cultural background to learn how to overcome domestic violence. This powerful book is not only for women who are being abused, were abused, or know a victim of abuse. *The Power to Break Free* is for anyone who believes domestic violence must end now!

Kiran Bedi
New Delhi, India
January 2012

Preface

Many of us avoid discussing the dark, unpleasant, and uncomfortable subject of domestic violence based on one simple principle: *out of sight, out of mind*. In our ignorance, we fail to appreciate this topic affects all of us when we expand our definition of family and community. It is easy to turn a blind eye at first, but when it affects our mothers, our sisters, our daughters, or ourselves, we realize it is real; it is cruel; and it claims innocent lives. The rich intricate tapestry of human life binds every heart and each spirit in the most delicate and profound way, connecting us through our suffering.

How many lives will be lost before we become cognizant of these global atrocities that occur every minute of every day? In the U.S. alone, a woman is victimized every twelve seconds. The epidemic of gender violence is the most preventable of all social injustices. We simply cannot afford to ignore these facts, especially when we have the ability to prohibit these crimes from being committed against innocent women and children and tearing apart families. If we do nothing actively to stop the violence, *we are* guilty of perpetuating the crime.

It is vital to raise public awareness of these issues and revolutionize the field of gender violence by initiating change at every level of society: family and friends, therapists and social workers, religious leaders and groups, shelters and agencies, medical personnel and caregivers, the legal system and law enforcement. We can prevent this injustice if every young woman is well informed before entering into a relationship as to the specific red flags of which to be aware, how to trust her instincts, and the importance of asking for help. Victims should be empowered to recognize when they cannot change the dynamic of their unhealthy relationships and leave when their safety is compromised. For all the women who feel trapped in their abusive environments, we *always* have a choice. We *can* find the courage to escape. Freedom is around the corner...

❖

I have chosen to tell my tale, because after surrendering my voice for seven years, I can no longer remain silent. The price of not sharing my story, not reaching out to other women who are suffering untold horrors, and not letting the world know what is at stake is simply too high. At my darkest moment of intense suffering, I made the decision to be the voice for all the victims who never had a chance to express themselves, the opportunity to share their pain so others could learn from their misfortune, or live to tell their tales.

In my mind, I was the last person who could ever become a victim of abuse. I was strong, confident, independent, well educated, and from a respectable family. I believed in fighting for women's rights and violence should *never* be tolerated. How then could this happen to me? I realized if I could be victimized, then anyone could. My quest to answer this burning question that every victim asks herself was all-consuming. I needed to uncover the psychology of abuse, expose the mysteries and ignorance behind it, and decipher the precise steps that led to my victimization. Despite researching numerous informative books on the topic, I believe the perspective of survivors is essential to offer new awareness and insight on the field of domestic violence.

    I was not keen on sharing my private struggles of abuse with the world, but I reasoned if my story could be the catalyst to awaken other victims and set them free, it was worth my personal sacrifice. For the women who live in a world of confusion, unable to decipher their partner's manipulative behavior, hopefully they will see their reflection in my story and begin to identify their victimization. So, I share with you my wavering mind and oscillation between hope and despair only to make you aware of the real inner world of the victim. I expose my wounds to not only reveal my fragility, but also demonstrate my strength and resiliency.

    A part of me died during my abusive marriage that I will never recover, years of my life I will never regain. But when something perishes within us, something else is born. My passion to fight for life, freedom, and basic human rights has been ignited with an undeniable vigor and vitality. I hope my story will make society aware of the depth of torment we can experience at the deceptive hands of someone we love and trust. It is my humble wish this book will inspire you to act as part of the global family, take action on behalf of victims everywhere, and do your vital part in the fight to eradicate domestic violence that can end when we *choose* to end it.

Note to Readers

Domestic violence, hereinafter referred to as DV, is a crime that primarily affects women and so the victim is referred to in the feminine gender throughout this text. Although she can be in either a heterosexual or homosexual relationship, the perpetrator is denoted in the masculine gender. All victims, regardless of their ethnicity, are addressed, but there are subtleties and nuances of how abuse plays out within different cultural contexts. Developing sensitivity to these subgroups is essential.

There are distinctive issues, for example, in the South Asian population which is inclusive of people originating from India, Bangladesh, Nepal, Bhutan, Pakistan, Sri Lanka, Maldives, and diasporic communities such as Fiji and the Caribbean. Even within this collective, there are variations within each subgroup. I distinctly focus on the plight of the Indian Hindu woman to later shed light on my own personal story. Other South Asian victims who do not identify with being Hindu will still relate to common cultural themes that overlap with their experiences.

Part 1 reveals the complex psychology of abuse with groundbreaking information that has never yet been presented in this field. Chapters 1-4 define abuse, identify its various forms, signs, and manifestations, dispel society's ignorant myths and misperceptions, and elucidate the intricacies of the newly revised cycle of violence. Chapters 5-7 elucidate the systematic creation of an abuser and how his abusive personality is shaped by his inner world of thoughts and emotions and his outer world of duplicity, manipulation, and deception. Chapters 8-11 explore the step-by-step creation of a victim, her role in co-creating and perpetuating abuse, layers of her wounding, and the challenges of separation.

Chapters 12-14 explain the fundamental role of all seven levels of the community in how to support a victim and hold an abuser accountable. Chapter 15 discusses the five stages a victim must pass through to break free while Chapter 16 expounds on her profound journey of healing and recovery to finally liberate her from the vicious cycle of violence. I am not a psychologist, nor an expert on the field of DV, but I humbly offer my deep insight and perspective as a survivor. Because I can only speak from my own experience, I do not delve into topics such as sexual abuse or abuse of children, although these are significant issues.

Part 2 describes my victimization in my seven-year abusive marriage. I describe the insidious way violence crept into my life, my difficulty in recognizing I was in fact a victim, and my mental paralysis preventing me from taking action. After overcoming my isolation, silence, and secrecy, I reveal the obstacles faced in reaching out to the Indian community, my battles with the legal system in the fight for justice, and my long journey to heal and reclaim my freedom.

Part 3 documents the brave voices of Indian women who are survivors and courageously opened up to share their stories. Their tales reflect the common themes of abuse that play out within the South Asian community as well as the recipe for victimization that is common to all women who experience DV. Every poignant story offers insight and inspiration.

As a reader, I ask you to resist the temptation to bring your preconceived notions about abuse and victimization with you while reading this book. Just for a moment, place yourselves in the position of a victim. See what she sees, feel what she feels, and experience the world from her vantage point. It is only by doing so that you will empathize with her suffering, deepen your compassion for her journey, and open your heart to her struggle to find freedom.

❖

Disclaimer:

The names of people and places mentioned in this book have been changed to protect the privacy of all individuals involved.

www.mapsofworld.com

PART 1

THE PSYCHOLOGY OF ABUSE

CHAPTER 1 SHATTERING THE IDEALS OF MARRIAGE

Freedom and love go together. Jiddu Krishnamurti

Deep within a woman's heart, she holds the hope of finding true love. Young girls often cherish this ideal and eagerly await the day they will meet their soul mate and best friend to marry. In Indian culture, the concept of marriage is more than a romantic notion. It is accepted that multiple factors are involved in choosing the right partner and love will come later in the marriage. Indians marry not for love necessarily, but to ensure a successful alliance.

The old adage, *"marriage comes first, love comes second,"* is drilled into young minds. Although this concept may be difficult for Westerners to comprehend, it is readily accepted by the Indian mind. Ultimately, marriage is not simply a union between husband and wife, but more importantly a contract between both families. Grasping the significance of this contract and the types of marriages in Indian culture is essential to later understand the implications of their dissolution.

Arranged, Introduced, & Love Marriages

Sustainability, the hallmark of Indian marriages, is based upon selecting a suitable mate who will allow the family lineage to flourish. The tradition of arranged marriages, which has existed for centuries, upholds this idea of union to foster strong alliances so as to ensure stability and security for generations to come, sometimes for the sole purpose of increasing social and economic prospects.

Relying on the wisdom of elder family members, the prospective groom is examined along with his family. Countless criteria are considered: the groom's age, height, education, caste, family background and values, appearance, fairness of skin color, health, religious nature, career, reputation, social and financial standings. A woman's beauty will be prized the more closely she resembles the fair-skinned Bollywood film actresses who are the Indian epitome of attractiveness. Roughly 95% of marriages in India continue to be arranged.[1]

In ancient India, the tradition of *swayamvara* was when parents announced the intention to have their daughter wed and invited potential suitors to attend a competition. The girl would garland the suitor she most fancied. In medieval India, *gandharva* marriages required the mutual consent of both parties. "As the Vedic religion evolved into classic, orthodox Hinduism, …society moved towards patriarchy and caste-based rules. Women were stripped of their traditional independence... It is at this time in India that arranged marriages rose to prominence in 500 B.C.E."[2]

This concept of arranged marriage has evolved with each subsequent generation and especially with the Indian diaspora to the West. It is unusual now to see alliances solely determined by the families for their benefit without the couple meeting before the wedding day. More commonly, an Indian woman is allowed to meet a prospective groom a few times and there is greater flexibility to meet several suitors and choose one who is acceptable.

More often than not, the groom possesses more power in selecting a mate and may reject many girls before he opts for one he fancies, while the bride has less ability to be so discriminating and reject a potential suitor if she is chosen since family pressure to accept him will be strong. This process can last anywhere from a few days to several months or years depending on the family's preference for the timing of the marriage. In contrast, "love marriages" occur when bride and groom mutually select each other without any family involvement. Although historically this is not common and statistically constitutes 5% of marriages in India, the frequency of this type of union has increased with second-generation Indians in the West.

With the evolution of the concept of arranged marriages abroad, a more popular term is "introduced marriages" where the couple is set up by family or friends for the purpose of meeting for betrothal, however, they are free to reject each other. This is similar to a blind date except the intention is to discuss marriage. After being introduced, some couples may choose to date for a period of time to get to know each other before their engagement.

For many, the idea of marrying a non-Indian is not considered a viable option due to parental expectations. Roughly more than 50% of second-generation Indians growing up in the U.S. still choose to marry Indians reflecting the pervasive ingrained belief that marrying within the community will guarantee a more stable long-term marriage. There is currently no data to show what percentage of these marriages are arranged, introduced, or for love.

The Business of Marriage

These ideas may seem foreign to Westerners, but marriage, in essence, is viewed as a business transaction. The marriage industry involves several methods of matchmaking. Matrimonial ads describing appearance and qualifications are placed in newspapers or more recently posted on matrimony websites. Matchmakers or marriage brokers have lists of potential brides and grooms from which families can peruse. Vedic astrologers are consulted to determine promising periods for alliances, compare charts of the potential bride and groom for compatibility, and fix an auspicious marriage date and time if the match is deemed favorable.

Immigration to the West has created variations to the theme of arranged marriages. Men who have either immigrated or grown up in the U.S. will travel to India to "shop" for traditional girls who more closely resemble Indian ideals. They may return to the U.S. within a week or two with their overseas brides who leave behind their families and the only lives they have known. Finding a groom who is a U.S. citizen is considered a promising match, allowing a bride's family to increase their societal status and often be viewed with envy.

Indians take pride in holding the lowest divorce rate globally at 1.1% compared with the U.S. at 54.8%.[3] This statistic demonstrates the inherent sense of trust and the prevailing Indian mindset of making a marriage work that has allowed the arranged marriage system to thrive and prove sustainable for centuries. Until the last two decades, it was rare to hear of divorce within the community.

Indian parents, burdened by the responsibility of fulfilling their duty, feel the pressure to marry off their daughters as soon as possible, although the same is not true of sons. If a daughter is still unmarried in her early twenties, she is considered a burden on the family and the stigma of being single or undesirable can persist, decreasing her eligibility to attract a decent husband. If she is married after the age of 25, it is considered a "late" marriage, but in America, this label has been delayed for those who are 30 years of age if not older.

Despite the trend of the current generation to wait until their thirties and focus on educational pursuits and careers, experiment with dating, and not rush into marriages, the unspoken pressure for early marriages persists. This cultural conditioning should be examined so the emphasis is finding a truly compatible partner instead of rushing into a quick decision to be "settled" early.

Limitations of Matchmaking

Despite the creation of many successful alliances, several drawbacks to the arranged marriage system should be noted. In *Speaking the Unspeakable*, Abraham says: "The very process of selecting a mate, especially in arranged marriages, often exhibits women's lower status and role in society."[4] The entire matchmaking process can be degrading as women suffer rejection from many suitors, thereby causing them to lose hope and confidence in themselves, feel unworthy, and diminish their self-respect. Judged by her skin color, "women who are dark-complexioned often face the humiliation of a society that is color conscious and uses color as a marker of class, beauty, prestige, and femininity."[5] The desperation that can prevail made one woman admit, "I had reached a point where I was just willing to marry anybody at all."[6]

Unable to resist parental or cultural pressure, she marries in the name of duty. Losing her voice, her marriage is not of her own choosing but an orchestrated act between two families with their own personal interests in mind. Thus, she is at a disadvantage to begin with by deferring to her parents' authority disguised as wisdom.

Traditionally, not only does she take her husband's surname in marriage, she also adopts his first name as her middle name in some parts of India. During the marriage ceremony, he may be given the liberty to change her first name if he so desires. Thus, the marriage may commence with both a loss of her identity and a power imbalance if she is submissive and deferential. Marrying a complete stranger, there may be no love to begin with, let alone respect.

Value of Marriage

Young Indian girls are raised with the understanding that they must marry when they come of age and blossom into exemplary daughters-in-law and eventually mothers. Marriage is the ultimate goal. Emphasis during their upbringing and education focuses on increasing their eligibility by cultivating the following ideal virtues that every Indian wife is expected to uphold:
- Obedient, dedicated, patient
- Humble, chaste, pure, loyal
- Adjusting, supportive, nurturing
- Tolerant of husband's beliefs and behavior
- Docile demeanor, conforming, submissive to husband's will
- Sacrifice individual needs in the spirit of service and surrender
- Prioritize family unity
- Place the needs of children, husband, and in-laws first
- Endure hardship without complaining
- Restrain emotions and feelings
- Maintain all aspects of the household
- Bear responsibility for upholding family life and cultural traditions

As a single female of marriageable age, the option to remain unwed simply does not exist since very few societal models encourage surviving independently without the support of a man. "Cultural conditions, marriage laws, economic realities, physical inferiority-all these teach women that they have no direct control over the circumstances in their lives... they are subjected to both parental and institutional conditioning that restricts their alternatives and shelters them from the consequences of any disapproved alternatives."[7] Hence, the pervasive stigma of being single or unmarried is to be avoided at all cost. The status of a divorced woman is even worse as she has lost her purity and is considered "damaged goods," minimizing her eligibility for re-marriage. Traditionally, even widows have been shunned from society for this very reason.

Immense value is additionally placed on preserving a young woman's virginity by avoiding premarital relationships. The article *Virginity is Everything* declares: "A woman's premarital virginity ensures her family's honor in alliances between families secured through marriage, the legitimacy of heirs, and the maintenance of caste purity. Consequently, general modesty is encouraged, sexuality is controlled, and interactions with the opposite sex are discouraged."[8]

Hindu Wedding Ceremony

As the auspicious day of the wedding approaches, lavish preparation ensues for days filled with extravagant festivities and customs. The actual Hindu ceremony is an elaborate production, each ritual imbued with rich meaning and significance. The wedding is held under the *mandap,* generously decorated with fresh colorful flowers and four pillars symbolizing the bride and groom's parents who have been the pillars of their lives.

The captivating sound of the *shennai*, the radiant colorful *saris*, rich ornate outfits of all attending, and excitement of both families fills the wedding hall. Amidst the chanting of sacred Vedic hymns to invoke the deities, the bride enters and stands opposite the groom. Anticipation builds until the cloth partition separating them is removed, the couple garlands each other with exuberant flowers, and the crowd showers them with grains of rice to bless the propitious moment.

Kanyadaan, the giving away of the bride, is a symbolic gesture during the ceremony of leaving her natal family. A bride is considered a goddess offered as a gift to the groom's family. Standing in a circle, flowing water is poured from the hands of the bride's parents to the bride and groom, symbolizing the flow of life. After exchanging vows, the groom ties the *mangalsutra,* traditional necklace worn by a married woman, around the bride's neck. The groom's family welcomes the bride as a blessing to their home.

In *mangal fera*, the couple join hands as the groom leads the bride around the sacred fire three times, followed by the bride leading the groom around the fire a fourth time. With each circle, they make a resolution to attain the four goals of life known as the *purusharthas* that they promise their parents they will strive to fulfill as a couple:

(1) Upholding *dharma*-one's life purpose
(2) Creating *artha*-material prosperity
(3) Finding *kama*-fulfillment and pleasure
(4) Attaining *moksha*-spiritual liberation.

Hand in hand, the bride and groom take seven symbolic steps known as *saptapadi*, to symbolize the seven commitments they pledge to uphold in their life journey together. These are:

Step 1 Harmony & sharing the responsibilities of married life together
Step 2 Strength & courage to accomplish their goals
Step 3 Material prosperity for the benefit of the family
Step 4 Health and long life
Step 5 Blessings of healthy children
Step 6 Cultivate happiness, joy, peace, and spiritual values
Step 7 Ever-lasting friendship

At the completion of the ceremony, the couple seeks *ashirwad*, or the blessings of the priest, parents, elders, family, and community. This is significant because the marriage is not simply a union of two people but of both families and their larger communities. Wedding guests shower the couple with grains of rice symbolizing fertility, abundance, prosperity. Performed countless times over the centuries, this elaborate Hindu wedding ceremony offers the promise of the ideal spiritual union and marital bliss blessing generations of brides and grooms to begin their new lives together.

Commitment of Marriage

Within the institution of marriage comes an inherent struggle to unify two individuals into one seamless life regardless of one's nationality. Irrespective of a couple's different personalities, ages, backgrounds, families, dreams, ambitions, desires, or careers, there must be a common thread joining them. A couple understands seeking harmony is an engaging daily process to ensure a successful marriage because harmony is a dynamic state. Authenticity is the foundation for establishing intimacy. A relationship evolves only as much as each individual is willing to be honest and develop spiritually. Feeling secure and complete, there is no inherent power struggle or desire to dominate the other. Safety is inherent with a sense of love and compassion. Watching their parents interact, young girls learn what to look for in an ideal husband and young boys gain knowledge of how to treat women respectfully.

Essential traits for a healthy relationship derived from several domestic violence (DV) publications include:[9]

- Trust, intimacy, empathy, patience, compassion
- Mutual support, encouragement, praise
- Share decision making and daily household responsibilities
- Freedom to express opinions, tolerance, willingness to listen to other viewpoints
- Personal feelings and experiences are validated and acknowledged as real
- Communication involving honesty, negotiation, compromise
- Respect individual values, beliefs, ideas, expression
- Pursue individual interests, hobbies, activities, goals, friendships
- Encourage relationships with family, friends, social support network
- Healthy boundaries, respect individual space and privacy
- Physical contact is non-threatening, expresses love, safety, comfort, assurance
- No verbal abuse, criticism, judgment, ridicule, or name-calling
- Receive an apology if hurt, spouse not made a victim of one's rage

Mutual respect is tantamount for creating a healthy relationship. Culturally, young Indian girls are taught to respect their elders, whether it is their parents or grandparents, aunts or uncles, or elder siblings. These are elegant teachings, and it is understood and expected that an Indian wife will have this respect for her husband, but the reverse is not always true. Although many compassionate Indian men enormously revere the mother of their children, there are many husbands who neither respect their wives nor treat them with dignity. Despite the beauty of the rich philosophy of the Hindu wedding ritual, how does this ideal of marriage get shattered? How is it so many marriages are not based on this foundation of love and respect? As we will observe, traditional gender roles are partly responsible.

Gender Inequality Patterns

Traditionally, after marriage, a bride leaves her natal family to move into her husband's home while a son continues to live with his parents even after marriage and take care of them into old age. *"As daughters, women are cherished as temporary guests in their parents' home."*[10] Thus, a daughter is considered a burden or responsibility to be passed on from father to husband, a transfer of property. The traditional logic prevails: a son is an asset while a daughter is a liability.

Young Indian girls quietly observe how they may be valued less than boys, burdened with additional responsibilities and household chores, while their activities and privileges are restricted outside the home. She watches as her brother is treated more favorably, waited on eagerly by the women in the family, and generally permitted more freedoms. From a young age, specific gender inequality patterns are enforced as girls witness and accept the reality of male privilege where men are bestowed the position of power, responsible for the women of the household.

Although the ideals of an Indian wife are elaborated on, in contrast, not much is stated about those of an Indian husband. He fulfills his traditional role of being the patriarch of the family, the protector, decision-maker, ultimate authority, and material provider. He is also duty bound to take care of his parents and look after their needs, especially if he is the oldest son. His role is to instill discipline and obedience in the household, but he is not necessarily expected to make any adjustments.

Inequality is fostered by men who view women as inferior, expect submission and deference, and believe in exercising ultimate control as head of the household. This belief is perpetuated within families from father to son, generation to generation. Growing up with this sense of entitlement and male privilege as young Indian boys makes it increasingly challenging as husbands to accept equality in a marriage with their wives. The reign of male hierarchy continues as fathers are influenced by cultural norms and subconsciously perpetuate the subjugation of their daughters.

Four Aspects of Indian Female Identity

Essentially, a woman's role within the family structure is dependent on and shaped primarily through her relationships with the dominant male of the household-first her father, then her husband, and later her son. Her identity can best be disseminated into four parts depicted as expanding concentric circles.[11]

(1) Broader cultural identity as Indian female who assimilates ideal stereotypes of Hindu women that emphasize submission, sacrifice, and surrender.
(2) Identity as part of family unit defined by relationships to parents and siblings and later husband and children.
(3) Individual identity not prioritized nor given much expression.
(4) Core spiritual self not easily accessible or repressed if living with abuse.

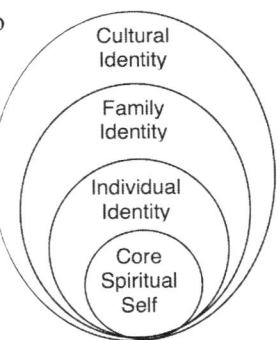

In contrast to the individualism of the West, Eastern cultures emphasize the collective family unit that suppresses a woman's individual voice. The cultural expectation is to uphold the virtues of being a dutiful wife. Many women revere their husbands as the person who defines them. The common expression *"Your husband is your god, without him you're nothing"*[12] runs through her head. Unfortunately, this same belief traps many women in unhealthy marriages who learn to tolerate abuse by accepting their subordinate place within the marriage. Later, it will be examined how all four parts of the Indian female identity are involved in and add a certain level of complexity in the process of breaking free from an abusive marriage.

Theme of Sacrifice

Living up to the ideals, cultural values, and community expectations, Indian women often embrace a model of subservience, striving to please her husband irrespective of his behavior. The pressure to do so is especially high if it is a favorable alliance marrying a man in the U.S. or someone of higher status or caste. It is ingrained in her that *"the primary burden of any adjustment in a marriage must come from the woman."*[13] She knows her sacrifice will be rewarded by accumulating *punya* (good merit/karma). This glorification of suffering in silence provides an added incentive to keep the family together at all costs.

Hence, it is ingrained and expected that she prioritizes the needs and wishes of her husband and children. Motherhood is an essential aspect of her identity and sense of duty. Praised for becoming fertile, her status is elevated if she can bear sons to continue the family lineage. It is only after fulfilling this first responsibility to her spouse and household that she can even entertain the idea of having a career or an independent life of her own. Without her husband's permission, she must resign to being a full-time housewife. Even if a man approves of her following her ambitions and a potential career does not pose a conflict, she may still be at the mercy of respecting her in-laws' wishes living in a joint household. A wife learns the adage early on: *"The less you expect in a marriage, the happier you will be."*

This common theme of sacrifice is deeply influenced by Hindu mythology, religious texts, cultural plays, and even Bollywood films where women are portrayed as meek, fragile, timid, and helpless, always needing a man's protection. Hindu mythology is abundant with stories of heroines who embody the virtues of sacrifice and surrender such as Sita, in the Sanskrit epic *Ramayana*. Her loyalty, purity, and chastity are expected of all Indian women. Even Draupadi, the wife of the Pandava brothers from the epic *Mahabharata*, is the essence of wifely service and devotion. Every Hindu goddess represents an embodiment of Shakti, a wild and fierce female force that must be tamed and controlled. Hence, the popular goddesses are always seen with their male consort: Parvati and Shiva, Lakshmi and Vishnu, Saraswati and Brahma.

Seeds of Abuse

The ramifications of these gender inequality patterns reveal emergent themes that inadvertently foster and sustain abuse. Ultimately, an Indian wife is bound in the name of duty to stand by her husband, maintain the relationship at all costs, and protect the family unit. Ensuring a lasting marriage is the goal she has been groomed to reach since childhood. As a consequence, she silences her voice in a culture promoting male dominance, accepts her suppression, surrenders her dreams, and passes this understanding on to her daughters. Breaking free is an extraordinary measure requiring her to overcome her perception that she has failed as a wife in fulfilling her duty.

To some, these gender roles and stereotypes may seem outdated or inaccurate in the modern world, but they are overarching traditional patterns of behavior that are still extremely predominant in Indian culture. With the diaspora to the West, immigrant Indians who settle in the U.S. seem to cling to cultural values and strict gender roles even more tenaciously. By no means, however, is this lack of equality restricted to India. Male hierarchy is a predominant global phenomena, especially in many traditional Asian or Hispanic cultures. The pervasive influence of patriarchy cannot be underestimated; virtually no country or culture has been spared. Despite the emerging movement for women's rights within the past fifty years or so, patriarchal biases still dominate.

As the effect of the women's empowerment efforts ricochets around the world, it is impressive that some women have succeeded in breaking through traditional cultural shackles. Even in India, there are growing numbers of women who are independent, driven, career-minded, and not necessarily financially dependent on a man; these are modern women dedicated to their families while still balancing their professions and passions. A minority may also choose to stay single or not become mothers, an option and freedom not exercised in previous generations. Nonetheless, for every woman who is free of these gender restrictions and inequalities, there are millions who continue to live in repression.

Just as this chapter highlights the foundation for abuse in Indian marriages and specific cultural biases, the next chapter reveals the common denominator for abuse that evolves and seeps into marriages of any culture, country, or continent. The inherent lack of respect for women is responsible for creating an environment that not only fosters but also sustains abuse. Essentially, "disrespect is the soil in which abuse grows."[14] Violence cannot occur where there is genuine love and respect. "This kind of love is incompatible with abuse and coercion."[15] True love, then, is an expression of freedom.

CHAPTER 2 SHEDDING LIGHT ON ABUSE

Safeguarding the rights of others is the most noble and beautiful end of a human being. Kahlil Gibran

Every human life is sacred. The sanctity of the human body, mind, and heart should be treated with reverence. A person is born with the inalienable right to live in freedom and safety, to exist peacefully with dignity, and to not be harmed physically. The harsh, undeniable reality is that these basic human rights are violated every single day all over the world, a fate millions of women cannot escape.

Human Rights Abuses

All violence against women occurs on a broad spectrum from abortion of female fetuses, female infanticide, crimes against women in war and armed conflict, to femicide or murder of women. Sexual violence includes dating brutality, stalking, rape, incest, sexual assault and harassment. The practices of racial discrimination, slavery, polygamy, and domestic violence are crimes as old as humankind. Trafficking, the modern day version of slavery, has grown at an alarming rate. These are not merely crimes against women but crimes against humanity.

Each culture also dictates its own specific restricting practices. Female circumcision, the violation of reproductive rights, and mutilating vaginas, a common practice in some African countries to prevent women from experiencing sexual pleasure, are atrocities worth mentioning. Traditional practices such as honor killings are still common in Arabic culture for women who dishonor their families by losing their virginity, even if they are raped. In China, it was most often the mothers themselves who enforced the ancient art of foot binding on their daughters to promote this notion of beauty and increase their marriage prospects.

The Indian practices of child marriage, dowry deaths, and caste-related violence are infamous crimes. The regrettable ancient practice of *sati*, officially banned in 1892, was when widows were burned on the funeral pyres of their deceased husbands because of the belief that a woman could not survive without a man and her duty was to follow her husband even in his death.[16] In *Breaking the Silence: Domestic Violence in the South Asian-American Community*, Nankani says, "All of these are part of the larger rubric of violence against women."[17]

Globally, violence against women continues as Mother Earth is raped, her lands pillaged, her forests destroyed, her bodies of water poisoned, and her atmosphere polluted. Every form of violence is interconnected and intertwined; the warpath of destruction remains unchecked. Abuse has the potential to exist wherever there is a lack of equality. It is a sickness that exists in the minds of those who desire power and control over another for personal satisfaction and is thereby transmitted in families from one generation to another.

The widespread oppression of women and these deplorable crimes are a result of the predominant global model of patriarchy. "Violence against women is rooted globally in beliefs in male dominance over women. Like other patriarchal systems, the South Asian cultural context is characterized by inequalities in male-female roles, legitimized and institutionalized by social norms that place men in dominant positions in the lives of women."[18]

Sexism is the explicit or implicit assertion that men are superior to women, relying on traditional gender roles as a basis for discrimination. In the U.S. for example, women continue to earn 20% less than their male counterparts even though they constitute 50% of the workforce.[19] Conversely, modern women are also expected to be self-sufficient, supplement or contribute equally to the household income, and yet carry the additional responsibility of raising the children and maintaining the home. Whether it is discrimination in the work or home environment, both visible and invisible forms of violence against women are thus perpetuated from generation to generation.

Epidemic of Violence

Women are also guilty of subjecting themselves to forms of violence through the debasing institutions of prostitution and pornography, reduced to selling and portraying their bodies as objects of pleasure for the sole sexual gratification of men. Eating disorders abound, such as anorexia, where depriving the body of food and nourishment is seen as justified to achieve the desirable svelte and slim figure Westerners are obsessed with.

Historically, the practice of wearing corsets in the name of fashion to reduce waist size, alter the natural shape of the body, and appear more attractive to men not only demonstrated women could be restrained but had serious physical consequences such as restricting vital air flow to the lungs. In addition to these self-inflicted forms of punishment, many women are driven to substance abuse or attempted suicide as a desperate means to escape abuse in their lives.

Violence against women has become an epidemic deserving of immediate global attention demanding society overcomes its insensitivity. In *Speaking the Unspeakable*, Abraham states, "Each individual woman's oppression is closely interlocked with cultural and structural oppression."[20] Justice must be sought, whether it is oppression by an individual or collective, a government or social system. Society cannot look the other way as these pervasive crimes continue and women senselessly lose their lives to both ancient and modern forms of cruelty. We, as civilized and compassionate people, are a part of the global collective struggle for women to find their voice, fight for respect and equality, overcome oppression, and end all forms of violence against women.

Defining Abuse

Along this spectrum of violence, abuse takes many forms. ***Abuse can be defined as any systematic pattern of behavior employing various strategic tactics that use power and control to exert dominance over another being.*** It is a pattern of assaultive and coercive behaviors that can manifest in multiple ways including verbal, emotional, physical, sexual, social, religious, spiritual, or financial control. Approximately 85% of domestic violence victims are female.[21]

Abuse pervades cultures, countries, and continents. Regardless of race, ethnicity, religion, gender, nationality, age, educational background, or socioeconomic status, the same predominant power struggle plays out in an abusive relationship with remarkable similarity. Using any form of coercion or force over another person is violent behavior. Violence in any form is destructive: destroying a woman's self-worth and dignity, sense of trust, and eventually corrodes her heart and mind. Its insidious nature makes abuse difficult to recognize in the early stages, but without fail, it always escalates over time.

Abuse by In-Laws

The nuances of abuse in Indian marriages take on a different context as this definition expands to include the abuser's family as well. Power and control by in-laws or extended kin is a common theme intensifying the victimization one might experience and augments the difficulty in recognizing the abuse. This leaves the victim subject to control by multiple family members when living in a joint household, complicating her situation further. Her isolation may increase if she lacks support from her family and is geographically isolated or settled abroad. In-laws may often exploit this fact and feel less accountable for their actions.

Dasgupta, author of *Body Evidence: Intimate Violence Against South Asian Women in America*, states, "At times, the husband may be a participant or observer of his wife's abuse at the hands of his parents and siblings."[22] "Often the extended kin are partners in the husband's crime, whether through their silence or their active involvement in the perpetration of the abuse."[23] A mother-in-law, for example, may exert control in various ways to display she is the dominant woman of the household and that her son's loyalty is to her rather than his wife. After a lifetime of being powerless, submissive, and deferential to her husband and in-laws, a mother-in-law finally gains respect as the matriarch of the household. It is her chance to exercise control in family life. Alas, it is common to see elder women abuse this position of power.

She may monitor the activities, free time, ability to work, and time spent with children of her newly acquired daughter-in-law. The husband's siblings may exert similar control displaying their higher status in the household, especially if they are older. When a spouse is a passive observer witnessing his family's abusiveness, this falsely leads a victim "to believe that the removal of the in-laws would end all violence in her life."[24] Any man who condones abuse of his wife by others is indeed capable of being abusive himself. If a victim confides in her husband, his attitude may change from a supportive partner to one who is defensive of his family being criticized.

Types of Abuse
Abusive behaviors can manifest verbally, emotionally, physically, sexually, socially, religiously, or financially. Each one has its own unique expression of varying degrees of aggression and hostility, and frequently, these various forms of abuse coalesce into a complex multi-layered destructive pattern. Verbal abuse is always a precursor to physical abuse. Regardless of the abusive pattern, each type of abuse is devastating in its own way and exacerbates with time. Ultimately, each form is a method of control to keep the victim on a tight leash. All abusive behaviors are conscious, calculated strategies the perpetrator implements to overpower and subtly manipulate his victim's mental state.

- **Verbal/ emotional abuse**-the use of threats, profanities, derogatory comments, and name-calling to injure, wound, insult, and dehumanize.
- **Physical abuse**: various forms of domination (such as intimidation and restraining tactics) and physical control that can cause serious bodily injury or harm, visits to the emergency room, or in extreme situations, results in death.
- **Sexual abuse**: includes rape and other forms of coercion and sexually violent behavior that goes against a victim's will and infringes on her reproductive rights.
- **Social abuse**: includes public humiliation, degrading one in front of family, friends, peers, social groups, or in the work environment.
- **Religious/ spiritual abuse**: using religious beliefs, ideologies, or sacred texts to support abusive behavior and discredit or trivialize personal beliefs.
- **Financial abuse**: using financial means to exert control and restrict financial freedom.

Domestic Violence
Differentiating between various terms or labels of abuse that are often used interchangeably is critical. The dictionary defines abuse as: "to treat in a harmful, injurious, or offensive way. To speak insultingly, harshly, and unjustly to or about, to revile, malign."[25] This can occur in situations of marriage, dating, cohabitation, or with friends and family.

While abuse can have multiple manifestations, DV emphasizes physical abuse that injures or violates one's partner who is living in the

THE PSYCHOLOGY OF ABUSE 15

same household, and more commonly refers to men assaulting women. Although domestic violence is the most commonly used term throughout this book, it can also be referred to as domestic abuse, spousal abuse, intimate partner violence (IPV), family violence, conjugal violence, marital assault, or gender violence. It is paramount to recognize violence against another person is illegal and punishable by law.

Common legal terms associated with domestic violence crimes are outlined below:[26]

- **Assault**-a crime occurring when one person tries to physically harm another in a way that makes the person under attack feel immediately threatened. *Actual physical contact is not necessary*; threatening, fearful gestures that would alarm any reasonable person can constitute an assault.
- **Aggravated assault**-the crime of physically attacking another person and causing serious bodily harm; or assault with a deadly or dangerous weapon. Aggravated assault is typically a felony.
- **Battery**-the act of beating or pounding. The unlawful and unwanted touching or striking of one person by another, with the intention of bringing about a harmful or offensive contact.[27]

Myths of Abuse

Unveiling the silence and secrecy surrounding domestic violence involves confronting the stereotypes of abuse perpetuated by the community. It is imperative to dispel these myths with enhanced social awareness, rigorous education and outreach.

(1) The number of women who undergo abuse is insignificant.
(2) If there is no physical violence, a relationship is not abusive.
(3) Sometimes it is justifiable for a husband to hit his wife.
(4) Unless a woman has physical injuries or requires medical care it is not abuse.
(5) Educated people are not abusive.
(6) Abuse only occurs in low-income families and does not affect the middle-class or wealthy.
(7) The wealthier a couple is, the less severe the abuse.
(8) Anyone involved in an abusive relationship must have grown up in an abusive family.
(9) Abuse is limited to those in heterosexual relationships.
(10) Cultural stereotypes and beliefs do not affect abusiveness.
(11) Battered women imagine, exaggerate, deliberately fabricate, or initiate the violence.[28]
(12) Battered women somehow provoke or are to blame for the violence.[29]
(13) If children do not directly witness the abuse, they are not affected by it.
(14) The abuser never targets the children or uses them to manipulate his partner.

(15) An abusive father is better than no father at all.[30]
(16) It is easy for an abusive relationship to change for the better.
(17) Domestic violence is about a loss of control and anger management issues.

Culturally Specific Myths Related to Indian Marriages
(1) Cases of abusive marriages among Indians are extremely rare.
(2) Abuse cannot occur in the Indian cultural group because it is a model minority in the U.S.
(3) Domestic violence only occurs in India, not to those who have immigrated to the West.
(4) Abuse only occurs to Indians who are poor, villagers, low-caste, or live in slums.
(5) Love marriages are free of abuse. Abuse only occurs in arranged marriages.
(6) If there is abuse in a love marriage, the wife is to blame for her poor decision in selecting her husband without her family's approval and support.
(7) The women are always to blame if their husbands are abusive.
(8) All Indian women are free to make their own decisions in a marriage.
(9) Abuse by in-laws only occurs when they are living in the same household.
(10) If the in-laws are abusive, the spouse will always intervene on his wife's behalf.
(11) If abusive in-laws are removed from the equation, the wife can lead an abuse-free life.
(12) Abuse will end once the couple moves abroad, obtains a green card, has children, careers are established, and they are "settled."

STATISTICS on Domestic Violence
Many myths are readily dispelled by verifying the facts. Staggering statistics reveal the severity of abuse and the alarming number of women subjugated to these crimes.
- Domestic violence is a worldwide crisis. According to a 2000 UNICEF study, 20-50% of the female population of the world will become victims of domestic violence.[31]
- The United Nations Development Fund for Women estimates that at least 33% of women globally will be beaten, raped or otherwise abused during her lifetime. In most cases, the abuser is a member of her own family.[32]
- Nearly 1 in 4 (25%) women report experiencing violence by a current or former spouse or boyfriend at some point in her life.[33]
- In the U.S., at least 2 million women are battered by their partners each year.[34]

Refer to Appendix 1 for additional statistics regarding those affected by domestic violence, profiles of perpetrators, incidents of abuse, separation violence, homicides, injuries, effect on children, economic consequences, and more.

History of Domestic Violence Movement

Until recently, DV has been considered a private matter of the home, a well-kept family secret, and one in which the government or authorities should not be involved. Understanding the history and progression of this movement to aid women in escaping violence in their homes and marriages is essential. In the past twenty years, this crisis has been recognized with an explosion of shelters and organizations that have spread throughout the U.S. Refer to Appendix 2 for a detailed timeline on the history of this movement.

Model Minority

Many Indians take great pride in their reputation as a model minority in the U.S., but this label impedes recognizing its susceptibility to abuse just like any other minority. The ancient 5,000-year-old civilization of India is known for respecting women as mothers, worshipping numerous goddesses, revering female saints, and electing the world's longest-serving female as prime minister. It is a community distinguished by its close-knit family ties, penchant for higher education, hard-working zeal, professional drive, and financial success. Preserving cultural identity and traditions has been maintained as a priority.

Representing the wealthier sector of Americans, the Indian minority is a group that has "achieved a measure of success that approximates the American ideal."[35] Thus, it may come as a surprise that many South Asian Women's Organizations (SAWOs) report many of the DV victims they work with are highly-educated doctors, engineers, scientists, attorneys, accountants, Ph.D. holders, and come from many other professional backgrounds.[36]

The model minority myth that is perpetuated is this group is "free of social problems such as gang violence, teen pregnancy, domestic violence, broken households, and drug abuse,"[37] but maintaining this image is problematic. It creates a scenario where "members of the community are preoccupied with maintaining cultural integrity and cohesion, as well as a positive image to the outside world."[38]

In maintaining this illusion, the community is reluctant to openly discuss issues such as domestic violence or deny that they exist all together. "The segments that don't fit the 'success mold' experience a sense of shame, deficiency, and failure."[39] Dasgupta states in *Body Evidence*, many physicians serving victims in emergency rooms are "surprised to learn of the magnitude of domestic violence in South Asian communities"[40] because it is a secret so well hidden.

Upscale Violence

Just as abuse can occur in model minority communities like Indian Americans in the U.S., it can also exist in the wealthier class. In *Not to People Like Us: Hidden Abuse in Upscale Marriages*, author Weitzman coins the term "upscale violence" that deserves mention. Going against the stereotype of victims being women who are less privileged, from lower socio-economic levels, lack higher levels of education, are helpless and weak, or from abusive homes, Weitzman reveals the opposite can be true as well. In her research of screening 50 women, she discovered several criteria to distinguish this group:[41]

(1) *"Income*: A combined marital income of at least $100,000 per year.
(2) *Residence*: Marital residence in a neighborhood ranked in the top 25% of its statewide area according to U.S. Census Bureau data; or, in some cases, neighborhoods highly ranked according to commonly held reputation.
(3) *Class status*: A self-perception of being in upper-middle class or upper class.
(4) *Education*: A minimum of a bachelor's degree."

She notes one reason for underrepresentation is because "women who fit these criteria fall between the cracks when it comes to the filing of police reports, the computation of statistics, and the pursuit of research studies on domestic violence."[42] As will become apparent, there are numerous parallels between the plight of abused upscale women and Indian or minority women.

Upscale women are married to successful and wealthy men in their community and often maintain a societal image of being a happy, supportive couple. For these women to break their silence and reveal the secret of abuse in their marriages, they jeopardize both their own and their husbands' success, careers, and reputations while running the risk of the community not believing prominent men would be capable of being abusive.

Most upscale women "stated that their silence was due to the fear that others would doubt their stories because 'marital abuse doesn't happen…to people like us…with education…in this neighborhood.'"[43] Or they would make comments such as "I'm too intelligent to be abused."[44] "The majority of upscale violence is emotional rather than physical, but it is often the physical aspect that brings the woman to treatment (even though, paradoxically, she won't speak about it). By comparison, in research studies on reported cases of wife abuse among lower-income families, the physical assault tends to be more prominent and more readily identifiable."[45]

Theories of Abuse

What creates abuse-friendly families, societies, cultures, or environments in the first place? Various perspectives highlight a range of theories for the origin of abusive situations. In reality, it is essentially a combination of influences that play an intricately interwoven role.

(1) **Feminist perspective**: The misuse of power by men and the global prevalence of patriarchy and accepting domination over women are especially emphasized within certain traditional cultures. Sexism maintains the subordinate position of women.

(2) **Family background:** Abuse is learned behavior boys are exposed to during childhood while witnessing family violence. Whether they are abused themselves or witness their fathers or male authority figures being abusive towards others, they imitate what they observe. As mentioned in *The Gift of Fear*, "Some child is being taught that violence has a place, learning that when it comes to cruelty, it is better to give than to receive."[46]

(3) **Social perspective**: The overexposure boys have to violence in all forms of media, whether it is through destructive video games, offensive musical lyrics or videos, assertive advertisements, aggressive television, cartoons, or Hollywood movies, leads them to believe violence is acceptable, common, and part of macho behavior. Sports also glorify violence and contribute to a pervasive atmosphere of tolerance. "By the age of 18, children in America will have witnessed 200,000 acts of violence in the media."[47] Society is obligated to play an active role in reducing this alarming exposure to violence. A child "may be controlling because he has learned how to in a culture that celebrates it."[48]

(4) **Psychological perspective**: Individual character flaws include an inability to manage emotions such as anger and rage, poor impulse control, and an inability to successfully cope with internal and external stressors such as "lack of goal fulfillment, unemployment, poverty, or cultural deprivation."[49]

(5) **Biological perspective**: There is a belief these men are programmed for violence genetically and there may be certain deficits in their brain due to inactive neurological centers that create a lack of remorse and affinity towards using violence. Research has shown "the elongated D4DR gene is present in assassins, bank robbers, and daredevils,"[50] but whether genetics plays a role remains inconclusive in batterers.

(6) **Ethno-gender perspective**: Cultural and patriarchal belief systems in Indian marriages as well as other cultures may promote tendencies towards chauvinism. Women may come to accept suffering in silence as part of their duty since divorce is not considered an option.

(7) **Upscale violence theory**: Men feel a sense of entitlement, have a tendency to narcissistic behavior, and display an attitude that they can get away with anything that drives their violent behavior.

(8) **Blame the victim approach**: The Western psychological focus for many years emphasized the stereotype of battered women as helpless, weak, and dependent. It was believed they were from abusive childhoods, prone to repeating the cycle of victimization, and set themselves up to experience violence in relationships. Some psychologists had the audacity to say these women "liked" violence and sought abusive relationships. The author, however, strongly opposes this offensive theory.

Whether there is a genetic predisposition to violence, "a chemical imbalance in the brain, mental illness, or personality problems"[51] that shape a perpetrator are valid questions, but research remains limited and inconclusive. Regrettably, violent offenders often use these same theories as excuses to avoid accountability for their actions. Exploring definitions and various manifestations for abuse, abundant myths, startling statistics, realities of it affecting model minorities and upscale communities, and theories for how it evolves, demonstrate the complexity of issues that must be investigated to begin to comprehend domestic violence.

CHAPTER 3 RECOGNIZING SIGNS OF ABUSE

Injustice anywhere is a threat to justice everywhere. Martin Luther King Jr.

To recognize the signs of abuse, it is essential to first understand the relationship between a perpetrator and his victim, differentiate between conflict versus abuse, examine the wheel of power and control, and identify the various categories of violent behavior.

Relationship Between Abuser & Victim

There are essentially three critical elements that characterize an abusive relationship:
(1) Constant dynamic of power and control
(2) Disrespect leading to a lack of real intimacy or empathy
(3) Unhealthy attachment often mistaken for love or affection

An abuser uses deception and manipulation to cleverly disguise these elements making them difficult to identify until a victim is sufficiently worn down and ready to break free. During an abusive interaction, when he exposes his vulnerabilities and reveals his fragile inner self, the only way to redeem himself is to prove he is exactly the opposite. It becomes imperative to display his dominance.

Creating an unhealthy power dynamic whereby he purposefully undermines her confidence and individuality, dominates conversations, and suppresses his victim is his sole objective. Treating her as an object or property allows him to feel in charge. Dismissing her opinions, talents, abilities, and desires is easy when he does not consider her an equal or feel any empathy towards her plight or suffering.

Every interaction is characterized by his attitude of disrespect towards his partner. As Bancroft aptly writes in his book, *Why Does He Do That? Inside the Minds of Angry and Controlling Men*, "Abuse and respect are diametric opposites: You do not respect someone whom you abuse, and you do not abuse someone whom you respect."[52] "The more a man abuses you, the more he is demonstrating that he cares only about himself. He may feel a powerful desire to *receive* your love and caretaking, but he only wants to *give* love when it's convenient."[53] An abuser lacks the ability to develop any real intimacy in a relationship. A victim may feel a strong sense of attachment mistaking it for love, but it is not true intimacy.

Conflict Versus Abuse

Abuse is often mistaken for a lack of conflict resolution skills, but they must be clearly differentiated. In a healthy relationship, conflicts are resolved through communication, understanding, attempting to see each other's perspective, and appreciating each other's concerns. Both partners accept responsibility for the part they play in a conflict and mutually concede to reach a middle ground. If no solution is reached, a resolution is not forced and they do not seek to dominate or control each other. In stark contrast, tension remains unresolved in abusive situations.

Hence, abuse cannot be mistaken for a conflict where a woman's right to express herself freely is stifled. She is not respected for her own feelings, thoughts, opinions, and values. The abuser denies accountability for his role in creating tension, and instead, blames the entire incident on his partner. In many instances, abuse arises even in the absence of conflict. Contrary to common belief, there may be no disagreement, opposing views, nor any significant reason to trigger a violent altercation. The perpetrator is not necessarily provoked. It is his abusive mentality that creates conflict in the first place and his choice to behave in an abusive manner that instigates violence.

New Wheel of Power

The wheel of power is a schematic diagram created by the Duluth Institute depicting eight methods an abuser strategically employs to gain power and control and can be found at *www.theduluthmodel.org*: (1) emotional abuse, (2) economic abuse, (3) using male privilege, (4) using children, (5) using coercion and threats, (6) using intimidation, (7) using isolation, (8) minimizing, denying, and blaming. This original wheel used in domestic violence education for years is slightly misleading because it includes types of abuse *and* specific tactics. A new wheel of power is proposed here that expands to six broad types of abuse while the pyramid of power differentiates three primary principles influencing an abuser's tactics.

Pyramid of Power

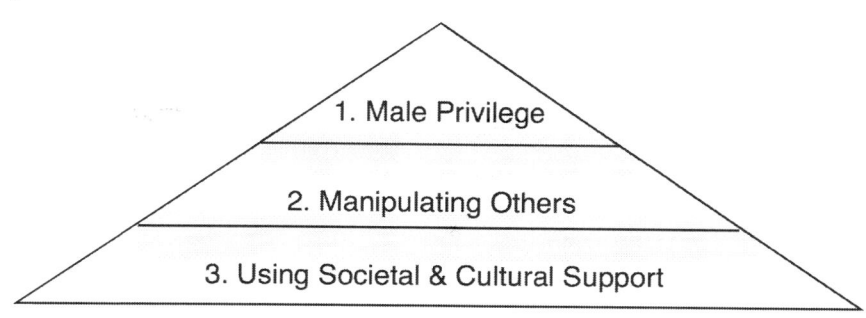

```
        /\
       /  \
      / 1. Male Privilege \
     /_____\
    /  2. Manipulating Others \
   /_____\
  /  3. Using Societal & Cultural Support \
 /_____\
```

(1) **Male privilege** is a common tactic employed by a perpetrator to establish his position as head of the household or "king of his castle." This idea of entitlement can be culturally-based if he has been raised with traditional gender stereotypes making it exceptionally difficult in Indian households, for example, to have a sense of equality. He clearly defines his wife's subordinate role as a servant to do his work and bidding. Oftentimes, he has grown up in a household where the male claims ultimate authority and may mimic the way his father treated his mother, without genuine love or respect.

(2) The **principle of involving others** can take many forms as his manipulation escalates but most frequently implicates children. He makes his wife feel guilty by threatening to take them away or hurt them, uses them to relay messages, or later employs visitation rights to harass her. He may threaten to harm pets, use violence against them to emotionally upset her, or claim he will hurt friends or family. In the case of Indian marriages, when in-laws and extended family are involved, the abuser feels supported. He can manipulate them to continually side with him or refuse to acknowledge the abuse. A perpetrator can also rely on local law enforcement to his advantage persuasively convincing them *he* is the victim.

(3) **Using society and culture** is another principle he derives power from. His religious beliefs and values may support his sense of entitlement and male dominance through various rituals or traditions. He may quote passages from religious texts about female subordination or rely on support from his spiritual or cultural community. A victim may be rebuffed by religious elders who chastise her for failing to be a dutiful wife. She may be asked to practice forgiveness more readily, be tolerant of his temper, and cultivate understanding and leniency towards her husband. Thus, violence can be perpetuated by society, community elders, and religious leaders who fail to accurately gauge the situation or downplay the immediate danger a victim may be in.

Verbal Abuse

Verbal abuse is highlighted first because usually some element of it is established in the relationship prior to all other patterns of abuse emerging. "Most abusers verbally attack their partners in degrading, revolting ways. They reach for words that they know are most disturbing to women, such as b*tch, wh*re, and c*nt, often preceded by the word fat... These disgusting words carry a force and an ugliness that feel like violence."[54] It is the context in which these words are used that creates uncertainty, alarm, shock, disgust, and fear. "That someone would intrude on our peace of mind... speak words so difficult to take back... exploit our fear... care so little about us... raise the stakes so high, that they would stoop so low-all of this alarms us, and by design."[55]

Most victims admit verbal scars are more damaging long-term than physical scars. Healing from the insidious and brutal psychological cruelty the assailant has inflicted can take years to recover from. Once he has established his control, even if the physical battering ends, emotional abuse can serve as a substitute for physical violence. With this conditioning, he may no longer need to be physical. A mere reminder of a previous battering incident, such as displaying a weapon he used, can effectively frighten a victim.

In *The Gift of Fear*, de Becker uses the acronym *TIME syndrome* which stands for "threats, intimidations, manipulations, and escalation."[56] He may intimidate a victim by expressing his intent to harm her, but remember, "threats are rarely spoken from a position of power. Whatever power they have is derived from the fear instilled in the victim, for fear is the currency of the threatener."[57]

Manipulation, a key component of verbal abuse, is a strategy that allows the perpetrator to gain the upper hand so his victim feels weak and vulnerable. He may interrupt her, belittle her opinions, ridicule her, or block discussions. His perplexing, contradictory behavior can vary from being cold, distant, and secretive, to suddenly becoming caring and affectionate. The abuser may engage in risky behavior such as driving recklessly, using drugs, or not seeking medical care to increase his partner's concern so she is forced to be attentive to his needs.

The **seven types of strategies for control** through verbal abuse are highlighted with the acronym *CONTROL-to criticize, oppress, neglect, trivialize, ridicule, order, and lie.*

CRITICIZE: He may begin with minor comments that are not necessarily harsh but make a victim start to doubt herself, remarks such as her clothing is too flattering or draws too much attention. Without realizing it, subconsciously she chooses not to wear her favorite outfit as often or when she goes out with him. If the abuser does not appreciate her makeup or hairstyle, she may slowly alter details about her appearance to please him or simply to avoid his criticisms. He may put down or mock those she is closest to so slowly she distances herself from anyone of whom he disproves. He may praise her friend claiming she is not as beautiful or intelligent as her. When the barrage of comments reaches a climax, the aggressor excessively critiques his partner's faults and inadequacies. Nothing she says or does is ever good enough. He creates unrealistic standards that are impossible for her to meet, discrediting her career, interests, or passions so she feels utterly worthless. Harping on old issues and annoyances, he refuses to let go of past incidents.

OPPRESS: His oppression bears many forms and seeps into every aspect of a victim's life-her interactions with others, caring for the children, running the household, pursuing her career, even managing her free time. The comments about managing her life escalate until his advice becomes excessive to the point of dictating what she can and cannot do. Because of his skill and persuasive abilities, she might initially mistake this interaction as genuine concern for her well-being. Later, as he restricts her freedom and independence, interferes with her ability to make decisions about her own life, and claims he knows what is best for her more than she does, a victim feels suffocated by his presence. He exercises control over whom his wife can see, where she socializes, and in what activities she participates.

Dominating discussions, he leaves his partner no chance to speak or offer a word in edgewise. Refuting her beliefs and values, a victim may feel she cannot even "hear herself think." Many experts say verbal dominance is one of the first warning signs of domestic violence. When a woman attempts to raise her concerns or voice her emotions, her perpetrator cleverly changes the subject to his grievances to play the victim. Often he speaks with "a tone of absolute certainty and final authority defining reality."[58] His impatience builds when his wife does not share all his opinions, resists his recommendations, or refuses to follow his advice. In this sort of stifling environment, he strips away the right to express herself freely or discourages her from retaining any autonomy.

NEGLECT: Oppression turns to neglect as he negates his partner's experiences, accomplishments, goals, and dreams. His constant undermining makes her feel unworthy, as if she can never meet his approval. Creating diversions in the conversation prevents her from deciphering what is on his mind. By ignoring his partner when she speaks, pretending she does not exist, or refusing to acknowledge abusive incidents by acting as if nothing has happened, he avoids genuine discussion or confrontation to face his actions. This is his intent.

He continues to neglect his spouse when he refuses to participate in family activities, childcare, or household responsibilities. He may withhold affection, access to finances, or healthcare so she feels she is completely at his mercy. Lacking support and validation, her spirit deteriorates and she forgets these are essential aspects of a "normal" healthy relationship. In *The Verbally Abusive Relationship,* Evans summarizes, "In truth, a verbally abusive relationship is more or less a constant invalidation of the partner's reality."[59]

TRIVIALIZE: When an abuser trivializes what his partner says or feels, discounts her emotions, ignores her concerns, and makes light of her interests or activities, she feels insignificant and worthless, as if she does not even exist. His "indifference, criticism, disregard, and so forth are all felt as a kind of rejection by the partner."[60] Plagued with insecurity and self-doubt, these attempts to constantly deny her reality and experience are extremely destructive. This is precisely his goal. In contrast, a woman feels acknowledged, respected, and validated in a healthy relationship.

Evans remarks, "Interestingly, abusers who trivialize their partners often brag about them to others as they would brag about a possession."[61] He may treat her like a trophy to be displayed and flaunted in front of others but subsequently discarded in private. She also opines: "The abuser invades your boundaries and moves into your psyche by telling you that what is meaningful to you has little meaning-what is valuable to you has little value. He attempts to dilute meaning and value in your life."[62] It may take years for a victim to decipher his insidious behavior especially if he feigns innocence.

RIDICULE: An abuser may taunt his wife in the "spirit" of being fun or entertaining by lashing out hurtful comments. When she reacts, he asserts he is not being hurtful, makes light of his jokes, and declares she is too sensitive, does not know how to take a joke, or fails to appreciate his sense of humor. But as the teasing escalates, his tactics undermine her, shatter her confidence, and destroy her self-respect. When this aspect of his abusive behavior is full-blown, he will roll his eyes, express sarcasm, and possibly make jeering facial expressions. All forms of ridicule such as name-calling, put-downs, mocking, and jeering are designed to humiliate and dehumanize her. "A name caller does not have, and may not gain, the requisite emotional development to love another in a healthy relationship."[63] As difficult as it may be for a victim to hear this, this type of man is incapable of true love or intimacy.

ORDER: His cultural or societal bias leads him to adhere to strict domestic role structures, demanding and expecting his wife to behave in certain ways. This can relate to meals, housekeeping, entertaining, raising children, finances, or any number of household tasks. He uses these issues to initiate abusive incidents when his specific demands are not met. His idealistic expectations of a subservient wife who waits on him assiduously and is completely devoted to serving his needs is a typical belief for macho, domineering men who are a product of patriarchal cultures. The vast majority of upscale husbands try to mold their wives to adopt a certain appearance, style, and behavior to fit in with societal expectations.

THE PSYCHOLOGY OF ABUSE 27

A perpetrator might falsely believe his need to control every aspect of his partner's life as caring deeply for her and hence justify his controlling behaviors. Believing she has fundamental flaws, he "assigns himself the role of 'helping' her. He may 'explain' to her the emotional issues she needs to work through or analyze her reasons for 'mistakenly' believing that he is mistreating her."[64] In reality, overseeing every detail of her life makes him feel secure and in a position of ultimate authority. The extent to which he will go to establish control can be hard to believe: he can use technology to his advantage by monitoring her computer activity, using live web/ nanny cams to spy, and even using cell phone calls or GPS on her car to track her whereabouts.

LIE: Similar to the actions of a con artist, an abuser becomes an expert at hiding the truth and manipulating facts to his advantage. He distorts what she says, insists she is lying, and makes false allegations. When it is time to defend himself, he will twist the truth to avoid accountability so his partner seems at fault. He will lie to mislead her or others about his intentions and motivations to create confusion. Denial is a major aspect of his lying behavior.

He will deny his words and actions or abusive incidents altogether, making his wife question her sanity when her reality of what just occurred is continually discounted. "Forgetting involves both denial and covert manipulation. The declaration by the abuser that what occurred didn't occur is abusive... Consistently forgetting interactions which have a great impact on another person is verbally abusive denial."[65] These various strategies of control are applied without discrimination by perpetrators in all types of coercion.

Other Types of Abuse

An abuser gains power by cleverly employing strategies of control that break down a victim's resistance, and eventually her mind and spirit. These can include a wide array of subtle and overt behaviors that are arduous to recognize at first because abuse can be expressed in a sincere and concerned way. Hence, she lowers her guard and defenses, shuts off her instincts, and ignores her inner voice. Because he is so convincing, she may believe what her spouse says is in her best interest.

The following tables throughout the chapter serve as checklists for what a victim or concerned family, friends, and the community at large should look for to recognize and identify abusive conditions. It is imperative we realize these behaviors are conscious strategies; he is not out of control as he may like his victim to believe. His behavior tactics can be remembered with the acronym for POWER: *Projection. Oppression. Will. Entitlement. Rage.*

Physical Abuse

Physical abuse is by far the most dangerous and extreme type of violence leaving scars and wounds that may never heal, serious injuries, or in extreme cases resulting in death. In roughly 50% of verbally abusive cases he is physically abusive as well.[66] "Research studies indicate that the *best* behavioral predictor of which men will become violent to their partners is their level of verbal abuse."[67] Physical abuse involves contact and violence directed specifically at a victim, intimidation tactics warning of abuse to come, or exerting physical restraint against a woman. Direct violence can include but not be limited to punching, pushing, shoving, or wrestling. Violence is sometimes perceived as being pummeled or slapped but it can be as simple as a pinch or a poke. If it does not seem appropriate or one feels violated, it may well be abuse.

"Evidence of physical abuse may include, but is not limited to, expert testimony in the form of reports and affidavits from police, judges, medical personnel, school officials, and social service agency personnel."[68] Most victims are not in the frame of mind to collect evidence and do not realize its necessity when the time for legal action arrives. Thus, many women are denied restraining orders on the grounds of insufficient evidence, unfortunately leaving their batterers to walk away as free men.

Intimidation Tactics: It is the context in which these actions occur that constitute a pattern of violence.

- ❑ Blocks doorway or corners her in room so there is no escape
- ❑ Locks her in home so she cannot leave
- ❑ Locks her outside home without access or way to get in
- ❑ Bullying response
- ❑ Cuts or tears her clothing, photographs, personal items
- ❑ Destroys her personal property, possessions, and anything that is meaningful to her
- ❑ Displays weapons to scare her
- ❑ Invades her personal space by getting too close so she feels uncomfortable
- ❑ Kicks doors, windows, or objects
- ❑ Makes her flinch
- ❑ Points his finger in her face
- ❑ Punches wall or other objects to show his strength
- ❑ Raises his fist menacingly as if to hit her
- ❑ Stalks her so she has no privacy
- ❑ Threatens to hurt her, the children, family, pets, or others
- ❑ Throws objects at her
- ❑ Towers over her
- ❑ Walks towards her in an intimidating way
- ❑ Wildly gesticulates when he is angry and waves arms at her

Methods of Physical Restraint:
- ☐ Holds her down
- ☐ Pins her against the wall
- ☐ Places his body weight on top of her
- ☐ Prevents her from moving or leaving
- ☐ Restricts her freedom of movement
- ☐ Uses contact with her body to control or intimidate her
- ☐ Blocks her from using self-defense

Contrary to the idea he is out of control, his actions and strategies are quite calculated. There are seven distinct choices he must make that influence his behavior patterns:[69]
- ☐ **On whom**: he can get away with victimizing
- ☐ **When**: specific activities such as girls' night, visiting family, or other activities when she is independent expose her vulnerabilities
- ☐ **Where**: so it is hidden from others, not in public
- ☐ **How**: so others will not notice
- ☐ **How much**: just enough to keep her in submission
- ☐ **By what means**: what type of abuse is more his style
- ☐ **Who will witness**: does not want to jeopardize his reputation and image which is at stake

Sexual Abuse

Although this category of violence is beyond the scope of this book and deserves special attention due to its complexity, a brief introduction is provided. Sexual abuse includes sexual harassment, sexual assault, or other sexual coercive acts and methods to degrade a woman or be psychologically destructive. "On average, almost 500 women are raped or sexually assaulted" daily in the U.S.[70] Sexual assault or forced sex occurs in approximately 40-45% of battering relationships.[71] Marital rape can include battering before, during, or after the sexual assault. "Experts have long believed that sexual assault, when combined with battering, is associated with a high risk of potentially lethal violence at some point in the future."[72]

Ultimately, sex is simply another way for an assailant to establish his power and dominance over his victim. He objectifies and depersonalizes her so she feels less than human. As Bancroft states, "A woman can sense the fact that in her partner's mind she has ceased to exist as a human being."[73] He "assaults her humanity, reducing her to an animal, a nonliving object, or a degraded sexual body part... By depersonalizing his partner, the abuser protects himself from the natural human emotions of guilt and empathy, so that he can sleep at night with a clear conscience. He distances himself so far from her humanity that her feelings no longer count, or simply cease to exist."[74]

He may find ways to continuously degrade her or control her reproductive rights. One woman said, "'By making me pregnant time and time again, he was trying to tie me down to him.' (He defines her) sexual relationship as primarily oriented toward motherhood rather than toward her own sexual desire or gratification."[75]

Sexual Tactics: Use the following checklist to determine if sexual abuse is occurring:
- ☐ Rape
- ☐ Battering before, during, or after sexual assault
- ☐ Drug facilitated sexual assault
- ☐ Forcing a woman into sexually coercive or perverse acts
- ☐ Intentional exposure to sexually transmitted diseases
- ☐ Degrading her sexually
- ☐ Sexual harassment
- ☐ Promiscuity, flirting with other women
- ☐ Threats of infidelity
- ☐ Objectifies and depersonalizes her
- ☐ Controls access to contraceptive use
- ☐ Interferes with or "sabotages" birth control
- ☐ Forces her to have an abortion
- ☐ Forcibly impregnates her against her will
- ☐ Refuses to let woman be part of decision-making about whether to terminate or continue a pregnancy

Injuries

Injuries victims can sustain as a result of physical violence vary on a spectrum from mild and subtle symptoms to severe, life-threatening damage involving visits to the emergency room. In the most horrific scenario, violence results in death. Statistics on injuries include:
- About 50% of all female victims report an injury of some type, only 20% of them seek medical assistance.[76]
- Women experience 2 million injuries from IPV each year.[77]
- 25% of women's visits to emergency rooms are due to domestic violence.[78]
- Nearly 75% of battered women seeking emergency medical services sustained injuries after leaving the batterer.[79]

The Battered Woman, by Lenore Walker, was one of the first publications to emerge on domestic violence in 1979. Walker elaborated on several categories of injuries:[80]
(1) "Serious **bleeding injuries**: wounds requiring stitches around face and head, facial wounds, bruises, swollen eyes and noses, lost teeth.
(2) **Internal injuries** cause bleeding and malfunctioning of organs such as damaged spleens, kidneys, or punctured lungs. Includes concussions, loss of consciousness, and surgeries.

THE PSYCHOLOGY OF ABUSE 31

(3) **Bones**: cracked vertebrae, skulls, and pelvises. Also includes injured ribs, collarbones, arms, legs, and broken jaws.
(4) **Burns**: from cigarettes, hot appliances, or scalding liquids.
(5) **During pregnancy**: mutilated vaginas, sliced off nipples, repeated blows to abdomen, miscarriage, stillbirth, infants born deformed as a result.
(6) **Sexual Injuries**: injuries to the genitals, lacerations, soreness, bruising, torn muscles, fatigue, vomiting, bladder infection, sexually transmitted diseases, and fistulas.[81]
(7) **Psychosomatic ailments:** backaches, headaches, stomach ailments, respiratory problems, skin rashes, hypertension, etc.
(8) **Emotional disorders**: includes anxiety attacks, palpitations, hyperventilation, severe crying spells." *Additional emotional symptoms discussed in Chapter 9.*

Financial Abuse
Still very much in the trenches of a patriarchal society, many men retain control of the financial resources. "Economic leverage is part of the control."[82] The day-to-day mundane affairs of maintaining a household and keeping track of finances is unfortunately not exempt from the reality of his exploitation. Eventually, abuse seeps into every aspect of a woman's life. Upscale women with more resources tend to develop strong attachments to their homes and material possessions thereby increasing their denial. Many victims will state they do not wish to lose their home, compromise their financial stability and material comfort, or deny their children this privileged upbringing. As the painful reality of financial abuse sets in and she struggles with resources and basic survival, she sees the truth: he is not capable of truly loving or caring for her.

Financial Tactics: The following list is partly adapted from *Free Yourself from an Abusive Relationship: Seven Steps to Taking Back Your Life.*[83]
☐ Controls how, when, and where money is spent
☐ Restrictive allowance dictates amount she can spend
☐ Intensely critical of how she spends money and what she purchases
☐ Limits access or refuses to share income
☐ Cuts off access to credit cards or bank accounts
☐ Makes subtle or overt financial threats
☐ Restricts decision-making abilities and spending rights
☐ Spends money freely on himself
☐ Withholds information about finances
☐ Purposely drains her assets to maintain control and ensure her dependence
☐ Takes economic advantage by forcing her to work and hoarding all the income
☐ Economically dependent on his wife to support the household

- ❏ Indian marriages specifically-forbid sending money to her family in India while he may spend extra money on himself or his family
- ❏ Refuses to let his wife get a job or makes it difficult to keep her existing job
- ❏ Restricts access so all bank accounts are in his name only
- ❏ Limits access to basic resources or necessities
- ❏ Denies finances for medical bills so she does not get adequate health care
- ❏ Regulates her activities and behavior through money

Religious /Spiritual Abuse

This form of mistreatment includes tactics that exploit personal ideas, principles, and values a woman holds sacred. By undermining her beliefs, he attacks where she is most vulnerable. The list below has excerpts from *It's My Life Now: Starting Over After an Abusive Relationship or Domestic Violence.*[84] Use the following checklist to determine if religious abuse is occurring.

- ❏ Denies her religious beliefs
- ❏ Defiles or destroys religious books
- ❏ Discredits or trivializes ideas, opinions, and values as unimportant, silly, or unrealistic
- ❏ Uses religion to intimidate: *"If you don't do as I say, you'll go to hell."*
- ❏ Justifies his controlling behaviors by using religion
- ❏ Rejects her cultural or ethnic heritage
- ❏ Ridicules her religion or religious beliefs
- ❏ States his beliefs are the only "right" beliefs
- ❏ Prevents her from observing holy days and rituals
- ❏ Forbids her from visiting temple/church, attending religious services, or participating in sacred ceremonies
- ❏ Uses sacred texts to justify the abuse
- ❏ Undermines her by garnering support from religious authorities

Warning Signs

Disregarding the red flags, a victim ignores her instincts as she repeatedly gives her partner the benefit of the doubt. Given all these signs for various types of abuse, how does she recognize early on if a man has the potential to be an abuser? The following list adapted from *Ditch That Jerk: Dealing with Men Who Control and Hurt Women* includes early warning signs that should be on a woman's abuse radar screen when she first meets her partner.[85] Checkmark all signs that are appropriate. Refer to Chapter 4 for a list of danger signs when violence escalates.

- ☐ Verbally dominant
- ☐ Sense of male entitlement
- ☐ Narcissistic personality
- ☐ Jealous or possessive
- ☐ Moody and unpredictable
- ☐ Critical, perfectionist, and tries to control everything
- ☐ Blames others for his problems and always plays the victim
- ☐ Victim mentality-believes the world is unfair and everyone is always out to get him
- ☐ Oversensitive to small slights
- ☐ Demands respect and is angry when he does not receive it
- ☐ Pressures a woman for sex
- ☐ Resists change, inflexible, unwilling to compromise[86]

CHAPTER 4 CYCLE OF VIOLENCE

To conquer oneself is a greater task than conquering others. Buddha

Power Struggle

Mistakenly, abuse is often identified as isolated, random incidents of violence, loss of control, explosions of anger, or irresolution of conflicts. This flawed perspective ensnares a victim in a destructive relationship until she can appreciate abuse is a *pattern* of behavior where her partner seeks to systematically establish his dominance. His control is reinforced with every abusive incident, creating a power dynamic whereby he claims his authority and purposefully weakens her through oppression. As much as he attempts to convince her otherwise, "Abuse is not a product of bad relationship dynamics… Abuse is a problem that lies entirely within the abuser."[87]

The beginning of a marriage involves an adjustment period where newlyweds learn how to compromise, but a victim makes more than the typical marital adjustments without realizing it. Since the concept of submission is so culturally ingrained for Indian women, they are at a disadvantage from the start. Indian men, who have grown up exercising male privilege from a young age and witnessing their mothers deferring to their fathers' authority throughout their childhoods, become quite comfortable with this seemingly natural power hierarchy. Thus, equating the existing power imbalance as a precursor to abuse is not so straightforward.

Insidious Onset of Abuse

"Many women report living with their batterers prior to marriage without experiencing abuse."[88] If there is no violence or altercations during the dating or engagement period when he most often is deceptively charming, statistically it will commence within the first six months of marriage. For Indian couples, a man can hide his true self with ease since the couple is not encouraged to spend any time alone together before the wedding and dating is still considered taboo. Early warning signs of abuse can be apparent as early as the first meeting or the honeymoon but often these red flags are disregarded.

Power can begin to shift in subtle, undetectable ways since a perpetrator is adept at concealing his controlling behaviors. "Abuse creeps into a relationship in an insidious, gradual way, over months or years. A precise moment or single event that defines the beginning of the abuse rarely exists."[89] At first, a woman may only notice a general sense of unease but cannot identify its root. Healthy boundaries blur as her partner dictates decisions, directs family life, and becomes increasingly demanding refusing to tolerate any opinion besides his own.

He might subtly or overtly pressure her to change her clothing, hairstyle, circle of friends, or quit her job. Research "found that the first violence is usually a single blow and is treated by both partners as exceptional; no one expects it to continue."[90] Walker states in *The Battered Woman*, "Having struck a woman a first time seemed to make it easier for the man to do it again. It is as if a taboo is broken and the behavior, once unleashed, becomes uncontrollable."[91]

Stages in the Cycle of Violence

Once his behavior quickly establishes itself, their relationship progresses from this first seemingly random violent episode into a deliberate, repetitive, abusive pattern coined the "cycle of violence." The original cycle used in domestic violence education has four stages but it is modified here to include five distinct recognizable stages in which tensions build, violence escalates, and the process is continually repeated. If unchecked, without any interventions, abusive patterns become firmly entrenched with time. These five stages are outlined below:

New Cycle of Violence

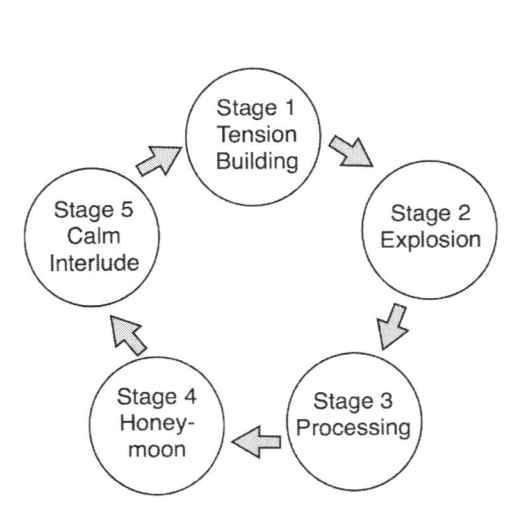

Stage 1
Tension building stage:
pressure builds, warning signs manifest
Stage 2
Explosive stage:
unpreventable and destructive explosion, abusive incident
***Stage 3**
Processing stage: critical stage where both come to terms with abusive incident differently, *not included in the original cycle of violence
Stage 4
Honeymoon stage:
false hope and apologies, builds emotional attachment
Stage 5
Calm Interlude:
everyday "normal" life and routine resumes as if abusive incident never happened

Once violence occurs, escalation is inevitable. Each stage is the batterer's attempt to deliberately acquire or maintain power when he feels it slipping away. In the beginning, this cycle may repeat itself unpredictably or irregularly. As the violence becomes progressively more predictable or regular, incidents escalate in frequency and intensity. Hence, the "good" periods in between become shorter and further apart as time goes on. A victim may experience this cycle repeating itself every twenty-four hours or every few weeks or months.

This cycle cannot be confused with the normal ups and downs that arise in a healthy relationship when a couple disagrees and may need time to reconcile their differences in a mature, adult-like way. In this scenario, tension may build in stage 1, but it is followed by a problem-solving approach in stage 2 instead of an explosion. Even if there is an outburst of emotion, violence is not involved, an apology is always sought, and feelings are reconciled to avoid such an incident in the future.

STAGE 1 **Tension Building**

A woman senses increasing pressure in her daily interactions as escalating tension creates a hostile, unpredictable environment. In *Not to People Like Us*, Weitzman calls this phenomena "shifting sands,"[92] where the very ground a victim stands on can be pulled from underneath her. His contradictory behavior keeps her hyper-vigilant, attempting to predict the next eruption where his moods can shift dramatically and abruptly during the buildup. She remains ever on guard, fearful of her spouse, recognizing from the warning signs that an explosion is inevitable. Living in this state of perpetual anxiety takes its toll.

In *The Battered Woman*, Walker avows, "Many couples are adept at keeping this first phase at a constant level for long periods of time. Both partners want to avoid the acute battering incident. An external situation will often upset this delicate balance. Many battered women recognize this and go to great lengths to control as many external factors as possible."[93] Thus, the focus shifts to her behavior rather than his.

Consequentially, she develops strategies for self-preservation such as: being emotionally withdrawn, keeping him calm, anticipating his every need, avoiding triggers for previous outbursts, or evading him completely. Despite the unpredictability of his explosions, a woman might do anything at this point to trigger an incident instead of waiting for him to unleash his rage when she least expects it since the anticipation can be too much to bear. This affords some slight measure of control in her life.

Regardless of her actions, the reality is there is nothing she can do to prevent an abusive incident. Her actions do not provoke his abusiveness, and she can never truly know what will set him off as much as he would like her to believe. According to *Why Does He Do That?*, "the abuser's problem is not that he responds inappropriately to conflict. His abusiveness is operating *prior* to the conflict: it usually *creates* the conflict, and it determines the *shape* the conflict takes."[94] Essentially, he tests her tolerance level, adjusting his behavior according to what he ascertains she will give him permission to do. On some level, when a woman adapts her behavior to prevent his outburst, she inadvertently becomes his accomplice. By choosing not to walk away, she co-creates a reality of abuse with him.

Jacobson and Gottmann, authors of *When Men Batter Women*, chronicle phases of an argument that contribute to the tension-building stage culminating in violence. The following is a summary of the **six phases of an argument** adapted from their book.[95]

(1) Unpredictability of abuser's fluctuating moods.
(2) A woman holds her ground rather than become passive or docile while tension builds, attempting to preserve some semblance of normalcy in her life.
(3) Abuser's unwillingness to be influenced no matter how reasonable and gentle she is. The more she asserts herself, the more aggressive he becomes.
(4) Her calm response contrasts with his typical outburst of anger if insulted or degraded.
(5) Absence of a withdrawal ritual-No matter how she may try to compromise, her actions have no effect once the violence starts. Unlike normal couples who take a break or separate themselves physically to cool down, a victim is unable to withdraw beforehand.
(6) The inability to defuse the situation leads to violence as the abuser's way of reestablishing control. Nothing his partner says has any impact on his behavior except to ignite his explosiveness further.

It is common for all couples to dispute about control but "the majority do not resort to violence as a means of enforcing their right in these areas."[96] Jacobson and Gottman designed SPAFF, a specific affect coding technique to analyze particular behaviors to predict violence. They discovered that "belligerence (taunting, challenging remarks designed to provoke another) and contempt commonly occurred prior to violent episodes. When belligerence and contempt are combined with another SPAFF behavior, domineering, …the batterer is signaling that he is close to crossing the line" and initiating violence.[97]

Contrary to common perception, minor battering incidents can and do still occur during this stage, often with great frequency. As a victim's conditioning grows, she accepts these smaller incidents with relief, grateful they were not any worse. By minimizing, another survival strategy, she views them as isolated random situations perhaps not even acknowledging them as abusive. With time, these coping strategies lose their efficacy so it is increasingly difficult to shield herself from his rage. The effects of residual tension building include suppressed anger she cannot safely express.

STAGE 2 **Explosion**

When tension reaches a critical point and fails to respond to any controls or coping techniques, an explosion is inevitable. The abuser lashes out, releasing the underlying tension raging within, not caring about the consequences. At her expense, he feels better after this unhealthy release. Major destructiveness is a defining trait that distinguishes his behavior from minor abusive episodes occurring in the first stage.

He may arbitrarily vary the intensity and frequency of incidents at his discretion, but there is no way to predict the magnitude or severity of violence that occurs. A perpetrator will target his victim, exposing her weaknesses and vulnerabilities to inflict maximum emotional damage. In many instances, a "man cannot stop (himself) even if the woman is severely injured... The woman's screaming and moaning may excite him further, as may her attempts to defend herself."[98] She learns from experience that self-defense will only magnify the violence.

"The cycle of abuse disguises an abusive relationship until violence becomes extreme. This is because, typically, the abuse increases very gradually over time, making it difficult to recognize exactly where or when it began."[99] Relying on her fight or flight response, nervous system in overdrive, a victim may recognize the peril she is in. This is the most dangerous stage but the opportune time to take action. If ever there is a chance to flee, this is it. The odds of escaping during any other period are minimal at best due to the unhealthy attachment binding the perpetrator and victim. Women who do leave are most likely to do so during this stage. Bystanders make the mistake of only recognizing this phase and not understanding how the other stages of the cycle inherently contribute to the perpetuation of domestic violence.

In *The Battered Woman*, Walker provides a detailed narrative of the abusive incident from the victim's perspective. "Distortion of time seems to play an important part in (her) attempt to control what happens... During an acute battering incident... she is able to prevent inciting him further... In most instances, she does not resist; she tries to remain calm and wait out the storm. She does not feel the pain as much as she feels psychologically trapped and unable to flee the situation... There is also a sense of distance from the actual attack... The dissociation is coupled with a sense of disbelief that the incident is really happening to her. An enormous amount of detail is remembered about the attack, suggesting an equally enormous amount of concentration on the actual movements that are occurring. Perhaps this helps (her) to stay alive... The one feeling that consistently comes across is the futility of trying to escape."[100]

STAGE 3 **Processing**

This critical stage that profoundly perpetuates abuse is not included in the original cycle of violence that has only four stages. However, in between the abusive incident and the honeymoon period, a significant interim occurs within which *how* both parties come to terms with the explosion differs radically and is indicative of the separate realities in which they live. From the author's own experience, processing this experience is the pivotal key that locks them in the unhealthy relationship and co-creates the reality of abuse.

Almost immediately after the explosion, the assailant enters a stage of denial, which may be conscious or unconscious. This may include: the absence of any struggle to face what he has done, time to examine his actions, or the opportunity to take any ownership for the situation at hand. Because he is incapable of any accountability, his projection leads him to blame the entire incident on his victim or external triggers. Afterwards, he will claim she is oversensitive or over-reactive to minimize the seriousness of the assault. By minimizing the extent of his actions, refusing to discuss the incident, or in severe cases pretending nothing has transpired at all, she is at a loss.

The victim's response is more complex since she mimics his denial first, and later resigns herself to acceptance after being broken down. Her denial can be for obvious reasons. Being paralyzed with shock since the severity of the altercation may be too much to process or being distracted by her intense physical symptoms does not leave her the option to dwell on events. Denial also sets in if she remains isolated for the first twenty-four hours after an incident and does not reach out or seek immediate assistance. Research shows victims may wait to contact counselors or seek nonemergency care after an initial delay period of several days.[101] Essentially, this delay period reinforces the abusive pattern as she inadvertently keeps the reality of abuse a secret and maintains her isolation. This is *precisely* what her spouse desires.

When the shock wears off, she may search desperately for a way to cognitively process what unfolded. As she struggles to make sense of the assault and maintain a "normal" life, she puzzles over the trigger and how to prevent another recurrence. When he persistently denies her reality, perception of events, and emotions surrounding an abusive incident, her invalidation is insurmountable. By learning to trust her partner's version of reality instead of her own instincts, she further surrenders her power. She is left doubting herself, her emotions, and her reactions to the abuse. Her desperate need to reestablish intimacy, feel loved, and build trust and affection after the psychological trauma may factor into forgiving him. She longs to forget the incident as quickly as possible, holding onto her dream of the normal, healthy relationship she desires.

The power of this stage is illustrated in *The Gift of Fear*: "Like the battered child, the battered woman gets a powerful feeling of overwhelming relief when an incident ends. She becomes addicted to that feeling. The abuser is the only person who can deliver moments of peace, by being his better self for a while. Thus, the abuser holds the key to the abused person's feeling of well-being... the worse the bad times get, the better the good times are in contrast."[102] "He gives punishment and reward unpredictably... Does he do all this with evil design? No, it is part of his concept of how to retain love. Children who do not learn to expect and accept love in natural ways become adults who find other ways to get it."[103]

A victim's denial eventually leads to her acceptance. It is not that she simply succumbs to the violence in her life out of a sense of helplessness; it is after the complex psychological process of mental deterioration has taken effect, her efforts to communicate have been futile, and she has exhausted all other options of reconciliation. This breakdown is systematic. His verbal dominance erodes his partner as he continues to attack her when she is at her weakest, blaming her for the explosion even when she knows she is not at fault, declaring something is wrong with her since nobody else triggers him.

A victim may believe him seeing there is truth in what he says; he is only abusive with her and not with anyone else. "The great majority of abusive men are fairly calm and reasonable in most of their dealings that are unrelated to their partners."[104] Being perfectly composed in public only adds to her confusion. Hence, a victim examines all potential triggers for the altercation to cognitively rationalize what happened. "As long as (she) believes the abuser is being honest and sincere, she remains a victim of verbal abuse… The partner who does not recognize her mate's hostility may simply assume that he just sees things very differently from her."[105]

If only the batterer admitted at this point to the abusive incident and the damage he had done, recognized her hurt feelings, and made amends to reconcile, he would in effect be validating her reality. He would show her respect and compassion. This perpetual hope entraps all victims. A woman may also fall into a pattern of accepting his blame because of his persistent denial to assume any accountability. Easier to become the scapegoat so he will leave her alone, she may assume responsibility to keep peace. Hence, with time, she unconsciously becomes tolerant of violence. Stage 3 is thus a pivotal period whereby their subtle tacit agreement to co-create the reality of abuse perpetuates the pattern.

As a result, she is "frequently left with a sick, hurt feeling that is never really resolved. There is no feeling of closure. Upsetting incidents may reoccur in confusing flashbacks because they haven't been fully understood or resolved."[106] In this weakened state, she may feel defenseless, unable to take further action. Essentially, the perpetrator feels empowered and justified since she has not walked away. Unless and until she does, the abuse continues unchecked because she has to some degree given him "permission" to behave violently and get away with it. This may be difficult for a victim to hear; she may voice her protests persistently and tell him his behavior is unacceptable, but her continuing physical presence *is* her silent acceptance of co-creating this reality.

STAGE 4 Honeymoon

The honeymoon stage is more than an apology. At the critical moment when an abuser senses his partner's continuing doubt and suspects she may walk away, he deftly changes his tactic. He may go to great lengths to win back her trust and loyalty and diligently pour on the charm by turning into the kind, loving man with whom she once fell in love. Knowing he must appease her, he begs for forgiveness and claims he has gone too far. Playing on her guilt, he may dramatically declare he cannot survive without her. With the smoothness of a con artist, his promises are compelling; he seems genuinely sorry for his actions. To some degree, he may truly believe this. His false encouragement for a "future" without abuse systematically hooks his victim.

This stage is especially dangerous and deceptive. Any defenses a victim constructed with the "fight or flight response" during the trauma are now effectively shut down. Even instinctively if she senses she must be vigilant, pure exhaustion from her victimization may put her off guard. He may beg other family members to plead his case and force the victim to stay with him. Bystanders may wonder how she continues to forgive her assailant and not abandon him at this point, but they underestimate the bond of attachment. As she chooses to believe his nice behavior in Stage 4 is his true nature, the strongest bonding takes place and entrenches her deeper into the abusive pattern. They both fool themselves into believing "two people who love each other (can) surmount overwhelming odds."[107]

This is often the most challenging time to end the relationship because the marriage is seemingly at its best. It would also seem natural after the trauma of an abusive incident that a woman might be discouraged from any sort of sexual relation with her perpetrator. Surprisingly, she may seek intimacy as a way to connect, be consoled there is salvation for her marriage, and desperately seek solace and reassurance. This rekindled bond allows the trauma of abuse to fade.

In some situations, however, the abuser will skip this step and not even bother with an apology or attempt to make amends if he is a narcissist or when his sense of entitlement is exceptionally strong. In the case of many Indian women and in upscale violence, it is frequently reported this stage never occurs. This lack of apology or acknowledgment of the abusive incident is incredibly emotionally devastating for the victim.

STAGE 5 Calm Interlude

When the intensity of the assault diminishes and the makeup of the honeymoon phase dies down, life returns to "normal" as much as that is possible. For an assailant, this is not challenging since the explosion is out of sight and out of mind for him, relegated to the past. This calm interlude is also known as the "good period" in between altercations, allowing a brief respite before the cycle repeats itself and the next violent event occurs. However, if the cycle reoccurs every twenty-four hours, there may be no respite. Bancroft states, "To understand abuse you can't look just at the explosions; you have to examine with equal care the spaces *between* the explosions."[108] This is critical to appreciate the abuser's hold over his

THE PSYCHOLOGY OF ABUSE 43

prey. These time periods may be deceptive for a victim as she starts to falsely believe her relationship is functional.

There is no motivation to leave during this stage with intermittent periods of positive reinforcement while she feels hopeful he will change. As a woman sinks deeper into the process of victimization, the altercation fades into a distant memory. She fights to hold onto the part of her relationship that brings relative happiness, desperately clinging to whatever is positive. Yes, there can be periods of "happiness" in an abusive marriage, but they serve as hooks to cleverly bait a victim and magnify her unhealthy attachment. She may deceptively feel genuine love and compassion for this man who she does not yet realize is incapable of reciprocating the same.

A woman may get used to this calm interlude, caught off guard by a sporadic insult or minor abusive incident. But soon, any sense of harmony disappears. Stage 5 blurs into stage 1 as tension mounts once again and her unease grows. No matter how long these "good" stretches may last, the undercurrent of violence remains constant in the relationship. When a victim has the clarity to see this, she holds the key to breaking free but the trauma of repeating this cycle will eventually erode her spirit.

Obstacles to Recognizing Abuse

The first crucial step to freedom is for a woman to recognize she is a victim. It may take years for her to come to this conclusion and bystanders often question, "how does she miss the obvious?" How is she not aware she is being abused if her partner is beating her or yelling at her? This seems so simple and straightforward, yet the psychology of abuse should not be underestimated. There are numerous reasons why it is challenging for a woman to process she is a victim or hesitates to label her experience as abuse:

(1) **Insidiousness**: The nature of abuse is subtle. By constantly invalidating her perception of reality, he makes it challenging to see through his manipulation and deception.
(2) **Secrecy:** A perpetrator conceals his motivations and disguises his behavior well while possibly maintaining the outward appearance of a supportive, doting husband.
(3) **Blame:** A victim may accept partial blame when her spouse tactically turns her attention towards not triggering him instead of analyzing his behavior.
(4) **Denial:** It is inevitable she mimics her partner's denial when he constantly avoids admitting to the abuse and she starts to doubt her sanity.
(5) **Conditioning:** With time, she adapts to the intensity of the abuse, accepts the escalation of violence, and minimizes or denies events.
(6) **History:** Never having witnessed violence, she may lack perspective to identify behavior that is so foreign to her. Or, if she does come from a background of abuse, this further complicates the situation,

impairing her ability to distinguish unhealthy relationships as undesirable.
(7) **Media:** Biased by extreme horrific images of domestic violence, she may not relate unless she has severe, brutal injuries or visits the emergency room.
(8) **Hope:** The eternal undying hope that her situation will improve with time characterizes all victims. She believes her partner's convincing promises he will change because he persistently and persuasively affirms this and has faith her marriage will work in the end.

Through his dense web of lies and manipulations, he essentially disarms his victim by destroying the weapons she most needs in battle: her instincts and clarity. It is no wonder then that it becomes so problematic to see abuse for what it is. The incredible women who recognize abuse during the first incident, possess the courageous strength to walk away, and refuse to tolerate his behavior should be commended. They possess clarity other victims lack. It can take the average woman several times of being victimized to establish an identifiable pattern to the abuse after believing for so long that each incident is a single, separate, unconnected event. This awareness is a critical turning point in her relationship.

Part of the inherent difficulty in pattern recognition is the fact that a victim lives in a separate and distinct reality from her perpetrator. Although the abuse inherently prevents any real intimacy, they may share the external façade of a relationship: living in the same home, raising children together, sharing household responsibilities. She believes in the false illusion of a real relationship. In her social interactions with friends, others may not be able to detect any discord or may even view them as the perfect couple. A woman may continue the façade by letting others believe she is happily married to a wonderful husband and her marriage is flawless. She may reason every couple has its problems and feel her marriage is no different than her friends'.

As a victim progresses through the stages in the cycle of violence, there are certain opportune times when it is easier to break free. During stages 1 and 2, as tension builds and the explosion occurs, she is aware the relationship is unhealthy or undesirable. If the cycle of violence only had these two stages, it would be so much simpler to walk away. What traps her in this cycle is not reacting while she is processing both her denial and acceptance in stage 3, believing the deception of stage 4 during the honeymoon phase, and fighting for normalcy and sanity in the calm interlude of stage 5.

Signs of Abuse Becoming Worse

As the cycle of violence progresses, a woman develops coping strategies and adapts to the violence but abuse only exacerbates with time. The reason for this escalation is simple, he "adapts to a certain degree of mistreatment of his partner, his feelings of guilt nag at him less and less, so

THE PSYCHOLOGY OF ABUSE 45

he is then able to graduate to more serious acts. He becomes accustomed to a level of cruelty or aggression that would have been out of the question for him a few years earlier... He then increases his abusiveness because he sees that it takes more to frighten or control her than it used to."[109] The perpetrator gains confidence knowing he will essentially get away with his cruelty. This harsh fact is in direct opposition to the false hope she possesses that their situation will improve as her instincts and clarity deteriorate. It is imperative every woman pays heed to imminent danger signs that should be on her abuse radar screen.

Danger signs: (Some excerpts taken from Bancroft's *Why Does He Do That?*)[110]

- His behavior becomes increasingly suspicious, more threatening, or extreme.
- She feels increasingly nervous around him but is not necessarily sure why.
- Her isolation is more noticeable as her contact with family and friends is increasingly restricted. He may claim they do not need anyone but each other.
- He reacts strongly to any steps she takes to separate from him or end the relationship.
- His isolation builds and there is no one to whom he is really close.
- He becomes increasingly withdrawn, depressed, or suicidal.
- He becomes progressively obsessed with monitoring her activities.
- He refuses to let her go to work.
- He starts to stalk her.
- He takes an interest in weapons or gains access to weapons.
- The violence escalates in frequency or severity.
- He becomes violent during her pregnancy for the first time or the violence intensifies as he feels increasingly threatened.
- He starts to abuse substances more heavily.
- He obtains personal contact information or addresses for people she knows.
- He threatens violence against other people.
- She discovers her partner has hit someone he has been involved with before.
- He has a history of being in fights, demonstrating he is not afraid to use violence.
- He is known to have abused animals.
- He acts like her rescuer and claims she is no one without him.
- Resorts to threats, intimidation, and bullying.
- Becomes suspicious of others and believes they will convince his wife to leave him.
- He breaks or strikes things in anger and uses symbolic violence such as tearing a wedding photo.

Breaking the cycle of violence requires tremendous determination, courage, and clarity. "Experiments have shown that it is most difficult to stop behavior that has been intermittently reinforced, especially on a random and variable schedule."[111] More often than not, a victim desperately requires the help of family, friends, community, and many times law enforcement to break free.

CHAPTER 5 THE CREATION OF AN ABUSER

Perhaps everything terrible is in its deepest being something that needs our love. Rainer Maria Rilke

The Enigma
    Violent men strategically shroud themselves in a cloak of mystery and create the illusion they are impossible to figure out, their true nature concealed from discovery. In *Why Does He Do That?*, Bancroft says, "To get away with his behavior and to avoid having to face his problem, he needs to convince everyone around him-and himself-that his behavior makes no sense. He needs his partner to focus on everything *except* the real cause of his behavior.
    To see the abuser as he really is, it is necessary to strip away layer after layer of confusion, mixed messages, and deception."[112] This chapter attempts to break down the carefully constructed enigma and illuminate the deception the perpetrator so deftly uses by discovering the precise set of ingredients that create an abusive personality.

Myths & Stereotypes of Abuser
    The myths that conceal an abuser's true nature are oftentimes perpetuated and upheld by the aggressor himself to create confusion, portray himself as the victim, seek sympathy from others, and defend or justify his behavior. For example, the low "self-esteem myth is rewarding for an abuser, because it gets his partner, his therapist, and others to cater to him emotionally."[113] Here are common myths partially adapted from *Why Does He Do That?*[114]

(1) Loses control easily, quick to anger, uncontrollable temper
(2) Aggressive personality by nature
(3) Violent in all of his relationships
(4) Low self-esteem, trust and intimacy issues
(5) Internalizes feelings and has difficulty expressing them
(6) Poor communication skills
(7) Tremendous stress from his work environment, mistreated by boss or colleagues
(8) Masters of the hard luck story
(9) Difficult childhood filled with struggles
(10) Abused as a child
(11) Hurt by previous partners
(12) Afraid of intimacy and abandonment
(13) Only abusive to those he loves and cares for the most

(14) Hates women and does not have close relationships to the women in his life
(15) Substance abuser, may be addicted to alcohol or other drugs
(16) Mentally ill or personality disorder
(17) Victim of racism or prejudice
(18) Not religious minded or active in his religious community
(19) Assumed he cannot be well respected, a leader, or in a powerful position in society
(20) Can still be a good father to his children despite mistreatment of his wife
(21) Rarely targets children or uses them as pawns to manipulate his partner

Culturally Specific Myths
(1) Pious Indian men who are devout Hindus are not abusive towards their wives.
(2) Within the Jain community, a sect of Hinduism that emphasizes non-violence, these husbands would never dare to inflict violence on their wives.
(3) Living in a joint household, husbands will always treat their wives well.
(4) A husband will always step in if others mistreat his wife.

Family Background Statistics

A fundamental question that must be asked is whether abusive behavior is learned or originates from innate tendencies towards aggression. Although there is no definitive answer, "Men who are most likely to grow up to abuse women are probably those who grow up with an abuser as an important role model and who *also* get especially heavy doses of destructive cultural training."[115] Understanding how power is distributed within a family, various roles family members play, emphasis on survival as a unit, and the pressure to keep family secrets contributes to multi-generational patterns of dysfunction. The following statistics reveal:

- "Studies have found that nearly 50% of abusive men grow up in homes where their father or stepfather is an abuser. Home is a critical learning ground for values and sex-role expectations."[116]
- More than 60% of all domestic offenders had either seen their mothers abused or been abused themselves as children.[117]
- Boys who witness IPV are twice as likely to abuse their own partners and children when they become adults,[118] than sons of nonviolent parents.[119]

What about the assailants who do not grow up in abusive households? They demonstrate the roots of a man's violence may originate from other equally valid contributing influences.

Foundation for Abusive Behavior

Abusive personalities are molded in the early formative years of childhood development and involve multiple dynamics that uniquely affect each perpetrator. His need to assert power and control through strategic tactics must be seen in relation to numerous coexisting factors. *The Gift of Fear* elucidates: "Violence is a process that evolves over time; it is not a condition or a state."[120] A series of five sequential steps is proposed here for a man to become an aggressor. At each step there are critical layers of influence that shape his inner mental landscape and external behavior patterns. Although these steps attempt to reflect a partial chronological progression, many of these influences do occur simultaneously.

Summary of Sequential Steps to Become an Abuser

STEP 1 **Exposure** to violence or destructive tendencies creates a memorable impression whether it is through:

STEP 1 EXPOSURE
Family Background
Socialization
Societal & Cultural Influences

↓

STEP 2 VALUES
Abusive Attitudes
Entitlement

↓

STEP 3 INJURY
Personal Inadequacy
Distorted Self-Esteem

↓

STEP 4 DEFENSE
Seeks Praise, Prestige, and Power
Creates Dominant Personality

↓

STEP 5 ENABLED
Experience Benefits of Abusiveness
Feels Supported by Community

Layer 1 Family Background
a. Observe dynamics of unhealthy relationship between parents
b. Witness father or role model being abusive and learns to imitate him
c. Possibly victimized or abused himself which leads to feeling powerless
d. Lack of quality psychological nurturing by parents who may be unreliable, unstable, unpredictable, absent emotionally or physically, or excessively critical

Layer 2 Role of Socialization
a. Being bullied, teased, and dominated by others
b. Socially isolated and ostracized by peers, interact superficially, and usually become loners
c. Self-esteem diminished and feels socially inadequate

Layer 3 Societal/ Cultural Influences
a. Patriarchal society emphasizes the subordinate status of women
b. Religious hierarchy may highlight male dominance and beliefs in sexism
c. Cultural or ethnic beliefs in male privilege or bias of traditional gender stereotypes
d. Media glorifies violence and portrays women as sex objects

STEP 2 **Values:** internal mental environment and core elements of abusive mentality shaped

Layer 4 Abusive Attitudes
   a. Learns disrespect for women and lack of empathy
   b. Adopts oppressive mentality and distorted thinking

Layer 5 Sense of Entitlement
   a. Inflated ego can result from being raised with overindulgent praise and "excessive admiration that is never balanced with realistic feedback."[121] A child becomes dependent on excelling in his parents' eyes when he feels their love is contingent on his performance or achievements. Many Indian boys are raised with this sense of entitlement.
   b. Develops superiority complex and believes he is always right, so by default, his spouse must be wrong. His rigid thought pattern makes him intolerant of any opposition or conflicting view.

STEP 3 **Injury:** internalizes and represses internal conflict as a young child

Layer 6 Distorted Self-image
Distorted self-image can result from feeling unimportant, unloved, and unvalued

Layer 7 Narcissistic Injury
Must find a way to respond to threat of narcissistic injury (*discussed in Chapter 6*).

STEP 4 **Builds Defenses** to fiercely protect his wounded, fragile self to avoid being hurt again.

Layer 8 Self-worth
Becomes deeply dependent of others' views to shape his self-worth.
   a. Consumed by deep-seated need for acceptance, approval, recognition, and constant validation, whether his ego is inflated or deflated.
   b. Seeks praise, prestige, and power to compensate for his sense of powerlessness, insecurity, and unworthiness.

Layer 9 Dominant Personality
Creates a dominant controlling personality to portray a confident image.
   a. Works overtime to compensate for his defect and prove himself.
   b. Adopts strategies such as a deceptively charming personality to serve as a decoy.

STEP 5 **Enabled**

Layer 10 Benefits Experience benefits from abusive relationship
   a. Learn that abusiveness is rewarding and makes him feel powerful
   b. Destructive pattern reinforced with time and each successive relationship

THE PSYCHOLOGY OF ABUSE 51

    c. Learns how to justify his behavior, make excuses, and deny its destructive effects

Layer 11 Enabled Community inadvertently enables perpetrator

    a. Learns he can get away with being abusive and not be held accountable for his actions

    b. Family, friends, peers, or society appear "tolerant" of abusive behaviors when they do not take a definitive stand or speak out against him

    c. Religious leaders/community may condone his actions

    d. His therapist may validate him so he feels supported

    e. Legal system and law enforcement may enable or protect the abuser's rights

Three Types of Abusers

    This struggle for power is not identical for all men. It will vary according to his background, personality, style, and strategy. Many theories abound regarding various profiles to analyze and identify perpetrators with more ease. Differentiating aggressors from non-abusive men who may merely be immature, highly reactive, obstinate, or possess explosive tempers is critical. The distinction in these situations is that a woman does not give up her voice, compromise who she is, or feel threatened by his behavior.

    Stereotyping abusers, one might mistakenly believe the media-dominated portrayal of men who "show no remorse, exhibit little conscience, (have) much less empathy for others, and usually have a criminal history. Even their brain scans show flat brain stem activity, which is different from normal men."[122] While these traits may apply to some men, many perpetrators do not necessarily fit this mold. The challenge with categorizing these men into exact profile types is that many share overlapping characteristics. In reality, each abuser is more a blend of traits from each of the three principal personality trait groups: (Adapted from series of personality types in *Why Does He Do That?*)

(1) **The Player**-maintains a tough macho exterior and views women as delicate, inferior, in need of protection, and to be kept in line. He is flirtatious, jealous, possessive, and disrespectful towards women. His partner feels violated, debased, used, or treated like a sex object. He is selfish, callous towards her feelings, and inattentive to her desires. He can be dishonest, irresponsible, or engage in risky behavior.[123]

(2) **Dominating/ Mr. Right**-is entitled, arrogant, condescending, and believes he is the ultimate authority on everything. His highly distorted self-image leads him to believe he is above criticism and reproach, has no faults, and cannot be challenged. He is intolerant of others' opinions and is personally offended if his partner

disagrees with him. Dominating conversations with his opinionated views, he harps on her faults, thrives on debating, and offers relentless advice on every aspect of his spouse's life. He can be demanding, threatening, intimidating, aggressive, and manipulative. His general attitude is that his partner exists to serve all his needs and should feel grateful and lucky to be with him.[124]

(3) **The Victim/ Mr. Sensitive**-claims he is constantly misunderstood, bullied by everyone, and truly believes he is never at fault. He complains life in general is unfair, feels underestimated, and blames his wife and everyone else for his problems.[125] Playing the victim, he appeals to her compassion and constantly focuses on his hurt feelings to avoid discussing his partner's. It may be challenging for others to imagine this type as abusive because he is not necessarily outwardly aggressive, may act calm, and never raise his voice. If he appears soft-spoken and supportive,[126] his partner may be confused as well. When he does express himself, he may label it as anger and not abuse and claim innocence. His subtle tactics include a steady stream of emotional assaults that may be difficult to identify and leave a victim perpetually confused.[127]

Cobras Versus Pit Bulls

Although many men can be described as the Player, Mr. Right, or Mr. Sensitive, the abuser's profile can be further dissected. Jacobson and Gottmann, authors of *When Men Batter Women,* discovered in their groundbreaking study in 1998 that violent offenders could be divided into two groups based on their style of violence: cobras or pit bulls. Their study monitored the physiology and heart rates of men during abusive incidents and what they uncovered was startling: 20% were cobras who strike with slow deliberate pre-meditation versus 80% were ferocious pit bulls always in attack mode.

"Like the cobra who becomes quite still and focused just before striking its victim at more than 100 miles an hour, these men were calming themselves internally and focusing their attention, while striking swiftly at their wives with vicious verbal aggression."[128] "Their lowered heart rates during arguments probably function to focus their attention, to maximize the impact of their aggression. We suspect that cobras are not only in control, but that they use their control over their own physiology to strike more effectively."[129] In contrast, pit bulls are highly aroused when they strike and do not exercise as much restraint or precision.

The following table illustrates major differences between cobras and pit bulls according to research presented in *When Men Batter Women.*

	COBRAS	**PIT BULLS**
Style	Two aspects to style: calm ferocity and explosiveness. Pre-meditated. Swift escalation until explosiveness unleashed. More emotionally aggressive at the start of the interaction. Learns emotional abuse quiets partner quickly with minimal effort.	Slow, gradual escalation of internal aggression until temper flares and loses control. Unlike cobras, internally aroused when behaving aggressively. Prone to fits of rage, and less calculated in their use of violence than cobras.
Degree of Violence	More severely violent, but always stay in control. Cannot always be judged by the trail of blood left behind.	Less severely violent, but lose control easily. Do not display calmness.
Motivation	Motivated by desire for immediate gratification to fulfill his needs.	Motivated by fear of abandonment and feeling threatened.
Dependency	Less emotionally dependent on wife. Withdraws in relationships and does not fear abandonment. Often economically dependent on wife.	Insecure, clingy, and jealous to the point of paranoia. Emotionally dependent and fears abandonment and betrayal in wife's every move.
Length of marriages	More long-term stable relationships.	Highly unstable short-term marriages. Almost 50% dissolved after two years in study.
Wife's role	Wives are for superficial commitments: gratification of sex, social status, and economic benefits. Increase violence when she will not be controlled. Many wives still crave loving relationship but he has no interest or ability to provide intimacy.	Demand changes in wife's behavior, but does not reciprocate with her requests. Dependent on her to meet his excessive need for approval. Expresses his demands through abuse and uses fear as a barometer of control.
Separation	Harder to leave in short run but easier in long run.	Safer to leave in short run but more dangerous in long run.
History	Severe antisocial, criminal-like traits, highly sadistic in aggression. More violent toward others in their lives. Chaotic family histories, abused as kids, or drug abuse. More in contact with criminal justice system.	Learned behavior towards women viewing father batter his mother. Not as likely to have criminal records or be delinquent adolescents.

This detailed breakdown is commendable but the primary critique is regarding their history. One would conjecture that pit bulls who act without prior deliberation would be more inclined towards violence against others or criminal behavior involving consequences with the justice system. Thus, the following analysis uses these labels of pit bulls and cobras and interjects some of the author's personal beliefs.

Low-income abusers who tend towards physical abuse more than verbal fit the pit bull profile better, which is, oftentimes, easier to identify.

Higher-income abusers who may be equally verbally and physically abusive can fit both profiles, but a higher percentage of them will fit under the cobra category than low-income abusers. Because they have more at stake, their violence is calculated to strategically avoid getting caught. Cobras are not as easy to identify and can cleverly disguise themselves so no one will ever suspect they are aggressors. At some point, everyone will hear a pit bull barking, but not necessarily see a cobra striking. It can be reasoned the more an assailant stands to lose with his status in society, the more sophisticated his strategy of violence will be.

In addition, these men can be differentiated into two types of hunters. The first type of hunter goes after the weakest prey and fancies the quick and easy conquest providing immediate satisfaction. Pit bulls are akin to this category. The second type of hunter delights in a challenge and pursues hard-to-get prey who require more skill and expertise to capture. They gravitate towards self-sufficient women who are confident and in control. Their domination in some ways is even more sophisticated. Cobras resemble this second type of hunter.

As a result, victims can also be divided into two basic categories: weak prey or hares who are easy to capture, and hard-to-get prey or foxes who require more domination. Assailants are sophisticated predators but uncovering the pattern and purpose to their behaviors deciphers their mystery. In *The Gift of Fear*, the author states: "Scientists marvel at the predatory competence of the great white shark, praising its speed, brute strength, sensory acuity, and apparent determination, but man is a predator of far more spectacular ability. The shark does not have dexterity, guile, deceit, cleverness, or disguise. It also does not have our brutality, for man does things to man that sharks could not dream of doing."[130]

Narcissistic Personality: Distorted Self-Image

Despite the various categories for these men, there is one common element to an abusive personality shared by all. It stems from a distorted self-image that results from fundamental flaws in their thinking. Chapter 6 explores the tormented thoughts and feelings responsible for creating conflict in a perpetrator's inner world that are the foundation for his violent behaviors. Although some of these men suffer from low self-esteem issues, others have the opposite issue. The term narcissism refers to a personality obsessed with self-esteem, ego, image, superiority, and vanity. This can lead to a sense of self-righteousness and others often describe him as arrogant, entitled, and pompous.

Although not all narcissists are abusers, all abusers have certain inherent narcissistic qualities and can be divided into two categories: the closet narcissist or the exhibitionist.[131]

(1) **Closet narcissist**-low self-esteem, deflated, inadequate self-perception, greater awareness of emptiness within, seeks constant approval from others, need to please others.
(2) **Exhibitionist narcissist**-high self-esteem, inflated, grandiose self-perception, little or no conscious awareness of the emptiness within, seeks perfect admiration all the time from others.

To correlate this with the previous discussion of abuser types, pit bulls resemble the closet narcissist who seek attention while cobras approximate the exhibitionist type who do not necessarily seek approval. The following table summarizes this breakdown.

Cobras	Pit bulls
Upscale abuser	Low-income abuser
Hunter who wants a challenge	Hunter who wants easy conquest
Exhibitionist narcissist	Closet narcissist
Less dependent on victim	More dependent on victim
Relies on emotional abuse more	Relies on physical abuse more

Narcissistic Personality Disorder

The *Diagnostic and Statistical Manual of Mental Disorders* defines narcissistic personality disorder (NPD) as "a pervasive pattern of grandiosity (in fantasy or behavior), need for admiration, and lack of empathy, beginning by early adulthood and present in a variety of contexts, as indicated by five (or more) of the following traits."[132] Although there is a spectrum of severity, traits 1-4 may not necessarily apply to all perpetrators, but traits *5-9 most certainly do.

(1) "Grandiose sense of self-importance (ex. exaggerates achievements and talents, expects to be recognized as superior without commensurate achievements) although often feigns modesty or humility.
(2) Preoccupied with fantasies of unlimited success, power, brilliance, beauty, or ideal love, distorted self-perception.
(3) Believes he is special and unique and can only be understood by, or should associate with, other special or high-status people (or institutions).
(4) Requires excessive admiration, constant need for attention, insistent that others see them as they wish to be seen.
(5) *Sense of entitlement and superiority, ex. unreasonable expectations of especially favorable treatment or automatic compliance with his expectations.
(6) *Interpersonally exploitative, manipulative, controlling, cunning, pathological liar, ex. takes advantage of others to achieve his own ends.

(7) *Lacks empathy, callous, total disregard for others, shameless, lacks any sense of remorse or guilt, unaware of others' needs and the effects of their behavior on others.
(8) *Often envious of others or believes others are envious of him.
(9) *Shows arrogant, haughty behaviors or attitudes, self-absorbed."[133]

Etiology

Most theories about narcissism reflect childhood behavioral conditioning rather than a chemical imbalance as the root of this disorder. The creation of a narcissist can stem from being either undervalued or overvalued in early childhood. His sensitivity to others' perceptions of him shapes his fragile sense of self. The idea that he is flawed is often a "belief held below their conscious awareness: such a person would typically deny thinking such a thing, if questioned. In order to protect themselves against the intolerably painful rejection and isolation that (they imagine) would follow if others recognized their supposedly defective nature, such people make strong attempts to control others' view of them and behavior towards them."[134]

Being recognized, valued, and cherished by a loving adult during the key developmental stages for a child is pivotal in his sense of self. As de Becker points out, "The moment that a child sees his own worth reflected in the eyes of an encouraging adult… inside that child a new view of self might take hold. He is not just a person deserving of neglect or violence, not just a person who is a burden to the sad adults in his life, not just a child who fails to solve his family's problems, who fails to rescue them from pain or madness or addiction or poverty or unhappiness. No, this child might be someone else, someone whose appearance before this one adult revealed specialness or lovability, or value."[135]

CHAPTER 6 PSYCHOLOGY OF THE ABUSER'S INNER WORLD

A life unexamined is not worth living. Socrates

One layer that molds an abusive personality from a young age is the inner mental landscape of his beliefs, habits, attitudes, thoughts, and emotions. What is really going on in the mind of an aggressor? This is the key to glimpse his true motivation for seeking power. "The truth is that every thought is preceded by a perception, every impulse is preceded by a thought, every action is preceded by an impulse, and man is not so private a being that his behavior is unseen, his patterns undetectable."[136] His tormented inner world is rife with emotional conflict as he struggles between feeling powerless and seeking power, experiencing a spiral of negative and destructive emotions, and being forced to create layers of defenses as he sinks deeper into denial.

Power Versus Powerlessness

A batterer is inherently driven and consumed by his quest for power. Abuse "is the mentality of oppression… that excuses and condones bullying and exploitation, that promotes superiority and disrespect, and that casts responsibility onto the oppressed."[137] His pursuit for total domination stems from his deep-seated fear of being totally powerless. He must compensate for the underlying feeling of inadequacy stemming from his childhood. He may repress these feelings unconsciously at a young age, but as he matures, he attempts to make his world predictable and safe. This seductive mask of power serves as a temporary survival strategy at best to create a false sense of security. It is no wonder, then, he feels threatened by a woman who feels confident, powerful, and secure.

Differentiating between real power versus the illusion of power is essential to understand the assailant's inner conflict. Unaware of true power that is derived from a sense of security, spirituality, and inner knowledge, the abuser resorts to fulfilling his imagined, false sense of power by dominating others and having to prove himself. To maintain the illusion he is not powerless, he must search for a victim to subjugate to his domination. Alas, this leads to a relentless battle to prove and maintain his control. In *Ditch That Jerk,* Jayne says, "Here's the rest of the paradox: he's also afraid of being in charge. Even when he dominates, he's afraid that if he doesn't sit hard enough on (her), she may have the strength to get back up. Because his domination of others is a sign of his actual powerlessness, his life becomes a constant struggle for him and anyone with whom he is involved."[138]

Thus, he relies heavily on his dependency to her and steadily builds this unhealthy attachment by quashing his partner's autonomy. If she dares to step out of this dynamic, it threatens his fundamental sense of self, exposes his vulnerability, and leaves him feeling utterly insecure. He fears his reputation will be tarnished, his secrets will be exposed, and he becomes apprehensive about losing his source of power. The perpetrator's vigilance over her life increases in direct proportion to his level of emotional dependency. Truthfully, he is hardly capable of creating a genuine emotional connection. His inability to form this bond leads to chronic dissatisfaction and frustration. In a way, his continued violence is his misguided attempt at establishing intimacy and an emotional connection.

Distorted Thinking Patterns

The contrast between his projected confidence and his fragmented self becomes apparent by his obsession with inflating his ego. A narcissist will often put down others, minimize their abilities, insult, degrade, or diminish them. One may hear him boast "at length how superior he is to other people, what fools they are, and that the rules of society (do) not apply to him."[139] At the same time, he seeks constant validation and praise from his partner to boost his injured ego. "Thus he relentlessly demands from his victim professions of respect, gratitude, or even love."[140]

This distortion leads him to describe himself in glowing terms, often in a very different light from the reality of what his wife experiences. In *The Verbally Abusive Relationship,* Evans says, "He also hides his abusive behavior from himself. His ideal image denies the reality of his motivations, his compulsions, and his actions. For example, an extremely tense, angry, and explosive abuser may describe himself as easygoing and relaxed. A critical, judging abuser may describe himself as accepting of everyone-taking people as they come. An undermining and trivializing or coldly indifferent abuser may describe himself as supportive of everything his partner does. And a countering, discounting abuser may describe himself as very open to differing views. Many verbal abusers describe themselves in the positive light of *all* of the above while they indulge in all categories of abuse."[141]

Denial is a survival mechanism designed to avoid confronting his true self and preserve his frail ego. "He wants to see himself as a generous and thoughtful partner, one who does not use or disrespect women."[142] To genuinely critically self-examine himself would require immense courage of which he is incapable. The depth of his denial cannot be underestimated: his capacity for convincing himself he is free of any blame is astounding. It becomes his only method of self-preservation to avoid a complete identity crisis. The effect of repeated denial of abusive occurrences takes a toll on his victim, can be quite destructive, and is one of his most effective tactics to invalidate her reality.

Abuser's Emotions

Looking deeper, a perpetrator's thoughts are formulated based on impulses and feelings. His abusive mentality, attitude, and beliefs are founded on his emotions, the precursors to his distorted thinking. Although anger is the predominant emotion that defines aggressors stereotypically, it is a misperception that tackling abuse simply involves reining in a bad temper. Anger can be a healthy emotion when it is expressed in a mature way that is respectful of others without being hurtful, accusatory, or destructive. Experiencing anger in response to conflict or an injustice is healthy. Unfortunately, an abuser lacks the emotional maturity to express his emotions in a healthy way.

Although it is true these men are most comfortable expressing themselves through rage, this is merely a surface emotion to act as a protective shield. Underneath this deceptive surface lurks a range of threatening emotions including: depression, anxiety, fear, insecurity, low self-esteem, unworthiness, and abandonment issues. Admitting to their existence would be akin to revealing his fragility and vulnerability. Because he truly lacks any genuine self-awareness, he is incapable of self-reflection or critical self-examination. He simply cannot face this reality that would emotionally cripple him and admit he feels impotent.

There is a misconception perpetrators are not in touch with their feelings or unable to express them when in reality the opposite is quite true. He believes nothing is more important than discussing how he is feeling constantly, effectively distracting his partner from examining her own inner state. Bancroft says, "Many of them express their feelings more than some non-abusive men. Rather than trapping everything inside... they have an exaggerated idea of how important their feelings are, and they talk about their feelings-and act them out-all the time, until (she is) exhausted from hearing about it all... Her life crises, the children's sicknesses, meals, birthdays-nothing else matters as much as his feelings. It is not *his* feelings the abuser is too distant from, it is his partner's feelings... For decades, many therapists have been attempting to help abusive men change by guiding them in identifying and expressing feelings. Alas, this well-meaning but misguided approach actually feeds the abuser's selfish focus on himself, which is an important force driving his abusiveness."[143]

Narcissistic Injury

Part of the assailant's survival strategy involves covering up the deep dark secret of his wounded inner self that he loathes and refuses to face. Only in the privacy of his home with his intimate partner does he feel safe enough to expose his true self. A narcissistic injury occurs whenever he feels threatened or his fragile sense of self is exposed. In *Not to People Like Us*, Weitzman says, "The fear (from this fragmentation) may be so severe that he can think of no action sufficient to help him recover equilibrium. As a result, he experiences a tidal wave of rage that knows no bounds, and violence seems the only outlet."[144]

Unable to deal with rejection or humiliation, he reacts strongly with rage or defiance to any criticism, whether it is real or imagined. To circumvent dealing with the emotions he desperately wants to repress, his fury acts as an effective buffer and familiar expression that provides comfort and security. In response to this threat, the narcissist is overwhelmed by the need to protect himself in a process known as self-righting.

In *Ditch That Jerk,* Jayne says, "Some guys describe anger as a rush of adrenaline, which certainly sounds better than feeling scared, lonely, unloved, or insecure."[145] It is easier to make his victim a scapegoat of his rage rather than face the turbulence of emotions churning within him. He gets a high from the adrenaline enabling him to feel in control and someone to be feared. Lashing out is the optimal psychological tactic to break her down.

This is about winning for him no matter what. His survival depends on it. The narcissist interprets even an insult or simple criticism as incredibly offensive, and is threatened by his partner's views, perspectives, or opinions. He "refuses to allow any woman to penetrate his armor... Anything could set him off. He reacted to any reasonable request as if it were a threat to his sense of honor. He was hypersensitive to any (of her) attempts to influence his behavior."[146]

It is evident every abusive incident is deftly designed as an attempt to protect himself from self-reflection, facing his inner conflict, and avoiding the painful reality of his fragmented self. His emotional explosion cleverly projects his energy outwards and shifts the attention away from himself. Directing his rage onto his spouse becomes his best self-defense. Thus, he justifies the rage that allows him to feel in control, restore his sense of power, and build his deflated self-esteem. This emotional volatility creates tremendous instability in his inner world. It is clear that "batterers choose to be violent at particular times and for particular reasons... The anger served a cleansing function for him. It was cathartic. He felt better afterward."[147] His release of tension is satisfying; he has protected his wounded self to a certain extent.

There is nothing a woman can do at this point to mitigate her situation or appease him. He will be infuriated by any action she takes. A narcissist believes she is to blame for threatening his fragile sense of self and not preventing the narcissistic injury from occurring in the first place. Whatever her response may be to his rage, "he feels irreparably injured; he is wronged, and no expression of regret or act of contrition on his wife's part will ever repair the damage."[148] Narcissistic rage is characterized by an inability "to distinguish his own issue or problem from the other as a separate entity."[149] The assailant regresses to behaving like an infant because he does not have the maturity level of an adult. The victim becomes merely the projection of his flawed fragile self.

"The abusive man feels cheated, ripped off, and wronged, because his sense of entitlement is so badly distorting his perceptions of right and wrong."[150] Because his thinking is rife with distortions, an abuser views any self-defense on his wife's part as an act of aggression and feels justified to take any action he deems necessary. He believes she is the cause of the problem and his self-entitlement prevents him from considering that he may be the one at fault. "All he notices is that you don't seem to be living up to his image of the perfect, all-giving, deferential woman."[151]

This is the narcissist's perpetual trap. Any violence towards him is once again a threat to his fragile sense of self that he must keep intact at any cost. In his mind, he thinks, *how dare she try to hurt him?* The only valid response he feels is to fuel his fury so it becomes even more explosive. His violence reaches a level of intensity at this point that becomes so destructive a woman's very life can be at stake.

Lack of Empathy

The aggressor's selfish behavior and lack of remorse is typical for a man who feels no empathy for his wife's plight or feelings. Part of this process involves shutting down a part of himself that feels and can relate to others. "An abusive man has to bury his compassion in a deep hole in order to escape the profound inherent aversion that human beings have to seeing others suffer. He has to adhere tightly to his excuses and rationalizations, developing a disturbing ability to insulate himself from the pain he is causing, and learn to enjoy power and control over his female partners."[152] "Denigrating you, dehumanizing you, making you into a nonperson so (he) can hurt you"[153] is an essential part of this process.

He views significant others in his life as a mere extension of himself who exist only to serve his own personal needs. "Such profound blindness to the other as a living, breathing human being is the expression of the narcissistic husband's sense of entitlement that is so integral to his emotional makeup."[154] He does not respect his wife as a separate individual with her own feelings, desires, or interests. Thus, when he does lash out at her, all the self-loathing he has kept in for so long finally comes to the surface. She provides him the perfect opportunity to project his emotion and find a release. "The worse a man feels about himself, the worse treatment his partner will receive… The injuries he causes her are a direct reflection of how he feels about himself."[155]

Anger Fix

The burning question a victim asks herself repeatedly is "What is the trigger for these explosions?" The answer is quite simple. Bancroft says, "He explodes when he gives himself permission to do so."[156] Because temporarily this outburst of anger seems to remedy the situation, abusers tend to increasingly rely on it to avoid facing the issue at hand and avoid accountability. The "explosion and release of tension-allows the anger addict to maintain his equilibrium."[157]

As his rage exacerbates, he becomes increasingly addicted to this anger fix. Hence, a narcissist rarely apologizes because that would involve giving up his fix and admitting he is wrong, which he refuses to do. Over time, his violence inevitably intensifies to elicit a heightened response from his victim who has become conditioned and tolerant. His obsession with gaining power and control is ever consuming and when he feels it slipping he tries with an even mightier vengeance to regain it.

To justify his actions, batterers often quote the myth that the cause for his behavior is his feelings. If this was true, everyone who expressed their feelings would be abusive. These men fail to differentiate between unhealthy feelings and destructive actions. He uses his anger as a weapon to intimidate and lash out at his scapegoat. "If you hurt someone out of anger, that doesn't make you less guilty. You're still responsible."[158] It is critical his partner observes his anger is not the cause; it is a side effect, a defense, a mere excuse to be abusive. His outburst "is actually being driven by his lack of empathy for *your* feelings, and by a set of attitudes."[159] He *chooses* to act violently. It is imperative she understands his motivation to truly be able to break free of this abusive dynamic.

In *The Verbally Abusive Relationship*, Evans says, "She then becomes as he once was, wounded and without a witness to her wounding."[160] Then he is not alone anymore in his pain. He finds comfort and solace in the fact someone else is suffering as much as he is. This defense mechanism is one an abuser relies on with growing frequency and contributes to his strategy of increasing his victim's confusion.

Negative Cycle of Emotions that inherently perpetuates abuse:

Evade repressed emotions such as depression, anxiety, insecurity, fear, low self-esteem, or abandonment issues
⇩
Need to protect fragile sense of self from being exposed
⇩
Process of self-righting to heal narcissistic injury
⇩
Use anger as a shield to avoid facing uncomfortable, scary emotions
⇩
Lash out in self-defense to avoid feeling inadequate, humiliated, disrespected, or inferior
⇩
Project rage onto victim to feel powerful instead of powerless
⇩
Addicted to anger fix to release tension and shift attention away from himself
⇩
Intensity and frequency of abuse worsens with time as anger fix intensifies.

CHAPTER 7 PSYCHOLOGY OF THE ABUSER'S OUTER WORLD

The reality of the other person lies in not what he reveals to you, but what he cannot reveal to you. Therefore, if you would understand him, listen not to what he says, but rather to what he does not say. Kahlil Gibran

An abuser skillfully projects and mirrors the tormented world of his inner conflict onto the external conflict he creates with his victim. She is merely a pawn in his power struggle; there is absolutely nothing she has done to instigate his maliciousness. In direct contrast to this inner struggle is the fabricated confident image he portrays to the outer world to ensure his emotional survival.

To understand the psychology of an assailant's outer world, his behavior, manipulative strategies, defenses, and complex dual personality must be examined. Abuse is perpetuated by the benefits he believes are inherent in continuing his behavior and being enabled by both his victim and the community in numerous ways. Therefore, a perpetrator's ability to change is extremely challenging when he lacks motivation or true sincerity.

Abuser's Behavior

The major behavior patterns characterizing a batterer are:

(a) his unwillingness to resolve conflicts with his partner non-abusively,

(b) his persistent choice to use violence against her, and

(c) his manipulative techniques.

The common myth that perpetuates abuse is the idea perpetrators are out of control, act unconsciously, and are unable to manage their tempers. Even though this is what he would like his partner to believe, this is simply not true.

Although some beliefs and thoughts that drive his behavior may be partly subconscious, many actions are calculated and premeditated. It is critical a victim observe his behavior is a choice, every action designed with a deliberate strategy. After being conditioned to accept the abuse over time, the only way to break through his brainwashing and have a chance at ending the cycle of violence is for a victim to remind herself repeatedly that he is consciously *choosing* to use aggression and violence against her.

According to Bancroft in *Why Does He Do That?*, "An abusive man is not *unable* to resolve conflicts non-abusively; he is *unwilling* to do so. The skill deficits of abusers have been the subject of a number of research studies, and the results lead to the following conclusion: abusers have normal abilities in conflict resolution, communication, and assertiveness *when they choose to use them*...They don't *want* to handle these kinds of issues non-abusively when it involves their partners."[161] The undercurrent of rage and tension present in all his interactions distracts her from appreciating his underlying motivations.

These men are masters of manipulation who "thrive on creating confusion, including confusion about the abuse itself"[162] to keep her off balance. At first, he will do this in subtle ways so she slowly begins to question her sanity and later in overt ways by threatening to leave, divorce, harm, or kill her. If it is not violence directed at her, his manipulation can lead to threatening self-injury or suicide to play upon her sympathy.

His unpredictability and fluctuating moods leave her guessing constantly, never knowing how to decipher his conflicting and contradictory behavior. Ultimately, he utilizes the sophisticated strategy of a con artist designed to wreak havoc with her mind so confusion seeps into every aspect of her life. "After a manipulative interaction she may have little idea what went wrong: she just knows that she feels terrible, or crazy, and that somehow it seems to be her own fault."[163] This leads her to feel increasingly isolated, not just from others, but from her own judgment, clarity, and sanity.

Whether he is avoiding accountability or simply in denial of his behavior, he lies and distorts events to feign innocence, adjusting the story to his advantage. His account is designed to draw sympathy, force others to forgive him, absolve himself of any blame, and render his partner guilty somehow. To convey his behavior is rational or acceptable, he may declare: "*I couldn't help it. It was not my fault. I had to do it to protect her.*" Do not believe him! Nobody *has* to resort to violence with a loved one. With the adept skill of a con artist, it is amazing how many people succumb to the persuasive lies he weaves. His narrative is so convincing that he may himself end up believing his fabrications and distortions. In the end, his manipulations have only one purpose: to exploit his victim.

Abuser's Excuses

He manufactures excuses to legitimize his actions, reinforce his intense denial, and repress his emotional conflict. Batterers are not only masters of making excuses, they feel entitled to do so. Their excuses serve a specific strategy: to distort reality and augment his partner's confusion. The more perplexed she is, the less clarity she has to see through his act. Excuse making includes: a) avoiding accountability, b) projection, c) justifying his actions, and d) refusing to apologize. Bancroft says, "The reasons that an abusive man gives for his behavior are simply *excuses*. There is no way to overcome a problem with abusiveness by focusing on tangents such as self-esteem, conflict resolution, anger management, or impulse control. Abusiveness is resolved by dealing with abusiveness."[164]

Every victim should remember, "If it is an excuse for mistreating you, it's a distortion."[165]

(A) Avoids Accountability

Coupled with denial, a perpetrator exerts great effort to avoid any blame or responsibility for his actions. They may "claim that they didn't know what they were doing and cannot remember anything (so) believe that they should not be held responsible... Temporary amnesia is one of the best excuses of all, because it's hard to argue with."[166] The reality is "most abusers do not have severe memory problems... He denies his actions to close off discussion because he doesn't want to answer for what he did."[167] He feels above reproach and resents being questioned after an abusive incident. "If his partner attempts to raise her grievances, she is 'nagging' or 'provoking' him. He believes he should be permitted to ignore the damage his behavior is causing, and may become retaliatory if anyone tries to get him to look at it."[168]

His inability to accept responsibility for his actions is almost pathological and his consistency with maintaining this position can drive his spouse crazy. He persistently avoids blame by shifting it onto her and justifying his actions. Checkmark any of the following behaviors of which an aggressor may be guilty.

Strategies to Avoid Accountability: Partially adapted from *Ditch That Jerk*[169]

- ❒ Denial can include beliefs, attitudes, dialogues, actions, or incidents
- ❒ Selective memory-conveniently unable to remember what recently happened or what came over him
- ❒ Minimize or downplay the abuse or its impact
- ❒ Justify abusive behaviors
- ❒ Distort and twist facts to play the victim himself
- ❒ Lie by claiming he was not abusive or convince others this is true
- ❒ Lie and invent an unbelievable story
- ❒ Feign silence to avoid discussing the situation at hand
- ❒ Get others to clean up the mess he has made

(B) Projection-Placing Blame on His Victim

Another safety mechanism to avoid facing himself and ensure his emotional survival is projection, a process whereby he labels his wife with his own fears and flaws. Because of his distorted sense of right and wrong, a batterer never feels at fault, always blaming his wife, others, or external circumstances and situations for his abusive actions, or frankly, for anything that goes wrong. He simply cannot accept the idea he is abusive and so is determined to find fault with everyone else. When she expresses her pain after an assault, he might typically respond by saying, "Now you are attacking me... A non-abusive mate would express deep concern, and would apologize, or would talk over the matter with empathy and understanding."[170]

Unwilling to face himself, "His anger, fear, and self-loathing grow in a secret hidden part of himself and, since he hides this part of himself from himself, he is unable to recognize the source of these feelings. When they do surface, their source, to him, is his partner."[171] Often he says, "*It takes two to tango*" to avoid being solely responsible. "To him, you need fixing every bit as much as he does (and probably more). He'd like to spread the problem and the blame around a bit to take the heat off him."[172] He may blame his hardships, but many people face these hardships without becoming physically abusive.

Typical excuses a perpetrator frequently resorts to include blaming:
- ☐ Stress from wedding and being a newlywed
- ☐ Anxiety, depression, or other emotional issues
- ☐ Low self-esteem
- ☐ Poor communication, misinterpretation
- ☐ Geographic moves
- ☐ Family pressure
- ☐ Job or career uncertainties
- ☐ Difficulty at work, pressure from boss, or job loss
- ☐ Blames the past or present
- ☐ Has to resort to violence to "protect" her
- ☐ Loses control and claims she is at fault for triggering him. Believes she is responsible for preventing an outburst by not upsetting him.
- ☐ Displeased when she irritates him and does not fulfill her "duties"
- ☐ Dealing with her first pregnancy and nervousness about being a father
- ☐ Substance abuse, blames his addiction for his mistreatment

(C) Justifying His Actions

Abuse becomes a means to justify his goal-ultimate control and dominance over his victim. A perpetrator will go to great lengths to justify his controlling behavior. For example, "Many men have decided that infidelity will not be tolerated and that violence is an acceptable and normal response."[173] They claim the outburst was not only acceptable but necessary to teach his spouse a lesson.

Any action that serves the purpose of bringing her under his control is validated in his eyes. "As a relationship progresses, the abusive man tends to get more comfortable with his own behavior and the remorse dies out, suffocated under the weight of his justifications."[174] He may revert to being silent if he cannot justify his actions. In *Ditch That Jerk*, Jayne notes, "You may notice that saying nothing is a typical response from men who can't think of anything convincing to say."[175]

Bancroft points out, "Abusers have numerous contradictory attitudes and beliefs operating simultaneously in their minds... His regrets

THE PSYCHOLOGY OF ABUSE 67

collide with his entitlement: 'women are fragile and in need of protection *but* they need to be intimidated from time to time or they get out of hand. My partner and I should have equal say over things *but* my decisions should rule when it comes to issues that are important to me. I feel terrible about how I treated her *but* I should never have to feel bad in a relationship, no matter what I did. I shouldn't raise my voice *but* I should have control over my partner, and sometimes I have to get loud to control her. You should never hit a woman *but* sometimes a man has no other choice.'"[176]

He views her as an object whom he has every right to control. Her independence, failure to accept his ultimate authority without question, or refusal to behave in a submissive way is a direct threat to his fragile ego. His attitude of disrespect for his partner defines the relationship. His mentality that control is justified perpetuates his mistreatment. Granting himself permission to take whatever action he believes is necessary, upscale abusers "felt entitled to their tempers and outbursts in exchange for the financial support and material accouterments they were providing-even in cases where the women were also high-earning professionals themselves. In some cases, the men repeatedly impressed upon their wives that they were 'bought and paid for.'"[177] The saying *"give her an inch, and she'll take a mile"* motivates him to hold a tighter leash and justify his control.

(D) Refuses to Apologize

After projecting all the blame from an abusive incident onto his partner, "he is convinced that he himself has been mistreated. Why should he apologize when he believes with every fiber of his psychological and emotional being that he is the one who has been wronged and injured? This is why he not only refuses to take responsibility for his abusive acts but also blames her for the violent episode."[178] He is incapable of a sincere apology because he cannot admit he is to blame when he is focused on feeling almighty. For a narcissist, his fragile sense of self would disintegrate.

If a batterer breaks through his narcissistic web to feel some remorse for his actions, it can be fleeting. If he genuinely feels concern for her, it may be too late after too much damage has been inflicted. By occasionally expressing remorse and asking for forgiveness, he plays the victim card to effectively shift his partner's attention, pull on her heartstrings, and garner sympathy. She may even wind up taking the blame as he somehow twists the truth. Perplexed, she is successfully distracted from processing the incident and getting in touch with her rage. Hence, the violence is perpetuated as she lacks clarity to see his underlying motivations. In reality, more than remorse, he may feel his pride is offended and his image or reputation tarnished after a public incident.

ABUSER'S DUAL PERSONALITY
Catching His Prey

In order to dominate a woman, he must first lure her in with bait by being deceptively caring and affectionate. Obvious signs of working too hard to impress one are a dead give-away he is seeking to compensate for some deficiency. He exudes a certain charm and his victim is intensely drawn to his magnetism. "To charm is to compel, to control by allure or attraction... People seeking to control others almost always present the image of a nice person in the beginning. Like rapport building, charm, and the deceptive smile, unsolicited niceness often has a discoverable motive."[179] In *Not to People Like Us*, Weitzman notes that upscale abusers "used their financial edge as part of courtship process... (to flaunt their) socioeconomic status, career potential or accomplishments, and prestige."[180] Many assailants possess a long list of fabricated, impressive qualities.

Attractive Qualities:
- Charming, exciting, captivating
- Playful, fun-loving, affectionate, kind
- Loving, attentive, warm, caring, devoted
- Sensitive, thoughtful
- Confidence, sense of ease, ability to take charge
- Magnetic personality, can mesmerize an audience
- Great sense of humor, entertaining
- Protective, acts concerned about her welfare
- Possessive, makes her feel special, like she is the only one who matters
- Well respected in the community, successful, held in high-esteem at work[181]
- Friends who look up to him and think the world of him[182]
- Close relationships to mother, sisters, or female friends[183]

Only after she is blinded by his charm and takes the bait does he reveal his true nature. In *Ditch That Jerk*, Jayne points out, "Their ability to conceal their true natures gives them an unfair advantage, since many women with whom they become involved don't know what they've gotten themselves into until it's too late. And, once involved, many women become convinced that their partners can and will change if just given the opportunity."[184]

As a master manipulator, he is quite persuasive and provides every reason to believe him. "The abuser often supports his ideal image by gaining agreement from others. He will let slip, in the natural course of conversation, how supportive and appreciative he is of his partner. It is no wonder that many battered women have been told how lucky they are to have such a wonderful mate."[185] By receiving praise from others, he ensures no one will believe his partner's victimization.

The Deception

To an aggressor, image is everything; many are stylish dressers, extremely conscious of their public persona. He desires being held in high esteem by family, friends, and the community. Skilled at the art of deception, he shares much in common with con artists who strive to uphold an unsuspecting image to society. The skill of concealing his abusive personality behind the façade of charm and confidence requires immense effort, persistence, and extraordinary levels of manipulation. The more upscale he is, the more sophisticated and convincing will be his deception until he himself actually begins to accept his lie as real.

Perpetrators "choose their partners very carefully. They are adept at finding women who are vulnerable to their macabre charisma, women whose lives are guided by a particular kind of dream, women who are down on their luck, new in town, or susceptible to an apparently attentive listener. (He) cannily figured out and then preyed on (her) particular vulnerabilities... His need for her was infantile, a need to know that he had the power to control her... The con job is persuasive; it can fool therapists, judges, prosecutors, probation officers, and the police."[186] Con artists similarly strategically choose their victims with great dexterity.

"Some abusers are so skilled at hiding their true selves that no one, no matter how informed and experienced, would be able to predict that they are capable of such abusive and violent actions. Other abusers may give off such subtle signs that only someone trained to know what to look for could detect them."[187] Why is it so difficult to predict who is a batterer? Because "most abusive men simply don't *seem* like abusers... He may simply not fit anyone's image of a cruel or intimidating person."[188]

In *Trauma and Recovery, the Aftermath of Violence,* Herman says, "His most consistent feature, in both the testimony of victims and the observations of psychologists, is his apparent normality... This idea is deeply disturbing to most people. How much more comforting it would be if the perpetrator were easily recognizable, obviously deviant or disturbed. But he is not."[189] It is remarkable the "depth of the psychological cruelty an abuser can perpetrate with little or no physical violence and keep hidden behind the most impressive façade."[190]

The closeness an aggressor might display with the women in his life can be extremely deceptive. He might possess unusually strong relationships with his mother, sister, and other female relatives or friends leading one to falsely believe he is respectful towards all women. Only when he chooses to behave violently towards his wife are his true attitudes exposed. It is interesting to note many of these men also possess a love-hate dynamic with their mothers. "The batterer's mother seems to have a good deal of control over his behavior; yet he will often abuse her, too. In fact, many women report that acute battering incidents are triggered by a visit to the batterer's mother. Often their rages are reminiscent of infantile temper tantrums designed by angry little boys to provoke their mommies."[191] Batterers may possess an unhealthy attachment and a sense of guilt for having separated from their mothers. This guilt may fuel his desperate need to be dependent on his wife. He fears abandonment even more than intimacy so his life essentially revolves around her. He needs her to feel powerful.

Duplicity

The assailant alternates between his dual personality: the charming, pleasant, and composed public persona versus his dark, hurtful, private persona. "Most men who batter their wives are generally not violent in other aspects of their lives."[192] They realize their behavior is inappropriate, would be condemned in public, and are typically only violent in the safety of their own homes where they cannot be observed. This contradicts a victim's false belief he is out of control and unaware of his actions.

Discussed previously in the section on narcissism, "They reveal their true nature only to the person upon whom they most rely for the maintenance of their sense of self."[193] He exposes his vulnerability only to his wife, an extension of his narcissist's web whom he must establish dominance over to feel powerful. This duplicity becomes an integral aspect of his personality and is the key to grasping why it is so challenging for her to walk away. She loves his sweet, affectionate, loving side that directly contrasts with his cruel, harsh, erratic side. Never knowing which personality will surface, he leaves her perpetually guessing with whom she will have to contend.

Everyone else thinks he is wonderful. "The pain of this contrast can eat away at a woman: enraged at home but calm and smiling outside; selfish and self-centered with (her) but generous and supportive with others; domineering at home but willing to negotiate and compromise outside; highly negative about females while on his own turf but a vocal supporter of equality when anyone else is listening; assaultive toward his partner or children but nonviolent and nonthreatening with everyone else; entitled at home but critical of other men who disrespect or assault women."[194]

His carefully crafted image essentially enforces his ability to get away with his unacceptable behavior. In the midst of a fiery rage one moment, he can seem cool, calm, collected, and even charming the next moment when the police appear. The fact he can shut off his behavior in an instant shows he is in complete control of his actions. A therapist may fall prey to his well-crafted image just as much as others and find it hard to resist his charisma. As he continues to deny his true nature, he uses his persuasive abilities to reinforce her belief in his favorable traits and gloss over his negative behaviors. Blinded by his dexterity at shaping her opinions, it becomes easy to minimize the abuse. Even after he confesses to his crimes, it may still be difficult to perceive him as a violent man. This is exactly what he desires, perhaps leading his therapist to defend him if others suspect him.

Alternating between this dual personality, the aggressor strategically sows the seeds of confusion in his victim's mind by wearing her down sufficiently. By clouding her vision, she fails to see through the dense haze he creates to accurately diagnose him. "So when a woman feels her relationship spinning out of control, it is unlikely to occur to her that her partner is an abuser."[195] Without realizing it, a victim mimics his behavior; the more he denies his true nature, the more she does as well. Essentially, she becomes trapped by her belief he is still a good person who needs help making it difficult to walk away even when the abuse escalates.

The mental shift she must experience to truly break free is to see the perpetrator in his entirety, the complete package beyond his deception. He might persuasively try to list all his redeeming qualities to win his spouse over, but she must see beyond the charm and the well-crafted illusion. No matter how many wonderful attractive qualities he may possess, they are overshadowed by his dark, abusive nature that can surface at any time.

In fact, she must realize that his dark side *is* his true nature he attempts to conceal. No one can honestly be *both* abusive and loving. His duplicity can only be sustained for so long after the schism and conflict created in his heart and mind. No matter how successfully he convinces himself he is okay, nobody can live with this level of guile forever. Eventually, an explosion becomes inevitable. Everyone has a breaking point, including the batterer.

Changing Abusers

Demanding change from perpetrators involves understanding three critical components: (a) his resistance to change, (b) what will truly motivate him to change, and (c) what true change entails.

(a) Resistance to Change

Change is not in an assailant's best interest as he finds abusiveness rewarding on many levels. He is perfectly content with his behavior and has no incentive to modify it. Why should he give up the benefits when they serve him and he is used to getting what he wants? Not only is abusive behavior satisfying his need for power and control and protecting his wounded self, it is also beneficial in other ways that a wife fails to notice: "because abusers are specialists in distracting our attention… If we want abusers to change, we will have to require them to give up the luxury of exploitation."[196] The following list outlines some of the perceived benefits a narcissist is reluctant to surrender unless forced to do so when his partner demands change or the community holds him accountable.

Benefits of Abusive Behavior: List adapted from *Why Does He Do That?*[197]
- ❏ Intrinsic satisfaction of power and control
- ❏ Getting his way
- ❏ Someone on whom to take out his problems

- ☐ Free labor from his spouse while he enjoys leisure and freedom
- ☐ Being center of attention with priority given to his needs and satisfying his ego
- ☐ Financial control
- ☐ Ensuring his career, education, and goals are prioritized
- ☐ Public status of partner/father without the sacrifices
- ☐ Approval of friends and relatives
- ☐ Ability to enforce double standards

Entrenched in his lifelong pattern of denial, it will take him time *and* outside intervention to recognize his abusive actions and how he has hurt his partner repeatedly. "In order to change, to develop empathy and understanding, to become non-abusive, he will need to work through all that has engendered within him his deep feelings of personal powerlessness."[198] For a narcissist, this proves a tremendous challenge. "Abusing is taking the easy way out... Nonviolence actually takes a lot more courage."[199]

Most perpetrators do not possess the courage, motivation, or the tools to face their insecurities or feelings of inadequacy. Examining himself honestly in the mirror is too scary. In *Ditch That Jerk*, Jayne says, "The task of helping men get beyond their protestations of innocence and into looking at what their lives are really like is a daunting and very difficult one... Abusers do not want to be thought of as abusive. The truth is that these men will go to great lengths to maintain an outward appearance of being all right. They go to even greater lengths to convince themselves. All this convincing requires so much energy that a man has little left to make any real change."[200]

(b) **Motivation to Change**

What will motivate a violent man to seek change? Because he is not suffering in the same manner as his spouse, he does not possess the same incentive to address his violent tendencies. A narcissist does not have the capacity to see how his violence affects his victim. He lacks genuine empathy and respect for her, and moreover, does not value her life. Blind to her suffering, in the end, he will only feel pressure when he sees how his actions hurt *him,* either through his reputation or legal consequences. It is no wonder he is motivated when his ego and reputation are at stake as he seeks respect and admiration from people he knows.

He builds his image in others' eyes so they will find it hard to believe he is violent and she loses her credibility. He knows society believes violence is unacceptable and will earnestly strive to maintain the image he is not a batterer. This places *pivotal* importance on the role of family, friends, and community to inspire him to change. The truth is, "abuse won't stop until people stop making exceptions for their own brothers and sons and friends."[201] Men are forced by external circumstances rather than self-motivation to change for the sake of their survival. "The men who make significant progress... are the ones who know that their partners will definitely leave them unless they change."[202]

(c) **What True Change Entails**

It is critical to grasp how challenging the task is of reforming a lifetime of abusive behavior. If it has taken years for an offender to become this way, it will take years to undo his behavior. To tackle deep-seated patterns of control, disrespect, and lack of remorse that have become a way of life for the aggressor is no small undertaking. It requires significant time to recognize these patterns before he can even attempt to change them. Most likely, he has never even thought about the power dynamics in his relationship before and takes usurping power for granted. He sees his actions as justified to keep things in check. He must learn how to develop empathy and compassion and put himself in his partner's shoes. The batterer must develop a set of ethics to differentiate between right and wrong.

Ideally, these are principles a person must learn at a young age. As he becomes older and set in his ways his patterns are only more obstinately ingrained. "Abusers are far more conscious of what they are doing than they appear to be. However, even their less-conscious behaviors are driven by their core attitudes... Abuse and respect are opposites. Abusers cannot change unless they overcome their core of disrespect toward their partners... Abuse grows from attitudes and values, not feelings. The roots are ownership, the trunk is entitlement, and the branches are control... Abusers are *unwilling* to be non-abusive, not *unable*. They do not want to give up power and control."[203] Moreover, there must be a deep fundamental awakening in the heart of the perpetrator, an intense desire to change and repair the damage he has created.

Some men will claim they want to change but just do not know how. Outside intervention is the only answer. Treatment within a batterers intervention program is still controversial and has limited improvement for some individuals. Unfortunately, some men use these classes to enhance their manipulation skills, becoming worse after participation in such a program. Ever the narcissist seeking approval and admiration from his peers, his goal is to convince others in the group he is not a batterer. He might appear to deeply self-reflect at each session, stop blaming his wife for his abusive behavior, seem remorseful, and even receive praise from his therapist, but then continue to be abusive when he returns home. "How can an abuser gain such insight into his feelings and still behave so destructively?"[204]

Victims should not falsely hold onto this belief that change is possible if she has no evidence to think so. Statistically, most offenders never get caught and never seek help. Of the small percentage that do enroll in programs for batterers, roughly a quarter of them do change.[205] "But it is virtually unheard of for an abusive man to make substantial and lasting changes in his pattern of abusiveness as a result of therapy."[206] This process of transformation is not easy or short and can average one to five years for significant change and that is only with a true desire to transform which is usually not present in most offenders.[207] Overcoming abusiveness is a lengthy process that takes years to reform abusive attitudes and behaviors.

Some men use their manipulative abilities to deceptively create the illusion of change. A victim deludes herself in her blind hope to believe he is different but when a man truly reforms there is a radical, undeniable difference. Only a perpetrator can ultimately decide if he is up for this challenge. "All you can do is create the context for change, and the rest is up to him. You are the best judge of whether or not he is truly developing respect for you and for your rights."[208] At the heart of change is true sincerity. "Shifting the blame to you, being overconfident or glib, refusing to talk about his behavior, or getting mad when you bring it up are all bad signs that in most cases indicate a lack of willingness on his part to change."[209] If he is truly sincere, there are certain actions he must be ready to take.

Checklist for Sincerity:
- ❑ Recognize his abusive behavior, admit his choice to use violence instead of another alternative, and see how his actions hurt her.
- ❑ Genuinely feel remorse, seek ways to make amends, build her trust, and ensure he will never be violent again.
- ❑ Stop blaming his victim and accept full responsibility for his actions and their consequences.
- ❑ Seek necessary help without his spouse having to ask him.
- ❑ Be patient if she is angry and allow his victim full freedom to express her healthy rage towards him.
- ❑ Deal with the abusiveness itself instead of all the excuses he makes.
- ❑ Be willing to let go of his need for power and dominance and having control over his spouse.
- ❑ Learn to have respect for her as well as for all women.
- ❑ Willingness to listen to his wife, allow her to express herself, and develop true empathy.
- ❑ Be truly motivated to be a better person and treat his partner well consistently.
- ❑ Actively seek personal change himself and not just because his wife, the community, or the legal system insist he do so.
- ❑ Be committed to therapy for the long haul and demonstrate how he has changed.
- ❑ He must willingly face himself, his insecurities, denial, fear, and his past.
- ❑ Accept that overcoming abusiveness is likely to be a lifelong process.[210]

CHAPTER 8 THE CREATION OF A VICTIM

We teach people how to treat us. Ben Franklin

In the same manner that Chapter 5 outlined the steps to create an abuser, a woman similarly undergoes a specific process to become a victim. This chapter explores the stereotypes of victims, common traits, and the steps leading to her surrender of power.

Myths & Stereotypes of Victim

The abundance of restrictive stereotypes about victims only serve to perpetuate abuse and prevent society from clearly recognizing a woman's victimization. Seen as a "damsel in distress," a woman is portrayed as defenseless, helpless on her own, and in need of rescuing. The following list of common myths include some that are grossly untrue while others do not fairly or accurately represent all victims of abuse.

(1) Low self-esteem, lack confidence, no self-worth
(2) Underprivileged, from low socio-economic class
(3) Not well educated or very intelligent, lack college degree or higher education
(4) Weak, timid, vulnerable, powerless
(5) Naïve, innocent, gullible, easy to take advantage of, too trusting of others
(6) Tolerant of violent behavior, conditioned to accept violence
(7) Grew up in violent households
(8) Abused as a child by father or dominant, influential male
(9) Feel the need to be protected by a man
(10) Drawn to domineering macho men, pattern of attracting abusive men into life
(11) Hurt by previous partners
(12) Prefer to be with abusive man instead of being single
(13) Enjoy being dominated and controlled by a man
(14) Believe she deserves to be abused
(15) "Would have left already if she did not like it"

Culturally Specific Myths for Indian Women:

(1) Fit the cultural stereotype or image of being passive, docile, submissive
(2) Wish to serve her husband and wait on him hand and foot
(3) Believe her place is in the home, taking care of the children, and not working

(4) Accept husband should make all decisions about home, finances, career, etc.
(5) Second-generation Indian American women are too well educated, independent, and career minded to become susceptible to abuse

These myths contribute to the classic image or media-generated portrait of a battered woman. A woman's inability to identify with these stereotypes that may be vastly inconsistent with her own self-image is one of the greatest barriers to accessing her situation correctly. If her wounds are invisible, she may reserve this label for someone with broken bones or severe injuries who requires hospitalization. She assures herself that she has no visible wounds or scars so is not a victim. Her self-image may be of a confident, successful woman who stands up for herself and does not let anyone push her around. This is especially true if she is affluent. As the upscale victim realizes her experience of being abused contradicts with her self-image, she feels increasing alarm and anxiety.

Having no one to relate to in her predicament, she may say, "This does not happen to someone like me." If she is well educated, has a college or advanced degree, or is very accomplished, she may declare, "I am too intelligent to be abused." One victim claimed, "It wasn't that I tolerated domestic violence because I was used to it-violence was so foreign to me that I denied it was possible."[211] Another victim confessed resolutely, "I wasn't *hurt* enough... I believed in my marriage."[212] It is this line of thinking that prevents a woman from identifying with her victimization.

Who Is a Victim?
The pertinent question that arises then is "Who is a victim?" Contrary to popular belief and the myths aforementioned, significant numbers of women do not fit the classic stereotype of a battered woman. In reality, *anyone* can become a victim of abuse. Whether a woman *chooses* to remain in the relationship will determine if she *stays* a victim. It is true daughters "exposed to their parents' domestic violence as adolescents are significantly more likely to become victims of dating violence than daughters of nonviolent parents."[213] If they are physically abused themselves during childhood, this increases the risk of future victimization among women and the risk of future perpetration of abuse by men more than two-fold.[214]

This begs the question do particular women have a propensity to being victimized? Are there certain commonalities in personality traits, childhood upbringing, belief systems, views on marriage, or outlook on life that victims share? Are there critical factors that differentiate her from other women who are not victimized? The following list outlines a few common traits:

Common Traits of Victims
(1) **Traditionalist-**about home, family values, and female stereotypes to some extent. Strongly believe in preserving family unit at all costs and upholding the institution of marriage. This is reinforced by the abuser's similar belief system.
(2) **Idealistic-**view marriage as an ideal to be attained and to strive for. May focus on his positive attributes to the point of idealizing him and glossing over any negative traits.
(3) **Vulnerability-**marked by being at a place of transition or uncertainty in life. She is influenced by predisposing factors such as loneliness, heartbreak from prior romance, homesickness, moving, life change, financial worries, job insecurity or loss, career changes, completing school, loss of a loved one, and naïveté about violence. There is a yearning desire to feel safe, secure, protected, and find a mate who provides this sense of belonging.[215]
(4) **Compassionate nature-**tendency to be kind, patient, loving, and give him the benefit of the doubt. Believe a nurturing disposition will change him but is unaware how he takes advantage of her generosity.
(5) **Power imbalance-**may admire and look up to spouse's position, wealth, or education, and feel dependent on him for reassurance and support. There is a belief he will help improve her self-esteem, financial and/or social status.

Two Types of Prey

Chapter 5 discussed perpetrators as hunters. No matter how charming he may seem, he senses her vulnerability just as a predator who hunts his prey. In *The Gift of Fear,* the author states, "The criminal's process of victim selection, which I call 'the interview,' is similar to a shark's circling potential prey. The predatory criminal of every variety is looking for someone, a vulnerable someone who will allow him to be in control, and just as he constantly gives signals, so does he read them."[216] Furthermore, "Every type of con relies upon distracting us from the obvious... The defense is to remain consciously aware of the context in which details are offered."[217]

Differentiated into two types of hunters, there are assailants who chase after the weakest prey and desire the quick and easy conquest (pit bulls) and those who take pleasure in pursuing prey that prove to be a challenge (cobras). This leads to the theory that there must also be two types of prey, those who are easy to capture and those who are more difficult to dominate. The former shall be referred to as the hare and the latter as the fox. All the myths and stereotypes of battered women describe hares, women who are weak prey. Although some women might fit this description, they are not the majority, and contrary to the idea they are helpless, many hares still adopt strategies of resistance. Women who have a history of abuse are more prone to being hares.

The more successful and independent a woman is, the mounting challenge she poses to the hunter and the more delighted he will be by the conquest. Essentially, a hunter feels increasingly powerful when he can dominate a fox, someone who may be well educated, possess a bachelor or masters degree, have a thriving career, and belong to a higher socio-economic group. In *It's My Life Now*, the authors point out, "Intelligence, background, upbringing, financial status, race, class, or any other individual factors are unrelated to who may abuse and who may become involved in an abusive relationship."[218] There are numerous examples of powerful, successful Hollywood actresses and famous artists and musicians who have been victims.

Process of Victimization

Unknowingly, a woman undergoes a specific process to relinquish her personal power and render her susceptible to abuse. The hunter gains increasing control in his quest for power in proportion to her submission. How does this occur? Genuinely puzzled, most survivors seem unable to answer this question. Every woman believes *"this could never happen to me!"* To reclaim her power, a victim must cognize the process whereby this occurs. This is an essential piece of the puzzle to offer her the clarity to break free.

In addition to the predisposing factors mentioned prior, there are nine progressive steps a woman experiences in the process of victimization and the transfer of power. Although there will be certain variations for each woman, these steps are part of her conditioning and simultaneously perpetuate the abuse. As will become apparent, the hunter's carefully executed strategy is behind each step as he seeks to systematically weaken his victim and hook her deeper into the relationship. Steps 1 and 2 are the precursors that build up to abuse while steps 3-9 occur as his partner experiences the stages in the cycle of violence.

***Step 1* Courtship**

Women must pay attention to how a man portrays himself from the first impression. Is he genuine or is he diligently striving to create a certain favorable image? In *Not to People Like Us*, Weitzman's research describes the "Cinderella factor," an idealistic tendency victims share that became apparent in the courtship process. "Despite (her) educational attainments and life experiences,"[219] many victims possess a certain naïveté and almost fairytale-like belief in being swept off her feet by a Prince Charming. In the fantasy of an idealized man, she is easily "impressed by suitor's prestige, power, charm, and charisma. In some cases, the men were as much as eight years older than their wives and seemed worldly and sophisticated."[220]

There is an intensity early on in the relationship that makes a woman feel special, like nobody else matters to him. Love-struck, she falls head over heels fairly soon after meeting. He appears "too good to be true."

THE PSYCHOLOGY OF ABUSE

Nine Steps of Victimization

STEP 1 COURTSHIP
Fall for abuser's charm and deception, believe in fairytale romance

↓

STEP 2 IGNORE RED FLAGS
Growing feeling of uneasiness and doubt, stop trusting her instincts

↓

STEP 3 ACCEPTANCE
Response to first incident of abuse sets the pattern

↓

STEP 4 INCREASING ISOLATION
Alienates her from friends and family

↓

STEP 5 GIVE UP HER VOICE
Choose silence and secrecy

↓

STEP 6 TRAPPED
Conflict of two opposing realities, confusion builds

↓

STEP 7 SHIFT PRIORITIES
Place him and his needs before hers as he conditions her to do

↓

STEP 8 TRAUMATIC BONDING
Develop unhealthy attachment and loyalty

↓

STEP 9 COPING STRATEGIES
Develop strategies to ensure safety and survival

This is an immediate warning sign that should alert a woman's abuse radar screen. If he places her on a pedestal and declares how perfect she is, he is already holding her to an unattainable ideal in his head.

What drives a victim to believe he is her soul mate and the man for whom she has longingly been waiting? It is the deceptive illusion he creates that she finds so irresistible. Speedy relationships that become intense and serious rather quickly or prematurely are a red flag. For him to secure his prize, he creates a compelling urgency to get married or be committed relatively soon. He may "expect the relationship to go on forever, perhaps using phrases like 'together for life,' 'always,' 'no matter what' (and)... refuses to accept rejection."[221]

Warning Signs During Courtship: List partially adapted from *Why is It Always About You? & Saving Yourself from the Narcissists in Your Life*.[222]
- ☐ Lose oneself the more one gets caught up in his fantasies and unreality.
- ☐ See people for who they are, not who one wants them to be. Potentially dangerous to insist on his goodness or good intentions when he is exploiting or hurting his partner. Issue is not whether they are good or bad but whether one can deal with his particular shortcomings.
- ☐ If he lies, cheats, disrespects, or hurts others, displays his lack of compassion, or betrays others' confidence, sooner or later, he will do the same to his partner.
- ☐ Do not feel assured one can change him or he will choose to change because of his feelings for his spouse.
- ☐ If a woman cannot control her own need to idealize, she may be standing in the way of her own happiness.

Weitzman observes: "The younger the (married) woman... the longer she tended to stay in the marriage... This may be related to the level of development of the woman's identity and sense of self prior to her bonding with her husband."[223] So the less formed her identity is, the more readily her sense of self will be shaped by her relationship with her partner. Due to cultural influences, Indian women are even more susceptible to this since there is usually no prior dating experience or involvement with men. An abuser is a predator who finds her vulnerability and search for reassurance appealing. As victims become increasingly dependent on their partner to boost their self-esteem, they expose their vulnerability.

"Sadly, many of these women believed that their mate would provide for them the parts of themselves that they felt were missing. But paradoxically, the very men who were supposed to support the women's weakened sense of self eroded it even further."[224] It is common for a woman to blame herself for being too blind, naïve, stupid, or trusting, but she should remember she is a victim of deception. Her assailant has expertly concealed his true nature with the skill of a con artist.

Step 2 Ignore Red Flags

As a woman spends more time with her partner, she senses a growing uneasiness that she cannot quite decipher. Because of the insidious nature of abuse, she doubts herself and ignores subtle signs that she cannot define or label. She dismisses her inability to identify that gnawing feeling to mean it is not real and she should not dwell on it. "When something is unnamed, and is seen by no one else, it has an aura of unreality about it."[225] Despite detecting something is amiss, she overlooks his behavior because she refuses to believe her relationship is in jeopardy.

Slowly, she trains herself early on in the relationship to ignore the red flags along the way that can appear as early as her first interaction with her partner, or if the courtship was smooth, then as early as the honeymoon. In *Not to People Like Us*, Weitzman says, in "courtship, there were tiny turning points along the way that pushed her more deeply into the relationship. These small decisions, almost indiscernible to others as well as to (her), reached a critical mass and became the couple's tacit agreement about what was to come."[226]

Thus, one of the pivotal steps to ensure her victimization is when she stops trusting her instincts and ignores her inner voice even if she senses impending aggression, violence, or danger. There is an irrational motivation to overlook her intuition that is both compelling and difficult to articulate for both foxes and hares. "Indeed, they all married despite this foreshadowing of violence."[227] The hunter strategically encourages this as he creates a deceptive illusion during courtship, discounts her feelings and perception of reality, and subtly influences her to not heed the red flags. Desensitizing her instincts for survival and failing to protect her boundaries is part of his strategy.

In *Ditch That Jerk*, Jayne says, "By calling your sanity and competence into question, a man can get you to wonder... if he has a point."[228] "Clearly, when there is no witness to one's experience and no validation of one's reality, one must rely solely upon one's own feelings and judgment. This is difficult for anyone... because the abuse itself diminishes her ability to trust her own feelings and her own judgment."[229] This is further reinforced if she believes she must accept his actions and behavior unquestioningly, out of respect or deference that is especially characteristic of the Indian wife.

Step 3 Acceptance

It is a woman's response to the first incident of abuse that sets the pattern. Any agitation prior is the buildup of tension she experiences in the first stage of the cycle of violence. As the perpetrator gives himself permission to explode in stage 2, he tests the waters during the first abusive incident and carefully gauges her reaction. If she chooses to leave him at this point, he realizes he cannot take advantage of her although he might desperately try to beg for forgiveness and ask for another chance.

By labeling it as a one-time event and making excuses for his behavior, his victim condones the abuse. If she *chooses* to stay with him despite his mistreatment, inadvertently, she has given him the green light. He feels confident and assured that her continuing presence is his victory. Even if his partner reacts to the abuse with anger, outrage, protests, or tears, it means nothing to him. He does not view her as an equal human being or respect her so he places no value in her response. As she copes with the abuse, the message she unknowingly sends him is she will tolerate his behavior, is willing to forgive him, can withstand the violence, will make an exception of her personal beliefs for him, and he can get away with treating her badly.

Reconciliation after the first abusive incident denotes a significant turning point at which battering becomes his personalized style. It is as if once this decision has been made it is a point of no return; the victim has now set the cycle of violence into motion. A victim fails to see that she inevitably validates her assailant by her decision to stay with him. For the narcissist: "She provides him with constant confirmation of her devotion that reinforces his inflated sense of self-worth."[230] His power trip is only threatened when his partner walks away from the abusive dynamic.

Step 4 Increasing Isolation

One of the perpetrator's most well-designed and successful strategies is to isolate his spouse, separate her from family and friends, even work or activities she was previously involved with, ensuring she loses contact with the outside world. The consequence of not having a job or any outlet outside of the home is she inevitably loses her frame of reference and perspective. Without realistic feedback from others who can provide an objective viewpoint, clarity evades her. Others may notice her withdrawal and without being aware of the full situation make comments such as: "*you have changed; you are not the same person; something is different about you.*"

A victim loses intimacy with people she was once close to and feels increasingly detached. One reason the isolation can be so frustrating is "because no one else seems to notice that anything is awry in her partner. *Her* life and her freedom may slide down the tubes because of what he is doing to her mind, but *his* life usually doesn't."[231] The pain of this contrast eats away at her and adds to her confusion as she feels utterly alone, as if no one else could possibly understand what she is going through. Her sense of isolation is inevitably reinforced when she fails to reach out for help and suffers in silence.

Step 5 Choosing Silence & Secrecy

Complicit in her subconscious acceptance of the violence is voluntarily surrendering her voice. She sacrifices the part of herself who stands up for her rights and dignity. If she is a hare, she might surrender meekly and feel she does not have options. This is especially true if she has been conditioned to accept violence while being raised in an abusive home. For a fox, despite her protests against the abuse, she forfeits her voice when she continues to stay with her partner. Part of this surrender involves choosing silence and secrecy to hide her shame that something like this could be happening to her. "Secrecy protects the highly valued intimate bond she has forged with her husband, however badly he has broken his vow to love, honor, and cherish her."[232]

There is a complex dynamic that contributes to the pressure a victim feels to maintain her silence. Without realizing it, she mimics her spouse once again choosing secrecy as a way of life. Weitzman says, "One of the hallmarks of upscale violence is the great pains to which these battered wives will go to hide it."[233] Culturally speaking, this is true of Indian women as well as other minority groups. The following list outlines numerous reasons victims find it difficult to admit the abuse to others and choose silence and secrecy instead.

Reasons for Silence & Secrecy
(1) Believes her predicament is unique and no one else will understand.
(2) Feels ashamed, embarrassed, and humiliated as she experiences the loss of her dignity.
(3) Blames herself for the abuse because he has conditioned her to do so.
(4) Unable to articulate her victimization because it is too painful to share the details with friends or family, she reasons it is easier to keep silent.
(5) Fears rejection if no one believes her, especially if they are enamored with abuser and constantly tell her how lucky she is to be with him.
(6) Seeks to preserve and protect her marriage and keep personal life intact.
(7) Feels ashamed to be perceived as a failure who could not make marriage work.
(8) Fears abuser's repercussions of betraying him if he discovers she has spoken about abuse to others.

These are valid, sensible reasons for a woman to maintain her silence. Even if she contemplates coming forth about the abuse, she may talk herself out of any attempt to reveal her secret for these reasons. The humiliation she feels can be overwhelming and hinders her ability to reach out to others. One victim claimed, "She felt too ashamed to admit that even as a therapist she could be trapped in an abusive marriage and not even recognize the extent of the problem."[234]

Another victim said, "My in-laws keep reminding me how lucky I am to have such a good provider for a husband. My lifestyle is the envy of my friends. Who would believe me if I said I was abused? Who could I tell who would not think I was demanding too much? And what would my children and I stand to lose if I betrayed my husband and talked about it?"[235] Inadvertently, a victim's silence perpetuates the myth that abuse does not occur in model minority communities or among upscale women.

Step 6 Trapped in Two Worlds

As a victim proceeds in the relationship, she continually witnesses two opposing realities. She feels "the wedding was a dream, but the marriage was a nightmare."[236] As Evans reveals in *The Verbally Abusive Relationship*, abuse "is crazy-making because it presents a double message. This is home-a safe place. This is where abuse takes place-not a safe place."[237] She observes the charming, wonderful side of her husband that she fell in love with, the image he portrays confidently to the outside world, versus the stark contrast of his dark, abusive nature that he reveals only in the privacy of their own home.

A woman's confusion builds as she tries to make sense of his dual personality: violent versus non-violent, cruel versus charming, powerful versus vulnerable. He cleverly deploys his manipulative strategies to keep his partner guessing so it is difficult to decipher his actions. She cannot blame herself that he is a hunter who knows her vulnerabilities and how to disarm her. Puzzling over his contradictory behavior, she constantly replays events in her head. Striving to make sense of his actions, she believes he is rational and offers him the benefit of the doubt. The *key* is to observe the inconsistency in his behavior when she is alone as opposed to in the company of others.

In addition to the dichotomy of living in separate realities in the public and private sphere, the fox or hare slowly arrives at the conclusion she does not share the same reality as her spouse. "His version of the abuse is worlds apart from hers."[238] She can live with him for years before having this realization. Trapped in this dual reality where there is seemingly no escape, she underestimates the extent of the situation and fails to see a way out.

A victim's attempt to save her marriage is futile. She cannot foresee the battle she is up against without identifying her victimization. This is the critical point when external guidance can make a tremendous difference, but if she chooses to keep her reality a secret no one can reach out to assist her. The truth is she is held hostage by the prison of her own mind; it is her own lack of clarity that prevents her from escaping and breaking free.

Step 7 Shifting Priorities

Gradually, her partner's conditioning succeeds and she falls for the trap of always placing his needs first, neglecting her own needs in the process. If she is an Indian wife, she has been told from a young age that this is her duty in marriage so she does it without hesitation. The assailant reinforces this repeatedly by prioritizing himself and making her needs secondary or not even acknowledging them at all. He will do this

THE PSYCHOLOGY OF ABUSE 85

consistently with career, family, weekend plans, extra-curricular activities, vacations, medical visits, etc. He strategically trains his partner to keep focusing on him and *only* him.

After an abusive incident, instead of acknowledging her emotions or how hurt she may be, he forces her to look at *his* emotion, *his* wounds, and *his* deeper need for healing, effectively shifting the attention away from herself. In the process, her personal boundaries erode as she loses herself. He enforces doubting her own feelings and needs, ultimately causing his wife to place more trust and faith in him.

Without realizing it, a woman increasingly depends on his version and interpretation of events, which is exactly what he desires. His denial heavily influences her, creating constant confusion in her mind. Every person has the need to be deeply understood on some level, but this is frankly not possible in an abusive dynamic where her partner refuses to acknowledge her as an equal. Bancroft says, "Your happiness in a relationship depends greatly on your ability to get your needs heard and taken seriously… You experience disappointment after disappointment, the constant sacrificing of your needs."[239] There is only so much a woman can sacrifice, however, until she reaches her breaking point. She can continue to survive for only so long in a relationship when her needs are not being met.

Step 8 **Traumatic Bonding**

One of the most puzzling interactions is the extreme closeness that develops swiftly in the abusive relationship. Despite the harsh conditions a victim may suffer, how does this loyalty form, especially under such tenuous circumstances? Traumatic bonding is a term coined to explain this unhealthy attachment and emotional dependency that takes root in the honeymoon phase. It is a powerful connection created in abusive relationships depending on four factors: [240]

(1) unequal power
(2) intermittent abuse (strongest form of reinforcement)
(3) cognitive dissonance
(4) masking techniques

Mistakenly, *both* the perpetrator and victim equate this attachment and dependency as love. This illusion of love is the most dangerous trap. It is difficult for outsiders to grasp the intensity of this bond. As Bancroft elucidates, "You can end up feeling that the nightmare of his abusiveness is an experience the two of you have *shared* and are escaping from together, a dangerous illusion that trauma can cause."[241] His clever manipulation keeps his spouse from turning against him. As a result, she develops a paradoxical love/hate relationship with her partner.

After the severe trauma endured in stage 2 of the cycle of violence, her isolation prevents her from reaching out to anyone. She seeks reassurance ironically from the perpetrator himself. There is an intense desire to connect with him, be reassured he did not really mean the nasty things he said, and did not truly mean to hurt her. The victim desperately holds on to the hope that their love is worth fighting for and the damage in their relationship can be repaired. So she convinces herself that any nominal gesture of affection will go a long way to soothe her troubled nerves and help her recover from the ordeal she has just withstood.

As Herman says in *Trauma and Recovery*, "He becomes a source not only of fear and humiliation but also of solace. The hope of a meal, a bath, a kind word, or some other ordinary creature comfort can become compelling to a person long enough deprived."[242] Ironically, a victim comes to perceive her batterer as her savior when he shows kindness because she is starving for affection and to be treated humanely. A flood of gratitude fills her heart for even the smallest kindness, albeit even if it is intermittent and unpredictable, that he may shower on her serving to reinforce the abusive pattern further.

The "oscillation between terror and reprieve"[243] in the cycle of violence creates an emotional dependency and intensely addictive quality to their interaction. As disturbing as this may sound, this is a crucial reason why it becomes challenging for a victim to sever the strong ties to her spouse and leave him no matter how ugly the abuse becomes. The Stockholm syndrome, whereby a victim begins to sympathize with her captor, is an excellent example of how four conditions must exist to create this dependency:

(1) "Victims are threatened with death or great physical harm and perceive the perpetrator capable of acting on these threats.
(2) Victims see no means of escape and, therefore, perceive that their lives depend on the captor.
(3) Victims feel isolated and hold little hope for outside intervention from family or friends.
(4) The victimizer offers kindness along with the violence, which increases the victims' perception of complete helplessness and dependence on the captor."[244]

Learned helplessness is a term that explains "how the process of victimization is perpetuated to the point of psychological paralysis."[245] This theory outlines how a victim becomes conditioned with time to feel powerless when she believes no response can result in a favorable outcome. Because she cannot exert any control to influence her situation or escape the abuse, she resigns herself to her predicament and does not even attempt to leave. Others may label her as helpless and submissive.

Research studies in which dogs and rats received repetitive electrical shocks demonstrated their lack of motivation to leave their cages. They were effectively conditioned to not respond. Similarly, when a woman experiences repetitive battering, she is cognitively trained to perceive any action on her part will be futile. In *The Battered Woman*,

THE PSYCHOLOGY OF ABUSE 87

Lenore Walker says: "Perhaps battered women, like the dogs who learn that their behavior is unrelated to their subsequent welfare, have lost their ability to respond effectively."[246]

Hence, this theory contributes to the stereotype of victims who are hares: passive, defenseless, submissive, compliant, and weak. Repeated conditioning over prolonged periods of time can transform even a fox who may be an independent, successful, goal-oriented professional. Blinded by her unhealthy attachment, his threats to kick her out of the home or divorce her may not be a strong enough deterrent.

She may respond with shock, denial, or rage but does not feel motivated to leave. However, the basic fundamental instinct for self-preservation and survival contrasts with this theory of learned helplessness. Most women do demonstrate strategies of resistance, do not accept the battering, and may even try to control the time and place of an abusive incident as a feeble attempt to have some control over the circumstances.

Interestingly, upscale and minority victims may possess other reasons to be attached to their assailants. Weitzman notes, "The upscale abused wife voices more attachment to her *lifestyle* than the traumatic bonding with her abusive mate. Very few... experienced abuse in their childhoods... In fact, it is this *lack* of experience with violence, rage, and abuse that makes this woman even more overwhelmed and unclear about how to cope with something so alien to her."[247] This same parallel holds true for Indian women who may not feel attached to their husbands but adhere to their traditional cultural upbringings and values to persist in a marriage.

Step 9 Coping Strategies

The final step that solidifies a woman's victimization is how she processes the abuse and survives in daily life. Chapter 10 discusses coping strategies she adopts for safety and survival that ultimately perpetuate abuse.

CHAPTER 9 LAYERS OF A VICTIM'S WOUNDING

The world breaks everyone and afterward many are strong at the broken places. Ernest Hemingway

Effects of Abuse

The psychology of abuse and the complexity of a victim's inner world are profound. The effects of living in the shadow of cruelty, whether a short-term or long-term relationship, cannot be underestimated. There are layers of trauma and wounding that take hold as the consequence of neglect and systematic violence intensely erode a victim's mind, body, heart, and spirit. This chapter elaborates on the emotional and physical wounding that occurs with time and makes escaping from abuse all the more challenging.

A hunter will always weaken his prey so any attempt to escape will be rendered futile. As the cycle of violence progresses, his partner becomes increasingly weak by his deliberate design. Her vulnerability heightens with each abusive incident until she eventually reaches her breaking point. If a woman was relatively confident and assured before, as a victim she may find herself struggling with her emotions and everyday life, as well as fighting to make sense of her predicament. It does not matter whether she is a fox or a hare. Every abusive incident wounds more deeply.

To maintain her composure of appearing strong and collected, she buries her pain beneath the surface. She becomes so adept at covering these wounds, she denies they exist. No matter how much she builds her tolerance to his mistreatment with time, the layering effect of pain is devastating and depletes her energy reserves. Later, when she decides to break free from the relationship, her healing will involve tackling each layer of pain. Each wound will need to be lovingly tended to.

Numbness & Masking

Before this healing may commence, a victim must penetrate the dense layers of numbness she created for her self-preservation. As a coping strategy, the numbness effectively serves its role as a temporary defense mechanism, providing a buffer of protection to minimize the impact of the abuse. Riding on a constant emotional roller coaster is exhausting and exacts a remarkable toll. Naturally, a woman shuts down because the shock from the trauma can be too much to absorb and her inability to cope overwhelms her. Without realizing it, she mimics her partner's inner world of torment and conflict by disconnecting, detaching, and denying. All of these enforce his clever strategy to systematically deplete her strength.

Masking is a defense mechanism to block her emotions from surfacing or deny they exist at all. Quickly she learns the more indifferent and detached she becomes, the easier it is to survive. She has learned it is safer to be silent and keep things to herself in the hostile environment he has created to minimize his violence. Whenever she does stand up for herself or state her beliefs, he irrevocably quashes her. Her entire focus revolves around evading an abuse trigger.

Ironically, while he trains her to repress her emotions, he continues to be overly expressive about his feelings in the typical fashion of a narcissist. By relying on this mask her assailant cannot penetrate, she has discovered a way to be "safe," endure, and continue to survive in her dangerous predicament. Even after she is courageous enough to break her silence and share her story with others, they will observe how she speaks in a detached way as if she is telling someone else's story. When she finally breaks free, it takes significant therapy, time, and healing for this numbness to dissipate.

Another form of numbness is disassociation, defined as a "psychological protection strategy… a powerful tool to create distance between yourself and the violence."[248] Understandably, a battered woman detaches from the present to avoid feeling the intensity of the pain. Many rape victims will describe witnessing their physical body from afar during the incident. Victims of abuse experience the same phenomena, sometimes with increasing frequency as the violence becomes severe. These layers of numbness, masking, shutting down, and disassociating must be penetrated for her to break free from the shackles of victimization and for her healing to begin.

Emotional Wounding

Beneath the numbness are layers of complex emotions swirling around within her in a dizzying daze of which she struggles to make sense. During the course of an abusive relationship or even within an abusive incident itself, a victim may experience the entire gamut of emotions that vary in intensity and complexity. With each layer, every emotion serves a specific role and purpose to help her heal and enhance her self-awareness. Essentially, to understand a victim's psyche, there are several key emotional layers that overlap and frequently blend together.

- Layer 1: Fear & Anxiety
- Layer 2: Grief & Depression
- Layer 3: Anger & Frustration
- Layer 4: Shame & Betrayal

Layer 1 **Fear & Anxiety**

When her awareness allows her to penetrate the external layer of numbness, the predominant emotions that manifest during the stages of the cycle of violence are fear and anxiety. Fear is her constant companion whether it is the buildup of tension, the abusive incident itself, the processing stage when she tries to make sense of what happened, or the anticipation after the honeymoon phase of the cycle repeating itself. She must realize fear is a natural response to danger when living with an abusive partner whose impulsive mood and unpredictability always leave her wondering about his next outburst and how he will retaliate.

Fear teaches survival-the need to take immediate action to protect herself and ensure her safety. She must embrace her fear as a warning sign of peril. The perpetrator instills fear as an intimidation tactic so she feels powerless, ensuring his reign of control persists. *The Gift of Fear* describes the terror that can haunt a victim. "After the shock of violence has begun to heal, victims will be carried in their minds back to that hallway or parking lot, back to the sights, smells, and sounds, back to the time when they still had choices, before they fell under someone's malevolent control, before they refused the gift of fear."[249] Fear is a reminder she has the ability to respond with awareness and make empowering choices.

Coupled with fear is the invariable anxiety creating an undercurrent of stress that permeates every area of a victim's life. All-consuming, she cannot remember a time when she lived without this adrenaline. She tries to anticipate her partner's next move, prevent another outburst, keep the children safe, and maintain her secret so no one else discovers the truth about her marriage. The stress on her physical system subsequently leads to other signs and symptoms such as palpitations, panic attacks, sleep disturbance, and irregular eating patterns.

Despite her hyper-vigilance and attention to every detail, something will inevitably trigger him and inflame his anger. She fears she is losing her mind and something must be seriously wrong with her. Another aspect of mimicking his behavior, she "internalizes a 'critical voice.' She feels a general sense that time is passing her by and she is missing something. There is a concern that she isn't happier and she ought to be."[250]

Layer 2 **Depression & Grief**

Underneath the surface emotions of fear and anxiety lurks the oppressive weight of depression. A wife might make her best effort to create the illusion her marriage is perfect, yet the depression suffocates her and slowly eliminates any sense of joy from her life. She feels hopeless, loses interest in daily activities, and finds in general life is meaningless. As she detaches, she develops a cynicism about the world and relationships. Despite going through the motions in her daily routine, there is an emptiness that seeps into the depth of her soul. Often her eating and sleeping habits might be significantly affected. Masking the pain of this emotion with anti-depressive or anti-anxiety medications has limited benefit. The real source of her depression is the violence she suffers at the hands of her partner.

Grief and depression go hand in hand. The sheer force of her grief when she taps into it can consume her, especially after restraining it for so long. Overwhelmed by her sacrifices and all the disappointments, she grieves the loss of her freedom and independence. She bemoans the loss of her spirit, the faded dream of a happily married life, and the heartbreak over a man she so deeply loves. She grieves for her children growing up in this hostile, unhealthy environment. Mostly she grieves because she cannot imagine a way out of her predicament. There is no escape from her misery as her anguish consumes her. "Grief is the conscious acknowledgment and realization of what the spirit already knows... When the victim of verbal abuse realizes she was not loved, only controlled, she grieves the lack of love because she knows that she is lovable."[251]

Layer 3 **Anger & Frustration**

After cycling through the stages of violence and repeating the pattern enough times, a victim eventually taps into the torrent of anger she feels deep within buried underneath the layers of grief. A quiet, smoldering rage builds steadily within her after each assault. Unsuspecting, she has no idea when she will erupt. Many women may not feel or express anger for many years until they are finally ready to break free. Her discomfort with expressing anger is for several important reasons:

(1) This is by far one of the most difficult emotions to get in touch with because she has trained herself to repress it. It has become second nature to deny her anger.
(2) Her abuser has conditioned her to believe it is not safe to be angry and she has no right to feel that way. She learns to associate anger with danger.
(3) He has successfully trained her to feel that any outburst of anger will only make him more irate and will trigger an abusive incident, which she does everything possible to avoid.
(4) By unleashing her anger, her deepest fear is she will lose control and mirror her partner. After detesting his explosions of anger, she refuses to stoop to his level.

As Bancroft highlights in *Why Does He Do That?*, "Your abusive partner doesn't have a problem with *his* anger; he has a problem with *your* anger. One of the basic human rights he takes away from you is the right to be angry with him. No matter how badly he treats you... the privilege of rage is reserved for him alone... He uses your anger against you to prove what an irrational person you are."[252] When a victim finally faces the intensity of this emotion, it can consume her and transform into a rage that knows no bounds.

A woman must learn "there is power in your anger. If you have space to feel and express your rage, you will be better able to hold onto your identity and to resist his suffocation of you. He tries to take your anger away in order to snuff out your capacity to resist his will... He perceives your anger as a *challenge* to his authority, to which he responds by overpowering you with anger that is greater than your own. In this way he ensures that he retains the exclusive right to be the one who shows anger... He isn't abusive because he is angry; he's angry because he's abusive."[253] A victim must differentiate between unhealthy, destructive anger that he possesses versus healthy, protective anger that serves her. She must learn "when (she) responds to abuse with a forceful 'stop that!' she uses her anger to protect herself. This constructive use of anger is quite different from destructive blame and accusation."[254]

When her fury finally penetrates the wall of numbness on the surface, it is the strongest catalyst for her healing. This emotion may surprise her, but it is absolutely critical to witness it has a power of its own. Releasing her rage will prove cathartic. This breakthrough point differs for each victim based on her level of tolerance and many other circumstances. Most survivors have fantasies of revenge and directing anger towards their partners for the violence they have endured. Instead of suppressing these feelings of vengeance, it is healthy to let them out. This does not mean acting out on these feelings or being abusive towards her spouse, but simply acknowledging them and finding healthy ways to release this pent-up emotion.

By suppressing her wrath long-term, her energy stagnates so she feels trapped in a doomed relationship. The only way to overcome this frustration is by giving herself permission to release her anger in healthy doses. A victim must feel and express her rage constructively, allowing it to serve as momentum to free herself. Having a physical outlet for release such as exercise or competitive sports can help immensely. Underneath her ire she will discover another layer of grief, and beneath that yet another layer of anger. These two layers are intricately intertwined and keep repeating themselves until she encounters the last layer of emotional wounding.

Layer 4 **Shame & Betrayal**

When she has pierced the dense layers of numbness and the intense combination of anxiety, fear, grief, depression, anger, and frustration, a victim reaches the very core of her emotion-an overwhelming sense of shame and betrayal. She witnesses her true wounding at the depth of her being. Mourning the betrayal she has suffered at the hands of a man she loved wholeheartedly, she laments her erroneous faith in believing in her marriage. Grieving the loss of her dignity, she is betrayed by the indignities her perpetrator made her suffer: basic rights of which he has stripped her and the general hopelessness that consumes her. The devastation of these realizations takes time to process.

Once she comes to terms with her partner's betrayal, she faces the betrayal by everyone else: friends and family who witnessed or suspected the abuse and did nothing, the community who adored and praised her partner while blind to his true nature, or the legal system that failed to protect her. The last layer of hurt, however, is facing her self-betrayal, the most challenging part of her healing journey. She is besieged with guilt and self-blame.

She asks herself: How did she stay in this marriage for so long? Why couldn't she see the signs? Why didn't she get out sooner? Why did she not ask for help? She betrayed herself by continuing to stay in the relationship and suffering for so long at the hands of her attacker who showed no mercy. The depth of her wounding that seems irreparable is her ultimate betrayal.

Breaking Point

Eventually, when the abuse has worn her down sufficiently, she reaches her breaking point. Whether it is a specific incident that is the "final straw" or a set of circumstances that is the trigger, she can no longer endure the trauma. "The decisive turning points and precipitating events that emerged fell into one of the following categories:"[255] (A victim should checkmark any that apply to her specific situation.)

- ☐ "His threats become increasingly severe.
- ☐ His public episodes of abuse are heightened.
- ☐ His violence increases and her injuries require medical attention.
- ☐ Her support network grows and she feels more confident about taking action.
- ☐ Her reasons for staying have been satisfied-ex. birth of youngest child or kids have graduated and gone to college.
- ☐ An extramarital affair reminds her she is desirable and not all men are abusive."

This low point "is often accompanied by shock, numbness, pain, forgetfulness, and the inability to carry out simple daily functions."[256] Surprisingly, this crisis is the catalyst for a victim's healing. When she feels totally defeated, this is the turning point to reclaim her rights, her health, and her life again. It is only after this collapse that she can begin to break through the layers of numbness and feel again. She commiserates with her pain, anger, sorrow, and the full extent of her suffering she has voluntarily blocked for so long. A victim should be gentle and patient with herself as it will take time to tap into the layers of emotions deeply buried beneath this wall of numbness.

THE PSYCHOLOGY OF ABUSE 95
Mental & Physical Wounding-Effects of Abuse
In addition to the emotional wounding are the mental and physical effects of abuse that compound a woman's victimization. This response has four components:
(1) Shock
(2) Exhaustion
(3) Stress and hormonal imbalance
(4) Physical symptoms

(1) The **shock** a woman experiences after a traumatic incident is frequently underestimated or simply not acknowledged. Others may be surprised by her lack of response and use that as an indication she is tolerating the abuse, enabling her partner, or acting helpless. From a physiological standpoint, however, the shock can be utterly paralyzing. Her initial gut reaction is to create a defensive and protective layer of numbness to block the pain of that wounding. In the moment, it may be the only reaction of which she is capable. In *It's My Life Now*, the authors say, "What happened was so out of context with everything she believed about life and relationships, it didn't fit into reality."[257] She feels she is living in a dream, a nightmare from which she cannot awaken. Her denial effectively blocks the abusive event from the conscious mind.

(2) **Exhaustion** consumes a battered woman as the effects of abuse destroy her systematically. She witnesses a gradual erosion of her emotional and physical strength preventing her from thinking clearly or choosing a productive course of action to extricate herself from this predicament. Her lack of resistance severely diminishes her capacity to break free. Others may interpret this lack of action as tolerance, but her fatigue is real and a strategic handicap.

Whether she is a fox or hare, her adrenals are taxed and she may experience adrenal fatigue, a precursor to chronic fatigue many victims suffer from unknowingly. She lacks fundamental energy to function and get through her daily activities that require enhanced effort. Symptoms include: difficulty awaking in the morning, continuing fatigue not relieved by sleep, lethargy, craving salty foods, low libido, diminished ability to handle stress, prolonged recovery time from illness, injury, or trauma, lightheadedness when standing quickly, mild depression, less enjoyment or happiness with life, increased PMS, symptoms exacerbated if she skips meals, diminished focus and concentration, less accurate memory, reduced tolerance, and deteriorating productivity.[258]

(3) **Intense stress levels and hormonal imbalance** are common debilitating symptoms. Due to the constant emotional fluctuations during the stages of the cycle of violence, the autonomic nervous system responds to stress with a complex chain of biochemical reactions known as the "fight or flight response": triggering the release of specific hormones, such

as cortisol and adrenaline, to cope with the immediate situation. As a result, her heart beats faster, her blood pressure rises, oxygen intake increases, more blood is pumped into the muscles, and she perspires more profusely. If stress is not regulated and control is not established, the system continues to flood the body with elevated hormones to achieve balance.

Physiologically, her "brain and body are working overtime to protect (her). These are by no means signs of weakness; they are perfectly normal reactions to having survived a terrible ordeal."[259] However, due to the steady stimuli of stress she is exposed to, the nervous system never gets a chance to shut off. Severe hormonal imbalance is inevitable. With time, she adapts to aggrandizing levels of stress and her dysfunctional coping mechanism for stress becomes routine. In *The Battered Woman*, Walker says, "The kind of generalized stress reaction that battered women live under day after day is an insidious form of physical abuse."[260]

(4) The **physical effects of abuse** are real. The shock from repeated trauma leads to a range of specific mental and physical symptoms indicative of post-traumatic stress disorder. "PTSD symptoms may result when a traumatic event causes an overactive adrenaline response, which creates deep neurological patterns in the brain. These patterns can persist long after the event that triggered the fear, making an individual hyper-responsive to future fearful situations. PTSD displays biochemical changes in the brain and body that differ from other psychiatric disorders such as major depression."[261]

A victim's response to trauma can be overwhelming, so she processes it by reliving the event repeatedly, a phenomena known as flashbacks or intrusive recall. These are moments that come suddenly without any warning and flood a victim's mind. Images or thoughts consume her and her recall of details can be quite lucid. She "typically has memories of what occurred that are clearer and more accurate than those of the abuser, because of the hyper-alert manner in which people react to any danger."[262] A survivor usually "remembered every word spoken and every blow delivered."[263] Her spouse works diligently to convince her she must let go, creating confusion so she cannot accurately diagnose her victimization. The trauma assaults her mental integrity and ability to cope. "Fear is an emotional, physiologic, and behavioral response to a recognized external threat"[264] that the trauma poses.

Exposure to severe or persistent violence can lead anyone to experience symptoms of PTSD. There is a delay period in which symptoms might not manifest for many months or years because the mind blocks the memory of the trauma. To accurately diagnose PTSD, symptoms must be reoccurring for one month or more "and cause significant impairment in social, occupational, or other important areas of functioning."[265] If it is less than one month it is classified as acute stress disorder: includes a "sense of numbness, blocked memory of traumatic event, feeling dazed (reduced awareness of surroundings), and a feeling that things are not real."[266]

Common Symptoms of PTSD, listed in the table following, include severe stress reactions and psycho-physiological complaints partially derived from *The Merck Manual*.

Anxiety	Restlessness, fatigue, poor concentration, irritability, muscle tension, disturbed sleep, uncertainty, growing self-doubt, loss of self-confidence, palpitations.
Depression	Withdrawn, not as involved in daily activities, lack enthusiasm, may be suicidal, flat affect or not talkative, trouble sleeping, poor appetite, can't experience other emotions, poor concentration, indecisive, helpless, hopeless, loss of sexual desire.
Fear	Intense terror, intimidation, or sense of being helpless. Anticipation can be terrifying, fearful of future events or relationships.
Disturbed sleep	Insomnia, restless sleep, difficulty falling or staying asleep, recurring distressing dreams, or nightmares.
Hyper-vigilance	Easily startled, heightened startle reflex, learns to be on-guard, defensive, distrusts spontaneity.
Flashbacks	Reliving thoughts and images of abuse suddenly without warning.
Numbness	Detachment, lack of emotional responsiveness, inability to feel.
Avoidance	Avoids abuse triggers or any stimuli associated with trauma, ominous feeling, intensely negative response to any abuse reminders, avoid talking about event, avoid people, places, or behaviors that might lead to distressing memories, inability to recall major parts of trauma. Desire to escape or run away, desire to not be "too sensitive," hesitancy to accept her perceptions, reluctance to come to conclusions.

Any untreated symptoms can subsequently progress to further imbalance. Extreme anxiety can develop into panic attacks that include the sudden appearance of at least four physiologic symptoms: "shortness of breath, palpitations or accelerated heart rate, chest pain or discomfort, profuse sweating, chills or feeling flushed, choking, dizziness, trembling or shaking, nausea, stomachache or diarrhea, numbness or tingling sensations, sense of 'unreality' or detachment from environment, fear of dying or going crazy or losing control."[267]

In extreme cases, some battered women become suicidal, unable to see any other solution to easing their suffering. Suicidal behavior includes: "self-destructive behaviors such as excessive drinking or drug use, heavy smoking, overeating, neglect of health, self-mutilation, reckless driving, criminal behavior."[268] Not having a social support system can be a risk factor. The lack of empathy her spouse displays takes a toll and destroys her self-worth over time. Many victims do not consider themselves suicidal but may repeatedly fantasize death as the only true escape.

It is impossible for any woman to tackle these severe symptoms on her own. She must seek professional help and acknowledge what she is experiencing is a normal reaction to the trauma endured. In some situations, anti-depressant or anti-anxiety medication might be appropriately suggested for certain individuals but this will only help superficially and temporarily. Supportive psychotherapy to face her trauma is also therapeutically essential. Long-term struggles women face during recovery relate to safety concerns, sexuality and relationship issues, and learning how to trust again.

Statistics on mental health care include:
- IPV results in more than 18.5 mental health care visits in the U.S. each year.[269]
- 37% of battered women have symptoms of depression,[270] 46% have symptoms of anxiety disorder,[271] and 45% experience PTSD.[272]
- The emotional effects of partner violence are a factor in more than 25% of female suicide attempts and are a leading cause of substance abuse in adult women.[273]

Refer to Appendix 1 for additional statistics.

Sense of Self

The deeper effects of both physical and emotional wounding significantly impair a victim's ability to heal and recognize the abuse. In *Trauma and Recovery* it reveals, PTSD "invades and erodes the personality. While the victim of a single acute trauma may feel after the event that she is 'not herself,' the victim of chronic trauma may feel herself to be changed irrevocably, or she may lose the sense that she has any self at all."[274] "Long after the event, many traumatized people feel that a part of themselves has died."[275] In *Why Does He Do That?*, Bancroft affirms, the "negative effects (of abuse) don't hold a candle to the emotional and physical pain, loss of freedom, self-blame, and numerous other shadows that abuse casts over the life of its female target."[276]

As mentioned in previous chapters, the parallel behavior patterns between a victim and her perpetrator are fascinating from a psychological perspective as she mimics him. At the core of his dysfunction is his distorted self-image and fragile sense of self. As the effects of abuse set in, her confidence or self-assuredness is replaced by a new sense of vulnerability and fragility. Step-by-step, her autonomy as an individual being is wiped away as she becomes merely a pawn in his narcissist's self-serving web. His narcissism dominates the relationship and leaves no room for anything but his ego. She is forced to surrender herself completely and lose touch with that part of herself that could set her free. His goal is to make her suffer as much as he does. If he is broken, he consciously or subconsciously wishes his partner to be broken as well.

Just as consuming poison will slowly infiltrate her bloodstream, so does the toxicity of an unhealthy, abusive dynamic seep into a battered woman subtly and gradually. She creates walls of defenses as her body, heart, and mind fragment. Her strength diminishes, her self-identity withers, and her integrity is shattered, permitting him to wound her deeper. Burying her true feelings, clinging to her denial, and repressing her wounded self becomes second nature. The erosion of her will and spirit creates irreparable damage and is a critical reason she cannot effectively or proactively respond to her situation.

The recovery period after an abusive incident takes time. Processing the shock and trauma can lead to a delay period of a week or several weeks to recover and feel normal again. This corresponds to stage 3 in the cycle of violence where there is an interval period before a victim might respond. Feeling dazed or as if things are unreal prevents her from taking any immediate action.

In *It's My Life Now,* the authors state, "Only later, when you were out of the relationship and safe, did something trigger your memory of the event and the full impact of what happened finally hit you. Perhaps days, weeks, or months later... Denial probably helped to save you."[277] Nobody's sense of self can be preserved and remain intact after severe trauma without developing strategies of resistance and defense mechanisms for protection. At some point after a woman breaks down, the need for self-preservation takes over and allows her to finally take the necessary steps to break free.

CHAPTER 10 PERPETUATION OF ABUSE

No one saves us but ourselves. No one can and no one may.
We ourselves must walk the path. Buddha

Abuse is perpetuated by the intricately intertwined roles of the perpetrator, the victim, and the community. This chapter breaks down the victim's specific role. To clarify, this does not mean she is blamed for the abuse in any way, but how her persistent decision to stay in the relationship *continues* the abusive dynamic and co-creates the reality of victimization. She is not responsible for the violence, but she partly perpetuates it in three primary ways:
(1) her coping strategies
(2) her belief system
(3) her rationale for staying or after separation-the reasons she may return to her partner.

Ensnared in the abusive relationship for numerous reasons, it adds layers of complexity to her dilemma that a bystander cannot even fathom. Part of reclaiming her own personal power is taking responsibility for what she creates, how she defines her reality, and the meaning she ascribes to her situation. As difficult as this might be to face, a victim cannot break free until she recognizes with complete clarity how she is an accomplice with her perpetrator in co-creating this reality. "If (she) can recognize her role in colluding in her husband's behavior, she can more quickly find a way to exit the marriage."[278]

COPING STRATEGIES

A woman quickly discovers the only way to survive in an abusive relationship is to develop coping strategies necessary to ensure her safety and survival. This is listed as the ninth and final step in the victimization process discussed in Chapter 8. Whether it is active or passive strategies of resistance, they provide an attempt at self-preservation and protection vital to guarantee she can function after severe trauma.

The very strategies she employs are both her strength *and* her downfall, because they ensnare her in an unhealthy dynamic. Her "efforts to adapt and cope serve to tighten the bonds to her tormenter."[279] Feeling isolated and lacking emotional support, there are essentially six fundamental coping strategies a victim heavily relies on, illustrated in the following diagram. Some are learned behavior adapted from mimicking her partner. But make no mistake, these defense mechanisms are doomed to fail with time. She may struggle to let go of them, but it is only *when* they disintegrate that she can truly break free.

Six Primary Coping Strategies

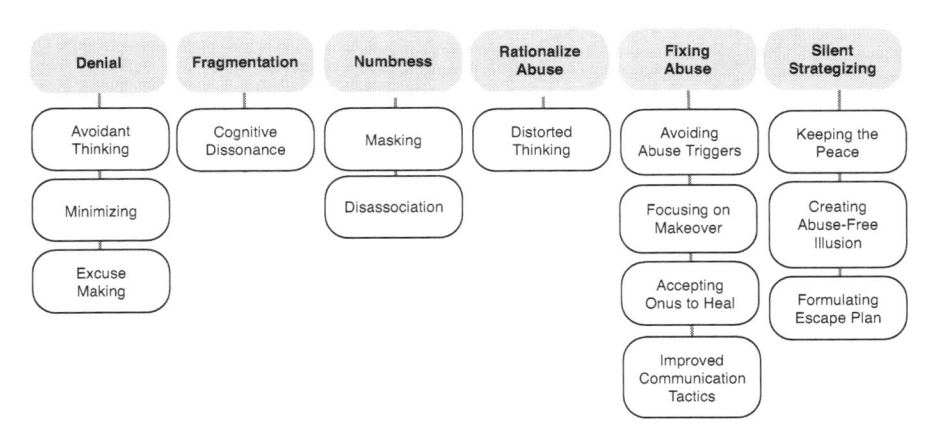

Denial	Fragmentation	Numbness	Rationalize Abuse	Fixing Abuse	Silent Strategizing
Avoidant Thinking	Cognitive Dissonance	Masking	Distorted Thinking	Avoiding Abuse Triggers	Keeping the Peace
Minimizing		Disassociation		Focusing on Makeover	Creating Abuse-Free Illusion
Excuse Making				Accepting Onus to Heal	Formulating Escape Plan
				Improved Communication Tactics	

(1) Denial

A victim's strongest form of protection is denial since her reality is too painful to accept. This tool ensures she can endure the abuse and find an effective way to cope in everyday life to a certain extent. Minimizing and denying the full impact of his mistreatment prevents her emotional breakdown. Alas, it is a false sense of security. At first, she learns to deny small, unsettling incidents she cannot quite label as abuse yet, feelings of doubt and despair she pushes out of her mind during Stage 1 of the cycle of violence.

As it progresses, she denies both her husband's aggressive nature and the abusive incidents themselves because she refuses to believe they are true. Avoidant thinking is easier than facing the painful and harsh reality of the truth. Why would she want to admit to herself that she is a battered woman married to a violent man or that her marriage is disintegrating? Why would she believe the man she is in love with can treat her so poorly and does not truly love her? Even for couples where abuse is not a factor it can take a long time to recognize when a marriage is failing.

After her sense of self-trust has been eroded strategically, she inadvertently allows her partner to define her reality with increasing regularity; she trusts his version of incidents over her own feelings. Lacking the ability to verbalize the abusive incident, she "comes to perceive that (her) torment lacks validity-as if it never really happened, or it wasn't all that bad, or it wasn't really 'abusive.' This diminishment, in turn, feeds (her) ability to compartmentalize the experience-until the mistreatment spirals out of control and reaches wildly dangerous levels that (she) is no longer able to keep secret or deny."[280]

Excuse making is another technique a victim implements to avoid looking deeply into her partner's abusive nature. Every step in a relationship is a choice. She makes the choice to accept the compelling excuses he feeds her: his difficult past, immaturity, inability to handle stress, or need to find an outlet for his rage. She believes the story he creates in which he is always the helpless victim, successfully avoiding any accountability for his actions. His persuasive, convincing skills as a con artist eradicate her lingering doubt as he insists she believe his protestations of innocence.

After observing his dishonesty with himself, it becomes easy for her to mimic his behavior. With conditioning, she adopts avoidant thinking, minimizing, and excuse making. All these aspects of denial are essentially learned behavior. Later, she denies her pain, emotions, and instincts, and this ultimately wounds her at the deepest level, fracturing her emotional integrity. At some point, a victim *will* pay the price for her denial and dishonesty.

(2) Fragmentation Process

Just as the plates of the earth rumble and shake along a fault line causing the earth's surface to split into two, the natural effect of denial is the fracturing of a victim's mind and spirit. She desperately struggles to find meaning in a life consumed by violence. It is inevitable that by accepting something that is utterly unacceptable, it creates a rift in her mind. Faced with the enormity of embracing two discordant realities, she has to find a way to perceive her world is not shattering. How does she accept two parallel realities: a life of abuse and the escape from the abuse? How does she come to terms with her husband's dual personality: his good side she loves and his evil side she fears? When a battered woman's mind fractures and holds onto contradictory realities simultaneously, she compensates by her "creative adjustment," a story or narrative that allows her to rationalize her world that has been turned upside down.

In order to survive and ensure mental cohesion, the victim comes to terms with the abuse through a phenomena psychologists label as cognitive dissonance. It "means that what was happening to you was so horrible, so far removed from your thoughts and expectations about the world, that it was dissonant, 'out of tune,' with reality. Because you were powerless to change the situation, you relied on internal, emotional strategies to try to make it less dissonant, to make it somehow fit. In other words, to survive, you literally had to change how you perceived reality."[281] "Research suggests that battered women have a greater tolerance for cognitive inconsistencies than other women."[282] Ironically, many victims will claim they have a "loving" marriage despite the extreme violence.

A victim unconsciously mimics her partner's inner conflict by adopting the schism of juxtaposing between a public and private persona. She switches between the wounded struggling victim versus the survivor who has the incredible strength to go on day-by-day proving she is capable to continue to take care of her family, manage the household, and possibly juggle a career as well. This places enormous pressure on her quest to maintain appearances that her marriage is sound.

If she is an Indian wife, she believes she has failed her cultural duty and will be blamed for any marital discord. There is familial and societal pressure to preserve the marriage at all costs. She may go to great lengths to not only convince others but also herself that she has the perfect marriage and is wonderfully happy. Eventually, the inevitable strain of maintaining this charade wears her down.

In essence, cognitive dissonance facilitates compartmentalizing her life, a diversion from recognizing the abuse. As a battered woman becomes tolerant of her spouse's behavior over time, she fails to notice the abuse worsening. Her mind has become conditioned to adapt to severe violence. A creature of habit, her mind and body become rooted in what is familiar, even if it is unhealthy. Despite her desperate attempt to avoid facing her victimization, deep down she acknowledges the abuse creeps into every aspect of her life and every part of her being no matter how much she tries to pretend otherwise. Just as it has taken time to become conditioned, it will require substantial time to heal, break through his conditioning, and unlearn her defense mechanisms.

(3) Numbness

Fragmentation leads to a natural shutting down process that is both conscious and subconscious. A victim becomes adept at ignoring her instincts, values, principles, and safety. As discussed in Chapter 8, disassociation and masking are part of this process of shutting down providing the ultimate strategy for protection and defense. She effectively masks her pain, her emotions, and the war that she wages internally.

(4) Rationalize Abuse

Along with the numbness comes a certain acceptance or resignation of her situation. After revisiting the stages in the cycle of violence repeatedly, there is a point when a victim finally accepts her fate. At this stage, she still might not label it as abuse, but she has at least recognized there is an established pattern to his behavior and the relationship dynamic, one that is not easy to change. The progression of a victim's reasoning from believing his excuses and recognizing a pattern to his behavior can take significant time.

How she interprets events and chooses to proceed in the abusive dynamic unknowingly perpetuates the abuse. "She gets drawn into the complexities of his inner world, trying to uncover clues, moving pieces around in an attempt to solve an elaborate puzzle. The abuser's mood changes are especially perplexing... When he's in this mode, nothing she says seems to have any impact on him, except to make him even angrier. Her side of the argument counts for nothing in his eyes, and everything is her fault. He twists her words around so that she always end up on the defensive"[283] and nothing she does ever seems right.

Despite her intelligence level or education, her thinking becomes distorted like his. "She held to the belief that her husband was a smart man, and she could not fathom that he would randomly get angry without good cause."[284] It is this notion he is rational that is a victim's gravest mistake and prevents her from accurately piercing his veil of excuses. Like most wives, she reasons she must give her husband the benefit of the doubt. But truthfully, why wouldn't she believe or trust the man she loves? With the smoothness of a con artist, he convinces her of his logic and manipulates her into feeling sympathy for him by rationalizing his outbursts.

A victim erroneously assumes the intensity of his anger clouds his mind and prevents him from being aware he is hurtful. She accepts that for a relationship to work there has to be 50/50 responsibility and willingly examines her role in the collapse of their marriage. She does not anticipate that down the road her spouse will not only refuse to do his part of the bargain or accept any accountability for his actions but will also hold her 100% responsible. In her defense, when she interprets her spouse's behavior, there are some actions that might not be considered abusive if taken out of context such as discussing the division of household chores. Weighing these isolated actions by themselves confuses her even more and she conjectures her marital problems are no different than any other couple's struggles.

In *Not to People Like Us*, Weitzman asks, are a woman's "attempts to cope and adapt actually becoming her way of colluding with her abusive partner? As she sought the means to 'make the marriage work,' was she simply getting herself more deeply entrenched? It is the continued denial and perseverance in the face of abuse that sets (her) apart from other women who are unhappy in their marriages."[285] A victim finds a way to persevere despite the abuse, which is no insignificant undertaking, but she will pay the price.

(5) Take Charge of "Fixing" Abuse

Despite falling prey to an abuser's brainwashing and conditioning, it is a mistake to think all victims hold themselves responsible. Contrary to the idea of learned helplessness, most women actively work to change the abusive dynamic by focusing on fixing the problem, keeping the peace, and sustaining the family unit. Even if she has reached the stage where she labels it as abuse, her fundamental incorrect assessment misguides her into believing it is something *she* can fix. A victim lives in a dangerous illusion that confines her until she has the lucidity to appreciate she cannot fix the dynamic by herself and she has not accurately diagnosed the root of the dysfunction: the abuse itself.

The irony in a victim's loss of power in an abusive marriage is her desperate attempt to hold on to some measure of control in her life. A battered woman must deeply examine whether this caretaker role stems from her personal beliefs, family upbringing, societal influence, or cultural hold. As the driven, success-oriented fox, she may consciously choose to take charge of the situation to resolve the abuse. To do so, her strategies, which are ultimately doomed to fail, include:

(a) Avoiding abuse triggers
(b) Focusing on her "makeover"
(c) Accepting the onus to heal him
(d) Improving communication tactics

(a) Avoiding Abuse Triggers

It stands to reason that if a woman can determine what provokes her spouse, she can influence his behavior. She may constantly replay incidents in her mind attempting to uncover the abuse triggers and causes for his outbursts. By minimizing these triggers, she hopes he will not ignite as easily over trivialities as he has conditioned her to do during Stage 1 of the cycle of violence. What she fails to see is that no outward triggers are necessary for his abuse; it is purely a manifestation of his dysfunctional emotional state.

(b) Focusing on Her Makeover

A batterer urges his partner to fix her "flaws" that he labels as triggers. Listening to his prompts, the pressure mounts daily until she realizes the conflict exacerbates regardless of what she does or does not do. It is not so much what she says but rather the fact she is speaking at all that infuriates him. She falls into the trap of always second-guessing herself. Even in retrospect, most women said "they were still not completely sure that there was not something they could have done differently that might have made the batterer cease his abusive behavior."[286] Devoting time to her self-improvement is just a distraction that buys the batterer time, removes the focus from himself, and weakens and depletes her energy, making it easier for him to maintain his power.

(c) Accepting the Onus to Heal Him

Part of his well-crafted power imbalance is projecting his innocence as the victim and blaming his wife as the culprit. When she lacks the clarity to identify him as the perpetrator, she places the onus on herself to heal him, sincerely believing he is capable of change if only she could steer him in the right direction. In *Ditch That Jerk,* Jayne says, "It's a powerful seduction to believe that a man has great potential if only you could reach him."[287] "This becomes another justification for loving him. Your partner seemingly needed you, and you thought that once you helped him heal, he would stop abusing you."[288] A victim cannot even begin to conceive he finds being abusive rewarding or the clever manipulative strategy underlying all of his actions.

(d) Improving Communication

Logically, a battered woman ascertains improving communication will help her spouse understand when his behavior is hurtful. It seems so simple, that after she gets through to him he will cease battering her. Possibly influenced by a marriage counselor, her misguided approach to implement better verbal strategies and facilitate mutual understanding is limited. Trapped in the endless and exhausting cycle of trying to explain her fear, disappointment, and pain, her frustration mounts as her search to find the appropriate words is inadequate. If only she could express herself better, eliminate "flaws" that trigger him, be more compassionate for his suffering, she reasons life will improve. This enforces a pattern where essentially she only makes more excuses for her perpetrator. A victim fails to see where communication is breaking down and somehow starts to accept this as a failure on her part.

(6) Silent Strategizing

"Secret strategizing," a term coined by Weitzman, involves implementing specific methods and conscious strategies to survive the abuse. [289] A battered woman harnesses a certain will power to be effective in the world that includes: (a) keeping the peace by pleasing her husband, (b) creating the illusion of an "abuse-free" life, and (c) formulating an escape plan when she is ready to leave. This idea counters or disproves the idea of learned helplessness or inaction once again that implies an environment in which she has no control. The "upscale abused wife is not a victim of learned helplessness. Rather, she makes specific decisions along the path to be involved in the abusive marriage, including silent strategizing as she chooses to stay or leave the marriage."[290] These conscious voluntary choices are how she participates in co-creating the reality of abuse.

(a) Keeping the Peace: All women relate to this role, not just victims. Whether they are foxes or hares, traditionalists strive to preserve a cohesive family structure whatever the cost. In the fictitious story a victim creates and rationalizes, she is forced to reason that if she can find a way to placate her husband, reduce his stress, help him overcome his past, or come to terms with his anger, their relationship will not only heal but blossom. She believes showing him tenderness, soothing his pain, and taking better care of him is what he needs. This is precisely his intention. She may apologize, do whatever he says, even praise him if necessary to diffuse the tension in Stage 1.

Attempts to please her husband and fulfill his wishes may be interpreted as submissive behavior, but there is an underlying strategy of negotiation at work. Redirecting her energy in this regard may prove successful on many occasions as she looks for solutions and ways to prevent triggering his explosions. Conflict avoidance is a value learned in a family system where keeping the peace is emphasized over resolving individual differences. This results in one person maintaining dominance while the other person thereby loses power. Being raised in this household creates a deeper pattern of compliance as a woman fights for her ideal by silently strategizing.

(b) **Creating the Illusion of an Abuse-Free Life:** As a by-product of her fragmentation, she employs tactics to distract herself in household chores. She may meticulously take care of the home, be the perfect, attentive mother, pour all her energy into specific household projects, or immerse herself in her career. She embraces any diversion that allows her to circumvent facing the reality of abuse. This provides some measure of control in her life, where command of her mind, heart, and emotions is slipping away at a rapid pace. In effect, she has created a world where she can escape the abuse while maintaining the façade of a successful marriage.

(c) **Escape Plan:** Chapter 14 discusses the essentials of formulating a survival strategy when a victim is ready to separate from her spouse.

TRAPPED BY BELIEF SYSTEM

Ultimately, a victim is ensnared by her belief system, held prisoner by her own mind. This can come as a shock after feeling trapped by her spouse for so long. It takes time to process this shift in perspective. There are several factors in her thinking that perpetuate abuse. The first two beliefs have previously been discussed.
(1) She believes her partner is rational and thus she rationalizes the abuse.
(2) She takes responsibility for "fixing" the problem that she incorrectly diagnoses.
(3) She is fueled by her desire to have a successful marriage.
(4) She blames herself for the failure of her marriage.
(5) The most critical factor is her undying hope that things will improve and change for the better.

Success & Failure

If a woman is a fox who is goal-oriented, ambitious, driven to success, and strives to resolve situations effectively, she is convinced she can play an active role in enhancing the quality of her marriage. Perhaps she has been this way with her education, career, projects, etc. Ever the achiever, she applies this same work ethic to her relationship, determined for it to be successful. Programmed to compromise, women are deeply ingrained with the notion of diffusing conflict, making their marriages work, and being nurturing.

A fox meets the challenge of marital strife with a fierce determination that consumes her. Entering problem-solving mode, she refuses to accept her marriage as a failure because she has never failed at anything in her life. Surrounded by family or friends with successful marriages, she believes if they can do it, she can as well. One victim admits, "I had pretty much succeeded at anything I had ever put my mind to, and here's a strong fear of failure at work with this marriage that is supposed to last forever."[291]

The belief that perpetuates her dilemma is her fixation on the ideal of marriage and fitting it into her world of accomplishment. She is blinded by this attitude that prevents her from looking at her relationship objectively. Burdened by the immense responsibility of the success or failure of her relationship, she cannot imagine her abusive marriage has no chance for success.

Self-Blame

The downfall of focusing all her energy on being successful is she inevitably sets herself up for failure. Internalizing her partner's unwillingness to cooperate or resolve conflict as her own personal failure is a victim's mistake. Indian women especially are trained from a young age to believe they carry this burden. As her vulnerability increases with every abusive attack and her partner's constant criticism, she may "readily believe and integrate her husband's accusations that she has caused his insults, rages, and assaults."[292] This is especially true of hares. For perfectionist foxes, they find failure unacceptable.

In *Not to People Like Us*, Weitzman points out that "for well-educated women, the sense of shame can also relate to the notion that they 'should have known better' or 'should have been smart enough to read the signs.' They are afraid of looking foolish, stupid, or ignorant at having 'chosen' an abusive husband."[293] She fears the rejection of friends and family. "The upscale abused woman may become a victim of her positive self-image: the ever-successful, resourceful woman who can do or fix anything... It is ironic that she doesn't readily use this self-image to propel herself into creating a new life."[294]

Self-blame is destructive, blocks her healing, and is a major reason for her silence, secrecy, and shame. "Women who report domestic violence more frequently have greater opportunities to discuss their problems with other women in the same situation-especially in women's shelters or domestic violence court."[295] On the other hand, minority or upscale victims fail to garner this support when they choose to remain silent.

"A puzzling commonality among (foxes) is that they fail to appreciate and lay emotional claim to their talents, accomplishments, and abilities. The way in which she inadequately assesses or even acknowledges her capacities and strengths dramatically affects her efforts at securing help. As a woman sits with feelings of isolation, embarrassment, and shame, as well as fears of being disbelieved and rejected, she discounts her personal resources."[296] Victims downplay their strengths because their perpetrators have conditioned them to do so.

Even when it comes to self-defense, a victim often blames herself for her actions. "If your actions did not harm, frighten, or control him, they (don't) fit the definition of violence. He labels you as violent in order to shift the focus to what *you* do wrong... Use your own behavior as a warning sign that you can't manage your abusive partner."[297] A victim's instincts for self-preservation and survival are considerably diminished or destroyed by her assailant. A woman who scratched her husband's arm in self-defense declares her attacker said, "'See, you're the one who's violent.' I was so ashamed he had those scratch marks. I thought he was right. I was violent, and I couldn't tell anybody what happened."[298] Feeling she must be tough and endure, she accepts her fate and does not want to admit to her "failure."

A victim must be aware she cannot accept responsibility for her spouse's emotions or behavior. He alone is accountable for his actions and their consequences. After suffering such injustice at the hands of her partner and succumbing to his control tactics, she cannot blame herself for acting in self-defense. She has done the best she could under the circumstances. When you love someone, you find a way to preserve that love and maintain your relationship at any cost.

Role of Hope

The ultimate paradox of feeling powerless is the victim's characteristic undying and persistent hope that perpetuates the abusive dynamic. This may sound contradictory, but this is the manifestation of cognitive dissonance once again. Even though she feels powerless in the abusive household, she is convinced she has the power to fix the unhealthy dynamic and save her marriage. She trusts the man she loves, believes his promises to change, and has faith he can be different. Despite all odds, she fiercely holds on to the notion her situation will improve, he will come to his senses and treat her better, and the pain will fade. Her innocence, idealism, and belief people are inherently good lead her to believe he will eventually do the right thing.

Influenced and conditioned by her partner, the tendency to live in the future traps a victim into believing a future change of circumstance will bring improvement. She repeats to herself: *"Everything will be great when or after... he gets a new job or a new boss, when their financial difficulties are over, when she gets pregnant, after their child is born, or after they move."* This cycle of hoping for change in the future never ends; it exists in all problematic relationships and is not unique solely to victims. Battered women deeply attach to this illusion with their perpetual hope, blinding love, and eternal optimism until they reach their breaking point and it becomes clear there is no salvation.

Reasons a Victim Chooses to Stay or Return After Separation

To reiterate, a victim is *never* to blame for her batterer's actions, but being cognizant of how her coping strategies and belief system perpetuate her victimization is the key to breaking free. Her choice to stay with her partner or return to him after separation prolongs the cycle of violence and is addressed in the following chapter.

CHAPTER 11 CHALLENGES OF SEPARATION

*Freedom is never voluntarily given by the oppressor;
it must be demanded by the oppressed.* -Martin Luther King Jr.

As a society, we often ask: *"Why do victims choose to stay with their abusive spouses or if they leave them why do they return?"* First and foremost, the commonly perpetuated myth that victims do not leave only creates more obstacles in offering necessary and critical assistance. Statistically, most battered women do eventually leave their assailants. It may take time for her to do so or several attempts, but 70% of battered women do reclaim their freedom.[299] It is not simply the issue of making the decision to leave. This chapter will highlight the numerous considerations a victim must take into account *before* she can leave and the importance of strategizing while Chapter 14 discusses why safety planning is essential. The list below outlines additional myths about separation.

Myths about Separation: Adapted from *It's My Life Now*.[300]
(1) Victims who do not leave an abusive relationship right away must have something wrong with them.
(2) Anyone who could love an abusive partner must be weak, insecure, and have other psychological issues.
(3) Once abused by her partner, all her love for him vanishes.
(4) There is no way for a woman to increase her safety if she continues to live with her spouse or if she separates from him.
(5) If there was no physical violence while she was in the relationship, there will not be any after she leaves.
(6) Once survivors leave their abusive relationships, they would never consider returning to their abusers.
(7) Any survivor who returns to an abusive partner is weak and any further abuse is her fault.
(8) Survivors of domestic violence are victims who just can't make it on their own.
(9) Once she is out of the relationship, she is out of danger.
(10) The emotional turmoil she experiences in the aftermath of an abusive relationship is brief and usually fairly mild.
(11) After leaving, a survivor is free from any interactions with her partner. He can no longer exert control over her and will leave her alone.
(12) Dealing with the loss of an abusive relationship is easy, a woman feels a sense of relief, moves on quickly, and her life becomes easier.

(13) Survivors of abusive relationships are doomed to repeat the cycle and are never again able to find a truly intimate loving relationship.
(14) Survivors become experts in predicting whether her next potential partner has controlling or violent tendencies.

Culturally Specific Myths:
(1) Regardless of whether one has a green card, immigrant Indian women are free to leave their abusive spouses at any time.
(2) Victims always have the opportunity to return to their natal homes and be welcomed by their families when separating from abusive husbands.
(3) Divorce is not a stigma in Indian culture and is an option women will readily consider as a viable solution to end abuse.
(4) Divorce is encouraged whenever abuse is disclosed.
(5) Returning home as a separated or divorced woman is acceptable in all Indian families.
(6) Remarriage for Indian women is equally as easy or viable as it is for men.

Factors a Victim Must Consider

The complexities of victimization reveal the numerous motivations and factors involved in a woman's resolution to persevere in a troubled marriage. She may need to weigh many difficult decisions. Especially in the case of the upscale victim, it is common to ask, "Why would women with so much going for them stay in such terrible circumstances?"[301] It is shortsighted for others to say she "likes" the abuse or she is too helpless to leave. Bystanders should reserve judgment until they grasp how arduous her struggle is to break free. They may also not understand that the perpetrator, of course, does not make it easy to leave him or stay away.

Making the challenging decision to leave her spouse is a courageous choice. Whether it is a short- or long-term separation, there are numerous reasons she might face an enormous temptation to return. She cannot judge or blame herself for this. "The very few upscale women who left after the first violent incident reunited with their husband shortly thereafter in an effort to 'make the marriage work.' This is understandable. Many women want to salvage a relationship they had pledged to be part of through good times and bad."[302] It can take several attempts before she leaves him for good. We should appreciate the sheer number of factors she must consider that reveals the intricacy of her situation.

"Many stay because of economic, legal, and social dependence. Others are afraid to leave because they have no safe place to go. Police, courts, hospitals, and social service agencies do not offer them adequate protection. Psychologists tend to counsel them to keep the family together at any cost… Both the batterer and battered woman fear they cannot survive alone, and so continue to maintain a bizarre symbiotic relationship

THE PSYCHOLOGY OF ABUSE 113

from which they cannot extricate themselves."[303] "The most likely predictor of whether a battered woman will permanently separate from her abuser is whether she has the economic resources to survive without him."[304] Victims who are financially independent often leave sooner, confident of their abilities to survive on their own.

The Gift of Fear elucidates, "Many women stay (because) until that night, no other possibility ever occurred to (them)."[305] "It is critical for a woman to view staying as a choice, for only then can leaving be viewed as a choice and an option."[306] A victim must be cautious and if she returns, only do so with her eyes wide open. To break the vicious cycle of violence, she must examine her resistance, her legitimate hesitations, and evaluate the price of breaking her silence.

Victims May Choose to "Stay" for 23 Common Reasons

(1) **Resist Change:** It is normal to gravitate to what is familiar, even if it means staying in an unhealthy situation. Of course, any change will be scary for a victim if she has been trapped in this pattern for years or her entire adult life. Amidst her struggle, staying or returning to her spouse may appear as the path of least resistance.

(2) **Safety:** Assessing her danger level, genuine fear for the personal safety of her children or herself if she attempts to leave is valid and appropriate. Statistically, separation increases her risk of violence.

(3) **Threats:** The prospect of facing his threats, imagining his retaliation, and dealing with his unpredictability is daunting. Many perpetrators resort to threatening a victim's children, relatives, or others she cares about, compounding her fears. Others may underestimate this risk and how much jeopardizing the safety of others weighs on her.

(4) **Paralyzed:** The sheer multitude of conflicting emotions a battered woman must process can be paralyzing. Her shock and confusion overwhelm her and make it impossible to take action or the first step to separate from her spouse and unhealthy environment.

(5) **Learned Helplessness:** There may be genuine passivity and a sense of overwhelming hopelessness that there is nothing she can do to alter her predicament. Although this may fluctuate with strategies of resistance she employs, at some point, acceptance and resignation may set in.

(6) **Love & Hope:** She may genuinely believe the myth that love conquers all and does not want to give up on her marriage. She holds on to his promises to change during the honeymoon stage. Falsely hoping the violence will end, she believes their relationship can be preserved whether or not she has any evidence to support this rationale.

(7) **Investment:** A victim carefully weighs everything she has invested into this relationship: her time, energy, love, and dedication. It is natural to not want to give up on that yet after many years of building a life and a marriage together. The natural human instinct is to preserve what one has. She may also consider the material life they share-a home, property, and possessions and be overwhelmed at the idea of dividing their belongings.

(8) **Illusion:** She may believe in the illusion of a real relationship with her spouse. Similar to other couples, they also share a home and property, have acquired many material possessions and attachments, and have children they are raising jointly. Functioning adequately in these roles of husbands and wives in public, they are viewed as a unit by their families, friends, and communities. A victim may assume she has an ordinary marriage with its typical ups and downs like everyone else. She may also rely on a satisfying sexual connection to establish a level of closeness and intimacy in her relationship that might not be expressed in other areas thereby deceiving her.

(9) **Traditionalist:** Whether she is a fox or a hare, she feels bound by the contract of marriage, committed to preserving the family unit, and does not consider divorce a valid option. This is reinforced by her spouse's similar beliefs. In some ways, it would be simpler to break free if she was only dating or engaged. One victim said, "I was in no way ready to leave our marriage. I've made my bed, and now I have to lie in it."[307]

(10) **Commitment to Children:** Naturally, any mother contemplates how her kids will be affected adversely by the separation, seeks to avoid breaking up the family unit, and feels pressure from herself/family/society to fit the traditional family model. The strong traditional belief children must be raised by two parents deeply influences her. Despite his mistreatment, she may still consider her spouse a good father. But keep in mind, "A good father does not abuse his children's mother."[308] She may also fear her husband's threats to take full custody of the children if she leaves.

(11) **Success Oriented:** Convinced she must try harder at saving her marriage, she puts the onus on herself to make the marriage successful.

(12) **Reputation:** Influenced by society, a victim may strive to protect her own reputation and that of her spouse. Jeopardizing his job or social status could have devastating repercussions for her as well. Fueled by her anticipation of rejection, fear others will disbelieve her, desire to save face, evade isolation, or be consumed by shame and

embarrassment, she maintains her silence. He may spread rumors to ruin his wife's reputation and destroy her credibility.

(13) **Support:** When others discover the truth, she fears the loss of ties to family, friends, community, and culture. Her loyalty to tradition might be questioned. Abandoned by those she loves most limits her avenues for help. She fears coming forth could aggravate her situation further.

(14) **Finances:** The harsh reality of separation is a battered woman may feel strapped without financial resources or support and hence, feel completely dependent on him. The inevitable change in her socioeconomic status and imminent financial losses she may suffer are intimidating. Not being able to provide for her children or herself or not being able to afford childcare may be an issue. "Untangling yourself financially from your abuser and establishing your economic independence can be a very complicated and confusing process... Worries about money should never force you to return to your abuser."[309] The assailant may threaten to ruin her credit or sabotage her job to maintain control. "According to the National Woman Abuse Prevention Project, in the first year after divorce, a woman's standard of living drops by 73%, while a man's improves by 42%."[310]

(15) **Limited Options:** Even if she wants to leave, she may have no place to go. Whether she lacks a support system, feels too ashamed to ask family or friends, or cannot find low-cost housing, she feels trapped. Shelters are often overcrowded due to space constraints or she may have already stayed there for the maximum amount of time permitted.

(16) **Independence:** If she has been co-dependent or married for some time, the fear of being on her own can be intimidating and overwhelming. The idea of finding a job, housing, or living on her own for the first time is scary. She may not have the confidence or know-how to survive on her own in the real world and support herself or her children. For immigrant Indian women, this is significant. The demands of everyday life and practical challenges can be overwhelming and drive her back reluctantly.

(17) **Being Alone:** Even if abuse is not an issue, separation or the ending of a marriage brings up many fears that are quite natural. She may fear being single for the rest of her life or that she will never be able to move on from this relationship. Emotional dependency complicates matters. In *The Battered Woman*, Walker says, "Feeling that it was better to have been married to a batterer than not to be married at all is pervasive amongst battered women, no matter what their age. The fear of being alone causes women to put up with indignities no human being would believe they could endure."[311]

(18) **Immigration:** If a victim is an immigrant, there may be language barriers and visa issues that increase her feeling of total dependence on her spouse. The idea of leaving the country is one she may not be prepared for.

(19) **Minorities:** A woman may be confounded by additional obstacles if she belongs to other minority racial groups or whether she is a bisexual, alcoholic, disabled, or elderly woman.

(20) **Legal Constraints:** With limited financial resources and possibly no money of her own, she may not be able to afford legal representation or find an attorney who is as skilled as her husband's. Her spouse will often use this to his advantage in legal proceedings.

(21) **His Manipulation:** She might also succumb to the sweetness her abuser displays as he tries to win her over. During a breakup or separation he will do everything he can to reel her back into the relationship much like the honeymoon phase. He might say he cannot live without her, promise to change, apologize profusely, or threaten suicide or other self-destructive behaviors. He coerces his partner to give him a second chance or sometimes asks others to pressure her. He will make her feel sorry for him and guilty for abandoning him.

(22) **Second Chance:** A victim believes in giving the man she loves and the man she married another chance. Even if she decides leaving her partner is in her best interest, clichés about love and fortitude run through her mind and convince her to stay a little longer. *"It takes two. Love conquers all. You can rise above it. Be glad you have a roof over your head. Take it with a grain of salt. Keep trying. Never give up. You can't expect too much. People don't always mean what they say. Keep smiling. He doesn't know any better. It's just a phase. Accept others the way they are. You create your own reality. Nobody said life was easy. For better or worse."*[312] A woman may feel she cannot abandon her husband after everything they have been through and because she adamantly believes he can transform into a better person.

(23) **Closure:** Unresolved feelings may drive her desire for an apology. She still longs to hear her partner admit to the abuse and confess how deeply he has hurt her.

Separation Violence

Statistically, the most dangerous time for a victim is when she chooses to separate from or leave her abusive spouse. Contemplating a life without her, his insecurity and vulnerability are heightened. The idea of her independence and breaking off the unhealthy attachment that exists between them is too much for a perpetrator to bear. Feeling the imminent threat of their separation, the narcissist will do anything to regain control. He may react even more explosively than previously. "Numerous studies have found that mistreatment of women by abusers tends to continue for a substantial period after separation and commonly escalates to levels worse than those when the couple was together."[313]

Statistics on Separation Violence: Refer to Appendix 1 for additional statistics.
- Although divorced and separated women compose only 7% of the population in U.S., they account for 75% of all battered women. They report being battered 14 times as often as women still living with their partners.[314]
- According to the U.S. Department of Justice, 75% of domestic assaults reported to law enforcement agencies were inflicted *after* separation of the couples.[315]
- According to the National Coalition Against Domestic Violence, nearly 75% of battered women seeking emergency medical services sustained injuries after leaving the batterer.[316]
- Other studies have found that women are most likely to be murdered when attempting to report abuse or to leave an abusive relationship.[317]

CHAPTER 12 ROLE & SUPPORT OF COMMUNITY

Too often we underestimate the power of a touch, a smile, a kind word, a listening ear, an honest compliment, or the smallest act of caring, all of which have the potential to turn a life around. Leo Buscaglia

Introduction
The role of community in influencing or ending domestic violence is often a topic that is neglected or devalued. We grossly underestimate the powerful role we play as a society in perpetuating abusive dynamics through our:
(1) Misperceptions, myths, and stereotypes
(2) Adherence to traditional gender roles
(3) Stigma attached to abuse or divorce
(4) Lack of support for victim

Let's be clear: *any* approach that does not stop abuse *is* promoting it. Ignorance is not a defense. Society ultimately determines what behavior is unacceptable and is responsible for enforcing these values. If we tolerate violence, it will continue to exist within our families and tear them apart. The hypocrisy of saying violence is deplorable and then looking the other way when it happens is unacceptable. Society's role or lack of involvement plays a direct contributing factor in impeding a battered woman's journey to break free. Ideally, she requires assistance from all seven tiers of community outlined in Chapter 13. As a society, we are the instrument of change and any support we provide is pivotal in ending the destructive cycle of violence.

Myths & Stereotypes on Community Involvement with Abuse
It is imperative to dismantle the following misperceptions regarding community involvement and society's attachment to clichéd myths that prevent true comprehension of the dynamics surrounding domestic violence.
(1) Women are not affected by cultural stereotypes and beliefs about relationship abuse.
(2) Abuse is restricted to certain communities such as lower socio-economic levels, certain ethnic groups, or specific strata of society.
(3) Turning to religious or community leaders for assistance will always prove useful for a victim. They will readily support her to make the right decisions for safety.

(4) Anyone a woman confides in or seeks help from, including friends and family, will support her unconditionally and not turn their backs on her.
(5) Those who support her will be understanding, not question her decisions or motivations, and will always approve of leaving her spouse.
(6) Health care personnel will easily recognize a victim of domestic violence and take necessary action.
(7) The legal system, police and law enforcement, and health care personnel are sensitive to victims' issues.
(8) When police are involved, they will always protect a victim.
(9) If community members are aware of abusive altercations, they will intervene promptly, choose to be involved, and call for help or assistance.

Culturally Specific Myths:
(1) Abuse cannot exist in an accomplished model minority community like the Indian population in the U.S.
(2) When a victim reveals the abuse to family members, they will support her without fail, encouraging and prompting her to leave an abusive spouse.
(3) If family members witness abuse, they will intervene immediately and stop the abusive behavior.
(4) Second-generation Indian women raised in the U.S. are more familiar with legal resources and will readily seek the help of law enforcement. They will not hesitate to obtain a restraining order.
(5) Compared to immigrant women, second-generation Indian women are more likely to seek the services of therapists or medical professionals.
(6) Victims will readily seek help from a mental health counselor given the opportunity since there is no stigma attached to therapy.

In *Not to People Like Us*, Weitzman's research demonstrates the prevalence of domestic violence in higher socio-economic groups still remains grossly underreported. Model minority communities such as the Indian population in the U.S. emphatically reiterate the common conviction that *"there is no way abuse exists in our community!"* The unfortunate reality is that violence pervades every community, socio-economic level, ethnic group, and country. There is no place free of this crime. Domestic violence does not discriminate. In *Ditch That Jerk*, Jayne says, "Abuse is a problem that is bigger than one man and even bigger than one country. It is deeply rooted in the way that most of the world view men and women and their respective roles."[318]

The pervasive cultural outlook of enforcing these traditional gender stereotypes promotes the idea of the aggressive male protector who has ultimate control and the passive nurturing female who surrenders and yields. "Popular thinking has it that women can save men from themselves and that they have both the power and the obligation to help their men change. Both men and women believe in this fairy tale, which is very convenient for abusive men, who can then blame their women when their transformation fails to occur."[319] Although this notion of gender roles is undergoing a makeover in the modern world, it has yet to infiltrate globally to all levels of society.

Stigma of Abuse & Divorce

As a society, we are guilty of allowing our misperceptions and stigma of domestic violence to impede us from recognizing or taking the necessary action to end it. We view abuse as an embarrassing secret, too shameful to be acknowledged. The conspiracy of silence surrounding it for centuries enforces the idea what transpires behind closed doors at home is a private affair. We can only blame ourselves for pretending violence does not exist or choosing to look the other way even when the signs of mistreatment are glaringly evident. Dispelling this stigma is the only way to encourage more victims to speak up and break free from the shackles of violence.

The stigma against divorce is equally obstructive where ending a marriage is less accepted in Eastern countries that tend to be traditional, patriarchal, and rooted in ancient values and beliefs. Although the trend is growing in Asian countries, divorce rates are still significantly lower than the U.S. at 54.8%. Comparatively, India has the lowest divorce rate globally at 1.1%.[320] The stigma we attach to divorce is believing these couples do not possess strong family values, are inept at or lack effort for conflict resolution, are not focused on preserving the family unit, or are not considering the best interests of the children.

Often, people express frustration that battered women stay with their abusers unaware that statistically 70% of victims do eventually leave.[321] Acknowledging a significant majority of victims possess this courage and do not let the stigma of divorce or abuse stop them from re-claiming their lives can dramatically alter our perception about divorce. We can end this stigma by affirming that a woman's fight to stand up for her rights and preserve her safety is more crucial than staying married or persevering with her partner in a destructive relationship. Choosing to stay can endanger her life.

In India, it is especially difficult to tackle the stigma of divorce given that cultural values emphasize preservation of the family unit, continuing the family line, inter-generational households, and the wife's responsibility to ensure family harmony. Divorce is not only frowned upon but viewed as a major disruptive and destructive action. Women who choose this path are viewed as selfish, going against fundamental cultural beliefs and values, prioritizing herself above her family, and ultimately to blame for any discord in family life.

It is understandable given this view why considering divorce is seen as a last resort for Indian women. Even worse, she is considered "damaged goods," someone who has lost her purity, and the chances for remarriage are slim or non-existent. It is common to hear beliefs reiterated such as "Being a divorcee-I would forever carry the stain of failure, of the inability to compromise, of not knowing how to keep the peace in a Hindu household."[322] The Indian wife feels she can never return to her natal home and be accepted. In *The Village Bride of Beverly Hills*, Daswani meaningfully captures this belief: "The only thing worse than being a single woman in India is being a divorced one. In America there is no shame in divorce. In India there is no shame in living in marital misery."[323]

Lack of Support for Victim

It is our fundamental lack of support that is the greatest impediment towards ending domestic violence. She may overcome insurmountable odds to break her silence, *finally* decide to confide in us, and reach out for help only to be re-victimized by our tolerance, silence, or indifference. If we respond with shock, or dishearten and discourage her, she feels betrayed and rejected. Our unwillingness or inability to acknowledge or recognize the abuse re-traumatizes her. A victim struggles to deal with a community that fails to appreciate the dynamics of an abusive relationship, does not believe it exists or the extent to which it does, and shows her no compassion. Often we shun, ostracize, or blame her for her predicament. Even if we do not take such a strong stand, our neutral stance can be just as detrimental.

Our misguided or ineffective approach that directly contributes to not supporting the victim includes **six common reactions or obstacles:**
(1) Sense of disbelief
(2) Shun or blame the victim
(3) Lack of action
(4) Neutral stand or silence
(5) Misguided coaching
(6) Enabling abuser

(1) **Sense of Disbelief:** Just as the shock of abuse can paralyze and traumatize a victim for years before she may gain the clarity or resolve to take action, those she confides in may also require time to process the shock of learning about an abusive situation. Especially if we are unsuspecting, it is natural for us to wonder who is really telling the truth and who is exaggerating. Reacting to a victim's confession, questions run through our minds such as: Why is she accusing him of this? Why should we believe her story when she has been married for so long, seemed totally happy in her relationship, and he seems like such a wonderful guy? Does she have something to gain? Is she just trying to hurt him? We judge her for taking so long to confess, tolerating this kind of behavior, and perhaps because she does not seem to fit our image of a victim.

If we have a particularly favorable impression of an abuser or have been swept away by his charm and personality, it can be distressing to integrate this information. It does not coalesce with any reality we know, especially if abuse is completely foreign to us. How are we supposed to make sense of this charismatic guy suddenly being labeled as a perpetrator? He might seem trustworthy, reliable, a doting husband and an adoring father; in other words, he does not fit the typical stereotypical profile either. This is in fact the majority of assailants. They are cunning masterminds at using their charm and deception to win people over and cloud their judgment in the same manner as when they courted their victim.

The batterer also knows most people will doubt the charge he is physically abusive and uses this to his advantage. No one wants to believe a prominent, respected, influential, well-liked man with a carefully groomed public persona could be violent. He relies on the myth that someone who is well educated or wealthy cannot be a batterer. Hiding beneath the façade he has worked so diligently to create, an aggressor gains the support of his family, friends, and community, so a victim is reluctant to reach out for support. He strategically attacks her credibility, spreads lies and rumors about her, and convinces people to turn against her.

In *Trauma and Recovery*, Herman says, "If he cannot silence her absolutely, he tries to make sure that no one listens. To this end, he marshals an impressive array of arguments, from the most blatant denial to the most sophisticated and elegant rationalization. After every atrocity one can expect to hear the same predictable apologies: it never happened; the victim lies; the victim exaggerates; the victim brought it upon herself; and in any case, it is time to forget the past and move on. The more powerful the perpetrator, the greater is his prerogative to name and define reality, and the more completely his arguments prevail."[324] He discredits her by turning around and accusing his partner of being crazy.

It may be hard to believe a victim if she hesitates to reveal emotion or speaks in a flat affect. After experiencing severe trauma, however, a person may respond in unexpected ways, unable to cry or respond when in shock. Doubting the victim and choosing to believe the perpetrator instead destroys her resolve. After the betrayal she has already undergone at the hands of her spouse, this insult can be devastating. As a society, we also discriminate between the foxes and hares, more readily believing women from lower socio-economic groups who come forth to receive assistance from domestic violence shelters, agencies, and law enforcement versus the foxes who do not disclose their circumstances so willingly.

(2) **Shun or Blame the Victim**: After doubting her, the next common reaction is to blame or ostracize her. The blame can be crippling. Instead of receiving the support and compassion she desperately needs, she is scorned. This is one of the most compelling reasons a victim does not come forth. In India, divorced women can be treated like outcastes, even

disinvited from weddings for fear of bringing bad luck. Approaches such as critiquing a victim's faults or weaknesses detract the focus from a batterer's accountability and support his distorted idea that she is at fault and not him.

After listening to her spouse repeatedly blame her, it takes a tremendous amount of clarity for her to irrevocably perceive the assailant is solely responsible for his actions no matter how much he tries to deny it. If only society promoted the idea a man has the choice to walk away instead of hit or abuse, we would then blame the offender rather than the victim. Alas, society does not integrate that idea into its belief systems, law enforcement, or judicial system.

The Battered Woman states: "These women were physically and psychologically abused by men and then kept in their place by a society that was indifferent to their plight. Thus, they were both beaten and then blamed for not ending their beatings. Told they have the freedom to leave a violent situation, they are blamed for the destruction of their family life. Free to live alone, they cannot expect to earn equal pay for equal work. Encouraged to express their feelings, they are beaten when they express anger. They have the same inalienable right to the pursuit of individual happiness as men do, but they must make sure their men's and children's rights are met first. They are blamed for not seeking help, yet when they do, they are advised to go home and stop the inappropriate behavior which causes their men to hurt them. Not only are they responsible for their own beatings, they must also assume responsibility for their batterer's mental health. If they were only better persons, the litany goes, they would find a way to prevent their own victimization."[325]

The hypocrisy of this outlook is the daily reality for women who do attempt to break free. The community is responsible for sending these continued mixed messages. We must accept that our beliefs as a society deeply affect and influence battered women. After she has been shunned and offered no support, she runs out of options and often does not know to whom else to turn but her spouse. We fail to offer her a helping hand and then have the audacity to be surprised when she chooses to return or stay in a violent relationship.

(3) **Lack of Action**: Why are we as a society so reluctant to acknowledge abuse? Our disbelief can lead to not responding to a victim's desperate plea for help. Typically, we may say, "*It is none of our business.*" This desire to look the other way after a victim's confession can occur for numerous reasons. Confronting abuse takes courage, and often we lack the proper social skills to comfort the victim or know how to handle the news. We may genuinely be unsure how to react, feel uncomfortable, or be paralyzed by shock or disbelief. Rightfully, we question what response is appropriate or not. The fear of saying the wrong thing or being hurtful can make us hold our tongues.

We may perceive being involved as inviting danger or threats from the perpetrator into our own personal lives. There might also be a natural desire to protect our family and prevent our children from discovering that the neighbors who seemed like the perfect family next door have this shameful secret. If a friendship is involved or if it is family, the idea of taking sides poses a problem. At other times, refusing to be involved may help us avoid our own issues if, perhaps, we have been victims of abuse ourselves. It might be too painful for us to confront our own past, pain, and victimization.

Remaining uninvolved, turning our heads to look the other way, believing the saying "*out of sight, out of mind*" may seem like the safest and easiest option but it is a purely selfish decision. There is no excuse for burying our heads in the sand when we understand a woman's life may be at stake. If ever there is a call to action-this is it.

(4) **Neutral Stand or Silence:** Sometimes the best solution appears to be taking a neutral stand, maintaining the conspiracy of silence, and refusing to take sides. This approach may be sensible when dealing with divorce or separation for couples whose relationship is free of violence, but it takes on an entirely different meaning for an abusive dynamic.

Not taking a stand against domestic violence *is* condoning the perpetrator and abandoning the victim. A victim is re-traumatized by our unresponsiveness, perceiving our silent acceptance of the abuse as a betrayal. This fundamental rejection causes her to be on guard, reluctant to confide in us further. As Bancroft aptly says in *Why Does He Do That?*, "Everyone should be very, very cautious in accepting a man's claim that he has been wrongly accused of abuse or violence. The great majority of allegations of abuse… are substantially accurate. And an abuser almost never 'seems like the type.'"[326]

"Neutrality serves the interests of the perpetrator much more than those of the victim and so is not neutral. To remain neutral is to collude with the abusive man, whether or not that is your goal. If you are aware of chronic or severe mistreatment and do not speak out against it, your silence communicates implicitly that you see nothing unacceptable taking place. Abusers interpret silence as approval, or at least as forgiveness. To abused women, meanwhile, the silence means that no one will help, just what her partner wants her to believe. Anyone who chooses to quietly look the other way therefore unwittingly becomes the abuser's ally."[327]

(5) **Misguided Coaching:** If we do choose to act, our misguided attempt to coach her is undermining. Perceiving her as too weak or unable to take necessary action, we may step in thinking we know what is best for her. After being controlled by her spouse and constantly told what to do by him, the last thing she needs to hear is another voice imparting instructions. This adds to her confusion, undermines her confidence about making her

own decisions, and deters her from taking charge of her own life. We act surprised and often fault her for resisting our advice. We may urge her to leave her spouse without understanding what is involved and the ramifications of such advice. We may encourage her to be patient, supportive, and tolerant.

There is a misperception that women need to be "dragged" out of their abusive marriages in the same manner as dogs in research studies that "could only be taught to overcome their passivity by being dragged repeatedly out of the punishing situation and shown how to avoid the shock."[328] "She becomes *emplotted* in the story that our culture has assigned her. 'Abuse doesn't happen to people like us, so make the best of your life.'"[329] This counsel is often received from religious community leaders and leaves a victim dumbfounded and prompts her to return to her partner. "You made your bed now lie in it. Marriage is forever. Divorced women are responsible for their marital failures.*"[330]* These judgments and mixed messages add to her perplexity.

(6) Enabling the Abuser: Without realizing it, we often inadvertently assist and enable the perpetrator further while denying vital help to a victim. When dealing with abusive families, "they may also accept abusive tactics as a way of dealing with problems and may even suggest that victims accept abusive behavior."[331] Keep in mind that a perpetrator can be quite convincing when he tells his side of the story and makes violent behaviors he is accused of seem impossible or a far stretch for the imagination. As a community, we often feel caught in between, not knowing whom to believe, and many times succumb to the persuasive skill of the abuser who convinces us of the following scenarios:

- She blows everything out of proportion and is a chronic exaggerator.
- She is oversensitive and creates drama over any incident.
- She is blatantly lying and fabricating stories.
- She just wants to be considered a victim to get sympathy.
- She is to blame for causing my outbursts, provoking me, and pushing my buttons.
- There is only so much of her behavior I can tolerate.
- Her goal is to ruin my reputation and hurt me in any way she can.
- She is intentionally attempting to ruin our relationship.
- Our problems are no different from any other couple.

It is amazing to witness how he turns any situation around to his advantage, distorting facts, and playing the victim so we feel guilty for condemning him. Being the clever con man, he is skilled at tuning in, reading our vulnerabilities, and knowing how to manipulate us. Despite all the indications or evidence he is violent, he convinces us otherwise. A victim must be extremely careful to whom she turns for help, because someone enlisted on the perpetrator's side could potentially endanger her even more.

Bancroft says, "It is impossible for a community to stop abuse while continuing to assist or ignore abusers at the same time. Protecting or enabling an abuser is as morally repugnant as the abuse itself."[332] Not only does the aggressor find abusive behavior rewarding, he is enabled by the support he receives from family, friends, peers, and the community. He finds allies among his therapist, law enforcement, attorneys, and courtrooms compounding the difficulty of instigating reform. He is enabled by "one of his core assumptions, which is that he can get away with it."[333]

The irony that many perpetrators are well respected and admired is not lost on the victim. After all, she was prey to his charm in the same manner as we were. The only difference is she has now detected his true nature that he keeps well hidden from everyone else. When she finally takes a stance against the abuse, the continued support her spouse receives alarms her. Before she felt trapped by her partner, but now she also feels ensnared by society's judgments, expectations, and response.

"The narcissist's insatiable demands and expectations seem justified by a society that gives the upscale, educated husband so many benefits. In addition to whatever material rewards he garners, he accumulates adoration from his professional associates and from his community. In our society, wealthy, powerful men are held in higher esteem than other men."[334] Most people are too timid to confront him, or if they do say something it is not direct or threatening. Society must overcome its shock and ultimately accept domestic violence exists in many more homes than we can ever imagine, and it is our duty to stand up and speak out against it.

Community's 5 Stages of Acceptance & Support in responding to abusive situations include:
(1) **Shock:** Experience shock, denial, and disbelief.
(2) **Process:** Need time to process and integrate information.
(3) **Guilt:** Blame ourselves for not seeing the signs sooner or taking action.
(4) **Acceptance:** Recognition that this is the reality of the situation.
(5) **Action:** Be ready for a call to action and ways to support a victim.

Four Steps to End Domestic Violence

We have already seen all the ways community does not help and as a consequence inadvertently fosters a culture where violence is "acceptable." There are four necessary steps for us to not only make a difference, but work towards completely eradicating domestic violence altogether.

Step 1 It is paramount to distinguish the various signs and types of abuse, stages in the cycle of violence, and the realities of both the victim and perpetrator's inner world.

Step 2 Become aware of the numerous ways we can reach out and be supportive of a victim's needs.

Step 3 If we are bold enough, take a strong stand against violence and the perpetrators of violence by demanding change and accountability from them and the systems that deal with them.

Step 4 Create a solid network and infrastructure to support an abuse-free community involving cooperation on many fronts.

Step 1 **How to Recognize Abuse/ Abuser/ Victim**

The intense destructive dynamics between a batterer and his victim can be so complicated that only outside intervention can shatter this bond. In the end, only a victim can truly break free, but any survivor will attest to how grateful she is for even the smallest gesture of kindness or assistance. Identifying abuse can prove challenging when there are layers of secrecy that both the perpetrator and the victim hide behind.

Even if confronted, there is a high probability a victim may deny being abused for various reasons: she is not ready to discuss it, has not admitted to herself yet that she is being abused, or fears for her safety by opening up. This can make a bystander who has the best intentions frustrated and eventually after enough attempts we may simply give up trying to "help" or intervene. Be patient if she is not yet willing to admit to the abuse and focus on emphasizing safety.

Be familiar with every form of abuse, how it takes shape, plays out, and the range of signs outlined in chapters 2 and 3. Appreciate the dynamics of power and the distinct stages in the cycle of violence outlined in chapter 4 that elucidates when it is most effective to reach out to a victim, when she stands a chance of breaking free, and when she is willing to listen to counsel. Timing is critical. We may even identify abuse before a victim does. Understanding the delicacy of the honeymoon stage and the bond between a perpetrator and his victim is imperative. A woman is less likely to feel in danger when she is focused on the love she feels for her partner. During stage 1, when tension builds, and stage 2, the abusive incident itself, are both when a victim is most ready to reach out and be responsive to outside intervention.

Be aware of factors that enable battering in society. Chapters 5-7 shed light on the perpetrator's personality, disguises, and the lengths he will go to win people's favor. We must train ourselves to see through his cleverness, charm, and deception. A man who goes overboard to impress us must have an agenda. Assess chapters 8-11 to deepen our compassion for the victim and know how much she must travail to break the cycle of violence. It takes courage, strength, and determination to walk away. Admire her for everything she has endured to choose freedom, to choose life, and let her know this.

No matter what, do not abandon the victim when she needs you the most! Know she may attempt to leave several times before she is successful. Do not give up on her when she gains clarity and undertakes such a monumental step. If she denies abuse or is secretive, watch for repeated injuries, constant excuses, growing absences from work or school,

THE PSYCHOLOGY OF ABUSE 129

personality changes, fear of conflict, or isolation. Understand the persuasion of the abuser and his manipulative hooks to make her stay. We can be the collective lifesaver she needs to pull her to the other shore. *We can prevent a preventable death*!

By reading this book, every reader should be able to identify the subtleties and nuances of abuse and take critical action to assist a victim who is struggling to break free and reclaim her life. As much as we would like to blame perpetrators who have taken the lives of their victims, in the end it is society as a whole who is responsible for condoning their behavior. We are responsible for every life that has been lost to the madness of violence because we failed to take a stand or reach out to a victim. These homicides are 100% completely preventable. We must do our part as a community; *we have no time to lose*. The next section tells us how we can make a difference.

Step 2 Supporting a Victim

It is crucial a victim feels loved, valued, respected, and cared for. Feeling this support is essential for her recovery. With all the psychological damage and neglect she has experienced with her spouse, she needs to know her life is worth saving, that there *is* something worth fighting for. Do not underestimate the power of others being involved. This validates her reality and provides the impetus to break free.

Accept that as someone close to the victim this will be a difficult process for you to witness and be a part of as well. "Because empowerment and recovery for an abused woman can be a long process, people who want to be there for her tend to go through periods when their patience wears thin."[335] We must acknowledge our personal biases and judgments when we hear a victim's story and learn to overcome them. The list below outlines ways for family and friends to be there when she needs them the most.

20 Ways to Be Supportive of a Victim:
(1) Don't blame her. Let her know she does not deserve to be abused. Repeating "this is not your fault," is very helpful for her to hear since she often blames herself.
(2) Offer to help her in whatever way *she* thinks is best. Trust she is the expert of her own life.
(3) Be empathic. Validate her pain and suffering. See her point of view. Believe her.
(4) Take time to listen to her. Let her tell her story if she feels comfortable and encourage her to break her silence when she is ready. This will facilitate gaining perspective on how volatile her situation might truly be.
(5) If she is not yet ready to break her silence, let her know you are there for her whenever she does decide to open up.

(6) Don't be afraid to reach out. Let her know she is not alone. After her isolation, just calling to "check in" can show you do care and are concerned.
(7) Be gentle. Any advice or criticism that is harsh or controlling, or dictates what she should or should not do, will remind her of her abusive spouse.
(8) Be aware that after what she has been through, "battered women fear conflict of any kind. They will often give up a friendship rather than fight with someone... They have difficulty with intensity in relationships."[336]
(9) Be patient allowing her time to heal, find clarity, and sort through her confusion and pain.
(10) Encourage her to feel confident and know she has the ability to make wise decisions for herself.
(11) Recognize when she is taking a step to protect herself.
(12) Respect and protect her right for confidentiality, meet in private, and develop her trust.
(13) Be persistent in letting her feel supported even if you doubt your ability to help. "You are making an impact... even merely by awakening her consciousness and affirming her reality."[337]
(14) Do not pressure her to leave her spouse. It must be her decision and hers alone. Let her know you are there for her whatever she decides and whenever she does choose to leave him. Emphasize safety planning as this is essential to minimize danger when she leaves.
(15) Do not denigrate or attack her spouse since being defensive of him may have been a natural tendency and established pattern.
(16) Prioritize her safety and focus on strategies to assist her. Offer her options and emphasize local resources such as domestic violence shelters or ways to keep the children safe. Express your concerns and fear for her safety as this will encourage her to be more vigilant.
(17) Help her appreciate her own strengths after she has been conditioned by her spouse to devalue them.
(18) Connect her with trained advocates who can educate her about the dangers of domestic violence escalating with time. Encourage her to call the national domestic violence hotline which is confidential and available twenty-four hours at 1-800-799-SAFE.
(19) Support her while she faces her fears about being a single parent and mourns the loss of her disintegrating traditional family structure. Many victims feel abandoned, left to raise their children on their own without economic or social support, even if they are the ones who initiated separation.
(20) Assist a victim in rebuilding her life again by learning how *she* specifically wants to be supported. Be prepared that she might not know yet or have the answers right away. Allow her to journey through her own process to figure this out for herself. Knowing we

are ready to help whenever she needs it will make a considerable difference.

Step 3 **Demanding Change from Abusers**

As a community, it is imperative we force him to confront his actions and hold him accountable for the damage he is causing. Every time we let him off the hook, his abusive behaviors are reinforced. Our firm stance validates a victim. She is often re-assaulted when she speaks up, so it is crucial a perpetrator hears us supporting her. There are numerous levels where this must play out: within our families, neighborhoods, workplace, religious and cultural centers, and legal institutions. Letting him know violence is absolutely unacceptable is the *only* way to take a strong stand.

His entitlement minimizes and change begins when he comprehends there are legal consequences that outweigh the benefits he experiences from being abusive. "Bringing about change in an abuser generally requires four elements: consequences, education, confrontation, and accountability."[338] "For some men, the fear of jail and the knowledge that abuse is against the law are the only reasons not to be violent."[339]

As Bancroft avers in *Why Does He Do That?*, "An abuser is not born; he is made. In order to bring about change in an abuser, we have to reshape his attitude toward power and exploitation. Abusive behavior is reinforced by multiple societal messages, some of which are specific to the abuse of women and some of which reflect the overall culture of oppression."[340] "Once we tear the cover of excuses, distortions, and manipulations off of abusers, they suddenly find abuse much harder to get away with… All forms of chronic mistreatment in the world are interwoven. When we take one apart, all the rest start to unravel as well."[341]

Step 4 How to create a solid network and infrastructure to support an abuse-free community is discussed in Chapter 13 and 14.

CHAPTER 13 SEVEN LEVELS OF COMMUNITY INFLUENCE

The problem with the world is that we draw the circle of our family too small.
Mother Teresa

Community's role in supporting the victim and taking a stand against the perpetrator is critical to end domestic violence. This chapter elaborates on each level of community's influence and how the collaboration between these segments is vital to inspire meaningful improvement in this endeavor. We have heard the expression, *"It takes a village to raise a child,"* but it truly *"takes a town to change an abuser."*[342]

Seven Levels of Influence in Responding to Abuse
Level 1 Friends and family
Level 2 Neighbors and coworkers
Level 3 Religious/spiritual leaders and associations
Level 4 Therapists and social workers
Level 5 Medical personnel and caregivers
Level 6 Law enforcement and legal representatives
Level 7 Social service organizations

Level 1 **Friends & Family**
This is the core support group a victim relies on during the long, arduous process to break free. We cannot abandon her when she needs us the most. Refer to Chapter 12 that outlines specific ways to be supportive.

Level 2 **Neighbors & Coworkers**
They might not necessarily be close, but they may see her frequently, first notice signs of mistreatment, and can be of influence before she is willing to come forth herself. Neighbors who witness or hear anything alarming should notify the police immediately since many times a victim cannot get to a phone herself or is too intimidated to call for help. Since many women receive harassing phone calls or visits at work, protocols for dealing with and reporting abuse should be mandatory in every work environment.

Level 3 **Religious Leaders & Associations**
A victim will often turn to her religious or spiritual community if she belongs to a church, temple, or mosque, especially if she is an

immigrant and does not have family nearby. She may seek advice or guidance from a leader or simply find solace in a group of like-minded individuals. She is often re-victimized by advice such as: *"You must return to your spouse, feel compassion for him, work towards preserving your family."* She may be instructed to pray more, renew her faith, and turn to God for the answers. Prayer and faith can play important roles in feeling stronger or at peace, but they are *not* a substitute for evading violence in a situation when danger is imminent.

Seeking advice from religious leaders should empower her to make the best decisions for her well-being without compromising herself or losing her own power. It is difficult for a bystander to judge the level of violence in a relationship or how much a victim's safety is at stake so the best policy is to assume the worst. The emphasis on marriage, duty, and sacrifice can coerce her to return to the vicious cycle of violence. Religious communities must urge her to be cautious and focus on safety rather than on saving or ending a marriage. Collaborating with local women's organizations and referring victims to seek out their services is imperative. Once she can clearly see she is in danger, it is easier to make the right choices to stay safe.

Level 4 Therapists & Social Workers

Therapists and social workers play key roles in offering guidance and direction whether through individual counseling, support groups, or batterers intervention programs. Being able to share her story and have a sympathetic ear listen validates her suffering and is pivotal in her healing process. When a woman is finally able to admit that her marriage may be abusive or at least identify something is wrong, it may still take time before she gathers the courage or the resolve to tackle her inner resistance and seek help. Indian women, for example, must overcome the cultural bias against therapy and discussing their personal problems with a stranger. A victim should not hesitate to question a therapist about her training, knowledge, and expertise working specifically with domestic violence victims.

In *Not to People Like Us*, Weitzman says, "The task of treatment (is) to help her assess exactly what (is) going on, to recognize what it means to live with an abusive partner, and to examine her role so she (can) make decisions about her next steps."[343] A therapist should be cognizant of the **key goals of therapy**:

(1) Be sensitive to the fact her initial visit might be the first time she is breaking her silence and acknowledge what a monumental step she has taken coming forth.
(2) It is critical to offer her an objective perspective on her situation that she lacks.
(3) Help her "recognize that the abuse she has endured is inappropriate, unacceptable, and criminal."[344]

THE PSYCHOLOGY OF ABUSE 135

(4) Empower her by focusing on her acceptance and choices that trap her instead of harping on her spouse's mistreatment and bad behavior.
(5) Gently show a victim her participation in co-creating the reality of abuse without blaming her or making her feel worse about herself.
(6) Do not dictate the speed through which a client must work through her issues. Respect her healing process on her timetable.
(7) After the abuser's repetitive denial of her experience, aid in facilitating the process for her to trust herself again, believe in her perceptions, and listen to her instincts.
(8) Recognize the stage where a victim is so your therapy is stage specific. In the earlier stage, she may seek therapy to learn better coping skills, techniques to impede the batterer's behavior, and enhance her resolution to save her marriage. Leaving her spouse may not be an idea she wants to entertain. Emphasize safety and building her strength and clarity to change her behavior patterns.
(9) In later stages, a victim should be encouraged to gain the independent skills she needs to break free. Remember, she is the expert of her experience and seek to guide her on her path of self-awareness, building confidence, and feeling empowered to move past her trauma.
(10) If she insists she wants to preserve her marriage and feels confident her spouse will change, gently ask her what proof she has of him changing. Asking for evidence to support her beliefs may force her to look at her situation more objectively without blind hope or unhealthy attachment.
(11) Help her build her strength, confidence, hope, awareness, and anything else that has been destroyed by her abuser. "The skilled therapist hooks onto that tiny glimmer of the positive and uses it in the healing process."[345]

Along with individual therapy, encouraging her to participate in support groups is an invaluable way to build solidarity among victims. They provide a means for women to break their silence, share their pain, and have others listen without judgment. After her isolation, connection with others is a critical part of healing. These groups discuss finding courage to leave the batterer, issues around separation, and facing immediate crisis. As women transition from being victims to survivors, the next stage these groups address is healing and rebuilding their lives again. The practicalities of living on their own, being a single parent, and daily struggles are discussed. As they move on, it is critical they learn how to trust their instincts, be comfortable in a new relationship, and be alert of warning signs of danger.

Inefficacy of Couples Therapy

In *The Battered Woman*, Walker writes, "Psychotherapy has generally emphasized the value of keeping families intact whenever possible. In working with battered women, however, psychotherapists must encourage breaking the family apart."[346] This is one of the main reasons marital therapy is ineffective for dealing with abusive dynamics. Here are several other reasons for its inefficacy.

(1) Couples counseling is designed for people with mutual issues that need to be resolved by working on them together.
(2) It is not possible for a woman to feel safe and open up completely when her aggressor is present. After the session is over, she may fear repercussions of his wrath for confiding their deepest marital secrets.
(3) He may feel increasingly justified in his actions and behaviors when a therapist identifies a victim's "issues" and points out what she needs to work on. This will affirm to him *she* is the cause of their problems.
(4) By not making the focus *entirely* on the batterer's behavior and accountability for his actions, therapy inadvertently strengthens his abusive tendencies.
(5) Empowered, the abusive dynamic becomes even more charged, leading to a dramatic escalation in frequency or severity of violence.
(6) He uses his powers of persuasion, manipulation, and charm to win over a therapist, make him/her the perpetrator's ally, and make the victim feel s/he has chosen sides. The victim "is forced to deal with yet another context in which she has to defend herself, which is the last thing she needs."[347]

The therapist thereby critiques the victim while becoming an advocate for the batterer. In one testimony, a woman said, "He had found a new ally in his efforts to shift his responsibility onto me. Needless to say, his abuse of me escalated horrifically. It seemed that my husband felt justified, even mandated, by the therapeutic world. I never expected that I would be abused by the psychologist I had enlisted to help, but this is exactly what happened."[348] Unfortunately, this re-victimization is quite common among many battered women.

Marital counseling, just like batterers intervention programs, teaches manipulative men how to say what victims wish to hear without him making any real progress towards correcting his abusiveness. To quote Bancroft, "Change in abusers comes only from... completely stepping out of the notion that his partner plays *any* role in causing his abuse of her. An abuser also has to stop focusing on his feelings and his partner's behavior, and look instead at *her feelings* and *his behavior*."[349]

Reform is absolutely necessary for the therapeutic community. "Many psychotherapists... have admitted not realizing that their clients were being brutally beaten over long periods of time."[350] Poor clinical training and failure to recognize the signs of abuse is unacceptable. "Half of all couples seeking therapy have at least some history of low-level violence."[351] Special certification and training in domestic violence coaching should be mandatory to distinguish them so victims can seek out their services directly.

Many victims approach couples counseling with the false assumption it will mend their marriage and end the abuse. It is imperative well-trained therapists speak to her individually and counsel her that couples therapy may aggravate abuse further. In addition, therapists should interface with women's shelters and organizations so they can direct and encourage their clients to focus on safety and using the legal system or law enforcement to aid their situation.

Batterers Intervention Programs

Instead of marital therapy, a therapist should refer an abuser to a batterers intervention program at this point because these programs are specifically designed for men to traverse beyond anger management issues and face their psyches. Therapy can focus more on his feelings while batterers programs confront his thought process, excuses, manipulations, and learning how to be accountable for his actions. "They address historical, social, cultural, and personal attitudes, beliefs, and behaviors toward women."[352]

Men are taught that violent behavior, focus on power, and insistence on being in control are *choices* they keep repeatedly making to harm their victims. They are not out of control as they might like to believe. "Denial and minimization are reasons that effective programs are usually mandatory and lengthy. Another reason is that participants' behavior can be monitored over an extended period."[353] It can take approximately two years in these programs to observe noticeable change.

Surprisingly, many perpetrators are quite aware of their abusive tendencies and tactics. Being masters of deception, some actually become more sophisticated in their strategies and adept at concealing them after participation in these programs. Victims should not be falsely encouraged by this, however, as the efficacy of these programs is limited and questionable. If it has taken years to create an abuser, it will likewise take years to change his behavior.

Level 5 **Medical Personnel & Caregivers**

Many victims do not seek medical care unless they sustain serious injuries that require visits to the emergency room. Oftentimes, they are unwilling to disclose the abuse even when questioned. Emergency room procedures should require a woman to be seen in privacy without her partner present so she has a chance to ask for help without him hovering over her. Staff should be aware that assailants often act overly attentive and extremely concerned about her well-being. If she does not reach out, medical personnel must be trained to read the signs of deep-seated anxiety and fear that accompany her physical injuries.

"One study found less than 3% of women visiting emergency rooms disclosed or were asked about domestic violence by a nurse or physician... this despite estimates that 37% of women seeking treatment at emergency rooms have come as a result of injuries inflicted by an intimate."[354] "A 1999 study published in *The Journal of the American Medical Association* found that only 10% of primary care physicians routinely screen for IPV during new patient visits and 9% routinely screen during periodic checkups."[355] Physicians are mandated reporters of DV in only a few states.[356] We need to encourage more states to adopt these practices.

Staff should be observant of carefully crafted cover-up stories or a woman's secretiveness or unwillingness to discuss details concerning her injury. Whether or not she shares the truth with her caretaker, they should provide routine education at every visit about statistics of violence, local shelters and resources, and the toll-free phone number for the national DV hotline. Letting her know she has somewhere she can go if she needs to can be monumental. Since it is common for abuse to commence during pregnancy, there should be standard procedures to question women who miscarry or have repetitive miscarriages to see if there are indeed any signs of battering.

Level 6 Law Enforcement & Legal Representatives

Law enforcement, whether through police involvement or use of the legal system, plays a critical role in taking a stand against the perpetrator, ensuring a victim's safety, and reassuring her she is not alone in her battle. The idea that abuse is solely a family matter was a notion not addressed in the legal arena until recently within the past two decades. Violence is reinforced when there is no punishment and a man feels he can get away with it. "The fact that batterers suffer no legal consequences for their assaults serves only to perpetuate their violent behavior."[357] One "study showed that 80% of the batterers were violent only in their domestic relations; 80% of them had never been brought before the criminal justice system prior to the battering incident."[358] The notion of establishing consequences for abusive behavior is where society's role is decisive. We need to send the message loud and clear that abuse is absolutely unacceptable and will not be tolerated.

Police Action

The legal domain of DV requires a cohesive integrated approach between both police action and the court system. Statistically, "only 10% (of these women) ever called the police for help. Of these, most stated that the police were ineffective: when the police left, the assault was renewed with added vigor."[359] It is understandable then why victims are under-confident calling the police is in their best interest, fearing retaliation after

THE PSYCHOLOGY OF ABUSE 139

the police leave. Mandatory arrest of one person has improved this situation.

Many women consider making that phone call a last resort reserved for a dire situation or only after she is severely injured. These crimes are underreported because research shows "we interpret violence perpetrated by strangers differently from violence that intimates inflict. Indeed, female victims of domestic violence are six times less likely to report the crime to the police or other officials than those who have suffered at the hands of a stranger."[360] If a stranger assaults a woman, it is assumed he will be arrested but we do not assume this of a spouse.

Upper-class women hesitate to involve the police in their personal problems for fear of ruining her reputation and the fact no one may believe her. She is conscious of being judged by the police who may look at her expensive home, luxurious surroundings, fashionable clothing, and life of privilege and refuse to believe her. She realizes that "the man of means has more resources to protect his rights, his privacy, and his 'castle'... And on the rare occasion when the battered wife involves the police or other outside authorities, the upscale husband can retain skilled legal representation to defend his actions with little retribution or fanfare."[361] Police must respond to batterers with more effective measures and not discriminate against women of different socio-economic backgrounds.

The reluctance Indian women feel to involve the police derives from their cultural training to always put their husbands first. To take a stand against him is seen as an act of disrespect, dishonoring him and betraying the family. Living in an extended family home with her in-laws, she is outnumbered and knows they will side with their son as witnesses corroborating his story. An Indian wife cannot take the chance of bringing this shame upon the family, forever angering her in-laws, and fearing retaliation from her spouse. In many ways, involving the police and/or obtaining a restraining order are steps she can take only when she feels there is no hope of saving the marriage and divorce is imminent.

One legitimate concern with intervention is the danger involved. "The largest number of police fatalities in the line of duty (approximately 25%) occur when police respond to domestic violence calls. That figure rises to 40% if all police injuries are included. Thus, not only do police agree that they are ineffective in providing alternatives for battering couples, but they also view responding to such requests as personally dangerous... Repeat calls to same residence are common."[362] "One-third of all police time is spent responding to domestic violence disturbance calls."[363]

Another dynamic is the frustration with repeat cases when women return to their partners. "Most police officers state that they lose interest in protecting battered women when the women repeatedly drop charges. They interpret this reluctance to press charges as a desire to remain battered rather than fear of violent punishment by their batterers for pressing charges."[364] Enhanced comprehensive training in domestic violence is essential for all police officers. Learning sensitivity to a victim's issues, the psychology of abuse, and compassion in these situations will help women feel they can rely on police officers with greater confidence. Developing cultural sensitivity for women of specific ethnicities is necessary to bridge the gap.

Restraining Orders

There is power in what the legal system can do that a victim cannot accomplish on her own. "The courts can place controls on a violent man that friends and family members cannot. They can send him to jail, levy heavy fines, restrict his bail, serve protective orders, and send him to a batterer's counseling program."[365] "Multiple studies have demonstrated that abusers who are prosecuted are more likely to stop their violence than those who are not... The only abusers who change are the ones who become willing to accept the consequences of their actions."[366] It changes everything when men know this crime is on their record and they will be held accountable. "A man should be required to complete an abuser program *in conjunction with*, not *instead of*, legal consequences."[367]

Orders of protection, also known as restraining orders, are essential to take a stand against abuse and let a victim know the government and community support her. Approximately only 20% of the 1.5 million people who experience IPV annually obtain civil protection orders.[368] Temporary Restraining Orders known as "TROs are issued in America at the rate of more than 1,000 every day... Police must urge extreme caution in the period following issuance of a TRO. That time is emotionally charged and hazardous."[369] Batterers may pretend the law does not apply to them, but there is proof of their efficacy; restraining "orders accomplish what the woman is seeking: restoration of her safety and a desperately needed break from the abuser."[370]

What other purpose does it serve? "The short-term benefits of restraining orders are greater than the long-term benefits... The men are deterred by the threat of arrest. Other times, TROs demonstrate the woman's resolve to end the relationship, and that convinces the man to stay away... Restraining orders are most effective on the reasonable person who has a limited emotional investment. In other words, they work best on the person least likely to be violent anyway."[371] In many circumstances it is better for victims to favor "law enforcement interventions such as arrests for battery, assault, breaking and entering, or other violations of the law. Charges for breaking the law involve the system versus the lawbreaker, whereas restraining orders involve an abuser versus his wife."[372]

The decision whether or not to pursue obtaining this order is one that should not be taken lightly and must be determined on a case-by-case basis. Every woman must decide for herself if it is appropriate for her. If he is reasonable, afraid of legal consequences, and will honor it, then it might be worth her while. For some victims, it can heighten the volatility of the situation and enrage her abuser further so she fears the worst. "In one study

THE PSYCHOLOGY OF ABUSE 141

50% of victims felt their cases were worsened by TROs."[373] "Many batterers find intolerable the idea of being under the control of their victims, and with a court order, a woman seeks to control her husband's conduct, thus turning the tables of their relationship."[374]

Unfortunately, many women are denied restraining orders on the grounds of insufficient evidence. Thus, the burden of proof is harbored by the victim. The law sides with the perpetrator that he is innocent until proven guilty. Reform could entail shifting our perspective from proving whether an aggressor is innocent or guilty to honoring a woman's request to feel safe and protected. Taking some extra measures to protect a citizen who feels endangered and provide additional security seems reasonable.

Even though the restraining order is merely a piece of paper, it does "contribute greatly to women's safety and peace of mind and has helped immeasurably in women's efforts to move on with their lives and be free."[375] Keep in mind the most violent offenders will harm their victim regardless of what protection she has and will not be deterred by a legal document. "Approximately 50% of the orders obtained by women against intimate partners who physically assaulted them were violated."[376]

Legal Action & Court System

It is ironic a victim's separation from her partner when she is at her breaking point and the weakest is when she requires the greatest strength to endure and face his wrath. She is re-victimized by making her private struggle a public affair, breaking her silence after so many years, and verbalizing unspeakable events that have transpired in her home. A woman will have to overcome so much to take a stand against her partner, possibly confronting him for the first time, only to find that the intensity of the battle has magnified and he *will* seek to destroy her by other means.

Understanding a domestic violence offender will use the court system to his advantage to manipulate his victim, intimidate her, draw out the battle, deplete her financially, threaten her, and take away custody rights from her takes this fight to a different level of which bystanders may be completely unaware. It is horrifying to see "how the abuser... maneuvers through the legal system, trying to prevent his partner from receiving empowering assistance and striving to avoid accountability."[377]

To add to her struggle, she must face an often, unsympathetic court system and deal with aggressive, insensitive attorneys. In addition, "The fact that they have continued to live under such brutality is used to their detriment in any legal proceedings, and knowledgeable family members often refuse their support."[378] This can be one of the most trying times for her, a period when she will often find the idea of returning to him to be easier than dealing with the enormity of the legal situation in front of her. Facing him in court for the first time since possibly their separation can re-traumatize her. Seeing the judge treat her spouse with respect or leniency because of his reputation or status in society re-victimizes her.

A woman learns if she "wants the legal system to help protect her rights, (she) needs to seek out assistance for herself and to be prepared to advocate for her own needs and interests."[379] We can help reform the legal process by providing "adequate police protection, easy access to restraining orders, facilitation of prosecution procedures by assault victims, provision for temporary support and maintenance, speedy divorces, regulated child visitation, and legitimate legal procedures for battered women as defendants."[380] We can support legislation that considers a stronger stand against perpetrators and denies them child custody for endangering their own children.

In *The Gift of Fear*, de Becker reveals: "About 15% of serious assaults are reported to the police... Only 78% of these reports lead to police action, this means that police come into contact with approximately 12% of all severely violent acts. But only half of these contacts lead to the criminal justice system. So, now ...only 6% of severely violent episodes lead to the batterer entering criminal justice system... In about 94% of the cases of severe assault, there are no legal consequences at all for the batterer... About two-thirds of cases that enter the criminal justice system end up in court. When cases do go to court, a conviction occurs (50%) of the time. But quite often the conviction involves either a suspended sentence or probation. When all these factors are taken into account only about one out of every 10,000 acts of battering result in a fine or a jail sentence." [381]

The article, *"Twenty Reasons Why She Stays,"* posted on the National Coalition Against Domestic Violence website outlines **flaws with the system:**[382]

(1) Assailants are still not routinely arrested in many parts of the U.S.

(2) Police still tell survivors that they must have a protection order before an arrest can be made (in jurisdictions where this is not true). This builds in a "free assault" system, since an arrest is not made until after a protection order is issued.

(3) Personal protection orders are often not enforced. Many police believe a survivor can "nullify" a protection order if she "invites" an assailant to her home or workplace.

(4) Female survivors of DV are often arrested when they are in fact acting in self-defense.

(5) Cases where a crime would in other circumstances (stranger assault) be charged as a felony are charged as a misdemeanor (because they are "domestics" and not as important).

(6) Courts do not assure that battered women are notified of their court dates. Then, when she doesn't show up, they blame her for dropping the charges.

(7) Some courts issue bench warrants and threaten to jail the woman for contempt if she determines she cannot continue with

prosecution, ignoring the terrorism her batterer is exercising over her.
(8) Some prosecutors will drop charges when the survivor calls them on the telephone to ask them to do so, ignoring the possibility that the woman is being coerced into the phone call, (or in some cases, that it is not the survivor on the phone at all).
(9) Some judges deny battered women custody even when the children have been abused by the batterer. There is a fallacious assumption that the woman will return to her abuser or will become involved with another batterer. Often judges are so impressed that a father wants custody of his children, they fail to consider the effects of DV on the children.
(10) Courts often believe that the woman is making up or exaggerating the violence. They often believe the assailant's story and go to great lengths to empathize with his problems.

Level 7 Social Service Organizations & Safe-houses

Advocacy groups, support groups, and women's shelters play a crucial role. The enormity of what these organizations can do to raise awareness, educate the public, establish political contacts and liaisons, or advocate legal change is tremendous. The creation of safe houses has proved to be one of the most invaluable contributions by the community to aid victims and make the war on abuse public. The first safe house for women to seek refuge from the violence in their homes was created in England in 1971. This radical idea soon spread throughout Europe. There are currently 2031 shelters in the U.S. according to a 2008 publication by the National Coalition Against Domestic Violence.[383]

In *The Gift of Fear*, de Becker rightly points out, "For every battered woman who makes the choice to leave, we as a society must provide a place for her to go... Battered women's shelters are the closest thing we have to homicide prevention centers."[384] Many women flee with their children and nothing but the clothing on their backs. They have no money, food, or personal items. Shelters provide women with immediate necessities and a much-needed escape from not just the violence but also the constant and insidious influence of her spouse. Suddenly, she finds she has some space to think, sort out her thoughts, put things into perspective, and possibly consider leaving for the first time.

Finding a community of other women who share her experience is monumental. It proves she is not alone, her story is similar to the plight of many others, and validates her reality and suffering. She learns for the first time her partner fits a profile and her experience falls under the category of domestic violence with very distinguishable and recognizable patterns. "Other women at the shelter will support you in your effort to change your life. They will understand the temptation to call or go back to your abusive partner. They will help strengthen your resolve not to go back to the violence, even if you love him-if that is what you want to do."[385]

Even after separation, a victim may still be bound to her spouse through her unhealthy attachment, traumatic bonding, and his ongoing manipulation. "About 50% who stay longer than one week in a safe house will not return to live with the batterers."[386] This corroborates the reality that independence from her spouse makes her stronger. Most victims average going back and forth with a safe house three to five times before being able to leave her spouse permanently.[387]

This slowly builds their strength and confidence. "Studies show that access to shelter services leads to a 60-70% reduction in incidence and severity of re-assault during the three to twelve months follow-up period compared to women who did not access the shelter. Shelter services led to greater reduction in severe re-assault than did seeking court or law enforcement protection or moving to a new location."[388]

Safe houses still have their share of problems that include: funding, operating costs, access to adequate resources for women, and a high staff turnover who are susceptible to burnout. Many women's shelters operate on the same model created several decades ago. Reform is necessary to offer more support and services for victim.

Creating an **ideal resource center for women** should include:
(1) Regular support groups that also target the needs of specific victim populations.
(2) In addition to therapy, speaking with other survivors will encourage her and build her hope that she too can make it through this arduous process.
(3) Providing access to a library of resources with recommended reading lists of DV books to each victim during her first visit will empower her.
(4) Provide educational media such as films and documentaries on DV at the library.
(5) A donation center where she can obtain immediate necessities such as clothing for herself and her children is invaluable.
(6) Legal advocates and free legal counsel to aid her with restraining orders, divorce proceedings, custody issues, or immigration concerns is imperative. This could be a mandatory requirement for law students to provide a certain number of volunteer hours toward this cause.
(7) Job and career training, housing options, and English language training, if necessary, will give her the tools she needs to be independent.
(8) Self-defense classes with a trainer will build her confidence and empower her to overcome her fear. A trainer can facilitate getting in touch with her physical body again and overcome her tendency to disassociate and neglect herself.

(9) Agencies should be able to effectively navigate resources and services for survivors and network with housing groups, legal resources, local law enforcement, and minority/religious communities.
(10) Providing stress management services such as massage, classes for yoga and meditation, and acupuncture for PTSD symptoms is a logical and invaluable way to make these shelters more holistic and health centered.
(11) Creating a DV education curriculum for victims to understand the psychology of abuse will demonstrate that her spouse's behavior is not a mystery but fits a coherent pattern.

Chapter 14 discusses how each of the seven levels in society must develop an effective strategy to tackle abuse and put an end to this oppression on a global level.

CHAPTER 14 COMMUNITY'S CALL TO ACTION

The difference between what we do and what we are capable of doing would suffice to solve most of the world's problems. Mohandas K. Gandhi

Chapters 12 and 13 demonstrate the critical role of all seven levels of community in taking a stand against domestic violence. This chapter discusses more specifically the essential contribution of social service organizations to create survivor-centered advocacy based on lethality assessment and safety planning. Addressing the special needs of specific victim populations, the effect of abuse on children, and the economic consequences of DV offer greater perspective. Society's response includes strategies for both intervention and prevention and crucial steps everyone can take immediately to end gender violence on a global scale.

Survivor-Centered Advocacy

Survivor-centered advocacy can be defined as sensitivity to support the needs of a victim in an empowering way without judgment or condemnation. Many women may not identify with the term "victim" or associate it with being blamed or shunned by society. They may perceive it as an unwillingness of others to work with them and as a consequence become withdrawn or less likely to seek services. Thus, many centers choose to call victims "clients" instead. Differentiating between these terms, a victim is someone who is still in crisis versus a survivor is in the process of healing.

Developing compassion and awareness to meet a woman where she is emotionally will empower her. We must learn to communicate effectively, in a way that is respectful and does not minimize her cultural experiences, keeping in mind her ethnic identity is central to how she defines her experiences. It is imperative we tackle our insensitivity, prejudices, and not discriminate against her.

Society must understand the barriers a victim experiences in seeking support. She worries about being blamed for her predicament, feeling ashamed and embarrassed, and social stigmatization. She fears disclosing her abusive situation might result in losing her job or employment discrimination, losing custody of her children, social isolation, and creating more conflict at home. She frets about jeopardizing her immigration status, the cultural stigma, issues of racism and classism, and a possible language barrier. The more sensitivity we can develop as a community towards these issues, the better chance we have of assisting her.

There are five necessary elements to survivor–centered advocacy:[389]
(1) **Validation**-listen to her story and offer empathy and support.
(2) **Evaluation**-gather information of her unique situation, specific risk factors, and identify her concerns and goals. Recognize and point out her strengths.
(3) **Lethality assessment**-tool to assess danger level of her situation and educate her about potential for increasing violence to herself or her children. Alert her of specific concerns for her safety and emphasize necessity for being alert.
(4) **Safety plan**-to help minimize danger, take precautions, create a workable plan, and give her back some control over her situation.
(5) **Ongoing case management**-continuing steps 1-4 while attending to her specific needs and informing her of potential options. Support and encourage her while reinforcing her strengths.

As a community, we must learn how to be compassionate and sincere advocates, coordinate services between different agencies, make referrals whenever necessary to address her specific cultural, religious, or ethnic issues, and provide translators if needed. To empower her, we must provide options that allow her to make decisions for herself. We are obliged to respect her right for confidentiality and support appropriate boundaries. Breaches of confidentiality can cause potential safety risks, endanger her, violate her rights, and jeopardize her trust and confidence in us.

Lethality Assessment
"The lethality assessment scale determines a victim's risk level and the likelihood of lethal violence. It serves to evaluate the abuse within her relationship, teach her how to protect herself in the future, reduce the risk of violence, offer a baseline measure from which to create a safety plan, and help personnel advocate for the most appropriate intervention or service."[390]

The firm of Gavin de Becker, a national expert on prediction and management of violence, provides security to many government officials and public figures and has developed MOSAIC-20, an "artificial intuition system that assesses the details of a woman's situation as she reports it to police. This computer program flags those cases in which the danger of homicide is highest... This system brings to regular citizens the same technologies and strategies used to protect high government officials."[391]

The statistics of lethal violence are alarming. On average more than four women a day are murdered by their partners in the U.S.[392] Between "1,500 to 2,000 women are murdered by partners and ex-partners per year, comprising more than one-third of all female homicide victims."[393] These casualties *are* preventable. The correlation between lethality and animal abuse has been documented in several studies where women reported that a pet had been threatened, injured, or killed by their

THE PSYCHOLOGY OF ABUSE 149

abusers. In another survey, 20% of women delayed leaving the abusive situation out of fear their pets would be harmed.[394] Refer to Appendix 1 for additional statistics.

"Research indicates that a woman's intuitive sense of whether or not her partner will be violent toward her is a substantially more accurate predictor of future violence than any other warning sign."[395] "The root of the word intuition, *tuere*, means 'to guard, to protect.'"[396] Developing intuition is listening to that inner voice most battered women have been conditioned to shut off. Helping her reconnect with her doubts, hesitations, and suspicions is essential to reclaim her voice and her freedom. She should be aware the absence of a risk factor *does not* assure a victim's safety. Escalation from non-lethal to lethal can occur without notice as the perpetrator's actions are always unpredictable while someone with all the signs may never become violent.

Identifying Specific Risk Factors:[397]
- Abuser is unemployed, has access to firearms, lives with his victim and her child by a previous partner, and forces sex.
- Woman has left or is about to leave.
- Restraining order is about to be served.
- Abuser has been released from prison.
- Abuser has been notified of a recent separation, divorce, or custody change.
- He finds out she has reached out for help for the first time; his behavior has become "public."
- Abuser is currently using alcohol or drugs.
- The woman is showing independence, job or promotion, bought a car, or started school.

If weapons are involved, the risk of lethality is immediately heightened. Determining whether a perpetrator has access to firearms is of paramount importance. If he brags about using them, flaunts them as a show of power, or threatens to exploit them against her, are all warning signs. Sometimes he might display his weapon to intimidate her and remind her he has the power to use it against her. These are not actions to be taken lightly. "*Never* underestimate your abuser... few survivors can be 100% safe... If you find that others... are more fearful of your safety than you are, be sure to take that into account too. It may be that you are not yet fully ready to acknowledge the true risk that your former partner poses."[398] The art of prediction involves looking at a perpetrator's underlying motivations-to achieve power in the only way he knows how-by trying to dominate another person. He believes that by initiating this kind of behavior a certain desirable outcome will be achieved.

Safety Planning

An advocate must assist a woman in creating an individualized plan to keep her and her children safe that will empower her and minimize risk level by creating a safety network and securing her home. Taking any extra precautionary measures is necessary. Specific steps from several DV publications include:[399]

- Avoid rooms without exits to have arguments
- Avoid the kitchen where knives can be used as weapons
- Change door locks, passcodes, and phone numbers
- Add a security system
- Be prepared with a list of contact numbers and a neighbor to call in an emergency
- Know how to contact a local women's shelter or agency
- Use a code word to alert family or friends to call the police if necessary
- Avoid staying home alone
- Vary routines and route to work
- Screen phone calls, save any messages he leaves to use as evidence
- Take photographs of injuries to use as evidence
- Notify children's school or colleagues at work of pressing situation
- If meeting assailant, only do so in public places where there are witnesses
- Determine escape plan if there is an emergency
- Plan how to stay safe and secure at a new location
- Pack an emergency bag with essentials to get away: include cash, credit cards, ATM cards, checkbook, house/ car keys, address book of contact numbers, copy of all prescriptions, and month's supply of medications. Copies of important documents should be taken: ID cards, driver's license, passports, green card or immigration papers, social security card, health insurance card, birth/ marriage certificates, divorce papers, restraining orders, custody orders, children's school records, bank account numbers, and car title, registration, and insurance information.

In *Trauma and Recovery*, Herman aptly describes how "survivors feel unsafe in their bodies. Their emotions and their thinking feel out of control. They also feel unsafe in relation to other people... Establishing safety begins by focusing on control of the body and gradually moves outward toward control of the environment. Issues of bodily integrity include attention to basic health needs, regulation of bodily functions such as sleep, eating, and exercise, management of post-traumatic symptoms, and control of self-destructive behaviors. Environmental issues include the establishment of a safe living situation, financial security, mobility, and a plan for self-protection that encompasses the full range of the patient's daily life."[400]

Special Needs of Specific Victim Populations

Developing sensitivity to the needs of specific victim population groups is essential to recognize when services should be tailored to accommodate individual requirements. This includes cultural competency and respect for religious beliefs and practices, addressing immigrants, the gay, lesbian, bisexual, transgender (GLBT) community, substance abusers, disabled, mentally ill, children, and the elderly. Each population group has its own unique issues that must be recognized and addressed for advocacy to be meaningful and effective and overcome the barriers each one has to seeking support. These obstacles can include lack of accessible treatment, limited transportation, or being dependent on her abuser as her primary caregiver.

Batterers often coerce victims to use substances and threaten to expose their use to others or to get the upper hand in custody battles. They may justify their violence as a way to control victims when they are drunk. When batterers misuse substances often battering incidents can be more severe and they will blame the substance as an excuse for their behavior. Victims can mistakenly feel it is the alcohol or substance that is to blame and not the abuser. Refer to Appendix 1 for additional statistics on substance abuse and victims with disabilities.

Effect of Abuse on Children

The greatest motivation we might have to get involved is for the approximately 15.5 million children nationally affected by domestic violence.[401] "The UN Secretary-General's Study on Violence Against Children conservatively estimates that 275 million children worldwide are exposed to violence in the home."[402] Additional statistics are listed in Appendix 1.

- On average, between 2001 and 2005, 38% of children witnessing IPV were young girls and 21% were young boys.[403]
- The National Woman Abuse Prevention Project reports that children are present in 41 to 55% of homes where police intervene in DV calls.[404]
- More than 90% of battered women said that their children have witnessed their battering.[405]
- Approximately 1 in 4 incidents (25%) of relationship abuse involves injury to children.[406]

Living in an environment where safety is compromised is detrimental for children and adversely affects their health whether they become victims of abuse themselves, sense tension between parents, witness the abuse, or are used as a pawn/weapon by the abuser to manipulate his victim. No matter how much a mother may try to shield her kids, they are silent witnesses who watch with horror as their fathers behave like monsters and injure their innocent mothers.

When there is nothing they can do to stop the violence in their own homes, they feel helpless, partly to blame, and intensely guilty. This is a heavy burden for a young child to shoulder, one that will stay with him/her possibly throughout adult life. They may fear abandonment living in such an unstable family dynamic and as a consequence suffer from other psychological issues. Exposure to violence and repetitive trauma affects children at different developmental stages. Research shows the physiological impact of violence on the brain leads to underdevelopment in certain critical areas.[407] The long-term consequences of this exposure are that they are more likely to become juvenile and adult offenders.

Many perpetrators also abuse their children. "In a national survey of American families, 50% of the men who frequently assaulted their wives also frequently abused their children."[408] We are all mandated reporters for abuse against children and must call the hotline at 800-96-ABUSE. "Fathers who batter mothers are twice as likely to seek sole physical custody of their children than are nonviolent fathers."[409]

A father's manipulation may include threatening their safety, turning them against their mother by fabricating lies, or accusing his partner of being neglectful. Before she blames herself, a victim should remember she has probably done the best she could under the circumstances to ensure survival and safety over being the "perfect" parent. The sacrifices women make in order to protect their children may even include rejecting child support to avoid disclosing their new location to their spouse.

Ways to Intervene with Children: outlined in *Not to People Like Us*[410]
- "Explain the situation in language children can understand.
- Tell them the violence is not their fault.
- Give them permission to talk about the violence.
- Help make a safety plan they can follow.
- Find someone outside the family with whom they can share their feelings.
- Let them know others have had similar experiences.
- Discuss the situation with domestic violence or protective services staff to find out how else you can help the children."

Economic Effects of Abuse

If we are stirred for no other reason than pure economics, the financial effects of domestic violence are staggering whether it is in health care or in worker productivity. Surveyed business leaders agree to the magnitude of the problem. In one survey, "66% of senior corporate executives believed their company's financial performance would benefit from addressing the issue of domestic violence among their employees."[411] Additional statistics are listed in Appendix 1.
- "In the U.S. in 1995, the health care cost of intimate partner rape, physical assault, and stalking totaled $5.8 billion each year, nearly

$4.1 billion of which is for direct medical and mental health care services. Lost productivity from paid work and household chores and lifetime earnings lost by homicide victims total nearly $1.8 billion in the U.S. in 1995.[412] When updated to 2003 dollars, the cost is more than $8.3 billion."[413]
- "Family violence costs the nation $5-10 billion annually in medical expenses, police and court cases, shelters and foster care, sick leave, absenteeism, and non-productivity. $2.5 billion of health insurance benefits are spent on injuries resulting from domestic violence."[414]
- "IPV victims lose nearly 8 million days of paid work per year in the U.S. alone—the equivalent of 32,000 full-time jobs and almost 5.6 million days of household productivity."[415]
- "According to the Bureau of Labor statistics, 12% of workplace homicides of women are committed by current or former intimate partners. Women with violent men in their lives took more time off, were often late for work, or had to leave early; 24% lost their jobs because of it."[416]

Society's Response-Strategies to Deal with Abuse

The question we must ask ourselves as a community is how can we change the ending of another victim's story? How can we avoid another preventable death? What must we do to ensure children are protected and do not have to live in violent homes? Society's response to abuse must be divided into two clear categories addressing both intervention and prevention.

Intervention strategies should be designed to focus on safety, empowering victims, and providing tools necessary to resolve their situations effectively. Comprehensive prevention strategies must address multiple levels of society. Our help should not be contingent on whether or not a battered woman agrees to leave her spouse. We must remember that is a decision for her alone to make. Her ability to choose freedom is determined by how empowered she feels.

Intervention Strategies include:
(1) It should be mandatory to report anyone suspected of abuse.
(2) **Family and friends**: do everything possible to let her feel comfortable, trust you will support her, and feel confident she has the power to change her situation.
(3) **National Domestic Violence Hotline:** everyone in the community should encourage women to take advantage of this twenty-four hour resource at **1-800-799-SAFE** and receive advice and coaching from trained personnel during a crisis. There are also hotlines for specific ethnicities who do not speak English.
(4) **Safe-houses:** create a warm, supportive environment for women to feel safe, restore their strength, receive crisis intervention counseling, and financial assistance if necessary.

(5) **Victim advocates:** direct her to resources required at various stages in her healing process and guide her towards appropriate intervention strategies.
(6) **Therapists:** focus on crisis intervention counseling, help her gain clarity of her situation, and see the pattern of abuse she has been trapped in.
(7) **Medical settings:** it should be mandatory to see women privately and assess whether injuries are due to domestic violence.
(8) **Legal involvement:** provide free legal advice at shelters about restraining orders and how they may help or hurt her individual situation.

Prevention Strategies include:
(1) **Community education and outreach:** is necessary at every level of society. Raise awareness about DV in our communities. The public must be able to recognize signs of abuse, understand the cycle of violence and victimization process, appreciate the reasons a woman does not reach out for help, and to what resources we can guide women. Gain insights from trained professionals such as emergency room physicians, judges, attorneys, legal advocates, therapists, safehouse volunteers, and most importantly, survivors themselves about the specific issues of domestic violence.
(2) **Education at school:** should be mandatory in every grade level, especially as dating and issues of rape and abuse become more relevant. Teach equality between boys and girls. Discuss the dynamics of abuse and why it is so insidious and hard to detect. Use effective media such as videos, documentaries, and online resources to increase exposure to DV education.
(3) **Young girls and women:** should receive self-defense training, be coached on how to respond to abuse if victimized, and be aware of available resources for intervention. Exposure to a DV curriculum annually will reinforce their instincts. Provide them with an opportunity to volunteer for women's advocacy groups and shelters to see firsthand the issues at stake.
(4) **Career opportunity:** Address gender biases, stereotyping, and promote equal opportunity for men and women. This should be reflected in all our roles including women receiving equal pay for work done by her male counterparts.
(5) **Religious community:** Interact with local agencies and shelters to direct women to appropriate resources trained and equipped to handle DV.
(6) **Agencies/Institutions/Societal influence:** Eliminate social problems contributing to abuse and reduce exposure to violence in all forms of media such as television, video games, or Hollywood films. Actively work to eradicate existing social myths.

(7) **Police:** Require training to be sympathetic to the needs of victims, understand the intimidation tactics abusers use to have control even in their presence such as giving her "the look."
(8) **Legal influence:** Introduce more effective legislation to punish abusers, grant restraining orders, and protect victims. Enforce new rules and regulations for treating women in the court system sympathetically. Emphasize protection instead of the burden of proof being on the victim to provide evidence of the abuse.

Ending Abuse on a Global Scale

Abuse is intolerable, unforgivable, and inexcusable. We cannot condone the actions of a single perpetrator. Domestic violence needs to be addressed more effectively and eradicated. This oppression of human rights perpetuates itself within society as long as we continue to look the other way or live in ignorance. Recognizing abuse is the first step. Expanding our definition of family, community, and what our role is, is the second step. Taking immediate action is the third.

Here are **seven immediate actions** we can take towards this cause:
(1) Support our local women's shelters by donating household supplies, clothing, or anything else they might find useful. Call them directly to ask what they need. Many agencies will have "wish lists" for their clients.
(2) Donate funds to women's resources and centers that are in dire need of adequate funding. Many donations are tax-deductible.
(3) "Adopt" a victim by asking your local shelter if they have this program. Your donations will go specifically to her immediate financial requirements whether it is legal bills, housing, or childcare.
(4) Volunteer time at local women's agencies to help with understaffing and the overwhelming response these centers have to adequately address victim's needs. Many centers can see approximately 1,000 new victims every month if not more.
(5) Inform and educate our religious institutions about partnering with DV agencies, when to refer to them, and how to support women.
(6) Speak to our children's teachers at school about increasing education and awareness about DV in every grade level and engage them in meaningful discussion as to preventing this crime.
(7) Discuss gender violence openly without deeming it taboo. Remove the shame and stigma so women are not afraid to break their silence.

CHAPTER 15 STAGES OF BREAKING FREE

A journey of a thousand miles must begin with a single step. Lao Tzu

Formula for Freedom

Breaking free and recovering from the trauma of an abusive dynamic is no easy feat. What is the formula for freedom? The challenge is to accept where she is at present, her point of ultimate surrender. Ironically, it is when she is the weakest that she will have to cultivate the strength and will to walk away. "The budding belief that life *can* be filled with something other than cruelty... grows a little stronger inside her."[417] Many former victims describe something infinitely more powerful that takes over at that moment, a glimmer of hope that is the seed to fuel her fight for liberation. Freedom happens one step at a time as she journeys through five distinct stages to break free:

Stage 1 Recognition
Stage 2 Break her silence
Stage 3 Stop the cycle of violence
Stage 4 Reclaim her power
Stage 5 Open to the healing process

***Stage 1* Recognition**

It can take multiple occurrences before a victim classifies her experience as an overall pattern of abuse rather than isolated incidents as her partner leads her to believe. Recognition surfaces on multiple levels:
(a) Understanding she is a victim
(b) Identifying *how* she has been victimized
(c) Comprehending her abuser's true nature
(d) Ascertaining whether his attempt to change is genuine or an illusion
(e) Grasping how she has inadvertently co-created this reality

Identifying the destructive patterns in the relationship dynamic and processing her victimization requires tremendous effort and determination, but there comes a point when she can no longer deny the obvious. At some level the truth seeps in, no matter how hard she tries to bury it and she finds it sets her free. When does this moment of clarity come? What is the catalyst? More than an abusive incident being the final straw, there is a certain shift in her consciousness when she "breaks free," gains insight, and has perspective for the first time of her marriage.

Many former victims describe waking up from a nightmare as an *"aha"* moment precipitated by either the first incident of violence, observing her child being harmed, or when she reaches her breaking point and knows she cannot withstand her unbearable situation any longer. Every woman's threshold varies, so there is no way to determine at what point an emotional breakdown or aha moment occurs. Culturally, this can vary as well, as there are different values about what is considered acceptable. It is when a victim's defense mechanisms that kept her marriage intact start to unravel that her path to liberation begins. The more self-aware she becomes, the less tolerance she has for her toxic, unhealthy relationship.

Her Victimization

It may be a struggle for a woman to confront her victimization after her perpetrator's persistent brainwashing and conditioning. Labeling his actions as abusive may still seem like a stretch but accepting she has been harmed is necessary for the healing process to begin. She cannot underestimate the traumatizing effects of his mistreatment, his exploitation of her vulnerabilities to gain the upper hand, and his manipulative strategies designed to weaken her.

She must grasp he has stolen something precious from her: her innocence, trust, faith, security, and joy. "You may need to become aware of your unmet needs for connection and intimacy and your right to be treated with courtesy, respect, dignity, and empathy."[418] Comprehending the victimization process outlined in Chapter 8, she begins to doubt her spouse instead of doubting herself. "When (she) recognizes that her mate has no determination to understand her, she has begun to understand him."[419]

In *The Verbally Abusive Relationship*, Evans points out that for some victims, "recognition and integration of what had occurred was still going on five, ten, and fifteen years later. Many had tried every avenue, every approach, to improve their relationship: explaining, overlooking, asking, begging, individual and joint counseling, living their lives as independently as possible, meeting their own needs, not asking 'too much,' settling for less and less, being undemanding, being understanding. Nothing seemed to work. The dynamics of the relationship were often still a mystery."[420] Processing her victimization allows her to move forward, build her strength, and use these lessons to shape her future life of freedom.

Abuser's True Nature

As a victim moves past all the confusion the aggressor has created, she steps out of the illusion he trapped her in and glimpses his true nature. "The chaos that often goes along with an abusive relationship is a distraction that can prevent you from seeing what might otherwise be very clear-the truth."[421] Suddenly, she sees her partner in a new light, comprehending for the first time how he has treated her inhumanely and how all of his actions have been based on dominating her. It can be a surprise for her to see the man she has been in love with as violent, cruel, ruthless, or domineering. Reacting with denial and shock is perfectly

THE PSYCHOLOGY OF ABUSE 159

natural since she cannot reconcile this reality with the image she has of the charming man with whom she fell in love.

Despite his tactics to continue to bully and intimidate her through the legal system or other means, she must remember he is weak and scared underneath his tough exterior. He has more to fear and more at stake than she does. His image, reputation, and career may be in jeopardy. Seeing him as a self-serving narcissist who is not capable of truly loving or respecting her puts things into perspective. His capacity to lie, be manipulative, and repeatedly deny reality has probably made her lose all respect for him. "You may decide that now that you're free of all the drama and emotional outbursts, you don't even like him anymore, and perhaps you never really did."[422] This can be a surprising revelation.

Grieving the loss of her marriage may be necessary before she feels she can take action. In the end, it is only the oppressed who can overturn an oppressive situation, not the one in power. Her partner lacks both the motivation and the ability to admit to or acknowledge the abuse. She must be encouraged to proceed at her individual pace as long as she does not neglect or compromise her safety.

If she is endangered, she must take steps to ensure her safety immediately. Confusion creates immobility while clarity empowers her and is the most potent tool she possesses to transform her situation. Revelation comes through perspective, insight, and self-awareness. The decisions she makes in her process to break free must come forth from clarity, not fear or confusion. We must remind a victim that at any moment she can *choose* freedom.

Evaluating Relationship

Part of recognizing domestic violence is stepping back to evaluate the unhealthy relationship dynamic and become aware of his subtle hold on her. For some women, it is not possible to confront the abuse until it is clear the marriage is terminating. She must examine the relationship through her partner's eyes: how it serves his needs, how being in power supports him, how he does not think of her as an equal, his double standards, and his profound lack of love and disrespect for her. How does he treat her compared to those he respects? Does he have unreasonable expectations? She must recognize his methods of domination and evaluate the "emotional hooks" he uses to bait her and increase her dependency.

A victim must closely examine her silence, sacrifices, and compromises. It is not possible to survive in a relationship if her needs are not being met. Only focusing on his needs, as he has conditioned her to do, leads her to lose her sense of self, identity, and independence. She must be honest with herself and realistically evaluate the pros and cons. It might be great to have a steady partner, a nice home, financial stability, but is the price of living with these things her own mental peace and safety?

A victim needs to evaluate herself, her spouse, the quality of their interaction, and determine either the healthiness of their relationship or the level of abusiveness. "Only when (she) can see what's wrong will she sense what could be right."[423] A therapist can work with a victim to gently plant these seeds of clarity and awareness in her mind when she is ready. By asking these questions, she can provide a victim with the insight she requires to break free. Refer to *The Power to Break Free Workbook* for additional exercises for victims.

Evaluating Abuse:
❏ How has the abuse affected your quality of life?
❏ What are the different ways he tries to control you?
❏ How often do abusive incidents occur?
❏ Does the abuse continue to escalate in severity or frequency despite your efforts?
❏ Are you compromising on the safety of your children?
❏ How does he make you feel threatened or unsafe?
Following excerpts taken from *Why is it Always About You? Saving Yourself from the Narcissists in Your Life.*[424]
❏ What buttons of yours does he push?
❏ What do your feelings tell you to do? Do you act on these urges?
❏ What have you tried in the past? What has not worked?
❏ Are there others who can help you?
❏ Consider the costs of remaining with him. What are you giving up? What are you getting in exchange?
❏ Is it worth it to continue to stay in the relationship?
❏ How has the abuse changed you? How has it impacted your relationships, ability to function, parenting skills, etc.?

Evaluating Change
❏ Is there any evidence he will change?
❏ If you ask him to examine his behavior, can he admit to his violence? Can he see how it has hurt you?
❏ Is he genuinely motivated to change? Why do you believe so?
❏ Is he willing to let you hold him accountable for his behaviors?
❏ Does he show a true sense of remorse? Has he worked to make amends for his behavior?
❏ Is he willing to do therapy, join a batterers intervention group, or take any other steps you feel are necessary?
❏ How effective have you been at changing the relationship so far?
❏ What, if anything, is different in your relationship now?
❏ Has the power dynamic between you changed in any way?

Real Change
Many women come to the point where they can label their situation as abusive, recognize their spouse needs to change, know they will not tolerate any more violence, only to discover he continues to subtly manipulate them. If a perpetrator declares he will change, a victim must

THE PSYCHOLOGY OF ABUSE 161

ask him directly what is his plan for change. He might promise to receive professional help and say all the "right" sentiments to convince his partner he is making progress but she must be able to distinguish between his façade and true change. "Illusions of change (can) keep you trapped... Real change looks very different from a typical good period... unless the man has also done deep work on his abusive attitudes."[425]

She must hold him accountable, look for genuine progress, and allow sufficient time for this transformation to occur. "Make the completion of a full batterers intervention program a requirement for any discussion of reconciliation... You need to arrange for the therapist who facilitates the batterers group to report your ex's attendance and progress to you directly."[426] He may convince his spouse to return and lead her to believe things will be dramatically different, but she must be acutely aware of not falling back into the same abusive patterns. A victim should require proof and set clear boundaries before.

Very few abusers are actually capable of genuine reform and those who do require at least two years statistically if they are enrolled and committed to an intensive batterers intervention program to recognize their hurtful actions, examine their fundamental underlying attitudes of disrespect, and feel remorse. "Even with effective treatment, abusers need time and a deep commitment to change. Unfortunately, many abusers are never able to break the cycle and they repeat the abuse with partner after partner."[427]

Ultimately, we cannot change anyone. A victim can only focus on herself and decide what she feels is acceptable or not. "He *may* change when he finds that you *do* know when you are being abused, that you *have* set limits, that you *mean* what you say, and that you *will not take* behavior you don't like."[428] If a woman is tempted to return, she should not blame herself; this is a common pattern while breaking free. A victim must "decide whether going back is worth the possibility of losing all that you have gained during your healing process... You *always* have a choice."[429]

The Victim Label

Identifying how she has co-created the reality of abuse is an extremely sensitive topic and one that a therapist or others should discuss with caution and compassion. After being in an abusive dynamic, it can take years before she realizes she has been victimized. When she "refuses to 'look at her part' in the abuse, she has actually taken a powerful step out of self-blame and toward emotional recovery. She *doesn't* have any responsibility for his actions. Anyone who tries to get her to share responsibility is adopting the abuser's perspective."[430]

So labeling herself as a victim is a critical turning point to be cognizant of her unhealthy situation and be motivated to leave. Bypassing this step only serves to validate the perpetrator and impedes a victim's healing progress. It is only after this realization has had time to really sink in that she can take the next necessary step in her healing journey-to see her participation in this victimization.

"It is fortifying for (her) to recognize the extent to which her own choices have kept her on the path-she is not necessarily a victim, and if she identifies how her decisions have contributed to staying, she can also see ways to escape the abuse."[431] This does not mean a victim should take the blame for the abuse but clearly see how she has assisted in perpetuating it and moreover, how she can take steps to end it. Even if these choices have been unconscious, she can bring them to the surface and see her line of thinking behind them. *The Gift of Fear* says, "The first time a victim is hit, she is a victim, and the second time, she is a volunteer."[432] This may be hard to accept at first, but acknowledging her participation is a necessary step to free herself.

Stage 2 Breaking Her Silence

A victim carries an immense burden keeping the reality of her marriage a secret from others as well as from herself. The relief from breaking her silence allows her to slowly admit to herself the severity of her victimization. By speaking her truth, she learns to listen to her voice that she had willingly surrendered and simultaneously reclaim her power. A victim must pay attention to whenever she forfeits this right to speak freely. It is only by reliving her tale and putting the pieces together that she ascertains how toxic her relationship is, glimpsing the pattern of abuse and horror she has lived through with a fresh transparency.

Having someone listen and offer empathy can be a turning point to overcome the barriers of isolation her assailant has so carefully constructed. "Validation must occur before (she) recognizes what is happening and take action on her own behalf."[433] Many victims report the external voices and continued support from friends and family were critical to her emancipation. Their input and objective perspective triggers the awakening of her inner voice and sense of self-trust that was repressed. By connecting with others, her world expands, she gleans options and choices she had not even imagined before, and salvation and freedom seem possible.

A well-trained therapist listens to how a woman constructs her story, the subtle nuances of words she chooses, the detached manner in which she speaks, the self-blame, and the tendency to minimize her abuser's behavior. "Feedback from an outsider helps (her) begin to crystallize her thoughts... The rationalizations she once relied on to sustain her within the marriage and to maintain the marital relationship begin to break down... She slowly rejects them as she confronts the *cognitive dissonance*-the contradiction between her own knowledge and what she sees going on... At this point, (she) is relieved to step away from her self-deception."[434] A therapist must skillfully deconstruct her cognitive dissonance by gently asking her to offer proof and evidence to distinguish her false hopes from reality.

In *Not to People Like Us*, the author says, "Yet these women retain a glimmer of their own truths and reality-no matter what the accepted cultural myth, no matter what their husbands tell them, and no matter how strong their denial. This disparity creates an inner tension. Interacting with others brings the inner truth to the surface, simply by acknowledgement and validation... For these women, talking and sharing breathed life back into their own perceptions, desires, and standards; it revitalized their moribund sense of themselves and their self-worth. After gaining this confirmation, over time they were able to reconnect with their own power and competencies."[435] We must encourage women to not be afraid to reach out and ask for help; this action could save her life.

Stage 3 Stop the Cycle of Violence

The only way to deal with a perpetrator and stop the cycle of violence is for a woman to disengage completely from the power dynamic he has created and thrives on. "Contact is fuel for the fire."[436] This entails stepping out of the reactionary mode he has conditioned her to be in. He desires a rise out of her to feel powerful and in control. Anything she says or does, any resistance or confrontation he encounters will only trigger an escalation of his domination tactics.

A victim must surrender the false hope she can effectively prevent or manage abusive incidents. She cannot appease his anger or defuse his explosiveness. Occasionally, she might succeed at thwarting an argument from escalating, but he will continue to behave in unpredictable and hurtful ways regardless of her actions or protests. She has no control over his level of abusiveness. Staying in the relationship co-creates the reality of abuse and gives her spouse permission in some ways to continue his violent behavior.

"Once abuse has begun, it usually does not disappear without intervention, treatment, and monitoring."[437] "There is also some evidence that certain treatment interventions are more successful if they occur at one phase rather than at another."[438] As discussed previously, a victim is more vulnerable during stages 1 and 2 of the cycle of violence while tension is building and during the abusive incident itself, thus, more readily influenced by outside intervention. As she slips into stages 3 to 5, processing the abuse, the honeymoon stage, and the calm interlude, her efforts focus more on reconciliation and survival so treatment strategies are less effective.

A victim should ask herself, what does it take to walk away? Examining her basic resistance to leave demonstrates how easy it is to be attached to what is familiar. "Pursuers are, in a very real sense, detoxing from an addiction to the relationship."[439] Just like detoxifying from substances, there is a strong pull to return to the addiction. Staying in close contact with her perpetrator impedes her healing progress, but often, he will not "tolerate breakup because on some level he senses that it is too healthy and healing for the woman. She might discover how much better off she is without him."[440]

Even after separation, she may still continue to be highly reactive to the abuse as if it were an ongoing daily occurrence. A trained therapist assists in identifying these conditioning patterns so a victim learns to trust that there will be a time that "in the future (when) abuse will no longer be such a powerfully painful part of everyday life."[441] Moreover, a victim should not let the strong feelings that consume her attention and energy interfere with assessing her safety. As Jayne says, "It's never too early to ditch a jerk, but it's sometimes too late."[442]

Guidelines to Disengage from his Power & Control Tactics:
- See how he actively tries to push your buttons. Identify how he tries to exploit your vulnerabilities.
- Stay detached from the negative feelings and reactions he attempts to trigger in you.
- Distance yourself from his projections, blame, and accusations and do not personalize them.
- Resist being in a reactionary mode and do not try to retaliate or challenge him in any way.
- Identify his irrational behavior and do not attempt to rationalize with him.
- "Do not negotiate, no matter how much he wants to. This is not a discussion of how to improve things, correct things, change the past, find blame, or start over."[443]
- "Seek and apply strategies that make you unavailable to your pursuer."[444]

A victim may require time to build her courage and craft a safety plan before she is ready to take action. "Like prisoners of war, such women find it soothing and emotionally sustaining to envision ways to escape."[445] She will need a well-thought out strategic plan of action. Ultimately, she discovers she has the power to make choices to set herself free.

Stage 4 **Reclaim Her Power**
(A) Set Limits, Establish Boundaries, & Demand Change

The challenge to reclaim her power involves relinquishing all the coping mechanisms she has employed until now to keep the peace, seek resolution, and not agitate her partner. She might need to clearly say, *"I'm not willing to take any responsibility for your actions or your mistreatment of me."* Boundaries are necessary to define, protect, and assert clearly what she will and will not accept. Her expectations of him should be straightforward. Whenever he violates her trust or assumes a position of authority, a victim should acknowledge this and be firm about holding him accountable.

"Asking for change is important (to) discover whether or not the possibility of a healthful relationship exists with your mate."[446] While developing effective strategies to deal with him, it is wise for her to anticipate resistance and danger in response to taking a stand. Especially if he is a narcissist, any step towards independence is a threat to his sense of self and can spark an increase in his intensity of violence. She should be prepared to separate if need be to protect herself if this occurs. This will recover her sense of self again.

Limiting time spent with him is crucial to avoid the toxic environment he has created. If she feels resistance, she must deeply examine her traumatic bonding. Surrounding herself with a healthier, supportive atmosphere where people accept her and do not try to hurt her will be healing. If she has been sexually abused, it is difficult to have clear boundaries and she will require the expertise of a trained therapist to guide her. By confiding in others who can offer support, they can check in within a specific time frame and determine what proactive steps she has taken to reclaim her power.

In *Not to People Like Us*, Weitzman states, "How does a woman proceed if her husband has stopped the abuse, is seeking help, and wants the marriage to stay viable? She learns to focus on herself first. She practices making demands of him in small increments with the goal of feeling safe and like an equal partner. She recognizes that the marriage will have its ups and downs, and she proceeds cautiously and assesses it daily. She learns to keep to her boundaries, setting up consequences such as leaving if he belittles her again or calling the police if he strikes her once more. She calls the shots for what she is willing to tolerate and is also willing to negotiate with him for change. Although she is patient, she is no longer a victim. However, she must be consistent in enforcing the consequences."[447]

(B) Assert Her Rights

The next step for a victim is to stand up for herself and notice unmistakably how her basic human rights for dignity, respect, and equality have been violated. It may be worthwhile for her to start documenting these abuses privately as it can be valuable when the time comes to take legal action. These violations constitute a loss of freedom. Part of her healing journey is appreciating true freedom on every level. The depth of this realization can only become apparent when she confronts what it means to be imprisoned by her abuser, as well as, by her own mind.

A victim has the right to be angry for what she has endured and the right to express her rage. She may have learned it was safer to stay silent, surrender her voice, and not show her anger, but it is a misperception to believe "you should have the ability to stay serene no matter how you are treated. Your serenity comes from the knowledge that you have a fundamental right to a nurturing environment and a fundamental right to affirm your boundaries."[448]

A victim compromises her integrity, another behavior pattern that mimics her spouse. In *Emotional Blackmail*, the authors say, "Integrity is that place inside where our values and our moral compass reside, clarifying what's right and wrong for us. Though we tend to equate integrity with honesty, it's actually much more. The word itself means 'wholeness,' and we experience it as the firm knowledge that 'this is who I am. This is what I believe. This is what I am willing to do-and this is where I draw the line.'"[449] Integrity has to do with integrated living between our inner and outer world that is the journey to wholeness we seek in our healing.

One platform to assert her rights will be in the legal arena, whether she seeks a restraining order, child custody, or divorce proceedings. She cannot be complacent any longer or fearful of confronting him. Accepting this as part of her battle for freedom is vital. "An abuser sees his partner's growing strength and independence as a sickness rather than as the harbinger of health that it actually is."[450] She must be strong, learn to speak her truth, and hold her ground. If he makes eye contact, she should hold his gaze, not back down, or give him any reason to believe he has the power to intimidate her anymore. The lesson is not the outcome but for a victim to reclaim her power and not be bullied by him, his attorney, or the legal system. She will find freedom from not being attached to the results or obtaining revenge.

(C) Personal Power

During this process of reclaiming her life and freedom, she glimpses the strong, independent woman she used to be and remembers her strengths. As she mourns the loss of her old self, she must actively take back what she has given away. A new creative identity will be shaped from the synthesis of her old personality and the wisdom she has accrued from her abusive relationship. This involves reclaiming every part of her self-identity. Chapter 1 elaborated on the **four parts of a woman's identity:**
  (1) Broader cultural identity influenced by ideal stereotypes of said culture.
  (2) Identity as part of family unit defined by relationships to parents and siblings and later husband and children.
  (3) Individual identity that is not prioritized nor given much expression in Eastern traditional cultures.
  (4) Core spiritual self that is not easily accessible if one lives with repression or becomes totally shut down in the case of abuse.

Breaking free from an abusive marriage involves reclaiming all four of these aspects of herself. Each one of her cultural, familial, individual, and spiritual identities must be nourished and tended. Reclaiming personal power is a process of self-discovery and identifying her individual armor. A woman must ask herself from where does she derive her power? What gives her strength and protection? The best weapon to arm herself with is education about domestic violence and developing self-awareness. Knowledge is power.

"Remember that there are very few situations in life where you are truly powerless."[451] A victim often limits herself to accepting only one path and thus resigns herself to her abusive union. She should create a vision for her future of living an abuse-free life, imagining what it would be like to live in freedom and not fear.

When a victim liberates herself from the prison of her mind, she glimpses a myriad of available choices. She can choose to live a healthy life and not be hurt again. The quest of human life is for freedom. Everyone searches for it whether one feels oppressed or not. As she realizes her freedom is not up for negotiation, she opens to the possibility of embracing freedom at every level. She realizes she has the right to choose her destiny and be the person she always wanted to be. If she is a mother, she can be someone her children can admire.

CHAPTER 16 HEALING & RECOVERY

And the day came when the risk to remain tight in a bud was more painful than the risk it took to blossom. Anais Nin

Stages of the Healing Process
After a victim has passed through the first four stages of breaking free, she is ready to embrace the healing and recovery process. Gaining clarity, breaking her silence, reclaiming her power, and establishing boundaries in the previous stages are intrinsic to recovery. Addressing the multiple levels of healing requires patience and persistence and involves peeling away layer after layer of trauma, buried emotions, and wounding.

Shifting her focus from her spouse to herself is crucial and may be challenging at first since her dedication and attention to her partner has consumed all her energy up until this point. Redirecting that energy towards herself is vital. There are numerous tools to assist with healing such as exercises and affirmations, various healing modalities, and the power of prayer discussed later in the chapter. The five essential layers to the healing process every victim must face are elaborated on first.

Five Layers to Healing Process:
(1) Face heartbreak
(2) Accept & process victimization
(3) Cope with layers of emotion, trauma, & wounding
(4) Practice forgiveness
(5) Embrace transformation & empowerment

Layer 1 **Face Heartbreak**
First and foremost, a victim must cope with her heartbreak over the relationship and give herself time and space to grieve the loss of her marriage. There are many life dreams, hopes, and desires they may have shared that can never be achieved together. She may experience a deep sense of loss for a love that could never be and for the possibility of a relationship that never blossomed. She may mourn for the loss her children experience after separation or imminent divorce.

The loneliness a woman feels may take her by surprise. She suddenly discovers in his absence she does not have someone with whom to share her life, speak to on a daily basis, accompany her for routine activities, or with whom to have an intimate physical relationship. There may be an aching void she cannot ignore. It is normal for her to recall the loving parts of their relationship and miss that side of him whether it was genuine or not. After all, if the marriage had only violent moments she would never have stayed. It is the tender loving aspects of the union that fostered the unhealthy attachment. However, these "happy" memories should not be confused with a reason to stay in the relationship.

Even for healthy relationships, recovering from heartbreak takes time. Part of a victim's anguish is her partner's fundamental rejection of her despite all the love she might have showered him with. He may have defused her attempts to share joy, express affection, and feel genuine pleasure. Regardless of her abuser's hostile feelings towards her, it is not easy to accept the man she truly loved was so cruel.

"All the justifications, rationalizations, and excuses you used and believed for so long…may even have strengthened your resolve to stay with him and continue loving him."[452] A victim may feel conflicted the more she begins to see his true nature, but she should have realistic expectations; she cannot stop loving him overnight. If he seems to be sincere about changing and has temporarily stopped the abuse, her wounding and trauma may be too deep to consider giving him yet another chance. She may have to accept it is too late to rebuild their relationship.

Layer 2 Accept & Process Victimization

One of the first questions every victim asks herself is: *"Why me? How did this happen to me?"* There is no easy answer. She asks: *"What happened to the strong, confident woman I used to be?"* She battles with her identity: *"Who am I? Who have I become?"* She is fueled by her desperate desire "to understand what had caused the abuse to occur; to make sense of a loving relationship that had gone sour; to figure out what could have been done to prevent the abuse; to find out if such abuse happens to others like her; and to help women in similar situations who (are) suffering in silence."[453] She might ask: *"What did I do to convince myself this was okay? What made me feel so trapped and powerless?"*

It is important for a woman to explore deeper emotional responses to these questions rather than only cognitively search for the answers. Realizing how much she has lost, what he has stolen from her, and that she can never reclaim those years of her life is devastating. Acceptance is not easy. A trained therapist will guide her to facilitate integration of the trauma. A victim cannot blame herself for the violence or disintegration of her marriage; to do so makes her no different from her spouse. Long after their separation or divorce, she may find she is still processing the abuse. She must trust the process and rest assured that the healing continues.

Layer 3 Cope with Layers of Emotion, Trauma, & Wounding

Part of healing is to let go of all the coping mechanisms and defenses that were her "crutches" or methods of survival for so long. The breakdown of these strategies catapults her out of her toxic, unhealthy environment that jeopardized her survival. "The recognition of abuse… brings both pain and shock. The spirit is wrenched from its foundations as mind and body confront the inconceivable, which must in the end be recognized as a reality, realized, and integrated. The longer the abuse has been perpetuated and the more intense it has been, the longer the process of recovery may take."[454]

A victim should look at herself with honesty, acceptance, and genuine compassion. It is time for her to shed her armor, expose her vulnerabilities, and surrender. When she realizes she has no idea how to go on, she has reached the most humbling part of the journey. When she feels truly broken, her genuine healing can begin. She must embrace the raw nakedness of being wounded. After masking her feelings and enacting the façade of a happy marriage, it is essential to be true and authentic. As difficult as it may be, she should be present with her discomfort instead of developing strategies of avoidance that deprive herself of the opportunity for authenticity.

Chapter 10 discussed four layers of wounding: fear and anxiety, grief and depression, anger and frustration, and shame and betrayal. In order to heal, a victim must process each of these emotions fully, allow them to surface and run their course, and address the layers of trauma buried deep within her subconscious. Suppressing or fighting these forces only intensifies them and postpones her denial. There should be no fear in expressing everything she has held back over the years. By granting her emotions permission and space to exist she allows this release to penetrate the numbness that has surrounded her heart for protection. Working with her emotions in a revolutionary way may be a slow process after feeling emotionally dead for years.

A victim should trust in the healing process: her repressed emotions and memories will surface as she is capable of handling them. She should respect and honor each emotion for its role to play in restoring her to a state of health and balance. Each one possesses the intelligence to flow through her system, tend to her wounds, and reinstate her self-awareness. "Through knowledge, awareness, and action we may heal the spirit... Psychological freedoms are usually won through emotional pain and feelings of loss... Even a plant seeks light and the most nourishing environment in which to grow. The survivor of abuse can do no less."[455]

A victim must experience healthy anger, a catalyst to reclaim her power and release her from victimization. Allowing her fear to surface, feeling how her pain and anguish move through her brings her to life. Even if it begets intense suffering, pain is a teacher to demonstrate her vulnerabilities and limitations. Gandhi said, *"You must go through the fire, but the fire will purify you."* Instead of avoiding pain and only seeking pleasure, we should know life and healing are about going beyond these dualities. Pain makes us deeply aware of the intensity of every moment and brings us to the present in a way no other experience can. Experiencing fully the amazing journey to go from being broken to being whole, no matter how painful it might be, is freedom.

With time, the intensity of these emotions diminish and surrender their hold on a victim's psyche. She can avoid the pain, deny it exists, try to medicate it, but at some point, she must choose to heal. That may seem hard to believe during a time of crisis but eventually pain fades like a distant memory as she moves gracefully through it. As she replaces suffering with new meaning and inspiration that she cultivates in her life, healing is inevitable. She will heal from the inside out.

Layer 4 Practice Forgiveness

Forgiveness is another crucial aspect of the healing process but plays out differently in the abusive dynamic. Is it necessary to forgive one's assailant? This is a highly contested and debated question. Some will say yes, until a victim does so she prevents herself from truly healing. Some will say no, she has no obligation to do so and she does not owe it to him.

Throughout her abusive relationship she may have already forgiven him countless times for unforgivable acts, but she felt everyone deserves a second chance and she believed his promises it would not happen again. She may have felt obligated by her role as a supportive and understanding wife. In many ways, her willingness to forgive actually perpetuated her victimization and contributed to surrendering her power. Realizing she can choose to not forgive him any longer may be empowering.

Deciding whether it is appropriate to forgive or not should be determined by three conditions:

(1) Are their acts forgivable?
(2) Will it help her heal to forgive them?
(3) Is she ready to forgive?[456]

No one can answer these questions for a victim. She might feel pressure from friends and family, religious leaders, therapists, or even healers, but if she chooses to forgive him it must be strictly on her own terms when she is emotionally ready. It is premature to do so before she has fully processed her rage towards this man for everything he has done.

It is natural and healthy to desire revenge when she realizes how much of her life this man has stolen from her and how deeply he has wounded her. Fantasies of revenge might float through her mind. She should acknowledge them and allow herself to feel the satisfaction of knowing she is no longer a victim. But knowledge is her greatest weapon. She must ask herself: does she truly want revenge or justice? The futility of revenge and resorting to any act of violence or stooping to his level makes her no different from him. Ultimately, the best revenge is to live well, allow herself to heal, and move on with her life.

A victim may never find justice; her abuser may never pay for his crimes nor be held accountable if he has cleverly manipulated the legal system. The vast majority of perpetrators fall under this category. She should take comfort in the fact there is a higher justice, and he will pay the price for his actions one day. Making her peace with this is necessary if she wishes to move on with her life. The idea of karma also mitigates any notion an Indian wife may have to seek revenge knowing she will reap the seeds she sows. Violence and hatred only begets more of the same.

Besides her partner, a woman grapples with also having to forgive others. How is she to make sense of and deal with others who supported him, remained neutral, flat out disbelieved her, or failed her at the most critical hour? Feeling abandoned by family and close friends may add to her pain and confusion. Unable to comprehend why they cannot be supportive, she realizes it will take time to heal these relationships as well but she must tend to her own healing first. She must not ignore her feelings of abandonment or feel obligated to maintain unsupportive relations. This is her fresh start to be selective about making new friends and keep people in her life who can truly be there for her.

The only person a victim must truly forgive is herself. The harshest judge she faces is the one in the mirror. She might be consumed by her self-blame for enduring the abuse for so long, repeatedly choosing to stay with her partner or return to him, or putting her children at risk. It is normal for all victims to battle these intense feelings of blame and guilt but she should know she is once again mimicking her abuser who has blamed her for all the strife in their relationship. A victim should practice genuine compassion, not self-blame. Given what she knew, she did the best she could under the circumstances. She cannot liberate herself until she gives herself permission to move forward in her life and not berate herself for the past.

Forgiveness comes naturally as she seeks wholeness after fragmentation. Using a daily prayer or affirmation will aid in this. As she acknowledges her wounding, grasps the damage is not permanent, and trusts she will recover and blossom from this experience, it is easier to forgive herself. For many women it can take years to reach this point, but after all they have suffered and endured, they deserve to be forgiven.

Layer 5 **Embrace Transformation & Empowerment**

"Helplessness and isolation are the core experiences of psychological trauma. Empowerment and reconnection are the core experiences of recovery."[457] Recovery, therefore, cannot occur in isolation. She must work to renew her connections with others; create a new social network to fill the void she might feel after separation. Connections bring her back into the world and facilitate healing. Developing the ability to trust and find empathy in her relationships will aid in moving past the trauma.

Listening to stories of other survivors and how they have crossed over to the other shore and rebuilt their lives shows her she does not have to traverse this difficult path alone. Learning from their experiences will inspire and guide her. Every victim must draw upon the strength of women who have already walked this path. Their strength is her strength. They serve as reminders there are strong, courageous, and confident women who found it possible to create new lives and start over after surviving their abusive relationships.

The isolation in the Indian community is especially pronounced since divorce and taking a stand against one's husband is still uncommon and culturally taboo. Others' perceptions should not influence her to fear breaking tradition, being divorced, or being single. It would make a world of difference if every Indian woman who took the bold, courageous step to deal with the stigma of divorce shared her struggles. Breaking free of cultural biases, perspectives, and stereotypes is part of empowerment. No survivor should be afraid to extend her hand to another victim and be her guiding light when it is her turn.

A victim needs to acknowledge her inner resources and know she has the power to transform her life. Empowerment is the opposite of vulnerability. "No intervention that takes power away from the survivor can possibly foster her recovery, no matter how much it appears to be in her immediate best interest."[458] Well-intentioned supporters respect this and offer advice but still encourage a victim to make her own decisions. After the false hope she has sustained throughout her marriage that it will work out for the best, she might have to battle the general sense of hopelessness she now feels. Rediscovering hope is part of healing.

As a victim fights this battle and moves on from her traumatic experience, she faces the challenge of transforming her tears into action. Research shows taking initiative for social action brings true empowerment. "The women who recover most successfully are those who discover some meaning in their experience that transcends the limits of personal tragedy."[459] Unification leads to collective transformation and global healing. No soul can be left behind. Victims, past and present, will only become stronger by walking this journey hand in hand.

By transforming her pain into educating and empowering other women to prevent such calamities in their lives, volunteering her time, or becoming a domestic violence advocate, she thereby creates deeper meaning out of her pain. Knowing so many victims are isolated motivates her to reach out to them. "Although giving to others is the essence of the survivor mission, those who practice it recognize that they do so for their own healing. In taking care of others, survivors feel recognized, loved, and cared for themselves."[460]

Implementing Tools For Healing

Exercises and affirmations are methods to develop clarity and self-awareness, build strength, and increase confidence in a victim's ability to heal and break free. Living with abuse erodes her spirit: she feels broken, wounded, neglected, in desperate need of nourishment. Repeating daily affirmations starts to shift the energy of her nervous system from that of a victim to a woman who possesses power and assuredness. Exercises that facilitate processing the abuse more effectively empower her. Refer to *The*

Power to Break Free Workbook for exercises and affirmations a victim can use.

List of Healing Modalities
A victim should not feel she must tackle her healing on her own when there are numerous resources at her disposal. The first step is therapy. Many women's crisis centers offer free or low-cost therapy for survivors. She might have already tried marriage counseling with her spouse and was discouraged by how ineffective it was. The benefits of finding a therapist who specializes in dealing with domestic violence is critical. She will guide a victim through the process of breaking free, aid in building her trust and self-confidence, help process the abusive incidents themselves, and provide a sympathetic ear to hear a victim's story. Feeling commiseration by speaking to a survivor or a therapist who has survived abuse herself builds support. A skilled therapist allows a victim to find clarity, strength, courage, and forgiveness.

Along with therapy, there are a plethora of healing modalities that address all levels of body, mind, and spirit. Incorporating these powerful tools facilitates integration into wholeness.
- **Acupuncture** is an excellent way to deal with trauma and symptoms of PTSD, reduce stress and anxiety, enhance energy, process various emotions, balance hormones, improve sleep, and boost immunity. This subtle energy work will assist in finding clarity and strength and powerfully facilitate inner transformation. Visit www.nccaom.org to find a local acupuncturist.
- **Somatic Trauma Resolution (STR)** is a technique developed to track sensations in the physical body to release unconscious trauma patterns that have become embedded in the psyche. Becoming aware of bodily sensations that might have been triggered during the traumatic incident itself and using those same sensations to rewire the nervous system heals the trauma. To find a practitioner, visit www.traumahealing.com.
- **Cranio-sacral therapy** is a potent technique designed to balance the central nervous system, release restrictions in the cranio-sacral system, and enhance physiology, by using gentle touch to stimulate the flow of cerebrospinal fluid. It is a powerful way to relax body and mind. To find a practitioner, visit www.upledger.com.
- **Massage** or any type of bodywork is grounding and centering. After the numbness and disassociation a victim has experienced, it is necessary to connect with the physical body again and be able to deeply relax. Her spouse may never have touched her in a comforting, loving way or with kindness and it is important to be able to experience this. To find a massage therapist, visit www.ncbtmb.org.
- **Yoga** provides deep stretching, physical conditioning, and body awareness. The mental and emotional benefits of yoga are profound and increase energy, improve sleep, and reduce stress and anxiety. To

find a teacher, visit www.yogaalliance.org or www.bksiyengar.com. In particular, restorative yoga uses the breath in certain poses held with supportive props to induce deep relaxation. To find a restorative yoga teacher, visit www.restorativeyogateachers.com.
- **Meditation**, a branch of yoga, involves training oneself to deeply relax at will. Breathing techniques and stress management exercises are centering and teach detachment from pain and suffering as one finds one's core of bliss. Developing self-awareness and cultivating inner peace is invaluable.
- **Ayurveda** is an ancient, holistic medical system of India that integrates understanding one's body type with dietary remedies, synchronizing one's lifestyle with natural rhythms, using herbal medications to balance mind and body, detoxification techniques to cleanse on every level, and bodywork such as marma therapy (acupressure). Refer to *Marma Points of Ayurveda* to learn simple self-acupressure techniques for relaxation. To find a practitioner, visit www.ayurvedicpractitioner.com.
- **Panchakarma** is a vigorous, detoxification technique used in Ayurveda that is a minimum of seven days long. It includes mono-diet fasting, herbal teas and remedies, yoga and meditation, daily massage with medicated herbal oils, herbal steam, skincare remedies, *shirodhara* (technique to calm the nervous system), and a number of other procedures customized to the individual and designed to achieve balance of body, mind, and spirit. To schedule treatment at a renowned center, visit www.Ayurveda.com.
- **Herbal therapy** uses various herbs to calm the mind, target the nervous system, resolve symptoms of trauma and stress, and restore balance on the cellular level. Only seek the advice of a well-qualified herbalist and do not attempt to self-medicate.
- **Aromatherapy** uses therapeutic essential oils that target different systems of the body and are deeply relaxing, grounding, and balancing for various emotions.
- **Martial Arts** involves learning self-defense techniques, cultivating discipline, building strength, and is empowering. Slow moving, graceful forms like tai chi create a sense of peace and stillness within.

Role of Prayer & Faith

The immense power of prayer and faith has the ability to shift consciousness and can be pivotal during both the time of crisis and the process of breaking free. Praying for a certain outcome may lead to disappointment, but praying for the power to face any outcome with poise, strength, and grace is invigorating. Asking for that which will guide our path and make us the vehicle of our own destiny is powerful. Many women say their faith and belief in God are what sustain them during this difficult ordeal.

Other women share the opposite experience; they feel their faith has been shattered and are unsure if they believe in a god anymore. Being abused is a betrayal and coming to terms with this can make her feel betrayed by the world, her faith, and her own higher power. This is an intensely personal experience and there are no rules as to how a victim should cope. If one's faith and beliefs have been challenged, part of the spiritual journey is to either renew one's faith and commitment or strike out on whatever new path is calling on the voyage of self-discovery.

For Indian women who are practicing Hindus, turning to images of the Goddess in all her forms can be inspiring and empowering. Each goddess is an aspect of the divine feminine energy or Shakti. Worshipping Kali or Durga in particular, goddesses who are emblems of fearlessness and undying strength, can help her find courage to tap into her inner power. Kali, the invincible goddess of death and destruction, symbolically represents transformation, the death of negative emotions, tendencies, and patterns. Durga, the fierce warrior seated on a tiger, sword in hand and ready for battle, assures one that victory is imminent. The legal divorce process is very much a battle requiring immense strength and focus. In the fight to break free from abuse, worshipping the images of these goddesses or repeating the *mantras* (sacred chants) that honor them cultivates these qualities within.

Strategies for Self-Care

Learning to start over and rebuild an abuse-free life is not easy. A victim has become a creature of habit, accustomed and conditioned to abuse, attached to what is familiar. It takes courage to embrace the uncertainty in her life right now, but as a victim choosing to stay in what is familiar can kill her. She must accept that any sort of change is stressful and breaking through these shackles can be overwhelming. So much in her life is evolving as she struggles to emancipate herself and release old patterns she has been holding onto.

The unfamiliarity she experiences in a new world where no one is trying to control her requires adjustment. According to one Gestalt psychotherapist, *"Confusion is the place in between what you thought you knew and new awareness coming in."* A victim should make the decision to not live her life in fear or make decisions out of trepidation but from a position of clarity and confidence. All the decisions she makes now shape the rest of her future. Becoming independent is not easy and requires immense effort on her part in multiple areas: taking care of her living situation, her children and their schools, seeking employment and training for new work, or creating financial security and stability.

She must discover for herself the steps to find freedom and the strategies to assist on her path. What works for someone else may not necessarily be effective for her. She should seize every opportunity to free her mind from her past trauma and her pain. Consistency of effort and committing to a future where she feels empowered is critical. Developing a community support network to rely on when times are tough and not feeling afraid to ask for help is essential. Investing energy and time into self-care will pay off. There are numerous suggestions for self-healing listed for victims in *The Power to Break Free Workbook*.

Making Progress

As a victim breaks free, she witnesses the organic, unfolding process of evolving into her full potential. Recognizing she is exactly where she needs to be at this moment in the course of her evolution is accepting the ups and downs. She must become her own teacher as she beholds the beauty of her healing. Facing her spirituality is a process of opening to her truth, to her heart, and the lessons she needs to learn.

Strength comes from knowing nothing can truly break her even when she feels the most wounded. She is still alive, still breathing. Her life, destiny, and freedom await her. There is an incredible sense of joy to find the desire to not just survive but thrive, to blossom into someone stronger and more beautiful than she could ever imagine. She learns to be open, for she never knows from where inspiration will come. In every moment, she can choose to be reborn.

Trusting the healing process, she witnesses her transformation unfold naturally. It is all right if she takes it slowly day by day and cannot look beyond that. She needs to feel safe and have time to tend to her wounds. It is comforting to know she will heal step by step and it is okay to ask for guidance. She cannot rush the process but must have realistic expectations. Her body and mind have the intelligence and wisdom to heal at the pace appropriate for her. There is no schedule or deadline to which she must adhere. A victim will be amazed by her resilience and ability to recover.

If she still lives or interacts with her abuser, she should be attentive, focused on trusting her own feelings, paying attention to her instincts, and heeding her inner voice regardless of his distractions. After the initial separation or divorce, she might be consumed with a feeling of euphoria, commemorate her liberation, and be pumped with adrenaline. After this fades, she finds herself facing yet another layer of introspection and reflection taking her deeper on her healing journey.

A victim should periodically check in and reassess at what stage she is. Recognizing she may still have a long way to go is healthy. By letting go of any preconceived notions of a storyline (what she thinks should happen), she allows life to unfold organically. At every step in her healing journey, she should acknowledge how far she has come. Appreciating her transitions and private internal victories that no one else can measure or see is important.

A victim will make considerable progress every day, every week, every month. She may even be surprised by her rapid integration into wholeness. Just like nature shows no resistance, she should have faith that her body's intelligence knows precisely what she needs to heal, surrendering to being a moth in a cocoon who needs time to metamorphose into a beautiful butterfly.

At some point, a survivor will be in a place to move on and commence a new relationship based on equality and respect. She should be cautious, heed any red flags, and keep her eyes wide open. She needs to set clear limits, restrict time together to specific planned activities, and not rush into a new relationship. Making sure to maintain individual friendships, activities, and independence is essential. Someone who respects her will take it slowly. As she becomes healthier, the law of attraction will bring a new partner into her life who can be present for her on every level. Ultimately, every woman should seek a partner who enriches her life, brings her joy, and respects who she is. Happiness is when she realizes there is nothing in her life she would change.

Spiritual Battle

As a survivor embraces her transformation and empowerment, she should be cognizant that breaking free from an abusive relationship is very much a spiritual battle. Abuse is about being trapped physically, mentally, emotionally, and spiritually. She surrenders her voice, relinquishes her identity, destroys her will, and perhaps loses her desire to live. There is no way for a human life to have meaning, inspiration, or drive when trapped in this oppression. The only purpose of violence is destruction. Nothing about abuse is acceptable or tolerable. There is absolutely no justification to ever treat another human being badly nor any reason for women to suffer at the hands of the men they love this way. Nobody should have to live through this horror. Everyone deserves a life of freedom.

A survivor's pain and grief are the soil through which her spirituality grows and blossoms, turning her weakness into her greatest strength and her suffering into her greatest weapon. She has endured the darkness so she may find the light again. Life is precious; it can be extinguished in a split second. Challenging herself to take this opportunity to evolve and viewing this experience as a gift in disguise for self-cultivation is an empowering shift in perspective. On some level, every experience brings to life a part of us that needs to be awakened, inviting us to look deeper. Even during our darkest moments there is always a reason to search for inspiration. We can view our years of living with abuse as a setback or see them as a time to catapult our spiritual progress and awakening.

We hold the key within us to find meaning in our suffering. We are the instrument of our own healing. Every encounter has the innate ability to heal and perfect something within us. Cultivating our spiritual practice leads to viewing every moment and interaction as designed for our personal spiritual liberation. This incredibly beautiful realization sets us free. Living through this spiritual battle teaches us how to find perfection in every moment. We are free at the moment we wish to be. In this moment, any woman can ... *choose* freedom.

PART 2

MY FIGHT

FOR

FREEDOM

Chapter 17 THE PROMISE OF LOVE

True love is when your heart and your mind are saying the same thing.
Leanna L. Bartra

My Dream

I had a dream-to find happiness, be married to a wonderful man who truly loved me, and start a family. It was a simple desire that grew in my heart and was no different than the dream of every other young girl, Indian or American, to create and share a meaningful life with someone I cared about deeply. After patiently waiting for many years to meet the man of my dreams, he showed up when I least expected it and in many ways had given up hope. After completing my masters in acupuncture training after college, I was prepared to relocate, start my practice, and establish my career. I was in my mid-twenties and ready to settle down, so to speak, for the "package" of marriage that included a husband, children, and sharing a home.

Destiny brought him to me effortlessly during the summer of June 2001. I flew home one weekend to visit my family in Chicago and attend a friend's wedding. At the ceremony, Chara Auntie, my parents' friend, approached me. Succinctly, she asked, *"Would you like to meet a tall, handsome Indian doctor who also practices acupuncture?"* It was remarkable to hear of another individual in the Indian community in my profession. I did not even have to think about my response, it was a definite *"Yes!"*

Even before meeting or speaking to him, I felt an instant connection. Chara Auntie knew Rakesh, my husband-to-be, through his family. She was best friends with his father's sister, knew his grandparents well, and had practically grown up in their home. When Rakesh finished medical school training in India and moved to America, he contacted her hoping she would introduce him to someone. Remembering me because of our similar professional backgrounds, Chara Auntie facilitated the typical Indian matchmaking story.

The Introduction

Surprisingly, Rakesh called the very next day. We spoke for a few hours about our training in acupuncture, our mutual interest in yoga and Ayurveda (holistic, traditional medical system native to India), and our passion for our Indian heritage. He seemed to read me very well and know exactly what to say to impress me. Being with someone who understood my "alternative" professional path and who respected my career choices was crucial for me. He seemed exceptionally supportive and admired my path. I was amazed we shared so much in common personally and professionally. Unbelievably, we were also both from the same city in India and spoke the identical mother tongue.

I went through the checklist in my mind of an ideal mate, and he seemed to have every quality I desired. I did not find him physically attractive, but I overlooked this because of his impressive "credentials": Rakesh was from a good family, well respected, with a strong educational background, a physician, religious-minded and quoted his favorite saints often. Someone with a spiritual nature was essential to me. It seemed too good to be true, a match made in heaven. I felt like the luckiest girl in the world. Being personally recommended by Chara Auntie, whom I have known since I was a young girl, was the final vote of confidence I needed. For two weeks, Rakesh and I spoke every night until we could meet in person. Our conversations were engaging, I felt we connected on a deep level, and there was a familiarity between us I had not expected so soon.

After two weeks, I flew to visit my best friend in Providence for the weekend. On Saturday I drove the short distance to Boston to meet Rakesh in person and have lunch. Our first few hours together were pleasant. It was obvious he was trying extra hard to impress me, but I assumed he was nervous about making a favorable first impression. This should have been my first warning sign he had an agenda.

On Sunday, we spent a leisurely day with his younger sister and brother-in-law at their home. Surrounded by company, he was charming, funny, and entertaining. I loved seeing this side of him come alive after he had been somewhat reserved the previous day when we were alone. Of course, I assumed he was less nervous. It would take many years before I would understand this dual personality of his, the duplicity between his private and public persona he could switch on and off at will.

My Decision

The following weekend we met in Chicago by pure coincidence while I visited my family and he planned to see Chara Auntie. Destiny seemed to be drawing us together. On Saturday, he met my family. I was overjoyed to visibly see my parents' happiness. Rakesh zealously attempted to impress them and appear like the "ideal candidate." My parents were pleased by his fluent Marathi and Hindi, his strong connection to his family, his educational background, his established job as a physician, and the fact he was financially well settled.

The only issue was his H-1 visa. Despite warning me against marrying someone who was not a citizen, they dismissed his immigration status after meeting him since he was such a "good catch" and strongly encouraged me to consider him as a potential partner. There was also the issue of our age difference since he was eight years older, but I convinced myself age did not matter if I felt a strong connection.

That night over dinner Rakesh told me simply, *"Anisha, I want to be with you and no other woman. If I cannot be with you, I am prepared to move back to India and be single for the rest of my life.*" It was not exactly a romantic proposal, no expression of feeling or emotion, but a simple matter-of-fact declaration of his decision. The next morning, I brought up his "proposal" and told him also matter-of-factly, "*I am ready. I do not want to wait to be married.*" In many ways, it was the truth.

Even before meeting him three weeks prior, I felt ready after waiting what seemed like an eternity to make his acquaintance. I thought he was perfect: my family liked him, Chara Auntie had introduced him and endorsed him, he had great credentials, and I did not want to go through the dating process and get engaged or married many months down the road. If I knew in my heart he was the one, I was willing to take a leap of faith and proceed forward with our future together. Rakesh was visibly surprised but pleased with my quick decision.

My parents were ecstatic and so was I knowing I had finally found the man of my dreams and marriage was around the corner. Of course, my parents had the desire, like all Indian parents, for me to find a suitable match sooner than later, but they did not pressure me into an early marriage. They knew I would take my time to find someone who understood my unique interests and pursuits. Elated I had finally found the man who would make all my dreams come true, I felt the wait was worth it. Many years later I would scoff at my naiveté, innocence, and idealism about love and marriage.

Jyotish Prediction

As part of Indian tradition, I consulted a *jyotishi* (Vedic astrologer) who assessed Rakesh's personality, heavily dominated by *mangal* (Mars). The energy of Mars is one who likes conflict, is drawn to challenges, and can be combative. It makes one passionate, opinionated, driven, and ambitious, but also hotheaded, argumentative, and with a difficult temperament. In extreme cases, it makes men abusive, violent, or destructive.

A person influenced by Mars has a tendency to create a dynamic of conflict in relationships, with a propensity towards power plays, authority issues, and legal battles. Struggle exists oftentimes where there is no need for one. I braced myself for my future husband's potential temper, however, I was too naïve to imagine how these other traits would play into our relationship. In hindsight, I regretted dismissing the opportunity to date so as these characteristics would have had a chance to reveal themselves over time.

Disappointingly, I discovered our horoscopes were only 50% compatible, not an ideal match. Despite believing in the wisdom of jyotish, I did not want to make my decision based on astrology alone. I told myself this was just a test to see if I would follow my heart. After all, I saw a bright future with this man and tremendous potential for our relationship. I did not want to say no to a match that seemed so promising because of an astrological prediction and let that dictate my actions. In so many ways we seemed like the perfect couple, and I wanted to trust my heart he was the one for me. The forces of karma were drawing us together with an unmistakable pull I could not deny. My heart was filled with joy at starting this next chapter of our lives together.

The Exciting Engagement

After meeting three weeks prior, we were officially engaged. Thrilled, we immediately called our family in India and shared the wonderful news with our friends. Because of my modern upbringing, many of my friends were surprised I would make such a traditional choice, but I had implicit faith in the ancient system of marriage that had operated for centuries. It did not bother me I barely knew this man and had not spent much time with him. If it had worked for so many generations and my family members, I had faith it would work for me, too. I had witnessed many "successful" arranged marriages based on common values that had endured the test of time. I believed in the Indian premise *"we would grow to know and love each other as husband and wife after marriage."* I accepted the old Hindi expression- *"pyar hota hai* or *love happens."*

Was ours an arranged marriage? No, not exactly, since it was still definitely my choice to marry Rakesh and I was not pressured to accept him. But yes, it was arranged in the sense we were introduced to each other in the typical Indian matchmaking fashion, met with the intention of finding a compatible spouse, received approval from our families, consulted our astrological charts, and were engaged and married soon after.

I must reiterate I agreed to marry a man I barely knew and had never spent time with because of the promise of a great match and the many qualities I was led to believe he possessed to make him an ideal spouse. He was, as they say, "perfect on paper." Due to my implicit faith in the Indian model of marriage, I allowed myself to overlook details I thought were irrelevant, red flags such as hints of his arrogance, sense of entitlement, and dominating personality. I dismissed these warning signs and told myself no one was perfect; everyone has flaws and I should learn to accept his.

The engagement lasted six months, and during that time, we spoke daily on the phone and met in person only twice. Rakesh visited me one weekend, and I traveled to visit him another weekend. Only once did he display a bit of his temper at the dinner table after I expressed my opinion on a topic he clearly disagreed with. He yelled, *"You are impossible to talk to!"* After which, he stormed off, but the outburst caught me by surprise and lasted so briefly I dismissed it. After some time, he apologized and we never discussed it again. During the six months of our engagement, that was the only time I witnessed his temper so it seemed like a one-time event, nothing to be concerned about. I should have known then I had my first clear warning sign of his explosiveness without any provocation that would subsequently become a regular pattern.

Planning the Wedding

The wedding date was set for December 2001 in India, but after the September 11 attacks on the World Trade Center, Rakesh used this as a convenient excuse to change our travel plans. The truth was he preferred a wedding in America so his mother could show up as a guest without any responsibility for managing the festivities. My parents gave him the respect due a son-in-law and told me to accept his choice. Surprisingly, Rakesh did not seem to care what I thought or take my feelings into consideration.

Since I was a young girl, I had expressed my desire to be married in India so my entire extended family could be by my side. The thought of all of them not being present at my wedding was unimaginable. He was not bothered my parents had worked tirelessly to make all the arrangements in India and we were forced to cancel it two months prior to our nuptials. Devastated by his decision, I chose not to remain silent and expressed my disappointment. Rakesh consoled me by saying the wedding in America would be just as wonderful.

This was the first battle I lost, the first time I surrendered my voice, the first time I resigned myself to his decision and felt like my dream and my wish did not matter. I told myself if this is what his family wanted, I should be accommodating and not seem like what many would perceive as a "stubborn American wife." This was my duty as an Indian wife to do what was best for his family. But my heart was heavy and I cried many nights as the date approached knowing it would not be the wedding of my dreams. There was no time to dwell on how sad I was about the circumstances or my dream not coming true. I had two months essentially to plan a wedding event for four hundred guests.

The Ceremony

Sunday, December 23, 2001, the wedding day I had dreamt of since I was a young girl had finally arrived. My relatives in America flew in from around the country and I was overjoyed by their presence for this great occasion. The cold winter weather deterred my relatives in India from embarking on the long journey to the U.S. The wedding hall was beautifully decorated, fresh flowers of every color surrounded the *mandap* (wedding altar), Indian statues of deities were strategically placed, and the sounds of the melodious shennai filled the air.

I wore a vibrant saffron-colored silk sari with intricate gold embroidery, decked in strands of exquisite gold jewelry, elaborate freshly painted henna designs covering my arms and legs. Smelling the garlands of fragrant jasmine flowers in my hair, I felt like a bride. The presence of my little sisters and close girlfriends meant the world to me. I was touched by their happiness for me on this big day.

My anticipation started to build knowing soon we would be officially married. As I walked down the aisle to the *mandap*, being led by my uncles on either side, my full concentration was devoted to not upsetting my husband-to-be. Rakesh had implied he would disapprove of tears at our wedding so I restrained my emotions because I did not dare ruin the ceremony. At the time, I did not know this set the stage for our marriage and the foundation for abuse had been laid on our wedding day. I intentionally gave up my voice to please this person who did not really care what mattered to me or give me the freedom to express the emotion I felt.

My husband learned early on he could make all the decisions and I would have to obey. Even if something was important to me such as being married in India, having my relatives present, or shedding a tear if I felt emotional, he assumed he could have control over me. What I felt or thought essentially did not matter because he did not give it any significance. The unequal power dynamic of our relationship was created and his lack of respect for me had manifested. Later, wedding guests would remark how unusual it was Rakesh had only a few friends present and the members on the groom's side were so few. Again, I dismissed that warning sign as well.

The Honeymoon

Flying to Hawaii a few days later for our one-week honeymoon, I reconciled my feelings up until that point. Despite my desire to have the wedding in India, we had a lovely, elegant ceremony in Chicago. So many wonderful people were present who sincerely wished us well. No matter where the wedding was, I told myself, at least I had still found the man of my dreams and our future awaited us. After the hectic festivities of the wedding ceremony were over, I was looking forward to spending some time alone together. I was perplexed that Rakesh was withdrawn, in a world of his own. Shouldn't this be a time of joy and happiness? But my sheer exhaustion from preparing for our wedding kept me from contemplating his behavior. I needed to focus on relaxing and recovering my energy.

I was not given much opportunity to rest, however, as the verbal abuse commenced on our honeymoon. Hawaii in December turned out to be colder than usual, and I was forced to wear a sweater. Having a tendency to always be cold, I did not think much of it but Rakesh used this opportunity to discuss self-improvement and character building. *"Obviously, you are not strong enough mentally if you are affected by the cold,"* he declared. It did not matter I only weighed a little over one hundred pounds. He insisted, *"You must overcome your weaknesses and make yourself mentally fit so nothing can affect you."*

This discussion occurred a few times during the week. I was a little surprised at his constant critiquing but reasoned maybe he was just being sincere. At the same time, I noticed he never critiqued himself. Apparently, I was the only one with a long list of flaws to examine. His badgering was cleverly disguised as concern for my well-being but my head was spinning with his constant concern/critique. Even though I tried to defend myself and my "right" to wear a sweater, I was silenced as he spoke indefatigably in long monologues without a chance for me to get a word in edgewise.

My mental and physical fatigue contributed to my decision to stop arguing over a sweater. His persistence continued until I finally broke down and exclaimed, *"Of course, I agree everyone should always want to work on self-improvement. Of course, I don't think I am perfect. Of course, I know I have flaws."* He behaved as though my admonition pleased him and acted like he had won a small victory over me. Many years later when I researched psychological abuse, I would learn verbal dominance was a common trait of batterers and a precursor to physical violence.

My Birthday

We had been married for exactly a week before my birthday on December 30. I was excited to spend this special day with Rakesh for the first time. Relaxing at the beach, our day was uneventful until the evening as we strolled through the hotel lobby. Admiring the elaborate display of Christmas decorations, I walked at a leisurely pace. Rakesh needed to find a restroom and his impatience was building, because apparently I was not locating one for him quickly enough. I was a surprised that he, a grown man, was demanding I find a restroom for him. Suddenly, he snapped at me and stormed off. I was stunned by the absurdity of his request and lashing out at me over something so trivial. Why would he chose to express himself in this manner? Perplexed by his behavior, I knew there was no reason to precipitate this degree of irritation.

When Rakesh returned a few minutes later, I was sure he would apologize for his rudeness. His unexpressed rage was palpable. Seeing his silence, I expressed how upset I was and my surprise at his outburst. What happened next shocked me even more. Instead of listening to my distress or apologizing, he attempted to justify snapping at me. I had never dealt with someone acting this immaturely before. Not able to control my emotion any longer after all the little incidents that had built up over the week, I burst into tears. It was our honeymoon *and* my birthday. Even on such a special occasion could he not treat me nicely? His lack of sensitivity was even more appalling. And now I was crying for the first time in front of him and I knew he hated tears. It would aggravate him more, although I did not even understand why he was offended in the first place.

Foundation for Abuse

Thus, a pattern was established early on when I started to think more about him and his emotions and began to neglect my own. The focus shifted from me to always being about him. After seeing me continue to cry, he comforted me saying, *"Anisha, I did not mean to yell. You are overreacting. Let's just forget about it."* I convinced myself it was a one-time misunderstanding. He persuaded me to let it go and I tried to only to avoid ruining the rest of our night, but my heart was filled with a heaviness I could not comprehend. Because I could not label this assault as something familiar and it seemed so trivial, I dismissed it. I rationalized he was probably overwhelmed by stress from the wedding and he truly had not meant to snap at me.

I did not fathom this was only the beginning of many incidents of abuse disguised as "misunderstandings" that would leave me totally bewildered as I attempted to rationalize the series of events. I was unaware that I would quickly learn to cope and adjust to these assaults by burying my feelings and denying or minimizing their severity. Despite these incidents during our six months of engagement and one week of marriage, I held fast to my dream.

The shadow of abuse crept up on our lives steadily, its tendrils enclosing me in their grasp, yet I would not give up on my dream no matter what. I had faith that regardless of the conflict that arose in our marriage, we would work through it like mature individuals. I believed strongly in the promise of love and finding marital happiness. After all, it was absurd to consider divorce after only being married for a week just because of the events that transpired during our honeymoon.

MY FIGHT FOR FREEDOM 191

Chapter 18 LIFE AS NEWLYWEDS

What matters is how well we have loved. President Barack Obama

Moving to Boston

Back from the honeymoon, our tenuous marriage was off to a rocky start. We flew to my parents' home in Chicago to retrieve my car and some personal belongings before our drive to Rakesh's place. Our first "fight" was over how to pack my things in the car. He seemed annoyed with my ideas, but undoubtedly, bothered I was proposing anything at all instead of accepting his suggestions with complete deference. Compromise was out of the question. He acted like I was being totally unreasonable and chose to walk away as the easier alternative than attempt to work out a resolution together. It did not appear he valued my opinion or respected what I had to say. This reinforced the dynamic of being insensitive to my emotions.

Abandoned and frustrated, I continued to pack the car on my own. My parents wondered why I was working by myself, but to alleviate their worries I claimed I had insisted on doing it that way, my first white lie to them. Rakesh seemed unfazed by my parents' concern or by my exhaustion being outside in the winter cold packing by myself. He was oblivious to the fact I was distraught by his response to the situation. I should have heeded the warning signs then if we could not figure out how to handle such a simple task like loading a car together as a team, there would be bigger problems down the road.

We drove to Boston in silence. Upon our arrival "home," I moved in with a suitcase full of clothes and a few belongings. In many ways, I felt like an Indian bride in new territory, leaving behind everything familiar, unsure what to expect. Now that the honeymoon was over, we would settle into our new life and routine together. I expected tension would abate now that the stress from the wedding and honeymoon was behind us. I had been looking forward to our first day in his home as husband and wife. This was a pattern I would find myself in throughout our marriage, always assuming our situation would improve and hopeful of change. This optimism, hope, or naïveté characterized my stance, blinding me from seeing the reality of what was happening as I held fast to my dream.

After lunch, I casually informed Rakesh I would call my family. Unexpectedly, he snapped, *"Don't you think you should call my family, too? Don't you think you should call them first?"* Stunned by his outburst, I had no idea why he would be outraged or find this unreasonable. Of course, I had every intention of calling his family and was just as excited to speak to them. I calmly explained, *"Rakesh, of course I will call your mother and sister. I just thought of speaking to my parents first."*

This incident left me perplexed. Why would something so simple trigger his fury? Why would he act as if I was being completely inconsiderate and disrespectful to his family? I knew I had not been offensive, but the seeds of self-doubt had been planted and I started to question myself with greater frequency. Over the next few weeks and months especially, he would nourish and water this seed systematically until it had taken root.

Isolation Sets In

During the first week of our marriage, Rakesh had a minor car accident. It was too costly to fix up his old, damaged car so he discarded it and conveniently started using my car. Suddenly, I found myself stranded in a one-bedroom apartment without any way to go out, in a brand new city where I did not know anyone. After growing up in America, always being independent, and living on my own for many years, this was a new experience. I felt isolated and trapped but I reasoned this was the experience of many overseas Indian brides, including my own mother, who learned to adjust to their new lifestyles. I was no different from them, right? But why was it no one else I knew from my generation who had grown up in America had experienced anything like this?

This set another pattern for the abusive marriage I did not suspect at the time. I lost my independence and the ability to have control over my own life. Essentially at Rakesh's mercy, I could use my own car only when it was convenient for him. I reasoned being frugal at the beginning of marriage was economical and we would save money with one car for the time being. I told myself to adjust as all Indian women are trained to do. After all, the definition of marriage was all about sacrifice, I reasoned, and this was only a temporary situation.

Being Close to Family

Like any newlywed couple, we spent significant time discussing our future dreams and aspirations. During these talks we also spoke about the roles of our families and how being close to them was important. Rakesh repeatedly stated, *"The two of us will always come first and our priority will be to each other over anyone else. After that, our children will come next, then the parents, siblings, and last our extended family and friends."* I appreciated making us a priority, but this was something I inherently took for granted as a couple and did not believe was necessary to spell out. I noticed Rakesh frequently mentioned this clear hierarchy in those first few weeks and months of living together after my family's phone calls triggered his irritation.

Exceptionally close to my family, my two younger sisters meant the world to me. Arya, three years younger, was my best friend, and Nandita, almost thirteen years younger, was only five-years-old when I left for college. I could not imagine going even a day without calling them to say hello. Rakesh reprimanded me for these frequent phone calls and asserted they interfered with us having time for each other. So I adapted, making it a point to call them when he was at work so I could speak freely without any pressure.

To my amazement, after that first month of marriage, he somehow convinced me to ask them to stop calling. I felt forced to abide by his request to prevent his rage. After that day my mother never called again not wishing to disrespect her new son-in-law's privacy, so she waited for my call. This should have been a major red flag that cutting off my family was not something I would ever consider. Suddenly, everything I did was starting to be influenced by how it would vex Rakesh. Of course, I did not see it that way at the time. The effects of being brainwashed were way too subtle, his manipulation too insidious to detect. Somehow this hierarchy of priority did not apply to his family; his mother came first even before us and was the exception to the rule.

The Mother-in-law

A few days back from the honeymoon, my husband declared his mother wished to stay with us instead of at his sister's home where she was not comfortable. She had the traditional belief her place was at her son's home, not at her daughter's where she did not want to disturb her son-in-law or interfere with their life in any way. Rakesh also made the case his mother was eager to be with us, witness us as newlyweds, and get to know me. He asked, *"Is it okay to fulfill my mother's wishes? After all, she just came all the way from India for our wedding and will return home in a few months."*

I was not expecting this development so soon after the honeymoon, but without hesitating, I complied. I had many reasons for doing so. I anticipated being just as close to his family as my own and genuinely looked forward to spending time getting to know his mother. Growing up in a traditional Indian home where my grandparents lived with us, an extended home felt natural.

I also sympathized with his mother deeply. Rakesh's father had passed away in the mid 1980s, leaving her widowed with a twenty-year-old son and a fifteen-year-old daughter. I could not even imagine the pain and suffering she must have endured. I admired her for her strength and courage after this adversity. Soon after that incident, Rakesh relocated to the U.S. and left his mother and sister on their own. After his sister also left India, I am sure his mother understandably felt lonely. I wished to ease her suffering in any way I could, the same way I would for my own mother. So, I agreed without hesitating the way any obedient daughter-in-law would do. My servitude to pleasing his family would be a continuous trend throughout the marriage. It was decided then we would bring her to our place the upcoming weekend.

In my heart though, I knew there was another reason I had made that swift decision. After spending a short period of time with my new husband, his quick temper was no longer a secret. I witnessed one outburst while we were engaged and another one during the honeymoon. I was tired of his constant critiques of my "flaws." The deeper realization that surfaced was I was scared of anticipating his next outburst, hesitant of spending time alone with him, and uncertain of how little I knew of this stranger I had married. His unpredictability worried me. Reasoning to myself that the arranged-marriage system had worked in India for centuries and one only got to know one's husband with time, I accepted my fate.

The Proverbial Third Wheel

My mother-in-law moved into our one-bedroom apartment one week after we returned from our honeymoon. We spent a considerable amount of time together, and I truly enjoyed her company. I was thrilled we shared similar interests in yoga, ayurveda, and classical Indian music. Rakesh made fun of how much we had in common. Those first few weeks I never had any time alone with my husband because of his demanding schedule working almost eighty hours a week, including weekends, in a busy physician's practice.

Returning late at night, he would speak tirelessly to his mother about his dreams in America and career ambitions. I gleaned right away they were both talkative by nature and had much to share with each other living apart in two different countries. She was lonely and longed to gossip about their relatives and her life in India. I tried not to feel excluded as I sat back and listened, convincing myself to be more understanding.

After spending the first month of my marriage feeling like that undesired third wheel in the relationship, I began to contemplate my situation realizing I was the new bride who had never spent time with Rakesh alone and was dying to get to know my husband. After everything he said about how we should come first, should that not apply especially as newlyweds when we were commencing our new lives together? Shouldn't it matter how I feel? Isn't what I want important, too? Finally, I mustered the courage to tell him, *"Rakesh, I would like to be able to spend some time alone to get to know you."*

I resented being put in a position to make this request, but I had no idea how else to get through to him. He dedicated his modest time at home to his mother and was oblivious to neglecting me. I could tell he was displeased and not keen on sending his mother back to his sister's home where she was uncomfortable. I accepted this, but I still felt strongly we needed time alone and held my ground. So we compromised. She stayed with us for one more week before returning to his sister's. We would have a few weeks to ourselves before she insisted on moving back in with us.

In the midst of all this, Rakesh's lease on his apartment expired. Because of his job uncertainty, I was forced to find us a short-term rental to move into during that first month. It was hectic and overwhelming, but I worked diligently to pack his belongings and handle the move by myself. I tried to be considerate about his busy schedule, but it would have meant the world to me to have a little support. This set another pattern in which I assumed all responsibility for managing our life independently so his time would not be affected. Of course, I was unemployed at the time so it seemed natural to do this and be accommodating like any supportive Indian wife would do.

Impending Lawsuit

While I attempted to adjust to all these changes in my new lifestyle, getting to know a husband I rarely saw, spending time with my new mother-in-law, losing contact with my own family, stranded in an apartment with no way to get out, living in a new city, handling a move on my own, I also walked into a lawsuit Rakesh was fighting against his employer at the time. Due to his immigration issues, his employer was not meeting the specific necessary visa requirements that could result in deportation to India for two years if he was in violation. That was the last thing I desired, although I was open to living in India if it was necessary. It was not until the time of our divorce that what I would perceive as his true deception would be uncovered. It seemed to me as if his only intent was to marry a citizen to enhance his prospects of obtaining a green card and to guarantee his stay in the U.S.

Rakesh discussed some details about his case while we were engaged, but as soon as we returned from the honeymoon, the lawsuit consumed our lives and what little free time we had was devoted to composing letters to his attorney, planning our legal strategy, and researching other jobs around the country. Because I could type quickly, he relied heavily on me. I reasoned that marriage was about helping the other person's dreams come true and I supported him in not fighting this battle on his own. Nothing in my life had prepared me for entering into a legal battle that was draining emotionally, mentally, and physically and destroyed any sense of being newlyweds or having a romantic start to our marriage. From the beginning, the tone of our marriage was set-it was a battlefield. We were always at war... just not with each other yet.

A meeting with his attorneys precipitated one of our first arguments, if it could even be called that. There were so many details specific to his legal case: names of doctors, hospitals, dates, and I struggled to commit these facts to memory. When I asked him to repeat something from the meeting, he exploded. I was shocked not only by his outburst but his inability to control himself in public. Didn't he know how to rein in his temper and keep his voice down in front of others? He yelled, "*I don't need your help to fight this lawsuit. You are nothing compared to me.*" How was asking him to repeat something suddenly becoming an attack against me? This came as a jolt, especially after devoting myself for countless months to work on his legal case.

Fighting a lawsuit is not the beginning to a marriage of which a new bride dreams. I could have chosen to not be involved, but I was committed to helping in any way I could. After yelling at me, he was silent for the entire car ride home. I had no idea what I had done wrong. Because I noticed he never apologized for his behavior, took any responsibility, or even acknowledged it was inappropriate, I started to question what I was missing. This reinforced a pattern where I kept trying to rationally understand his explosions. What had I done to upset him? There had to be a reason, right? I surmised he was a reasonable, intelligent man who would not act totally irrationally. At the time, I was unaware creating confusion was an inherent part of the abuser's strategy.

An Innocent Gesture of Affection

In those first few months there were other incidents allowing the dense fog of confusion to build. One weekend, we took a trip out of town, our first travel since the honeymoon. I looked forward to having time to ourselves and time outside of our apartment where I was trapped all week long. The trip was uneventful, but the journey back home took a sudden turn for the worse. On the plane, I casually put my head on Rakesh's shoulder. We had hardly much time together as newlyweds and not many chances to be affectionate. Most of our time at home was spent with his mother or on paperwork for his lawsuit.

His reaction to my simple display of affection was outrageous. Despite the fact passengers were next to us, he yelled, "*Don't lean on me. Get off of me. I don't like it. You are making me claustrophobic.*" The man sitting next to me was visibly surprised to see my husband's reaction but pretended he could not hear us to avoid it being more awkward. Despite my repeated attempts to ask him to lower his voice, I could not get through to him. He acted like he could not hear me and denied he was yelling.

After the incident, I remained completely silent the rest of the day. I could not process why he had reacted this way to a simple gesture of affection. Who was this man? This experience did not fit into any view I had of a normal relationship between a husband and wife. How could something so spontaneous and loving lead to such an eruption of insanity? I went through the rest of the day mechanically, cleaning the home, cooking dinner, but struggling to find meaning in these events. Finally that night, I could not bear the pain any longer. As we sat at the dinner table, I burst into tears and sobbed uncontrollably for how hopeless I felt, my confusion over events, and my inability to get through to my husband.

At that crucial point when I could have gained clarity, Rakesh was suddenly kind and comforting. He seemed truly heartbroken to see me crying so intensely and pronounced he would not yell again. He reassured me I could put my head on his shoulder anytime from then on. I wanted to believe him, yet my instincts did not trust him. I would always have to be cautious around this man and his eruptive personality.

I considered confiding in my sister or a friend about the incident but then realized how silly it was to quarrel over being affectionate. In what normal context would this ever be considered a "fight" or even a misunderstanding? I decided to keep it to myself since it was obviously too ridiculous to discuss with anyone. Simultaneously while my confusion was building, I felt caught between two distinct, emerging sides of my husband's personality: the "nice Rakesh" and the "evil Rakesh."

First Physical Incident

Within the short time frame of our two-month marriage there were enough signs with my husband's verbal dominance, powerful personality, impatience, tendency to snap at me on numerous occasions, and complete disregard for my feelings to see he was abusive. I should have recognized his abusive personality and prepared myself for what was to come, the inevitable buildup towards physical violence, but I could not. I had become so isolated up to that point, so weakened by his verbal dominance that I lacked the clarity and the strength to sort through my layers of confusion. I was too naïve to even consider violence as a possibility never having been exposed to it in my life. And then one weekend the inevitable happened-the abuse escalated and I experienced the beginning of his physical aggression.

During a casual conversation, I mentioned my eagerness to discuss acupuncture techniques and strategies together. It was exciting to share the same interest professionally, and I was curious about his training and specialized course for physicians. It appeared he was not keen on discussing this topic and seemed threatened by my request. For some inexplicable reason, this triggered his irritation and before I could process what was happening, he grabbed my arms forcefully, dug his fingers into my flesh, and shook me violently.

I was immobilized. His grip was too strong, and besides, I was paralyzed with shock. Why was he touching me this way? What had come over him? He shook me until it seemed he had released his anger and then abruptly left the room. I ran to close the door of the bedroom and cried silently for a long time. The pain in my arms was intense. No one had ever laid his hands on me before. In a matter of minutes, my world turned upside down. Yet, the idea this was abuse never entered my mind.

My mind flooded with questions trying to understand what had occurred and rationally decipher his reaction. What possessed him to be physical? What was the trigger? How could this discussion have possibly instigated such a reaction? What was my role? I knew I was not to blame, but I was simply too overwhelmed to see clearly or identify this as an assault at the time. This set a pattern of being so emotionally crippled by an abusive incident I could not think straight or comprehend his actions. I was not trying to make excuses for him or justify his actions, but I reasoned he could not manage his temper and it was an issue we would need to address. I did what any rational person would do which was to try and make sense of what had transpired.

After that incident, he returned and apologized profusely with tears in his eyes sincerely pleading, *"Anisha, please forgive me. I swear I have never ever done anything like this before and I never will again."* Truthfully, I believed him. Everyone was allowed to make mistakes, but I knew it could not happen again. It was a one-time incident. I would never tolerate this kind of behavior. I would never accept violence as a means for handling anything. I resolved to learn how to live with and manage Rakesh's temper so it would not flare up as often. I had to brace myself for the future. Determined to be a better wife to ensure our relationship would be more harmonious, I fell into the pattern of assuming more responsibility, the typical role to which every Indian wife resigns herself.

Chapter 19 DESTINY BECKONS

The only journey is the one within. Rainer Maria Rilke

Moving to Chicago

After three months of living in Boston, Rakesh succeeded in leaving his demanding job. We had no idea the lawsuit would continue for another three agonizing years, but we were moving to Chicago! My father had assisted in securing a job at a hospital fulfilling my husband's visa requirements to ensure he would not be deported to India for two years. We were all elated except for my mother-in-law who surprisingly seemed displeased that we would be near my family.

Although I had grown up in Chicago and my family lived there, moving back had never been in my plans, but it seemed like destiny was guiding us home. We believed it would only be for a year or so until his visa requirements were fulfilled and then hoped to relocate to a sunny locality. After moving into a cozy one-bedroom apartment, Rakesh commenced work at his new job and we settled into a comfortable routine. I made sure to restrict time spent with my family so the weekends would be free solely for him. I learned how to adjust my schedule to meet Rakesh's needs and be the ever-accommodating Indian wife.

During what ended up being a four-year stay in Chicago, there were numerous abusive incidents, but they were spread out with several months in between. These long stretches of time or "good periods," when life seemed harmonious, allowed us to concentrate on our careers. It made me consider our marriage to be relatively normal and merely had its ups and downs like any relationship does. I believed every marriage required effort and convinced myself to work harder at being happy when there was conflict. I told myself to be more patient and loving so my compassion would transform him.

The Dual Personality Emerges

During the good periods, Rakesh could occasionally be pleasant and warm. I chose to see this side of his personality as the "real or nice Rakesh." He was entertaining, charming, fun to be around, and made me laugh. I wished he would always be this way but this side of him tended to emerge only in the company of others. When he was abusive, I saw this side of him as the "troubled or evil Rakesh" who I believed would disappear if he put in the effort to address his issues. The real Rakesh was the one I loved, and I was convinced the troubled Rakesh would be transformed eventually.

This pattern of delineating his dual personality reinforced the abuse and kept me from identifying his true nature. What was so intriguing was Rakesh also supported this idea. When he admitted to being abusive, he would always blame it on something else-his anger, his past, his misfortunes, bad karma, or a dark cloud following him. There was an endless list of excuses preventing him from ever taking responsibility for his actions. The further away he removed himself from the abuse, the more I did, too.

Inadvertently, I mimicked his behavior. In retrospect, he fit the profile of the typical narcissist and con artist discussed in Part 1, but I could not identify it at the time. Persuasively, he was a mastermind at projecting his reality and I felt obliged to accept his excuses. I chose to believe in the good Rakesh who I married, fell in love with, and thought was real. Since I did not want to accept the evil Rakesh, I dismissed him whenever he surfaced.

After every abusive incident, I naively assumed it would not happen again. I regarded them as isolated episodes, unconnected to each other. Each time I forgave him, moved on, and learned to let go of the past and concentrate on having a positive future. When I brought up incidents from the past, their emerging pattern, or how distressed I was, he quickly shifted the focus away from his self-examination. His constant critique was, "*You don't know how to let go. You are hung up on the past. You have to learn to stop being so emotional.*" He made it seem like I was at fault for bringing up these incidents and urged me to work on improving my flaws, building my character, and fixing our relationship.

Somehow I started to believe him only because he persistently refused to accept any accountability. It was not until later I learned by turning the focus away from himself, the perpetrator gains increasing power and control. He had successfully distracted me from examining his behavior more closely. I was trapped assuming our stressful situations and circumstances were a trigger for the abusive incidents as he led me to believe. Erroneously, I concentrated all my energy on trying to make him aware of his actions instead of realizing he truly did not care.

Lashing Out Verbally

Our first summer in Chicago, I was co-writing a clinical textbook on acupressure and asked Rakesh for advice on some technical medical terminology. Without warning, he became impatient when I did not blindly accept his suggestion and was bold enough to mention how to improve on his word choice. I recognized then his anger was percolating, about to dangerously spill over. Realizing anything could ignite his explosions, I was still not prepared for his caustic insults.

He hissed, "*How can you question me? You are stupid!*" My jaw dropped as I attempted to process the venom in his voice. No one had ever insulted me before and the words he chose were devastating. For the first time, I guessed this man did not love me. His intense hatred and disrespect for me was paralyzing. Not only was his impatience unexplainable and unacceptable, he lacked the ability to understand or care how I was affected emotionally and justified his word choice instead of apologizing. After he walked away, the tension diffused, and I held back my emotions.

Later that day when I overcame my shock, I questioned him frankly. *"Why would you marry me if you thought I was stupid?"* He muttered, *"I was just angry and picked the wrong words. I did not mean it."* The frustration of continuing to rationalize these incidents was overwhelming. I still could not decipher the reason for his anger in the first place. Out of despair, I let it go. What else could I do? The emotional toll was too much to process, and I could not think straight anymore. The pattern of his denial coupled with my emotional devastation was convenient for him because he would walk away from these incidences untroubled. I was left trying to process the hurt and make sense of the verbal attack. Afterwards, he never apologized, but when I questioned him persistently he would say he did not mean it.

Each time he lashed out I began to wonder how these negative thoughts could even enter his mind if he truly loved me. Even when I felt irritated with Rakesh, I never even considered insulting him or calling him names. It was clear to me he carried tremendous unexpressed anger from his past and I was his convenient, unsuspecting scapegoat. By overpowering me, it seemed he felt increasingly confident, secure, powerful-traits he had desperately longed for before.

It was almost as if he felt the need to constantly express his "opinion" and was apparently threatened when I voiced mine. Debasing me and deflating my self-esteem seemed to validate him. Under constant scrutiny, I suffered his wrath and relentless judgment no matter what I did. But then at the crucial moment when clarity could have surfaced and I could have left him, the "nice Rakesh" emerged. This was the side of him I desperately longed to see and when he appeared I was grateful. No doubt, this was my weakness. All I desired was to quickly forget the "evil Rakesh" who was irrational, immature, and hurtful.

Abusive Patterns Set In

That same summer, his second physical assault occurred just six or seven months after the wedding. Following yet another simple discussion that inexplicably triggered his wrath, he grabbed my arms forcefully after promising me he would never do it again. There was nothing I could do physically to resist his grip. Even though this action was familiar, my shock utterly paralyzed me. I willed myself to remain calm and said, *"You are digging your nails into my arm and hurting me."* Surely he would snap out of his rage when he saw he was hurting the person he supposedly loved? However, the more I tried to get through to him, the more his denial increased. Once again, his irascibility created a wall I could not penetrate. It was as if he could not hear me. I assumed he was obviously too out of control to know what he was doing.

After he finally released his grip I showed him the nail marks on my arm to prove how much force he had used. His casual dismissal perplexed me. How could he blatantly deny his actions? His ire unleashed, Rakesh proceeded to insult me. It was bad enough being called stupid before, but I was unprepared to hear him swear. He bellowed, *"You are a piece of sh*t!"* I was dumbfounded. Never having tolerance for that kind of language, it was absolutely unacceptable to speak to one's wife in such a derogatory fashion. I was outraged and told him so.

I patiently explained, *"Rakesh, the human language is sacred. Words have the power to express beauty and the most indescribable emotions within. When we realize this, there can be no tolerance for destructive, hurtful language that only manifests when there is no value or respect for human life."* My words fell on deaf ears as he chose to nonchalantly walk away as if nothing had transpired and blatantly ignore me. The pattern was quickly established where he lashed out his insults and then denied anything had ever happened.

Over the years, the verbal abuse continued and escalated with regularity. The emotional toll of hearing these hurtful labels one would only use on one's worst enemy was devastating. Not only was I stupid, according to Rakesh, but also apparently I knew nothing about life, I was not a true Indian wife, I was spoiled, and many derogatory swear words were used. He called me "worthless, psycho, a f*cking idiot, and crazy." Each time it was distressing to hear these insults spewing from his mouth. Yet he continued to find new ways to degrade me.

He proved no day was sacred as the barrage of insults was unrelenting on birthdays, anniversaries, special occasions, or whenever I seemed to be in a good mood. Basically, there was never a day worth treating me with respect. Amazingly, Rakesh's indomitable ego and sense of entitlement prevailed as he repeatedly exclaimed, *"There is no one else in the world like me!"* How did he have the nerve to continue to praise himself despite his abusive behavior?

Processing My Shock

Hastily, after this incident, I grabbed my purse and ran out of our apartment to escape. I did not feel physically safe being anywhere near this man whose behavior was utterly bewildering. I drove to my parents' home as a refuge, hoping not to see Rakesh for the rest of the day. I failed to comprehend his denial and complete lack of concern for me. To my amazement, he had the nerve to show up after this incident for lunch and greet my parents as if he was still the perfect son-in-law. Evidently, he felt entitled to be served a hot Indian meal. Unable to stand his presence, I left in a hurry with the excuse of not feeling well. Knowing he was at their home, enjoying a nice meal, and acting like everything was okay made my stomach churn. I was sickened by his abhorrent actions. Unable to process my shock, I felt paralyzed.

I spent the entire day outside driving around aimlessly, wondering how to make sense of recent events. I considered spending the night at my parents' home just to be away from him but how could I admit what had happened to them if I could not fully admit it to myself? How could I bring myself to tell them the crushing news that no parent should have to hear? They loved Rakesh like their own son and regarded him so highly.

It seemed unnecessary to burden my parents when I felt confident we would successfully work through this madness. I made the conscious decision that day to keep what happened a secret, cover up my embarrassment, and protect him, our relationship, and my parents from knowing the truth. Only later would I learn my actions enabled my husband to become stronger, in turn weakening myself. Unknowingly, I sent him the message loud and clear he could be abusive and get away with it. I had tacitly agreed to co-create this reality of abuse with Rakesh.

I finally returned home in the evening, hoping all the time elapsed would have somehow brought him to his senses. I expected him to be calm and discuss what had happened like mature adults. Surely he would apologize to me, beg for my forgiveness, say he did not mean what he said. Then it would all be over and we could forget it ever happened. That was my only wish. I was surprised to discover he was not home at this late hour. I decided to write him a letter hoping this mode of communication would not risk triggering his temper.

When Rakesh finally showed up, his behavior puzzled me even more. He avoided eye contact and acted like I did not exist. Instead, he walked briskly around the apartment, searched for the telephone, and proceeded to dial someone's number. Why was he blatantly ignoring me? Why should I have to beg him to talk to me? I felt like screaming but I told myself to remain composed and asked him to face me. Upon my insistence, he finally read my letter but made no comment and refused to look at me.

From my logical frame of mind I could not rationalize events or assemble the pieces of the puzzle. I failed to comprehend logic does not apply in an abusive situation where an abuser is completely irrational. If I had known his lack of remorse was a characteristic factor, maybe I would have had clarity. I can accept it if someone makes a mistake when he is out of control and cannot face it. But so many hours after the incident, why had his anger not abated?

Why could he not make amends? Did he not see it was critical to make some effort? These questions flooded my mind. Somehow I felt more in shock by this than the abuse itself. The next few days were a daze. I lived in a fog, unsure of what to make of my reality. This became a common pattern: I still functioned in the outside world but inside I was becoming increasingly numb and paralyzed by emotions I could not safely express. That numbness was my coping mechanism.

Enabling Him

Unable to emerge from my fog of pain and devastation, my husband must have realized he needed to make amends so we could again go on as "normal." Slowly, over the next few days, the "nice Rakesh" emerged. He warmed up to me, consoled me, reassured me this would never happen again. I had a choice at this point to believe him or not, and I chose simply to believe him because the alternative was too incomprehensible. After all, if he did mean those nasty things, then my marriage would be meaningless. I refused to believe that. I could not process or come to terms with his abusive, violent nature. To stay sane, I needed to convince myself these were separate, one-time incidents when he lost control. Unknowingly, my pattern of denial started to develop and become ingrained as my survival response.

The emotional toll of these incidences along with my shock and incomprehension reinforced the denial. Because it was so foreign, I could not correlate these events to anything I had experienced in my life up until that point. I had never faced violence, been insulted, or had anyone treat me poorly. Reaching out for help never crossed my mind. This was a critical point when my cognitive dissonance emerged and I made a "creative adjustment" to accept something that was utterly unacceptable. I made up a story I needed to believe to preserve my sanity and ability to function in the world. It was a coping technique, a survival strategy upon which I increasingly relied.

Traumatic Bonding

It was not until many years later in my recovery period I heard of the term traumatic bonding. It helped explain why I became so trapped in my abusive marriage. After being physically and verbally abused by the man I loved, the only thing I wanted was comfort, to be soothed, to feel the pain go away. Naturally, I turned to the person I loved to provide this reassurance even though he was also my abuser. After being so isolated, I did not feel there was anyone else to whom I could turn. When the abusive incident was over, ironically, I sought comfort in *his* arms. I needed to hear he did not mean it and it would not happen again to stay sane, otherwise the shock of being treated so badly would have been insurmountable. In hindsight, I comprehend how this survival technique prevented my mental disintegration.

I recognize this created a pattern of abuse that perpetuated my weakness and vulnerability, while ultimately, he became stronger and confident he could get away with his mistreatment. Rakesh knew each time I would forgive him and we would move on. His denial, coupled with my emotional exhaustion, led each incident of abuse to be swept under the rug. I ask readers not to look at this as a weakness but as basic human conditioning that is a product of repetition. Rakesh had eroded me systematically in a way so subtle I could not see it happening.

Unaware of the insidiousness of abuse, I assumed violence was a black and white issue. I reasoned, if your husband hit you, he was a jerk and you got out of that situation as fast as possible. However, I was not being slapped, punched, or beaten yet and had no visible injuries. Being psychologically abused and weakened, I was too confused to identify when the first physical incident occurred. It was easy to recognize violence by a stranger, but at the hands of the man you love and trust it was utterly incomprehensible.

Drive to Ashram

Sometime later in 2002, another incident occurred while traveling to an *ashram* (Hindu religious retreat) Rakesh used to frequent. With evident pride, he wished to show me this spiritual place he attributed to shaping his devotional and religious nature. It was ironic to describe him this way, but I later learned many abusive men cleverly hide behind this disguise. This was one of the reasons I had been initially drawn to him when he had portrayed himself as a very devout Hindu. As a religion major in college fascinated by studying Hinduism, I thought this was yet another bond we shared.

On the highway, he yelled at me about the car door not shutting properly and subsequently lost control behind the wheel. He was screaming at the top of his lungs, swerving the car, and driving recklessly. Calmly, I said, *"Rakesh, I do not feel safe being in a car with you when you are acting this way."* My words had the opposite effect. He became enraged I had the audacity to speak and spat, *"I am in complete control."* It was such a contradiction. It did not matter what I said; he could not hear me.

At that moment, I resisted the compelling urge to open the door and jump out so I would never have to witness his madness again. That impulse should have warned me I was in a dangerous situation to consider an action that showed I was not in my right frame of mind. But I would never do something so rash. So I sat in silence, trapped with a lunatic, trying to ignore his screams, praying to every god I could think of that he would not swerve off the road. Once again, he never admitted to being out of control or raging like a rabid animal. He never apologized for his behavior or putting my life in jeopardy while he was driving. The irony this was happening on our way to an ashram was almost laughable.

During the course of our marriage my husband maintained his image of being a pious man, interested in studying scripture, conversing with holy men, and devoutly praying and visiting the temple. No one would have ever guessed this man could be abusive. He disguised his inner nature well while in public but even with close friends and family. I did not learn until later perpetrators often have this charming and friendly personality to discount suspicions of their abusive tendencies. Later when the victim reaches out to friends and family for support, it lowers her credibility and people believe she is lashing out to ruin her husband's reputation. I could not foresee this would be my experience at the end of our marriage when I found many refused to believe me.

Along this vein, we had several disputes about being involved with an Indian human rights organization which served to protect the rights of Hindus globally. We both believed in this cause, but Rakesh expressly forbid me from participating in any way saying, "*This is not the time. You need to learn how to manage your time effectively.*" By not allowing me to follow my passions, he found yet another means to control me. The irony of him promoting himself as an advocate of human rights only supported the deceptive self-image he cleverly tried to create.

Becoming the Perfect Wife

I took more initiative in trying to "fix" our marriage. Every time an abusive incident occurred, I became the therapist patiently explaining to him the pattern in which we were trapped. I was determined to appeal to his logical, rational side even though there was no proof it existed. Surely if he saw how this incident was similar to the last incident he would have more clarity. Right? My explanations, however, only triggered his anger more. He reprimanded me, "*You are too emotional. You are always harping on the past and cannot let things go.*" So I graciously forgave my husband and tried to forget these altercations so he would not accuse me of living in the past. I continued to work diligently on myself so we could eventually live an abuse-free life.

I strived to eliminate every flaw my husband commented on so he could not criticize or blame me for his ire. I took it upon myself to run the household, prepare a hot Indian meal every night, and manage our finances. So he would not be inconvenienced, I ran errands on weekdays and handled all our moves on my own so he would not waste time packing. I devoted my time attending to his needs, caring for his mother whenever she came to live with us for months at a time, and playing the role of an obedient Indian wife. I stepped out of the way so mother and son could bond and make up for all the lost years they had not seen each other even if I felt left out. I distanced myself from my priorities and immersed myself in doing everything I could for his family. I forgot what was important to me and neglected my own needs, losing myself completely in this process. It was only a matter of time before the inevitable disintegration of my being.

Chapter 20 ENDLESS BATTLES

In the midst of movement and chaos, keep stillness inside of you.
Deepak Chopra

Starting My Private Practice

Three years had passed since I graduated from acupuncture school. I was desperate to start working after putting my career on hold due to planning the wedding, all of our moves, fighting my husband's lawsuit, supporting his career ambitions, and working on writing my first book. I had dreamed of starting my own practice for years, and I did not want to wait any longer. To my amazement, Rakesh made it clear he would not help me financially in any way. This was the beginning of the financial abuse, but I did not recognize it at the time.

I took it for granted he would not contribute financially to my career pursuits but became accustomed to his use of our joint resources for his own needs, to advance his own career, and support his mother in India. Persuasively, he told my parents we needed funds to plan for the future, save for buying a home, and continue to fight his lawsuit with our mounting legal bills. He convinced my parents and me that relying on my father's help was the only way to start my career. So in March 2003, I moved into my father's office space for a period that would extend to three years. His generosity allowed me to pursue a career and for us to save a considerable amount of money.

Rakesh and I had several heated discussions before I commenced work to determine my schedule. I made it clear I was committed to doing whatever it took to have a successful career but to begin with working four days a week would make my practice schedule more efficient since it would take time to build my clientele. Instead of respecting my decision or giving my opinion any importance, my husband berated me over and over again. "*You do not know anything about business. You are not committed to being successful. You have to be there Monday through Friday!*" He badgered me on this issue constantly for several weeks until I eventually broke down defeated.

Frustrated, I could not get him to hear or appreciate what I said. Rakesh had made it impossible to stand my ground any longer. The only way to settle the issue was by emphatically saying, "*Fine, Rakesh, I will work Monday through Friday if that is what you wish.*" By capitulating and saying what he wanted to hear, I got him off my back, stopped the barrage of insults, eased the emotional assault, and could breathe a little easier. I had just learned a new survival technique-to give in, compromise my beliefs, and surrender some battles.

Threats of Divorce

The second summer of our marriage in 2003 events became worse after a lull of several months when it seemed the abuse had ended and I was unsuspecting. My guard down, I believed our heated incidents were relegated to the past. After a trivial discussion triggered his irascible temperament, he piercingly yelled and proceeded to threaten me with divorce. Rakesh bragged, *"If my friend could divorce his wife, then it is no big deal. I can do it, too."* Not only was there no substantial argument to precipitate this, I was paralyzed hearing him mention the word divorce. Divorce was just not an option in Indian culture nor in my personal belief system. I was devoted to this man for life and loved him. I never went back on my commitments. If there were problems, I was committed to fixing them. How could he even consider using such a word and on top of that brag about it?

I told him patiently, *"Rakesh, it really offends me to hear you mention that word. Divorce is a sign of hopelessness, not giving our marriage a chance, and not defending our love for each other. If you have the perspective we can work anything out with effort and dedication, then divorce should never come up in the conversation. Divorce is the easy solution. Do not use it as an escape from facing our problems. Please respect my request to not use that word."* Again, my words fell on deaf ears. Over the years he would use this word to threaten me mercilessly, apparently feeling more powerful when he saw how it effectively crushed my spirit.

The Assault

How was I to react to his threat of divorce? Caught off guard, what happened next was even more appalling. Within seconds his temper escalated, I could see the fire ablaze in his eyes. As Rakesh walked towards me aggressively, he smiled menacingly, grabbed both my arms forcefully, and shoved me vigorously onto the bed. I flipped over backwards in a somersault, landed limp on the other side with my head twisted, and felt shooting pain on the side of my neck. Possessed, he kept coming at me with what could only be described as a twisted smile. I knew I had to defend myself for the first time before he became more dangerous. Rakesh pinned me down with his body weight on top of me. I tried to shove him off but my act of defense only enraged him further.

Threateningly, he boasted of his strength. *"Who do you think you are to be fighting with me? I have fought people coming at me with knives. You are clearly no match for me."* I could not process his words. He was in another world, maybe reliving some trauma as a young boy in school with bullies cornering him. He could not hear me, calm down, or see I was hurt. He failed to observe I was lying pinned down and defenseless in front of him. Why would he boast of his strength at a time like this? Obviously I was no match for him physically. He was at least twice my weight and overpowered me completely. Could he not see that?

My Rationalization

The confusion, the overwhelming emotions, the hurt and devastation of his actions, it was all too much. To understand his behavior, my mind needed to rationalize an answer. I assessed the situation: (1) He was out of control. (2) He was unaware of his actions and their effect on me. (3) He could not hear me. (4) His emotions were too powerful for him to handle. (5) He did not have the ability to see what was happening in front of him. (6) He was in another world. (7) He was hurt. (8) He had not processed his anger from the past. (9) These incidents helped him release his past anger and hurt. It was not a justification or a defense of his actions but necessary for my mental survival. I had to create my own story or "creative adjustment" to make sense of reality.

I realized we lived in completely separate realities during these incidents. Looking back, it was amazing to witness how my rational mind still kept functioning despite my shock and how desperately I longed to make sense of reality. When I broke all this down it was a turning point to grasp Rakesh needed help. I felt empowered knowing I had finally "diagnosed" the problem. If I could find a way to communicate effectively and bridge the gap, he would become more self-aware of his hurtful actions. I reasoned if he truly loved me, then he did not mean to treat me this badly. His emotions clouded his judgment, and I felt confident I could bring him clarity.

I fell into a pattern of being the responsible, nurturing caretaker creating the false hope I could change Rakesh without accurately assessing my diagnosis was flawed; he was a batterer addicted to violence. I minimized these events and focused on him and his needs instead of mine as he had conditioned me to do. To clarify-this turning point came from a position of strength and not weakness with which victims are stereotypically labeled. I did not feel helpless, I felt empowered. I was no longer confused; I believed I had lucidity.

After that incident, I rushed to my parents' home for refuge even though they were out of town for the weekend. To process his assault, I needed to write and pour out my heart, unleashing all the emotions that had built up inside. I decided to write Rakesh a long letter and hoped this mode of communication would get through to him. I understood now my single purpose-to fix this "problem." Maybe this was why destiny brought us together I reasoned. I was a healer after all; this is what I did, help people overcome their issues and transform themselves.

Fighting Through the Pain

From the injury of being thrown across the bed, however, I developed serious neck pain. I kept writing through the misery and tried to finish my critical letter to Rakesh, but after awhile it grew into a full-fledged migraine I could no longer ignore. For a person who rarely had headaches, the migraine was an excruciating experience, a hammer that was a persistent blow to my head. My only thought was to return home safely so I would not be alone. Somehow, I used sheer will power to drive despite the pain, learning never to underestimate myself and what I was capable of. This ability to withstand tremendous mental anguish and physical pain and yet still function in the world became a characteristic trait of mine for survival.

Wracked with pain, the agony forced me to be completely dependent on Rakesh and reinforced the traumatic bonding pattern. I had no choice but to let go of the incident and focus on recovering. Rakesh lifted me out of the car, into the elevator, and then into the apartment. Without speaking, he placed me on the bed in a seemingly detached, unconcerned manner. Upon my request, he treated me with acupuncture and instantly I felt the throbbing pain dissipate. Physically drained, I fell into a deep sleep.

There was no time to contemplate the fact he never apologized, acknowledged his behavior from that day, or showed any remorse. We never spoke about that incident afterwards. This was now a common pattern to conveniently avoid discussing what had transpired because it was too difficult to face and he was unwilling anyway. The physical violence consumed my strength and I lacked the energy to battle his denial. My resolute focus was on survival, recovering from my injuries, and finding a way to endure.

Insults Continue

That summer, the abuse continued and his scathing insults seemed to intensify. Rakesh liberally lashed out at me whenever he was so inspired. People assume conflict provokes an argument, but this only holds true for rational, mature couples. To me, my husband was rapidly proving with each incident he was totally irrational and did not require any provocation. One evening at the dinner table he turned to me and said out of nowhere, *"You are not a true Indian wife."* That insult was more devastating than anything he had said previously. Being sworn at and called names was upsetting, but this was the lowest possible affront.

My attempts to explain how deeply hurt I was only led him to cruelly point out all my inadequacies that made me an "American wife" and justify himself. Blind to the tears streaming down my face, he had no ability to see what that term meant to me. In the midst of my shock, I patiently reasoned with him the way a therapist would, a pattern that was fully ingrained in me now. This effectively distracted me from my own pain. I held on to the belief I could somehow convince him of my perspective. If I had only known he had no desire to do so, I would have saved myself years of anguish.

I declared, *"My entire life all I have ever wanted to be and everything I have strived for is to be an Indian wife and mother and uphold my family's traditional values. It has been a struggle growing up in America, far away from my family in India, my Indian roots, and my passion for Indian culture and sciences."* But he already knew that I had worked extremely hard to be an Indian in every sense of what that meant to me. I continued, *"Rakesh, no American would invite her mother-in-law to live with her one week after her honeymoon or be fine with her moving in permanently. No American would accept her husband prioritizing his mother over his wife, live without a car, or be trapped in her apartment. No American would allow her husband to stifle her career opportunities!"*

It was only many years later when I studied the psychology of abuse that I grasped his apparent strategy of carefully choosing the exact words to create the deepest psychological impact. He seemed to know which words would be a dagger to impale my heart to inflict the maximum emotional damage. I did not appreciate then every move of his appeared calculated, every action and insult apparently designed to weaken me. Once again I noted his lack of an apology or sense of remorse but I had become accustomed to it at this point.

The Ice Bin

Up until this point, many incidents were on weekends or while we were traveling but it did not take long for the abuse to creep steadily and mercilessly into our everyday lives as well. One early morning over breakfast before he left for work we had a trivial discussion that irritated him. To shut me up, he came at me aggressively, cornered me behind the sofa, grabbed my hands and wrists vehemently, bent them backwards and applied tremendous pressure. It was excruciating and seemed to last for an eternity. I could not even cry out in pain.

He once again seemed to be totally unconscious of his actions, unaware he was hurting me. As soon as he let go I ran to the freezer and immersed my hands in the ice bin to numb the fiery pain shooting up my arms. I was terrified that day for the first time seeing him so out of control. Apprehensive of my wrists being seriously damaged, how would I practice acupuncture? What if he had broken something? Even if he had not, the next time he could. I was beginning to recognize his serious pattern of showing no concern for my physical well-being after unleashing his anger. It amazed me that even after I was physically hurt he could not seem to snap out of his fury, realize his mistake, or show remorse.

I felt a new emotion building inside me but I refrained from expressing my rage, choosing instead to suppress it deep within. My survival depended on it. Displaying my anger would only provoke Rakesh further. Still, despite grasping the gravity of the situation, it never occurred to me to seek help. My conundrum was how to explain these incidents when there was no context for our arguments or basis for conflict. I still did not label this as abuse. After all, I had no visible injuries, did not need to visit a hospital, and I was sure he had not intentionally meant to hurt me. My ignorance of the reality of domestic violence would come to haunt me later.

Niagara Falls

It was a grueling year and a half of marriage up until then. The summer of 2003 his mother and grandmother came to visit us from India for several months. I was looking forward to their visit, getting to know his grandmother, and welcoming them into our home. Deep down, I knew their presence also guaranteed my safety. When they were with us, my husband would be forced to treat me well. In the company of others, he was always funny, entertaining, and pleasant. I loved seeing the "nice Rakesh" emerge and it reminded me why I had fallen in love with him. I looked forward to a few months of safety without any violent altercations.

We planned a fun trip to Niagara Falls and my husband's sister and brother-in-law joined us. With four houseguests I went out of my way to make them feel at home in our overcrowded one-bedroom apartment. Rising early in the morning, I lent a hand to Rakesh's mother to cook *parathas* for our car ride. Working in the kitchen was never my forte but especially so early in the morning before a road trip was challenging. I then graciously volunteered to drive the caravan full of family members since Rakesh had an intense upcoming medical board exam so I knew he needed the extra time in the car to study. At this point, he took my generosity for granted and was used to me catering to his needs.

Exhausted from cooking in the morning and driving four hours, I hoped our trip would be enjoyable. Most of our time at Niagara Falls was uneventful until the end. My husband and brother-in-law went inside to get refreshments while all the ladies sat outside on the lawn. We wondered what was taking them so long, so I decided it would be nice to stretch my legs and went inside the café. I casually asked about the delay, not anticipating Rakesh's response.

Glaring at me, he was clearly upset by my presence. I should have backed away seeing the warning signs but before I could move he snapped. Even though we were in a public place, my sister who had also joined us was standing right beside me, and his brother-in-law was nearby, he did not care. He flippantly muttered under his breath, *"Stop following me and checking up on me"* and then stomped away. I was dumbfounded. What just happened? I was not checking up on him! How could he react this way to something so casual?

Even though I was confused by his behavior, I was also outraged by his response. It was not acceptable to treat me this way, especially in front of family or in a public place. After all the effort I had put into that day, everything I had done for his family and him, why was he being so hurtful? My presence should not trigger such an immature reaction. Ignoring me for the rest of the afternoon, Rakesh acted as if I had done something terribly wrong, did not deserve to be spoken to or acknowledged, and refused to even look at me. I felt trapped, unable to talk to him with his family present. Forced to remain silent, I restrained my emotions instead of confronting him like I usually did.

After being mentally and physically exhausted, the four-hour drive home was excruciating. It was too dark for Rakesh to read or study but he never volunteered to drive. He completely dismissed me, acting like I did not exist while he spoke to the rest of his family jovially. It took incredible effort to maintain the appearance everything was okay in front of his family. I felt obligated to be a convincing actress, forced to cover up what transpired, and restrain my emotions. Returning home there was no privacy with his family staying with us. Because it became customary for him to refuse to acknowledge the incident, apologize, or show any remorse, I let it go. Could I expect anything else from him at this point?

Possible Pregnancy

Soon after his family left I was no longer safe at home. One afternoon, he randomly pushed me vigorously off the couch and down onto the floor when his temper ignited. At the time, we thought I might be pregnant but were not sure yet. That did not stop him. After pinning me down with his body weight on top of me and shaking me repeatedly, I felt him pressing down on my rib cage. I could only surmise rage clouded his mind and he seemed unaware of hurting me or possibly our unborn child. I lay still, eyes closed, afraid to move a muscle.

Waiting patiently for his furor to lift, I prayed for him to get off me. I trained myself during these incidents to maintain my calm and focus on my breathing. I would watch from afar, outside of my body, where I was safe. I adapted this survival technique of disassociation to keep the violence to a minimum. The more I resisted, the worse his assault. When he finally heaved his massive body off of me, I ran into the bathroom and locked the door. He could have helped me up, asked if I was okay, or shown some concern for my well-being.

It was futile thinking he would eventually snap out of his tantrum. He displayed once again he was totally unaware of his actions, or so he had me believe. As he repeatedly pounded on the bathroom door and screamed at me to come out, I began to truly fear my husband. I stayed locked in there for at least thirty minutes until I felt Rakesh's ire had subsided. Fortunately, I was not pregnant but the fear his actions could hurt another being, especially our child, terrified me. I would never let that happen. It dawned on me I had married a veritable brute, but I did not know how to handle the craziness of our marriage. Nothing in my life had prepared me to deal with this. It would take many years before I realized there was a method to his madness.

Chapter 21 KEEPING THE SECRET

Although the world is full of suffering, it is also full of the overcoming of it.
Helen Keller

Trip to India

The year 2004 marked the third year of our marriage. I reassured myself things could only improve from here. With all the turbulence in our relationship, I felt I was losing a part of me slowly every year. I desperately needed to do something to feel inspired, so I opted to follow some dreams I had put on hold. Traveling to India for three months, I pursued advanced training in yoga and ayurveda and focused on my education and passions. It provided a necessary break from the chaos of my daily dysfunctional, abusive reality. It would be difficult to live apart from Rakesh when I was so committed to mending our marriage, but it seemed a minor sacrifice to make to have time for myself. Those three refreshing months filled me with a new vigor.

At the end of my stay I visited Rakesh's mother before returning to the U.S. From the combination of my exhaustion, traveling extensively, sunstroke, and dehydration I ended up in the hospital ICU for a few days hooked up to an IV. My only wish was to return home quickly after these intense three months and my hospital stay. I was homesick and missed my husband terribly. As the saying goes, absence makes the heart grow fonder and the abuse had faded into a distant memory. I took comfort in hearing the sound of his voice over the phone. Even though the doctor had advised me against returning to the U.S. earlier, I confided to Rakesh my heart's desire to change my ticket. Instead of understanding I was simply conveying my eagerness to be reunited and comfort me, Rakesh screamed vehemently on the phone.

Even though he was on the other side of the world, had not seen me in months, and knew I was in a hospital hooked up to an IV for god's sake, I was appalled he could be abusive. Did he not have a modicum of sensitivity? Could he not speak to me nicely even now? He spat, *"You are crazy to be thinking of coming home sooner. What is wrong with you? You are disrespecting my mother!"* I could barely hear his ranting as my mind flooded with questions. How could saying I missed him and want to be with him be perceived as an attack against his mother? Confounded by his harsh words, tears streaked my face. I could not believe he had the audacity to keep yelling at me. His mother saw me crying on the phone but never inquired about my tears.

Our First Witness

After my return to the U.S., a couple months of relative, uneventful calm made me believe the past was behind us. I was unsuspecting again after another deceptive "good period." One weekend we went to my office so Rakesh could receive an acupuncture treatment. As he laid with needles up and down his back, I asked him a question but could not hear his response. Asking him to speak louder surprisingly ignited his anger. Suddenly he yelled, "*Take these needles out. Do it faster!*" It seemed ridiculous to lose control at a time like this. I had no idea what came over him. I was beginning to see there was no pattern for his rage that was becoming increasingly unpredictable.

Despite removing the needles as quickly as I could, he lunged off the table and came towards me menacingly with a distorted smirk. Terrified, I had no idea what he would do but I wondered why he always smiled before his physical attacks. It was as if he enjoyed these moments and derived some sort of pleasure being the aggressor. I felt the "normal" panic, fear, and palpitations that I had become accustomed to surface. Somehow, Rakesh convinced me these physical symptoms were due to my insensitivity and inability to deal with my "uncontrollable" emotions. The irony of that comment was laughable when it was really his anger that was always out of control. It was not until much later that I identified my symptoms as a healthy response to fear alerting me of danger. In hindsight, I now view these comments as his systematic ploy to weaken me.

Rakesh once again grabbed my arms, pinned me roughly against the wall, and trapped me in a corner, a familiar scenario. I begged him not to touch me and struggled to break free of his grasp. Of course, he could not hear me. I resisted in vain, powerless against him. A doctor who shared the office space walked in right then and heard the commotion. I told Rakesh loudly, "*Please stop hurting me. Let go of me.*" He quickly walked out and I was left there sitting alone in tears. His growing apathy and loss of control in public places was distressing. The doctor knocked on the door of my treatment room and asked if I was okay. Trying to cover up my tears, I nodded yes. It was not clear how much she had heard. I was humiliated not only that someone had heard us, but also because I, a well-educated, independent, intelligent woman had landed myself in this predicament.

Fireworks

That same summer as we drove to a friend's wedding I looked forward to attending, I made a casual comment about which car we should buy next. Without warning, Rakesh's irritation flared and he proceeded to holler. There was no way to have a conversation with him without always walking on those proverbial eggshells. I was beginning to see it did not matter what we discussed; no topic was safe. He was not reacting to the comment as much as he was annoyed by my pleasant mood. Once again, I felt threatened being in a vehicle with a yelling lunatic who was out of control. Turning the car around abruptly, he drove us back home.

Disappointed I had missed the wedding, he seemed like he could not care less by the turn of events. I called my family and lied to them, *"Rakesh is not feeling well and we won't be able to make it."*

It was the Fourth of July. I needed to leave the apartment, be as far away from my husband as possible, and clear my head. At the park, watching fireworks by myself, the realization set in: I was truly depressed knowing how alone I was and how my marriage was not anything I had dreamed it would be. I had missed the wedding, lied to my family, and recognized it was one of the saddest nights of my life.

Not surprisingly, when I returned home Rakesh did not apologize for his outburst or care I was gone. He continued to ignore me and pretend nothing out of the ordinary occurred. His behavior led me to question my sanity as I felt myself slipping into confusion, unable to make sense of these disconcerting incidents. I contemplated how to get through to him, improve my communication, and change the dynamics of our turbulent marriage.

Family Illnesses

At this point, I considered telling my family the truth about my marriage, but there were too many reasons not to. My mother had just suffered from a stroke in the spring of 2004, and it had been devastating for all of us. She was the pillar of our family and the embodiment of strength. Witnessing her suffering and her vulnerability was too much for all of us to bear. Mindful of reducing her stress levels to prevent a second stroke, I felt it necessary to keep my secret.

A few months later that summer, we discovered my seventeen-year-old sister was diagnosed with a brain tumor. My family pulled together to be strong and supportive for her and keep her occupied to distract her from worrying about the upcoming surgery. Surprisingly, even Rakesh made it a point to play basketball and tennis with Nandita. It was endearing to see the "nice Rakesh" emerge as a caring big brother. I felt reassured I could count on him when my family most needed the support. I fooled myself into thinking the past was behind us when he showed this considerate side. Surviving an entire summer without an abusive incident made me falsely feel hopeful our marriage was improving.

August 11 was the fateful day of Nandita's surgery. When the medical staff rolled her away to the operating room we witnessed a few tears slide down her cheeks as she waved goodbye to us and smiled. Her smile broke our hearts. I marveled at her strength and bravery, especially for a seventeen-year-old. We did not know if the surgery would be successful, if we would see Nandita again, or what her condition would be post-op. For my family it was one of the scariest days of our lives. Time stretched painfully as we sat in the waiting room from 9 to 4 watching the hands on the clock barely moving.

Finally after seven hours, we were told Nandita had been transferred to the ICU and we could visit her. Seeing her in pain, the sparkle missing from her eyes, the smile erased from her face, I completely broke down emotionally. I fled the room so she would not see my tears. I sobbed my heart out in the hallway knowing they had taken the smile away from my beautiful, happy, cheerful sister. Here was a little girl in pain whose eyes were glazed over, who could not even function, and who did not even seem to recognize us. Her head was pounding so intensely she could barely have a conversation with us. Arya was the stronger sister that day whose grace and poise amazed me. She calmly called all our relatives in the U.S. and India to update them on Nandita's condition while I drowned in my tears.

Rakesh's Appearance

That day, Rakesh did not join us during the surgery. I had hoped after being supportive all summer he would have understood how much his presence would have made a difference. But apparently he did not see why he needed to be there and did not wish to miss work. I could not understand his decision, but I gave him the freedom to make up his own mind without insisting he be there. When Nandita woke up in the ICU and asked for Rakesh it devastated us to tell her he was elsewhere. She could not fathom either why he would fail to be by her side. After bonding with her big brother all summer she naturally assumed he would be present to comfort her.

Finally, he showed up later in the evening for a few minutes and spoke briefly to my parents. After a long day at work, he was tired and in a rush to get home for dinner. I thought of all the times Rakesh had spoken of how we must be supportive of our families, but he treated the operation lightly, barely acknowledging it or what I was going through emotionally. He always mentioned being supportive when it involved his mother and easing *her* suffering, anxiety, and loneliness. He justified her moving in one week after our honeymoon because of this.

I thought of how I had bent over backward since the first week of my marriage to please his mother, take care of her needs, and be understanding of her past suffering. I was beginning to see the disparity in his words and actions. How had it taken me three years to realize this or admit his apparent narcissistic tendencies? What about my sister's suffering in the present? What about my parents and caring for their needs? Wasn't having brain surgery a good enough reason to be supportive? What about feeling compassion for my emotional devastation?

I failed to understand Rakesh's actions that day but did not have much time to dwell on it. My heart and energy were consumed assisting my little sister recover from the ordeal she had just endured. Those next few weeks Nandita was in rehab, I juggled my work schedule, supported my family, cooked for Rakesh, and spent as much free time with my sister as possible. Our only goal was to help her get back on her feet, out of her wheelchair, into physical therapy so she could walk and function again. It was an exhausting and challenging time but we watched my sister slowly heal from her operation as the sparkle started to return to her eyes. Somehow, my family pulled through that arduous time together even though Rakesh remained aloof.

My Resolution

During that traumatic time I made the decision to never burden my parents or sisters with the personal problems in my marriage. They had so much else to deal with that my issues seemed trivial in comparison. I thought of my little sister's strength and bravery during the surgery and knew if I could only have a fraction of her strength I would survive. She was my hero and role model. I saw how much my parents had to endure emotionally at the possibility of almost losing a daughter. No, there was no reason to worry them, I assured myself. I resigned myself to keeping my secret. In my heart I was convinced somehow Rakesh and I would find a way to work things out. The past few months had been abuse-free. For some reason, blind hope in me persisted despite all the mounting evidence our marriage was not working.

Chapter 22 TIME APART

Darkness cannot drive out darkness; only light can do that. Hate cannot drive out hate; only love can do that. Martin Luther King Jr.

One-Year Vacation

After three years of living in Chicago, my husband's sense of entitlement had evidently magnified and he declared he needed a one-year vacation. To me, this was not a typical choice a grown, responsible, adult man would make. Everyone questioned our decision, wondered how we would survive without his income for a year, and how he could walk away from all financial responsibility. I sincerely believe when you love someone you set him free to make his own decisions and support him in fulfilling his dreams, not try to control him in any way. I wished to give him unlimited freedom to do what his heart desired, to give him the freedom I so desperately craved for myself. What my parents did not know was if I had expressed any resistance to Rakesh's decision, he would not have cared about my opinion anyway and would have pursued this time off regardless of my input.

Rakesh believed this vacation was essential for his health, restoration, and accomplishing his goals. In my opinion, he always portrayed himself as a victim of life's hardships: his difficult childhood, challenging move to America, concern for his mother living alone in India, struggle with his visa and job requirements, fighting his lawsuit, excessive stress from the jobs he found unsatisfying. Dealing with the loss of his father at the age of twenty left him feeling weak, vulnerable, and powerless, so he seemed desperate to feel in control of his life again. There always seemed to be some excuse for all the stresses in his life.

But now, his visa requirement was fulfilled, our lawsuit was over, and these challenges were behind us. He reassured me, "*Anisha, our life will improve now and I will treat you better.*" Compassionate and understanding about his hardships, I was committed to easing his suffering in any way I could. I truly believed I could help him heal. I was convinced this year of rejuvenation would transform Rakesh and turn our lives around like he falsely led me to believe. Even though we would have to sacrifice a year living apart and his income, I believed our marriage would ultimately improve as a result.

In my mind, I also knew the time apart would permit me space to breathe, not be under his attack and constant control, and allow me to feel safe again. So we left our apartment of three years, transferred all of our belongings into storage in my parents' home, and I moved in with them. My husband took advantage of my parents' generosity and never offered to pay rent. He apparently felt no guilt about being separated for a year, leaving me to manage my own business, or how living in my parents' home would affect them financially. At this point, however, I was used to his sense of entitlement where he only considered his own needs. During that time I maintained my thriving acupuncture practice and kept myself immersed in the work I loved to avoid reflecting on the disappointments and divide of my marriage.

Indiana

I supported Rakesh's decision to spend the first four months living in Indiana pursuing a research project with a famous physician he had aspired to study with. I believed it was important to help him heal by fulfilling his heart's innermost desire. During this time, I was still eager to spend time together and made the commitment to visit him in Indiana for one week every month. Although I thought this time apart would bring us closer together and we would fight less, disappointingly, I was wrong.

Rakesh still seemed unhappy about everything I said and did. The constant critiquing and lashing out at me worsened. He would yell profanities, tell me I was spoiled, and justify insulting me. Once again, he disregarded my feelings and every comment appeared well designed to wound me deeper. This continued to defeat my spirit. If I had been emotionally detached or uninfluenced by my traumatic bonding, I might have seen his abusive nature with transparency but instead I was distracted figuring out how to help him. The blindness from my determination to fix my marriage consumed me.

Running out of Excuses

After spending four months in Indiana, Rakesh returned for two months in the summer to stay at my parents' home. Absence had once again made the heart grow fonder and living apart for several months seemed like it had done some good. We had several weeks when everything felt tranquil and I enjoyed the company of "nice Rakesh" again. He would be leaving soon for India, and I wanted to enjoy what little time I had with him. Now, I realize these "good periods" were deceiving because it made me trust, lower my guard, and believe the abuse would not continue. I became increasingly vulnerable for the next attack because I was so unsuspecting.

That summer was a turning point in the abuse. All the excuses Rakesh had made before for his violence were no longer valid. He would say, *"When I am free, the stress will end and things will be better."* I believed him up until that point, but now that he was "free" with no job, no responsibility, no expenses since he was making me freeload off my parents, what excuse could he possibly have? He was not working, enjoying a one-year vacation, pursuing his dreams, and doing what he had always wanted to do. There was no possible explanation he could give for continuing to treat me badly.

I also pointed out to him how incredibly stressful my life had been. Besides moving numerous times and fighting his lawsuit, I had written my first book, started my first business despite his attempts to hold me back, witnessed my mother suffer a stroke and my little sister undergo brain surgery, *and* put up with all his violence and abuse over the years. Somehow he did not validate my stress or felt it compared to his. I pointed out how despite my stress I was still patient, controlled my emotions, treated him well, and never lashed out at him. As expected, there was no response to my argument. His silence spoke volumes.

Infertility Struggle

One evening, we discussed visiting Rakesh's relatives for a weekend. After all the months of living apart and working diligently in my practice to support us financially that year, I desperately craved some time off, just a weekend getaway, nothing fancy or expensive. It was ironic that while he enjoyed a one-year vacation he did not believe I was justified in asking for a weekend off. Even though I expressed my desire to him calmly and reasonably, it triggered an explosive reaction I could not have anticipated.

Let me provide some background as to our discussion. After three years of marriage, we decided we were ready to plan a family and began the process of trying to conceive. Because our marriage had been filled with so many instabilities: moving numerous times, job changes, living in different states, fighting a lawsuit, and starting my business venture, a few years had passed before we were ready to be parents. Why did I want to have a child with this man? Because I believed as all women do that having a child would be fulfilling and healing, change our family dynamics, and it would make Rakesh want to be a better person. I also reasoned if I could not find happiness in my marriage at least I could find it in motherhood. At the time we did not anticipate our attempt would turn into a three-year struggle with infertility.

Each month when I discovered I was not pregnant, however, I experienced a mixture of grief and intense relief. I never shared this with my husband because questions were churning in my mind. If he could not be a decent husband, how could he possibly be a decent father? If he could not provide a safe nurturing home for me, then our children would not be safe either and I would not under any circumstances jeopardize the life of my child. The realization I could not trust him and he would not be a good father was frightening. What was I doing in a marriage with someone who was not fit to be the father of my children? Unable to process these questions, my denial triumphed.

Back to the current discussion, apparently leaving for a weekend was unacceptable to my husband because he believed we needed to try to conceive. His response to my idea was to bellow, "*What is wrong with you?*" over and over as his voice continued to escalate. He kept yelling until I could not handle it anymore and desperately begged him to stop.

Rakesh had the audacity to holler, "*You are not fit to be a mother! Your priorities are all messed up.*" How could my desire to go on a weekend getaway mean I would be a bad mother? There was no logic or justification for his words or behavior. Devastated, I was too shocked to react.

Processing

Rakesh stormed out of the room, and for the next few hours, I knew I did not want to be anywhere near him. He needed time to cool down and for the first time so did I. Fuming inside, I managed to remain silent and repress my anger. Questions flooded my mind. Why was he so out of control? What was wrong with him? Why was he making these accusations? What did they have to do with planning a trip? I told myself to let it go, calm down, and reasoned he did not mean it. My only recourse was to ignore his unfathomable behavior since I was too exhausted to confront him.

After waiting patiently for a few hours, I expected him to return, hoped he would apologize, admit he did not mean those harsh words, and tell me I would be an excellent mother. Otherwise, why was this man married to me in the first place? What was the point of starting a family together if he thought so poorly of me? Finally, I decided to face him and ask these difficult questions. I was not prepared for what I saw.

Despite the time that had elapsed, his face was still seething with anger. His eyes had a fierce intensity to them I recognized all too well. How could he have not cooled down? His face warned I should keep my distance and not approach him, but seeing him so infuriated triggered my anger that I had worked so hard to let go. I was the one who had been victimized, yelled at for no reason, and had justifiable anger. After all the times he had lectured me about learning to let go, why couldn't he do the same?

I was upset by his immature behavior and inability to listen. Despite my best effort at communicating my wish, he made it clear my desire to go on a vacation was unacceptable. Rakesh proceeded to walk towards me in an intimidating and threatening way, shove his face in mine, and back me up towards the wall. Saying I was scared was an understatement. I held my breath as I realized it was happening again, the same pattern, the same cycle, the same palpitations. But for the first time I was also furious, an emotion I had not allowed myself to genuinely experience before. Fear had been my survival mechanism, but my rage took over and I snapped.

Four years of being a victim of this man's anger was unbearable. I could not tolerate it any longer. A pattern had been set and I could see this was unacceptable. I lost control after so many years of suffering his injustice and slapped him across the face. Could he really blame me after being patient with him for so long? But I instantly regretted my action and hated myself for losing control. The fear of becoming like my husband was daunting. What was happening to me? I was alarmed I could do something so uncharacteristic of me.

The Explosion

I did not have much time to ponder these questions, however, because Rakesh responded with an intensity and ferociousness I had never experienced before. Slapping him had clearly seemed to offend his ego. He was probably thinking: *"Who do you think you are to hurt me?"* This triggered a fervent explosion of violence making everything up until that point seem trivial. As he lunged at me, that ever-present sneer on his lips, my husband seemed to morph into a wild animal attacking me. He slammed me against the wall, threw me down forcefully on the wooden floor of the hallway, and grabbed my neck fiercely.

I could not breathe for what felt like an eternity and truly believed I would be choked to death. I had an overwhelming feeling this was the end and my whole life was meaningless to have brought me to this point. The fear of knowing he could kill me was terrifying to say the least but it numbed me to the point of paralysis. My life was in the hands of what I could only label a crazy, possessed maniac who I had sworn to love and be with for life. I had no choice but to mentally shut down.

Yet, I willed myself to be calm, gain control, and stay alert. Used to being hyper-vigilant during these times of danger, time slowed down as I watched events unfold in slow motion. The only way to survive the trauma of that moment was to disassociate, leave my body, and witness the violence from afar. Cognizant my life was at stake and any movement was critical of further endangering me, I did not utter a word or try to resist in any way because this had only triggered more violence. I let him do what he wanted as he took my head and banged it repeatedly on the unforgiving wooden floor. Possessed with what I would say was an uncontrollable rage, he used all the strength he could muster. As his fury intensified, it seemed he was once again totally out of control and unaware of his actions.

The pain of the impact ricocheted through my skull and traveled to my forehead and temples. It was excruciating, numbing, terrifying. I had never experienced anything like it. He beat my head on the floor nonstop until I felt myself drifting out of consciousness... Saved by the distant sound of my parents' car returning home, he stopped immediately. If they had not arrived, I truly do not think Rakesh would have been able to stop himself from pounding my skull into the floor until it was broken, until I was dead, until I could no longer resist his power. I imagined my parents finding me lying in a heap on the floor. I could not fathom what I would say to them after years of living with this man's torture. After what I had just endured, there was no way to even trust myself to speak.

Despite the ordeal I had just been subjected to, my thoughts still loyally revolved around protecting Rakesh because it was my natural, conditioned instinct, what I had always done, what I had been trained to do. I had to think quickly because I could barely move, was too weak to get up on my own, and hardly coherent. Trapped in a dense fog of pain and numbness, I had no choice but to ask him for help. He was pacing angrily in the hallway. Even though my voice was weak, I pleaded, *"Rakesh, please lift me up and take me to my bed."* Condescendingly, with venom in his voice, he replied, *"Yes, sweetheart."*

I was shocked by his lack of concern. Couldn't he see I was hurt or how much pain I was in? He lifted me mechanically, carried me down the hallway, and threw me forcefully onto the bed. I begged him to give me some aspirin. Again condescendingly, he icily replied, *"Yes, sweetheart."* Of course, there was no acknowledgement of what had transpired. He left the room to inform my parents I was asleep so they would not disturb me. It was obvious he could not take the chance of them discovering the truth. I fell into a state of deep sleep from sheer exhaustion and excruciating pain.

The Aftermath

The next morning, I went into complete denial of the events from the preceding night. It was simply too much to process. We spent the day running errands as if it were a normal, casual Sunday. My damaged glasses were the first physical evidence of the abuse. I went to repair them at the store and heard myself fabricating a story to the employee. As I covered up the abuse with this white lie, Rakesh stood next to me perfectly poised and expressionless. Understanding his complete denial of the incident, I knew things were serious and this was unacceptable.

For the next two weeks, I suffered from unbearable neck pain and headaches traveling along the same route from the occiput to the forehead and temples as I did during the incident. For the first time, I considered visiting a doctor because the persistent pain was so alarming. I knew I needed medical care. But where would I go? I could not visit the hospital where my husband worked and jeopardize him or his job. No, I realized then, I had to protect him no matter the cost.

Even if I went to another hospital, there were Indian physicians everywhere who were bound to know my family or me. I thought of the disgrace of admitting what was happening in my marriage and knew no one could find out. Trapped and helpless, I resorted to living with the pain until it eventually tapered off. Rakesh nonchalantly dismissed my concerns and made it clear he did not want to discuss the incident. I thought of confiding in my family but the same question surfaced: how could I admit it to them when I couldn't even fully admit to myself what was happening?

I should have called the police. I should have told my family. I should have received medical care. But I would only have taken those actions if I had complete clarity, if I could have woken up from the mental fog of confusion, understood my husband's true abusive nature, or diagnosed the problem correctly. But I simply could not. Four years of abuse had worn me down. I was mentally and physically exhausted, too weak and defeated emotionally. At the time, I did not suspect this was evidently his clever strategy.

After this incident I played the charade of the happily married wife, mechanically going through the motions since it had become easy to do in a way. Nobody would have ever guessed what was happening in our home or the internal emotions I battled. The more Rakesh acted like everything was normal, the easier it was for me to mimic his behavior. In essence, I learned to fragment my life into the part that was abuse-free and escape as much as possible into the realm of work and time spent with my family to avoid dealing with the harsh reality of violence in my married life.

Breaking My Silence

The intensity of the abuse and the realization my husband could kill me numbed me. I felt a kind of paralysis I had not experienced yet. I learned to live with the excruciating pain and convince myself all the reasons why I should not visit a doctor. I learned to put my husband's reputation, job status, and immigration status before my own immediate concerns for health and safety. The numbness was a tremendous coping mechanism and essential survival technique I depended on at that critical moment.

Almost being murdered was a turning point. This was the most brutal act of violence committed yet. Coming out of my paralysis and inability to act for several weeks, I recognized the gravity of our situation; it was a serious, concrete problem we could no longer ignore. Whereas before I deceptively believed they were separate incidents, now I knew I could not lie to myself anymore. Knowing my life was truly in danger scared me to death. I had to reach out because trying to reason with my husband had obviously not worked.

In the four years that had elapsed, the abuse had consistently worsened. Becoming proactive, I called his mother and broke my silence for the first time. I described Rakesh's irascible temper, mistreatment, and physical violence. She seemed surprised but responded compassionately, "*I will talk to him when he comes to India and address this.*" Relieved this would be taken care of, I felt reassured confiding in my mother-in-law. I trusted her. She was devout, pious, and with her gentle demeanor I was confident she would get through to her son. Surely when he heard his behavior was unacceptable from his mother, whom he loved and respected, it would have to stop. She would make him see the error of his ways and put things into perspective for him. I had hope again for saving my marriage.

Panchakarma

Before Rakesh departed for India, we had one more incident in the summer of 2005. Visiting me at work while I ate lunch in between patient appointments, I expressed my desire to take a week off and receive *panchakarma*, an ayurvedic detoxification program. This had been part of my training in ayurvedic school and I truly believed it was an essential therapy to undergo every year as a way to focus on health and rejuvenation. I knew it would be invaluable to detoxify from all the stress and trauma of an abusive marriage and also prepare me for a healthy pregnancy. Without any warning, this discussion ignited Rakesh's uncontrollable rage.

He snapped, *"It is ridiculous for you to even consider it. Don't you know how expensive it is? You have no understanding about finances!"* Not only was his emotion inappropriate but also his choice to express himself this way in my office setting caught me off guard. Why was he incapable of having a mature and calm conversation? I wanted to point out the irony of him taking a year off with no income to contribute to our lives while I was the one supporting us financially, all the money he was spending on himself during the year with his travels and just having returned from a week of panchakarma himself!

I did not realize at the time this absurdity was another aspect of financial abuse. I knew he was being unreasonable and felt frustrated by my honest attempt to communicate my desires with him. But the pattern had already been set throughout our marriage that my beliefs, desires, and dreams did not matter and should not be considered valid or equal to his. The discussion was terminated by his abrupt departure. Once again, I had to put on my mask to function and continue to see clients while trying to forget our upsetting interaction. He never spoke about this with me afterward.

Vacation in India

I supported Rakesh's decision to spend several months in India studying yoga and visiting his mother who was lonely and desperately craved her son's company. Time apart mended my wounds partially because I still missed my husband terribly. The strain of working nonstop all year without a vacation and the stress of living apart made me forget the daily tension to which I had become accustomed. Rakesh brainwashed me to let go of the past and so I worked hard at forgiving him in that absence. It was easy to repeat his own excuses: he was stressed, he didn't mean it, we'll get through this, it will be a thing of the past.

My husband encouraged me to visit him in India, take off a month from my practice, and declared I deserved a break. The "nice Rakesh" was making an appearance but despite his insistence, I was reluctant to travel, break the momentum of my growing successful practice, and miss a month of income when I knew I had to keep up with the expenditure from his one-year vacation. After many persistent conversations, I finally relented since he made it too difficult to say no.

I traveled to India full of excitement and anticipation to be reunited after so many months apart. Not surprisingly, his temper flared our first day together. Rakesh snapped at me in the hotel lobby while trying to get directions. It appeared I had undermined his authority by interrupting him to tell him I knew the way to our destination and he seemed threatened by my confidence. I do not know why I expected him to be any different. Disappointingly, I realized time with his mother had not changed him. When I broke down in tears in the cab, he assured me he would not lose his temper again. But my trust was rapidly fading and it was increasingly difficult to believe him. I questioned why I had let him persuade me to visit India in the first place and already regretted my decision.

That month in India was mostly uneventful. I confronted him if he had spoken with his mother about the abuse as he had promised he would but was distraught to hear Rakesh say, *"My mother was too upset to speak with me."* I felt betrayed that his mother had let me down after confiding in her, placing my trust in her, and turning to her for help before anyone else. On our last day before leaving for the U.S. she spoke to both of us briefly. *"You both must love each other and treat each other well."* Incredulous there was no mention of the abuse or the physical violence, I wondered how that was all she could say. She acted like we both needed to equally make an effort to improve our marriage.

Stunned, I knew I did not need any coaching about being a better wife or putting forth more effort. After four years of focusing on improving myself, I knew now it was a diversion from facing the real issue: Rakesh's violence. My husband needed to hear what he did was wrong and it was imperative he changed his behavior. I was surprised his mother would not come out and say this directly to him. Much later I would learn her denial and refusal to take a stand encouraged the abuse to intensify and allowed Rakesh to feel empowered and unaccountable for his actions.

Returning to the U.S.

Once we returned to the U.S. Rakesh lashed out, *"You shouldn't have come to India and took up my time. I could not accomplish anything there because of your presence."* I reminded him he had invited me and despite my reluctance he had insisted I visit. These facts did not matter to him. I was shocked, hurt, and confused. I pointed out, *"I respected your other commitments and never interfered with your daily plans. I did many things independently since you were unavailable. On a few occasions I expressed how much I missed you and my wish to have more time together, but was that really such a terrible thing for me to say? What wife would not want to spend time with her husband, especially after being separated for an entire year?"*

His only response was to scold me for being demanding since I asked him to spend one day shopping with me in India. He knew I disliked shopping, and on the rare occasions I did, it was always out of necessity. I laughed at the absurdity of his comment. *"One day? Even in America I can count the days we went shopping together on one hand in the past four years of marriage. You do not realize how undemanding actually I am as a wife and how I have never really asked you for anything!"*

I was beginning to identify his immaturity despite the fact he was forty-years-old. There was no other way to put it: he was purposefully hurtful, ruthless, inconsiderate, and lashed out at me whenever he felt like it. He had no regard for my feelings, did not care how his language affected me, and made no apologies. Instead, I felt he justified his insults with more hurtful accusations that wounded my heart deeper. Mindful his statements were unfair and inaccurate, it did not diminish the pain. My heart only bled more hearing him continue to speak this way.

Anniversary in Vegas

In December 2005, we traveled to Las Vegas to celebrate our fourth anniversary. It was a special milestone and I hoped some time together after a difficult year apart would do us some good. As we enjoyed ourselves, I decided to risk opening up to him because our "fight" from the night before still weighed heavily on me. I tried to let the incident go, but it was unhealthy to keep burying my emotions. I needed to honestly communicate how I felt without fear of his reactions. Surely talking to him when he was in a good mood would be safe in a crowded hotel lobby. As soon as I voiced my hurt, Rakesh stopped walking abruptly and turned on me. Seemingly unaware of the people surrounding us, he snarled, *"Let's take this upstairs and get this over with once and for all!"*

He grabbed my arm gruffly and kept me close to his side as we walked silently to the elevator. Shocked by his sudden change of demeanor, I had not anticipated this but I could only brace myself for what was to come. While he yelled and unleashed his anger in the hotel room, I remained silent hoping to avoid a physical assault. After he stormed out of the hotel room, I cried for a long time. Calling his sister in desperation, I confided about our fight as I had turned to her on a few previous occasions. Always sweet and comforting, she reassured me, *"Anisha, everything will be all right. I am sure it is just a simple misunderstanding."* Because the alternative was too much to process, I chose to believe her.

That night for our anniversary dinner we sat silently without acknowledging Rakesh's earlier outburst. I stared blankly at our food when it arrived realizing I was too devastated to eat. My heart was heavy knowing it was not safe to express how I felt. This did not fit into my idea of a normal relationship. Unable to maintain the charade our marriage was okay, tears trickled down my face. Knowing this would ignite Rakesh's ire and he would blame me for making a scene in public, I tried to restrain them. The last thing I needed was guilt about expressing my emotions or making a scene but I could not hold them back.

What upset me more was that it was our fourth anniversary, a special day. Did he really not care these episodes kept occurring on birthdays, anniversaries, and vacations? Shouldn't those days at least be sacred and free from him lashing out? Did they not have meaning for him as well? I realized they did not. I felt there was no basic consideration for my feelings or meaningful days. Later, I would understand that my happiness threatened him. No day could be free from abuse…. No day was safe.

Chapter 23 TURNING POINT

The important thing is to be able at any moment to sacrifice what you are for what you can become. Charles Dubois

Major Changes to Come

With a heavy heart, I closed my prosperous three-year acupuncture practice in the beginning of 2006. After being financially successful with my first business and creating many meaningful relationships with clients, it was a challenging step to take but I felt there was no alternative. Spending a year living apart from my husband, I missed him terribly and felt a strong pull to be together to mend our marriage. After living in Chicago for four years I said goodbye to my family, friends, career, and hometown.

To fulfill Rakesh's dream of pursuing a one-year fellowship to advance his medical career, we moved to Memphis to start a new chapter in our lives. After applying to several fellowships and being rejected by them all, he was finally accepted into one because my friend generously convinced his fellowship director to grant Rakesh admission. Once again, my family connections assisted Rakesh in advancing his career. I was hopeful a fresh start would allow us to put the past behind us and move forward. Always optimistic, I believed the abuse was over.

Isolation Sets In

That year in Memphis was another turning point in our relationship when I became increasingly isolated. We moved to a city where we knew no one, far away from home, living in an unfamiliar part of the country. For one year I accepted this sacrifice to make my husband's dreams come to fruition. While he was at work all day long, I remained trapped in our small apartment without a car. I considered working in an acupuncture clinic for a year but without a vehicle there was no way to pursue a career. Up until then I had used my parents' extra car for four years. I disliked taking advantage of their generosity but Rakesh claimed we could not afford a second vehicle and refused to pay my parents for the car I was using. Of course, his financial abuse was well disguised at the time.

Rakesh emphasized the importance of saving money for our future but our personal funds were depleted from his three-year expensive lawsuit, leaving his job, expenditure for his one-year vacation, and extra cash we would need to compensate his significantly reduced salary for his fellowship. I agreed with the principle of saving money so I was not opposed to owning one car, but I did wonder why we had to make so many sacrifices when the average American family owned two cars. He was a physician, I was an acupuncturist with a great income while I was working, surely we could still afford a second car. I resigned myself to the situation even though there was no way for me to get out, nowhere for me to go, and no one for me to talk to.

Another Divorce Threat

Relatively uneventful months passed and it seemed once again like the abuse had faded into the background. Out of the blue, one morning at breakfast my husband told me simply, *"I cannot put up with you anymore. You are driving me crazy. I want a divorce."* After numerous threats over the years, he declared his intention as if he could easily wash his hands of our marriage. Incapable of realizing the devastating weight of his words, he muttered under his breath, *"Get out."* A scowl befell his face and fire lit up his eyes. I registered the warning signs of his mood and behavior, but I observed this time was different from other incidences; he did not seem out of control and was not yelling. This time, I noted he spoke with authority, clarity, and chose his words precisely. I was speechless. Fighting the urge to yell, I calmly exited the room to avoid a physical fight. For the first time, I did not try to reason with him.

Overwhelmed by the thoughts racing through my mind, I questioned if this was really the end of our marriage. How was I supposed to process what was happening? Why was he kicking me out? What had precipitated this? Where was I supposed to go? Scared and confused, I realized deep down I was furious. How could he be this way after all the effort I had put into saving this marriage? I felt betrayed after so much insistence he would change and mend our marriage he could say this so casually. It all seemed so pointless… this could not be the end!

Silently, I searched for my purse and keys while I kept myself composed, but I was shaking inside feeling my life falling apart. I longed for a bag with some clothes, money, and important items. Unprepared, I could not make a fast getaway. Later, I would learn domestic violence centers always encourage women to create a safety plan to facilitate leaving quickly with essentials. This practical advice would have made a world of difference at that time.

Unable to think straight, my heart was racing. We only had one car. I did not know anyone or have any place to go. My only option was to start driving, maybe go to my parents' home, even though it was at least ten hours away. How would I get there? I had no cash, but that was not important. I simply needed to get out. All of my instincts told me to run. After a few minutes of frantically getting my belongings together, Rakesh told me in an unemotional, detached voice, *"Don't go. I didn't mean it."* Maybe he realized we only had one car and he would be stranded. So I stayed, not because I wanted to, but because my anguish paralyzed me and I was incapable of driving anywhere in my state of emotional devastation.

Emotional Toll

After years of living trapped with this man in an unhealthy relationship dynamic, I felt utterly defeated. I struggled with the constant emotional upheaval after Rakesh lashed out at me and then expected me to simply forget his hurtful comments. How was I supposed to keep mending my broken heart and heal my wounds? I strived to find meaning in these incidents, communicate my pain to him, and find a healthy solution as my idea of marriage kept shattering from one moment to the next.

His continual denial of his abusive nature made me truly question if I was going crazy. I grappled with returning to an everyday, normal life after these incidents, erasing them from my mind like they never happened, maintaining the charade of living in wedded bliss. Looking back, reliving these abusive incidents frequently in my mind was just an aspect of my post-traumatic stress disorder. Rakesh had succeeded at the typical abuser's strategy of systematically wearing me down.

It was clear we desperately needed professional help. I could no longer handle this on my own. Turning to his family for support made no difference. His mother and sister had spoken to him privately, but ultimately whatever transpired in those conversations I was not allowed to be privy to, failed to prevent the abuse from escalating. If anything, it seemed to have exacerbated it. I had suggested therapy on several occasions but Rakesh refused to participate, denying there was a problem. Later, after he had admitted to his abusive nature, he declared, *"A therapist will not be understanding of Indian cultural issues. It will be ineffective and a waste of time."*

I begged him for permission to see a therapist on my own if he was unwilling to attend couples therapy, but he claimed we could not afford it and made it into a financial issue. I desperately needed to talk to someone, vent my emotions, and release my pain. He insisted, *"Anisha, I am your best friend. You should be able to talk to me about anything. I will be patient and listen to you. I am committed to our marriage and things will change for the better."* Convincingly, he said exactly what I needed to hear at that moment to reassure me. Too weak to protest, I made the mistake of believing the "nice Rakesh." Blind hope in me persisted. In retrospect I would surmise his apparent motivation was to keep his true abusive nature a secret and protect his reputation at all costs.

Disillusioned

Something within me began to shift at this time. I witnessed with increasing transparency my husband was the one with the problem and not me as he had brainwashed me to believe. Rakesh had strategically distracted me for many years as I focused dutifully on self-improvement, addressing my multiple "flaws" and weaknesses. I mistook the rule everyone was responsible 50% in a relationship and failed to see that does not apply in abusive situations where only the perpetrator can be accountable for his violent actions. I misinterpreted the idea an Indian wife should be accommodating and suffer in silence, preventing me from taking action sooner.

In the meantime, the abuse had grown progressively worse year by year, but I was trained to not focus on him, to let go, to move on, failing to recognize this was just another aspect of the perpetrator's methodical strategy. No matter how much he tried to blame me for his violent nature, I began to slowly identify how he manipulated the situation and redirected the emphasis away from himself. No, I realized, even if he believed I was the most irritating person in the world, I could not be blamed for his anger, irritation, impatience, or violence. Only *he* could take responsibility for his actions and his lack of control over his emotions. This was a monumental step for me to break free of the shackles he had imposed on my mind and redirect the focus on him.

Family Vacation

In the fall of 2006, we joined my family for a weekend trip to the Gulf Shores, our first vacation with them. Up until this point, Rakesh had enforced his strict policy to not travel with my family. Exhausted after a long drive late at night, we then had to wait in the parking lot for some time due to a mix-up with our hotel keys. As I spoke about the room key fiasco, Rakesh silenced me in a low, irritable voice: *"I don't care what you have to say."* Simultaneously, he grabbed my arms and shook me. How could he talk inappropriately to me this way for no reason, especially with my family nearby? I tried to calm myself as he walked away, but I found myself following him. Demanding an explanation, I questioned, *"Why are you speaking to me this way? It is unacceptable!"*

As Rakesh's face contorted with emotion, I immediately recognized the rage lurking behind his eyes. Smiling viciously, he grabbed my arms again and squeezed them tightly. I could not escape his immobilizing grip. Once again, he seemed to be completely unaware of his actions and the pain he was inflicting. Numbness radiated down my arms, while he simultaneously stepped on my foot leaving me unable to follow him. Confronting him had only made things worse, instead of receiving the apology I knew I deserved. Once again, there was no concern for my well-being, no remorse, no apology. Why did I believe every time it would be different? I laughed at myself for still hoping he would come around even though his heartless nature was crystal clear.

Returning to the parking lot, I felt defeated, unable to confront him with my family present. I was forced to pretend like nothing had happened and assume my role of the perfect actress. At this point, I had maintained the façade for so long it was easy to do and in some ways the only thing I knew how to do. I watched amazed as Rakesh casually interacted with my family. The weekend was ruined but I could not spoil my family's vacation or tell them their perfect son-in-law was a jerk. I realized a part of me hated him for talking to me that way and continuing to treat me like dirt. It was the strongest my emotions had been so far, but I had no way to reconcile my feelings for this man who was my husband after all. I felt doomed to be stuck in this crazy marriage as I oscillated between hope and despair.

His True Nature Surfaces

Once again, we went through a good period of several abuse-free months. I spent that year in Memphis immersed in writing a fiction book, a new endeavor to express my repressed creative side. I waited patiently all year for Rakesh to show some interest in my work and desperately wished to share all the exciting new ideas taking shape in my story. One night I finally begged him to read a chapter. He yelled with intense irritation, *"Your book is not important. Stop bothering me about it. I have no interest in reading it. I don't want to ever hear you mention it again!"* Shocked, I tabled my emotions and patiently explained how deeply hurt I was by his lack of interest. Surely he would understand where I was coming from. No... it was apparent he did not care what was important to me.

Wasn't part of being married being interested in the life of one's spouse? He was inconsiderate of my feelings, immune to my tears, and completely unaware of his destructive actions. His cruelty and insensitivity amazed me. Rakesh was blinded by his anger and emotions to the point he could not see what was right in front of him-a wife who was wounded, hurting, in pain. He was a man with an ego made of steel, suffering from what I would deem the erroneous belief he was always right, no other viewpoint or reality was acceptable besides his own. This left me in a world where my own feelings had no reality, my own experience was always discounted, and I was perpetually confused.

Fateful Dinner Party

At the end of 2006, we had our first dinner party in Memphis, another turning point in our abusive union. We had invited over the only couple we knew from my husband's hospital, southerners who had never eaten Indian cuisine. I was nervous and questioned whether they would like the food, find it palatable, or be overwhelmed by the spices. Rakesh seemed irritated by my concerns and exclaimed, *"Anisha, you are too stressed out!"* His assessment was not inaccurate but I had no idea why this would trigger an intense explosion of anger.

Suddenly, he started yelling condescendingly and walked towards me aggressively. His eye were fiery and his glare sharp as a dagger. The pattern was all too familiar; I could more quickly recognize the danger I was in but I still felt trapped and defenseless. I knew I had to take precautions to get away from him. What bothered me most was the expression he wore. A smile, a smirk, whatever it was, it indicated to me that pleasure was derived from his actions. He jabbed his finger at my face and sneered, *"You-stop talking!"* Outraged, I said emphatically, *"This is not okay. I will not tolerate you speaking to me this way!"* Later, I would learn a victim's stance to defend herself is a turning point that threatens the perpetrator so he intensifies his abuse to regain control.

As he strode towards me menacingly, I backed up from one room to another but in a small apartment my options were limited. Escaping to the bedroom was impossible because he refused to let me get away. With every physical incident he always followed me and blocked my path. In retrospect, his apparent strategic tactic was to prevent me from disengaging from the dynamic that allowed him to feel in control. My escape would keep him from asserting his control over me, and in my opinion, he was addicted to feeling in power. When I walked away, it appeared he felt powerless. He had admitted many times to being cornered and bullied when he was young and victimized by other school kids. I believe one reason he had to victimize me was to feel better about himself to make up for the helplessness he had felt as a child.

The Full Length Mirror

Cornered by the bedroom door, I could not escape. Without warning, he threw me with all the force he could muster. I flew across the room, at least six or seven feet away. A full-length mirror was propped against the far wall. I slammed into it at full force. In slow motion, I saw my limp body make contact with the mirror. I floated above my body and watched the scene from a distance. Learning how to disassociate from the trauma was natural at this point. I listened to the crisp musical sound of the glass breaking.

I watched the mirror shatter into a million pieces as it came crashing down all around me like snowflakes falling furiously to the ground, enveloping everything like a blanket. This was not real; it could not be happening to me. Detached, I was witnessing a scene from a horror movie. Pieces of glass scattered everywhere, all over the room, covering my inert body. I lay crumpled on the floor and felt sharp pieces of glass piercing my skin, scalp, neck, arms, and legs. Overloaded by the trauma and the dangerous impact, I slipped out of consciousness....

As I woke up slowly in a daze I could hear his voice screaming from a distance. Disoriented and still not fully alert after the traumatic incident, I willed myself back to reality. I had no idea how long I had been lying there paralyzed, crumpled in a heap on a bed of glass. I listened calmly, trying to decipher his words, able to detect the furious undercurrent of anger in his voice as sharp and penetrating as the glass. He screamed *"Get up!"* over and over again while his wrath continued to build. Gingerly, I tried to move but every muscle in my body resisted me. I was sore; everything ached. I was afraid to move and lodge a piece of glass in deeper. I could not respond or get up. After all this, I couldn't believe he was irate I was not cleaning up the mess. How in the world did he have the audacity to yell at me after what he had done?

Seeing my unresponsiveness, he lifted me roughly out of the pile of glass and threw me flippantly onto the bed. I moaned in pain and explained, "*Rakesh, please be gentle. There are pieces of glass still stuck in me.*" It did not matter; he did not believe me and did not care. Over and over he bellowed, "*There is no glass!*" Slowly, I made myself sit up despite the pain and cautiously lift my neck so embedded pieces of glass could fall onto the bed. Despite my attempts to express I was bleeding and hurt, he kept denying it. How could he not see what was happening right in front of him?

The Evidence

Despite my wooziness, I carefully examined myself for cuts and pieces of glass since my husband clearly did not offer any help or believe I needed any. Blood stains covered my shirt where the glass had penetrated. Still dazed, I removed the shirt and attached pieces of glass. There were multiple cuts and scratches. The deepest cut on my upper arm was oozing and I reeled with disgust. I felt sick and dizzy just looking at it. Pointing to my arm, I asked him, "*Now do you believe me?*" He made no comment, showed no concern, and was not unfazed by my injuries. At the moment when I was so weak and vulnerable a little tenderness would have been comforting.

Meanwhile, Rakesh worked frantically to pick up the glass, stick it in a bag he could toss away, and make sure there was no remaining evidence of the incident. I threw my bloody torn shirt in the trash, disgusted by the sight of it. I wanted it out of my sight completely. It never occurred to me to think of this as evidence, take a picture, or keep the bloody shirt. The shock and trauma of the incident kept me from thinking with any lucidity. I could barely function in the moment let alone think long-term about how to protect myself or the consequences of discarding the evidence. Silently, he found a Band-Aid and cleaned the deep gash in my arm after I begged him to help me. I was grateful for his assistance.

After this traumatic incident, I maintained my composure. Once again, I put myself in the position of being a therapist, trying to rationalize with him. In a quiet voice I asked, "*Do you realize what you have done?*" To my amazement, he denied having any involvement in the incident. He insisted I simply tripped over my own feet and lost my balance. Patiently, I explained the law of physics: "*My body hit the glass with an intensity and force equal to the force you exerted when you pushed me. Even if I had tripped there is no way I would have landed on the other side of the room, traveled that far a distance, or hit the mirror with such an impact.*" He acted like he had no idea what I was talking about. I might as well have been speaking in a foreign language.

The Doorbell

My mind was reeling. How could he take no responsibility once again for his actions? How could he not acknowledge his destructive and violent behavior? His denial and lack of remorse stunned me. It did not fit into my rational, logical world. At that precise moment, the doorbell rang.

Our dinner guests had arrived. Under other circumstances, I probably would have been ready to reach out for help after this incident, maybe by calling my family or leaving for a women's shelter. I could barely function and was severely traumatized. If it had been company who knew me, they would have seen right away I was not myself. But these were total strangers I could not share something so personal with. Besides, what would I tell them? I had evidence-I could show them the broken glass or the bloody shirt Rakesh had stuffed into a trash bag, but I never thought to do so.

In slow motion, I made myself presentable to attend to my guests, and my training to be a good Indian hostess kicked in. The night was uneventful while I served dinner but I remained quiet and withdrawn. Consumed by my throbbing headache and achy body, every muscle hurt. My mind was in a fog. I could not think straight and felt numb inside. I was barely present but my husband made up for it by entertaining our guests the entire night. It amazed me to watch him be funny and charming, laughing without a care in the world. I honesty began to wonder who was this man to whom I was married?

Escaping to Chicago

The next morning, Rakesh drove me in silence to the airport. Luckily, I had planned a trip to visit my family and the timing could not have been more perfect for a getaway. I desperately needed to escape from my husband, our apartment, the uncontrollable violence, and the insanity of our lives. I could not look at his face or bring myself to say goodbye. He tried to hug me but I walked away without looking back. Frankly, I did not care if I ever saw him again. This was a monumental shift for me. He was a monster and I detested him.

I stayed at my parents' home for ten days. If it was not for that refuge I do not know how I would have continued living with him. I needed to be around people who genuinely cared for me, loved me deeply, and would never do anything to hurt me. I needed their comfort, protection, and safety. In my parents' loving home, I began to see what a contrast there was between my husband's behavior and the people who truly loved me.

This would have been the time to confide in my parents, tell them everything, ask them for help, and attempt to escape my marriage. But I was paralyzed by the trauma and kept my silence partly because it was so ingrained. How could I begin to convey the trauma I had endured, articulate my confusion, and share the truth about my sham of a marriage? My parents believed we had an ideal relationship. In their presence, Rakesh always treated me well, complimented me, praised me, and made it seem like he admired me in every way. He did that in front of everyone actually and I was frequently told, *"You are so lucky to have a husband who adores you so much!"*

There was no reason for my parents to suspect anything was wrong. All of our abusive episodes were private, isolated moments no one had ever witnessed. Who would believe me? I was humiliated, embarrassed, and confused. How could this be happening to me? For the first time I did not call Rakesh at all for those ten days while we were apart. My mom asked if something was amiss but I reassured her everything was fine. I wore long sleeve shirts to cover up the gash in my arm. Every day I fought my nausea at seeing the depth of my wound when I cleaned it, knowing what Rakesh had done. I tried to bury the weekend's incident but my flashbacks were intense.

I avoided looking into full-length mirrors as much as possible, but when I glanced at my reflection, I relived the trauma of that horrific experience. I saw myself lying crumpled on the floor with broken glass surrounding me. I was beginning to recognize my victimization and the effects of post-traumatic stress disorder (PTSD). *This was not okay. This was not love. This was not supposed to be happening.* I went through those days mechanically, numb, dead inside, unable to process my life. Something was shifting internally. I knew I did not trust my husband anymore and this realization was shocking. I could not forgive him for what had happened. But I was trapped; Indian women simply did not divorce.

A glimpse of clarity was finally emerging the more space I had apart from him. I was nearing my breaking point. More than five years of enduring this abuse was enough. For the first time, I identified these were the signs of physical domestic violence. I had never used that term before. This was a serious problem, a crime punishable by law. I could not keep living like this. But who would I tell? I had never once thought of calling the police and knew I could never involve them. Too much was at stake. I could not put Rakesh in jail. It would be humiliating for him and for our marriage.

Of course, the Indian thought ran through my mind, *"What would people think?"* No, he was not a criminal. The consequences for his job would be disastrous and he would certainly lose his medical license. His immigration status would be affected and he would not be considered for citizenship, or worse, he could be deported. What wife would want her husband to lose his job, his license, be put in jail, or kicked out of the country? Understanding these consequences somehow made me more resolute to fix our marriage.

After my ten-day stay at my parents' home, they left for a trip to India, and I was forced to return to Memphis. Perhaps if they had remained in the country, I would have stayed with them longer, because for the first time I was certain I did not want to return to the same home as that fiend, be a victim of his violence, or continue to live in peril. I had reached my threshold of tolerance. I did not possess the energy to pour infinite effort into saving a doomed marriage.

I could not pretend anymore nothing had happened and resume living a "normal life." For the first time, I grasped how much help I needed to recover from my trauma, feel safe, and mend my broken heart. The focus was starting to shift towards myself. It was groundbreaking to see I was truly a "victim" after my husband had repeatedly blamed me over the years and held me responsible for his unrelenting abuse.

Returning with a Heavy Heart

When I returned, Rakesh astonishingly tried to win me over with flowers and a poem declaring his love. I wanted to laugh. Is that all he thought it would take to fix things? Without commenting, I placed the flowers at the exact spot where both the full-length mirror and my heart had shattered into a million pieces. I needed to replace the memory of pain with something beautiful and symbolic of my heart healing. Later, I learned how an abuser redoubles his efforts at the honeymoon phase when he perceives his victim is gaining clarity and strength to walk away. I had heard of the cycle of violence with the buildup of tension, explosion, and honeymoon but never made the association with my experience since there rarely was an apology or make-up period.

Astonishingly, Rakesh now seemed sincere about changing, making amends, and acknowledging his abuse. This was a first. He had never made this much effort to win me back before. He tried to be attentive, patient, and allow me to voice my anger, frustration, and pain. Encouraged, my false sense of hope prevailed. At least he was trying, right? Maybe things were changing for the better, I told myself. I should give him another chance.

After all, this was my husband. I made a commitment to spend the rest of my life with this man. I could not just walk away, no matter how difficult it became. I could not throw away five years of marriage if he was willing to sincerely change. My strong personal beliefs to honor commitment and my Indian cultural values held me captive. Divorce was just not an option. I did still love him, and if he was sincere about making it up to me, truly changing, and being a new person, I longed to believe him.

Now that I understood this was domestic violence and could label it as such, we could receive professional help. He had a recognizable, identifiable problem we could address. Our situation was definitely out of our hands, but I was convinced therapy would make a difference. When I suggested visiting a therapist yet again, he staunchly exclaimed, *"We don't need it! Nothing like this is ever going to happen again."* Fine, if therapy was not an option, we would figure out another way. I resolved to patiently coach him and teach him right from wrong since I could not accept my marriage as a failure.

Surely if I just worked arduously enough we could fix our marriage. No relationships were easy; they all had their own trials and tribulations, yet everyone made it through them somehow. What I realize now is I once again shifted all my energy and focus to him, while neglecting my own needs, my own emotions, my own pain. This mired me more deeply into the abusive marriage. It was beginning to look like there was no way out of my misery.

Yet looking back, I realize he still never admitted to making a mistake. It was as if it was impossible for those words to come out of his mouth. He admitted to hurting me profoundly and upsetting me, but he never said he was sorry for physically assaulting me. He never accepted he had been the one to slam me into the mirror and still insisted I tripped and made a big mess for him to clean up.

It was obvious we lived in two different realities: he evidently lived in a narcissistic world where he was always right, where his own needs had to be met and mine did not exist, where his authority and power over me could not be questioned. He always justified his anger that defied logic. I lived in a world where I kept rationalizing events, letting go of the past, and practicing forgiveness. I still believed a relationship was a 50-50 partnership and I had to do my part at keeping the marriage intact not acknowledging I had actually been doing 100% of the work.

Chapter 24 DAWNING OF CLARITY

If we can really understand the problem, the answer will come out of it, because the answer is not separate from the problem. Jiddu Krishnamurti

Moving to Atlanta

After completing a year of fellowship training, researching possible jobs around the country, and flying for interviews, my husband accepted a job in Atlanta. Finally, after five years of moving around, being unsettled, and living with the majority of our belongings in storage, we were relocating to our final destination. The tide was turning in our lives and our new future awaited us. I recognize now this theme of hope for the future sustained me for many years and kept me from acknowledging the full impact of the abuse.

In March of 2007, we transitioned into a short-term apartment and by April Rakesh started his dream job with a lucrative income. It would still take two years to become a partner but he would be established with no more financial worries after many years of sacrifices. Now there could be no more excuses for his behavior, and I assumed our life would be abuse-free. Sadly, I was wrong.

Kindergarten Shenanigans

That spring the abuse took a new turn. After casually asking Rakesh a question and being ignored several times, I was perplexed by his blatant refusal to acknowledge my presence. Did he not care I was speaking? In a loud and clear voice, I asked him one last time, *"Rakesh, can you hear me? I am talking to you. Why are you not answering me?"* This triggered the most immature outburst I had seen yet. He made faces, mocked me, even imitated the way I spoke. I had never witnessed this before and was surprised by this level of juvenile behavior coming from a grown man at the age of forty-one. Calmly, I asked, *"Do you realize you are making faces at me? Do you see how immature you are being right now?"* Of course, it appeared he did not.

As if mocking me was not enough, he vehemently shouted, *"You are completely psycho!"* Despite being hurt by this insult, I forced myself to maintain my composure. *"Rakesh, how can I be psycho when I am just asking you to not ignore me?"* Reasoning was futile. He proceeded to walk towards me aggressively with that fiendish smile, back me into the bedroom, push me down on the bed, and grab my arms forcefully. Tired of this familiar routine and his only way of dealing with his purposeless anger, I let myself be passive and limp.

All I could do was wait patiently for him to calm down and let him do what he wanted to my physical body. Later, I understood I had reached the point of hopelessness victims experience when it seems useless to struggle or fight back. How had I come to accept this behavior as normal? Disgusted with myself, I realized that at least some emotion, even if it was disgust, was finally breaking my layers of numbness.

Taking a Stand

A few weeks later, I found myself trapped in another familiar abusive situation. The good periods in between had become increasingly shorter from a few months to a few weeks or less and an abusive episode always seemed to be lurking around the corner. In our apartment one night I tried to escape when Rakesh walked menacingly towards me, towered over me, and backed me into corners. His fiery eyes and possessed smile haunted me. I was sick of feeling trapped.

All I wanted was to put distance between us and give him space to cool down and gain control of himself. Why could he not understand this and let me be alone? Despite my repeated attempts to explain how his behavior made me feel uncomfortable, threatened, and unsafe, it did not register. I begged him, *"Rakesh, please stop putting me in these compromising positions and respect my wishes."* These attempts to break through to his rational, logical side proved ineffective.

Running away from him, I entered the bathroom but he stood staunchly blocking the doorway refusing to budge. At that critical moment, all the panic and fear of being a victim of his physical abuse for so many years kicked in. I could not take it a second longer. I was determined to protect myself, not be passive and let him do whatever he wanted to me again. I had been in this vulnerable position too many times. I knew I was fighting for my life. A new light was dawning as I saw with transparency the familiar patterns of his violent behavior.

Using all my strength, I was desperate to close the door and not let him come inside at any cost. I pushed the door repeatedly hoping he would leave, begging him to give me space. Refusing to surrender, that night was a turning point to reclaim my life and take a stand. Surprisingly, Rakesh finally backed away and I seized the chance to run to the bedroom and lock the door. Even though it seemed he wanted to make me feel guilty for what I had done, I won a small victory that night by not letting him overpower me. Astonishingly, it took me six years to realize he would never take responsibility for his actions or show remorse.

Panchakarma

Later that spring, we committed to a week together of *panchakarma*. Ideally, a husband and wife should purify their bodies through this ayurvedic cleansing and detoxification ritual before trying to conceive a child. This had been my dream for years. We had been married five years and attempted to get pregnant for more than two years at this point. Due to our impaired communication and his lack of sensitivity to my emotions, we never discussed our struggle with infertility but it did affect me deeply. After all the unhappiness in my marriage, I questioned why I could not fulfill this dream of being a mother. Only later would I see that this was a blessing in disguise.

During our week of panchakarma, which was supposed to be a time of relaxation and rejuvenation, we had several heated discussions and it was obvious all lines of communication were breaking down. I expressed my frustration about his lack of support for my career and new acupuncture practice. Emphatically defending himself, Rakesh hollered, "*You just don't recognize how supportive I am being.*" I tried to explain, "*The definition of being supportive is a subjective feeling. If I am not feeling it, that means you are not being supportive.*"

To clarify this for him further, I listed the ways in which he was unsupportive. "*You called me selfish for thinking of my own career before yours, although I have made endless sacrifices and put my life on hold for six years so you could fulfill all your dreams and get your dream job. I gave up my successful practice in Chicago and spent the previous year in Memphis living as a housewife trapped in our apartment without a vehicle. After our three-year struggle with infertility you tell me to wait until we have children and they are grown before working again! I don't see how you think you are being supportive with these absurd comments.*" Of course, reasoning with him was pointless. He still seemed convinced as usual he was always right. His apparent narcissistic personality made him unable to tolerate any opinion other than his own.

When his yelling amplified, I fled the hotel room to be safe. I could not stand to be near him. I drove aimlessly down unfamiliar streets in a new city with no idea where to go. From a parking lot I called my sister and told her Rakesh was being a jerk. It was the first time I had hinted of unhappiness in my marriage to one of my family members. I was attempting to reach out for help but was confounded how to ask for it after years of silence. After keeping a secret for so long, I could not bring myself to confess even though it was killing me inside.

If she knew the truth, my sister would never forgive Rakesh, respect him, or accept me living with a man who treated me poorly. It was important to me my family respected and liked my husband. Since I had nowhere else to go, I eventually returned disconcerted to the hotel room. Rakesh tried to comfort me without acknowledging his wretched behavior. I was mentally exhausted from this routine. How could this be happening during our week to rejuvenate, rest, and heal ourselves from all past traumas? I realized the past would keep repeating itself and haunting us. I would never be free of his violence. I would never find peace.

Our Final Move

In June 2007, we finally moved into our beautiful new home after much anticipation. I felt positive it would bring us a fresh start allowing us to put the past behind us. This was our last move after seven moves together in five and a half years. On our moving day, I was surprised my husband casually announced, "*I need to attend a volleyball tournament.*" Surely he did not expect me to do everything on my own even though I had done that for all our previous moves. Surely he would want to help when he realized how much work there was.

My philosophy was to allow him complete freedom and never restrict him. I truly believe when you love someone you set him free to be who he is and make his own decisions. Continuing the trend of depending on me to take care of everything, feeling no responsibility, and lacking the ability to see when I needed him, he left for the game. It was clear I was on my own once again.

The responsibility of having a new home, settling into life in a new city, and starting my own business was overwhelming to say the least. I knew I could not keep running the show on my own anymore. For the first time I vocalized, "*Rakesh, I need help. Running a home is simply too much for one person to manage. I need you to take on a little more responsibility.*" One afternoon when I was sick in bed I asked him to retrieve a package outside the front door and expressed my exasperation. "*It would be nice to have a little help with things around the home.*" Discussing chores and household responsibilities was a topic every married couple had to work out, but this was one of our first conversations in five years.

His response was to yell, "*You are making a big deal over something trivial. You are so controlling!*" This argument could be considered more typical of any husband/wife encounter and not particularly abusive, but with our history it just perpetuated the tone of abuse. He did not care I was sick in bed. He resented being asked to retrieve a package. Our new home, which I believed would be our sanctuary and provide a new beginning, would alas not be free of abuse. Our history would continue no matter where we were living and my hope for improvement was shattering.

To ignore the fact my marriage was falling apart, I kept myself busy. I spent the first two months in our new home immersed in furnishing it, buying essentials, and decorating. Both of our families planned to visit us in August to perform a *satyanarayan puja*, a ritual Hindu ceremony to bless our abode. Astonishingly, it was a struggle to convince my husband to agree to this. Once again, I had to fight for something important to me while my husband accused me of being demanding and unreasonable. I thought something so simple as blessing our home, a ritual every Indian family does when moving to a new place, he would have agreed to more readily and been supportive. I could not comprehend his objection, which he failed to clarify. I had at last caught on to his apparent drive to act on any chance to antagonize me.

Launching My Business

From August to December 2007, my mother-in-law moved in and her presence restricted us from spending any time alone together. During this time period, I struggled to start my fledgling business, spent five months negotiating an office lease with an unreasonable landlord, and found contractors to finish the flooring and build-out. Rakesh was not available to discuss any of the changes in my life. The distance between us was growing at an alarming rate. I noticed something in me had changed. Exhausted, I could no longer devote 100% of my energy into saving the marriage. After patiently waiting for six years and making endless sacrifices for Rakesh's career, I had to reclaim my life by pursuing my dream to have a career again.

In September, it was finally time to move into my office. I looked forward to this milestone with much anticipation and excitement. Our weekend was busy since Rakesh's relatives were visiting from out of town so I waited until Monday, Labor Day, to ask him for assistance. He had mentioned taking time off work if necessary to help me move and be supportive. This was encouraging but the timing was perfect to move on a holiday. That morning he declared, "*I can't help you move. My priority is to spend time with my mother. She is home alone all week and I need to take her out sightseeing.*"

After entertaining his family all weekend, I was stunned. I told him, "*I understand the desire to spend time with your mother but she is living with us for several months. There will be many weekends and numerous opportunities to do so. Can you really not help me just this one day? Do you really expect me to move into my office by myself?*" Finally, he relented but made it clear he was not pleased. Why did he always make it seem I was being difficult and demanding? My excitement quickly evaporated and I felt guilty for upsetting him and his mother although I knew I had not asked for too much. My life seemed to have become one disappointment after another.

Rakesh also made it clear I was not to use any of our personal funds for launching my business and declared I would once again have to rely on my father. I had tried to put aside the funds I had grossed during my three-year practice in Chicago into a separate account to use towards my anticipated next business in Georgia but Rakesh had protested. He depleted much of that money with legal bills and what was left I was not allowed to access. Defeated, I asked my father for a business loan so I would be able to work. Neglecting my needs, Rakesh would lavishly spend any amount on his whims, whether they were legitimate or not. Later, he claimed he required an exorbitant $10,000 to spend on holistic dental work for cosmetic reasons. He ignored my desperate plea for spending those precious funds on my start-up business.

Living as Roommates

For several months we fell into a pattern of co-habiting like roommates instead of spouses. I struggled to start my business, maintain our home without any assistance from Rakesh, and wondered how to prevent the complete disintegration of our marriage. He returned late in the evenings, had dinner, and then dedicated the remaining few hours chatting with his mother until bedtime, reminding me of being the third wheel all over again. He made no effort to spend any time alone with me, prompting me to finally express clearly, *"Rakesh, I need at least five minutes of your time alone every day without your mother present to talk to you."* Although it put me in an awkward position and I certainly should not have had to ask this of him as his wife, it had come down to that. He said okay rather reluctantly and unconvincingly.

One night, I asked him to speak to me privately in the bedroom. I needed to discuss matters regarding the home and my business but also convey I missed him terribly. I felt neglected. I needed him to make some effort, if not for the home or the business, at least for me. Didn't he feel the need to connect and know how I was doing? Sadly, I realized he did not. He showed up after an hour and I reminded him of my request for five minutes alone every day. He rudely responded, *"You are being demanding and unreasonable. My mother suffered a terrible loss twenty years ago when my dad passed away and I have to do everything I can to make it up to her and ease her pain."* I was taken aback. What did that have to do with spending time with his wife? Did he really think spending five minutes with me was unreasonable?

I sympathized deeply with his family and the loss they suffered but everyone I knew who had lost someone found a way to cope, deal with the loss, and move on with their lives. Rakesh's family was not the only one who had ever suffered. I had been more than patient in accepting this. For years, he had used his father's death as an excuse for being abusive to release his anger and pain, but the tragedy was not a reason I should have to suffer at his hands. Patiently I explained, *"There is nothing you can do for your mother now, twenty years later, to take away that suffering. That is not your role."*

I brought him back to our conversation and asked why he could not spend time with me despite what had happened in the past. He exclaimed, *"You are being unreasonable to ask that because my priority will always be to my mother. I cannot give you even those five minutes a day because of the tragedy of losing my father twenty years earlier."* His apparent crazy, illogical thinking was becoming crystal clear. This was not adding up in my view of what a true marriage was supposed to be. We essentially led separate lives for those five months, communication was nonexistent, and what was left of the marriage rapidly deteriorated.

Swinging a Broom

That fall, we threw our first dinner party in our new home. An hour before our guests were supposed to arrive, we rushed to clean the kitchen. My husband swept the floor and accidentally ran the broom over my foot. Casually I remarked, *"Rakesh, you should have warned me you were sweeping and I would have moved out of your way."* Surprisingly, he ignored me, something he had been doing more frequently this year and I could not fathom why. *"Rakesh, can you hear me? Do you realize I am speaking to you?"* There was nothing more degrading than the person you love acting as if you did not exist.

He approached me once again with seething anger in his eyes and that unnerving smile that were all too familiar. Swinging the broom in the air at me several times, I flinched, bracing myself for the impact. He was bound to lose control and I would inevitably have to pay the price. What kind of a husband hits his wife with a broom? Did he not care his mother was in the next room? Up until now I thought I would always be safe if I was not alone. He would not dare act this way in front of anyone else, right? He had successfully kept his true nature hidden until that time from even his own family.

At that moment when I flinched, the realization I was a victim of trauma jolted me and I woke up in a flash. I understood my symptoms of fear, flashbacks, and intrusive recall all these years were manifestations of PTSD. My persistent palpitations had returned, and even though I informed Rakesh about them, he blamed me for being too weak and sensitive. As a physician, how could he mock me and have no concern or regard for my physical well-being? I saw lucidly now how messed up our marriage was, how unconscious he was consistently about his actions, and how the identical patterns kept reoccurring.

This was not my first breaking point, but the culmination of these realizations slowly over the years that opened my eyes. Different pieces of the puzzle were assembling themselves rapidly in my head as his abusive pattern became more transparent. Exasperated, I needed to express my frustration. In a calm voice I said, *"Rakesh, please come to the bedroom so we can discuss this privately without your mother walking in. You've just done a million things wrong to upset me."* His denial was persistent. Instead of apologizing over the incident in the kitchen and acknowledging swinging a broom at his wife was not normal behavior, he grabbed me forcefully, shook me, pushed me down on the bed, and pinned me down with his weight on top.

Ganging up on Me

Hearing the commotion, Rakesh's mother rushed to break up the fight. Although she could not see us, the sounds coming through the door were enough to raise her concern. This was the first time a family member had heard us fighting. After opening the door, Rakesh shockingly did not cool down in front of his mother but proceeded to lie to her face. *"Anisha is upset I accidentally swept a broom over her foot."* He did not realize I could not have cared less about that incident and was enraged about him ignoring me, swinging the broom at me, and then the physical assault in the bedroom. His denial amazed me and I saw my husband in a new light. Not only was he abusive, hurtful, and violent, but I discovered he was a liar as well. His mother turned to me suddenly and said vehemently, *"Anisha, how can you be upset about something so trivial? That is not right!"*

How was I supposed to respond to this? I felt like they were ganging up on me. The truth was getting muddled. I had to defend myself when I had not even done anything wrong. After so many years of being calm, I was losing control and could not suppress my emotions or my tears. I was hurt, couldn't they see that? *"Rakesh, please tell your mother the truth!"* I begged him, but he refused. Several times I attempted to explain to my mother-in-law what happened, but she refused to let me speak and insisted I calm down. Why would she not let me simply tell her the truth? In frustration, I locked myself in the bedroom and cried hysterically. His mother forced him to apologize but he just screamed, *"I am sorry!"* I tried to point out he was yelling but they both emphatically said, *"Anisha, you are, too!"* This was ridiculous.

After awhile when I felt more serene, I went outside and heard Rakesh speaking to his mother in a hushed tone. He said, *"Do you see how she is? How difficult she is to deal with? Do you see how out of control she is?"* I couldn't believe it. Hearing these words was like a slap in the face. How could he possibly make this all about me? Was he really going to take no responsibility? Wasn't he going to tell her the truth about the physical assault in the bedroom?

This turning point demonstrated how strong his denial was, what he would do to defend himself and protect his image, how he would always put the blame on me. This was the first time I saw his denial in action in front of his own mother, the person he loved and trusted. He was capable of lying to her. This was getting uglier and more complicated than I could imagine. The difference from earlier abusive incidents was I always felt he was unconscious of his actions and out of control. What I could not deny this time was his conscious deliberate lies. My confusion was dissipating; there was no way to fool me now. There was not much time to process this incident before the doorbell rang. Our dinner guests had arrived.

Dinner Party

Once again, I put on my mask of the happy wife while we entertained our dinner guests even though my heart was heavy. I contemplated calling the police for the first time but realized it would throw a damper on the dinner party and my mother-in-law as a witness would likely zealously defend her son. I wondered why so many of these incidents were precipitated before socializing, and I realized Rakesh's insecurity must be at a high since he seemed threatened by the presence of others coming into our home. On guard, it was as if he had to ensure no one could detect his true nature by working extra hard to pour on the charm and act like the doting husband.

Rakesh also knew socializing was something I enjoyed so maybe he took pleasure in ruining it for me. Many of our friendships had been jeopardized by his insecurity that he covered up by confronting others, diminishing their opinions, and demanding they accept his authority unquestioningly. It was challenging to maintain friendships in this constrained, tense atmosphere.

That night my husband claimed he confessed the truth of physically assaulting me to his mother. I noticed he did this privately, disrespecting my wishes, refusing to include me in their conversations. Relieved his mother knew, I finally felt hopeful she would feel some compassion for my plight. I trusted now that she had partially witnessed our fight, she would make Rakesh see he could not treat me this way any longer. I was happy she asked him directly, *"Why are you treating Anisha this way?"* His response was to be expected, *"Because she irritates me and drives me crazy."* How could he keep blaming me for his use of physical violence and take no responsibility for his actions?

Lecture from Mother-in-law

The next day, my mother-in-law sat me down and had the audacity to lecture me for an hour. *"Anisha, you must learn to be a better wife. You cannot irritate Rakesh anymore. What do you do to irritate him?"* When I sat there silently unable to answer her, she deftly responded with her own ideas. *"Maybe you are too close to your family, maybe they call you too much, or you call them too much. Perhaps you travel too frequently or are too independent. Do you think you should spend more time in the kitchen? Maybe you don't cook enough and he is not eating enough Indian food. He says you are too selfish since you want to work and have a career. Maybe you should stay home more."* Did she really think our diet was the root of the problem?

I pointed out I had spent six years putting my life on hold and I did not think waiting any longer to work was justified. This did not faze her. Unrelentingly, she continued with her suggestions. *"Perhaps you are too controlling and demanding. Maybe you do not think of his needs enough. Maybe you need to do more for him and stop thinking about yourself."* It was a grueling hour, but I sat in shock listening to her. I had spent so many years of our marriage examining what I needed to change about myself, scrutinizing my role, feeling like I was partially to blame. It had taken me a long time to step back and say this was not my fault, the abuse was strictly his problem. But now his mother was making it all about me again.

I could only assume she had been brainwashed to believe her son and merely repeated his words to use against me. I was beyond frustrated. I was crushed, hopeless, and betrayed. I was puzzled why she was so tolerant of her son's violent behavior and did not react with more outrage as I would have expected. I thought about how I had turned to her over two years ago and hoped he would listen to the woman in his life who he loved and respected the most to be motivated to change his behavior. I thought of everything I had done for his mom over the past six years and wondered what had she really done for me.

Breakthrough in My Awareness

After that incident, I started privately researching domestic violence online when Rakesh was not home. I looked at websites, read definitions about abuse, studied profiles of abusers, and learned my rights to be safe in my own home. I discovered how to clear my browser history on my computer so he would not know which websites I had visited. I went through checklists and marked many behaviors on the list that applied to our marriage. I was appalled; we seemed to match an undeniable, distinguishable pattern.

With much trepidation, I called a hotline for a South Asian women's organization and spoke to a counselor asking to be anonymous. The counselor professed, *"Using violence is a conscious choice. Your husband is not out of control."* This was a revelation to me. What did she mean? All these years how could it be possible he was in complete control, consciously choosing to be violent if he loved me? His behavior only made sense if he did not love me at all. I could not make sense of this but her words stuck in my mind. I replayed them over and over: *"He is consciously choosing to use force and violence against me."* The realization was numbing to say the least.

I thought of all the excuses I made for him over the years: his temper, uncontrollable anger, hardships and obstacles he had to overcome, and the fact he was always misunderstood. I had reasoned he was opinionated, spoke forcefully, and had an aggressive personality. All the times he made it seem like he was totally out of control, or could not remember what he had said or done, it was a lie. I read profiles of perpetrators, learning they were experts of manipulation and deception. It came naturally to fabricate excuses, avoid accountability, play the victim, and blame others. I realized now Rakesh consistently *chose* to resort to physical violence during each encounter to purposefully hurt me and destroy my spirit.

It Takes a Neighborhood

My awareness was slowly increasing as I felt my fog of despair and confusion lifting. Settling into our new home in Atlanta for the past six months allowed us for the first time in our married life to socialize with other married couples. Living for years in isolation from our frequent moves from state to state prevented us from truly developing meaningful friendships. Attending social events in our neighborhood with other married women started to open my eyes to how abnormal my situation was in contrast and realize that not all marriages are created equal. I listened as these women openly talked about their husbands, problems with in-laws, and vacations they wanted to take. They spoke about their careers freely, and I discovered their husbands did not inhibit their ambitions or interfere in any way. They did not dictate which days their wives should or should not work or prioritize their mothers before their wives.

In my mind, I wondered how their husbands gave them so much freedom, permission to pursue their own dreams, and flexibility in making their own independent decisions. All the years of isolation had prevented me from seeing how many of my freedoms had been stripped away. I observed the natural progression of these couples growing relationships, embracing having children, and allowing their families to flourish. Quietly I reflected on how my marriage lacked any sense of growth and in fact was exactly the opposite, characterized by destruction. Exposure to these neighborhood women was a turning point to clearly see what a prisoner I was in my own home.

Visiting My Sister-in-Law

The rest of the year was filled with other incidents but the details were not so important. The same basic pattern repeated itself with increasing regularity. In November 2007, we visited my sister-in-law for a weekend. My mother-in-law approached me about extending her ticket to stay with us before returning to India. I felt trapped. I did not want to say no or be an inconsiderate daughter-in-law. I always did whatever I could to make her happy and accommodate her wishes, but something deep down inside of me knew it was a recipe for disaster. After spending five months in our brand new home with her and having no time alone with my husband, I could not honor her request. I desperately needed time alone with Rakesh to salvage our marriage in any way possible. We were at a critical breaking point and time alone together for real communication was our only hope.

I spoke to my husband privately and informed him of his mother's desire. I told him simply, *"Our marriage is falling apart and we need time alone."* I never said his mother was not welcome. Instead of hearing the desperation in my voice or understanding the meaning behind my words, Rakesh criticized me. *"How can you not respect my mother's wishes and make her our first priority? How can you not invite her into our home?"* I could not believe it. After everything I had done for him and his mother, this was the first time I placed my needs first. Did he really not care our marriage was deteriorating? Was it not as apparent to him as it was to me?

He proceeded to lie to his mother, *"Anisha does not want you to stay with us. We always fight when you come to visit because Anisha does not like your presence."* I was shocked by his blatant fabrications and immature way of handling this. How he could say this when I welcomed his mother to our home with open arms every time, had no ill feelings against her, and sacrificed so much time to devote to her needs? I was the one who spent the most time with her since Rakesh was at work. Why was he acting this way? This was the second time I had caught him lying to his mother. The realization my husband was a liar was rapidly bringing me clarity.

That night, in my sister-in-law's guestroom, I refused to sleep in the same bed as him. I needed distance. Being near Rakesh made me sick to my stomach. My feelings towards him were growing stronger; my anger and hatred were penetrating the frozen layer of numbness. Comprehending he was abusive, a liar, and did not love me was melting away my confusion. Refusing to let me sleep on the floor, Rakesh forcefully threw me on the bed and shook me. A wave of excruciating back pain coursed through me and I fell asleep in tears. *"I will never forgive you for this. I will never let you treat me like this again!"* Surprisingly, Rakesh apologized. *"This will never happen again. It was a mistake."* Six years of violence was not a mistake; it was calculated, methodical, and intentional. I knew better than to believe his empty promises.

Trip to Costa Rica

A month later, we were in Costa Rica on a one-week vacation at my husband's insistence. The last thing I desired was to be on a vacation with the man I despised but he had already booked the non-refundable tickets without consulting me since he did not care about my opinion. Spending six thousand dollars for this trip fundamentally clashed with my belief system of wasting that much money on a single week. I told Rakesh those funds would have allowed me to pay rent for my start-up business, buy a computer for the office, or allowed me to afford a second vehicle when I lived trapped in our apartment. He reassured me I would have plenty of money for my business once it was established. My argument did not matter; if he felt entitled to spend a luxurious amount of money on this one week for himself, I could not protest.

Thankfully, I had a brief respite from any abusive incidents. Our trip was the calm before the storm. Some part of me deep down felt it was our last time together as husband and wife. I could see the end was near. I was drained mentally and physically. I could not hold on much longer or sustain our charade. Costa Rica was a beautiful country and I chose to enjoy the landscape while engaging in many activities separately. Reflecting at the beach, I contemplated the direction of my life and searched for meaning. I questioned how my marriage was serving me. As I quietly kept to myself, I felt the distance between us growing infinitely bigger and watched our lives separate in a surreal, detached manner.

Coming Full Circle

Returning home from vacation, I quickly fell back into the routine of pretending my life and marriage were normal to preserve my sanity. I was overwhelmed by how much we still needed to do for our new home, and I knew I could not do it alone. For my birthday weekend I made a special request to drive to a neighboring city to shop for furniture and visit his relatives. I knew Rakesh hated shopping, but I had rarely ever asked him for help before. The day was uneventful but by evening his irritation levels reached an all-time high.

In a public parking lot, Rakesh suddenly blew up at me. Trying to avoid a scene, I simply turned around to get in the car and avoid engaging in any sort of discussion with him. I knew he would not be reasonable or speak calmly and I had no patience to listen to him be a jerk on my birthday. Enraged that I refused to engage in this charged dynamic with him, he proceeded to yell, *"You are a f*cking idiot. You drive me completely crazy. This marriage is definitely over. I am divorcing you."*

Completely taken aback, I was speechless. From his irritation over shopping he was suddenly divorcing me? Exactly six years after his first outburst on our honeymoon and on my birthday it was happening again. We had come full circle. A part of me felt like laughing inside at how ludicrous it was to still be with this man. Why was I so patient and understanding with a man who repeatedly showed he was totally unreasonable and treated me so wretchedly? I questioned for the first time whether I really still felt any love for my husband or was merely attached to what was familiar. Did I still care for this man who seemed to despise me and consistently demonstrated his disrespect for me?

No matter how much I felt like he was driving me crazy, I had never yelled at him, swore, or threatened him with divorce. I tried to be calm, patient, and understanding out of my love and respect for him, but now I was beginning to doubt myself. I resigned myself to sit in the backseat and cry my heart out as we drove back to his cousin's house. The intensity of my emotions overwhelmed me.

I longed to speak to my parents, break down and tell them everything, but they were in India. I craved their love and support, wishing desperately they could rescue me from the nightmare I was living. If only I could run to their home and take refuge in a safe place. I sobbed uncontrollably and felt my heart being ripped apart, realizing my husband did not love me, could swear at me even on my birthday, and feel no remorse or sympathy. Our marriage really felt over for the first time. Six years of effort and I could not do it anymore. The more I wept, the more he ignored me as I drowned in my heartbreak.

Silenced Again

It was not ideal we were spending the night at his cousin's home. I was determined to speak to someone and break my silence. I needed help. I could not cope with this emotional turmoil on my own. But I was exhausted, suffering from a splitting headache, and could barely think straight. What would I say and would they even believe me? Everyone believed Rakesh was the perfect husband who praised me, adored me, and respected me. He had successfully fooled them all.

I pleaded with him, *"Please break the news to your family we are getting a divorce. We cannot pretend like everything is alright all evening in front of them."* He refused with the declaration, *"My mom is the first person who should know so we will wait to tell them. You cannot tell them anything."* Defeated and silenced once again, I was too tired to play the perfect actress this time. I excused myself from the dinner table informing his family I had to retire early because of a throbbing headache. My husband enjoyed himself late into the evening, laughing and talking with his family. He never came to check up on me or apologize. He seemed to have entirely forgotten it was my birthday.

I recalled the surprise I had planned for his birthday just the month before. I flew his sister into town without him knowing, made Rakesh take the day off of work, and drove his family to Epcot Center in Orlando since none of them had ever been. His mother thanked me profusely for planning such a wonderful day and for always making such an effort to be considerate of them. Not once had my husband ever done anything special for me on my birthday or any other day. Not once had he ever done anything for my family.

The next day, we drove for five painful hours in silence back to Atlanta. I was trapped, suffocated by his presence, overwhelmed with my heartbreak. He lied to his relatives and claimed we had to leave early because of an emergency at work. I was astonished seeing how easy it had become for him to lie and cover up the truth constantly to protect his image in front of everyone. That night, New Year's Eve, was a blur. We stayed in separate rooms and did not speak to each other since there was clearly nothing left to say. Avoiding each other completely, we bided our time before the real storm would devastate our life.

Chapter 25 WAKING UP FROM A NIGHTMARE

It is never too late to be what you might have been. George Eliot

New Year's Day

A time of new beginnings, a fresh start, my undying optimism made me feel blindly hopeful there was some chance we might salvage our marriage. Two days had passed since my devastating birthday when Rakesh had declared our marriage was over and forced me to remain silent until he shared the news with his mother. Unable to keep living in this tense and charged atmosphere waiting for him to make a move, I decided to finally break the silence.

I begged him, "*Please call your mother in India.*" I had to hear him say the words "*the marriage is over*" to her simply because my mind could not accept it. I needed confirmation this time was final and different from previous threats. Part of me still secretly, desperately, hoped his mother could make things right between us. I wanted her to convince him to be reasonable, apologize, make it work, and not divorce me. I had failed but maybe she as a mother would not fail us now. Surely we did not struggle in vain for six agonizing years to have it end like this.

Rakesh blew up over my request. "*Stop badgering me. Get off my back!*" How could I possibly be badgering him when it had been two days since we spoke last? I could not fathom why he was angry when I was the one who had been treated poorly on my birthday and had justifiable anger. Why could he not just call his mother? I was enraged at how far this had gone. Six years of pent-up rage exploded inside me as I exclaimed, "*How dare you talk to me this way! How dare you treat me like this!*" It felt healthy to vent my emotions finally instead of staying calm and patiently trying to reason with him.

Enjoying the fact he had pushed my buttons, he taunted, "*Come on, hit me, take a swing, you can do it!*" What had come over him? Why was being physical the only recourse he could think of? Why couldn't he resolve this in a mature, adult fashion without involving violence? Over and over again he kept repeating, "*Hit me!*" Emphatically I replied, "*I do not want to hit you. That is not going to resolve anything. I do not want to resort to being like you. It is ridiculous you won't speak calmly with me!*" I was furious by this juvenile behavior I had tolerated for way too long.

He proceeded to walk towards me aggressively, put his face in mine, corner me, and demand I hit him. At my breaking point, I could not withstand his abuse anymore. I refused to let myself become his prey again. As he grabbed my arms wearing his venomous smile, I pinched his cheeks in desperation and asked, "*How can you just give up so easily after six years of being married and refuse to make any effort to fix things? Why don't you care about me or ever apologize when you've hurt me? Why am I the only one in the relationship doing all the work to keep it together? If you truly love me then isn't that worth fighting for? Don't you want to change?"*

Even though I had no intention of hurting him, my long nails left marks on his face where I had pinched him. I was ashamed and horrified at what I had done. What had happened to me? Later, I would learn victims who are violent in self-defense are often led to believe by their abusers they are at fault but if he is not intimidated or threatened by these actions, it is not abuse. My head was reeling with new insight. He did not know how else to handle conflict or how to behave in any other way. After years of trying to reason with him I saw he could not be reasonable or rational. Sadly, it dawned on me my husband did not have the skills, ability, or the desire to make the necessary effort to fix the mess of our marriage.

Betrayed by My Sister-in-law

Refusing to acknowledge my questions, my pain, or my tears, Rakesh left the house abruptly to go for a jog. Once again, I was perplexed by his actions and priorities. Why didn't he wish to resolve our issues? Abandoned, I faced the tremendous rage within me and knew something in me had snapped. Despite anything I had experienced previously, this was my true breaking point. I did not know how to continue with my meaningless life or face the enormity of my emotions. The only thing I was certain of was I could not go back to married life as I had known it up until then or survive another day with this man.

Clarity flooded my mind, and I knew it was critical to reach out for help. I considered calling the police but I remained reluctant to take any incriminating action against my husband. From online research I learned I could call the police even if he verbally threatened or pushed me. Looking back, there were countless incidents when I could have reported him, but I chose instead to protect him. In this scenario, I knew he would blame me for being the aggressor and had the nail marks on his cheeks to defend himself. Where he had grabbed my arms violently and shook me had conveniently not left any evidence.

In desperation, I called his sister and begged for help. *"Rakesh told me on my birthday two days ago he was divorcing me. Can you please speak to him and tell him to be reasonable?!"* Reacting to the panic in my voice she replied, *"Anisha, please calm down. You are making a big deal over something trivial. Everything will be fine."* How could she downplay my emotion as if nothing serious was happening? *"No. You are wrong! Nothing is fine, things are not okay, I am not safe, and I urgently need you to intervene. I could have easily called the police right now but my choice was to call you instead."* Her fiery response completely shocked me. *"Anisha, it takes two to have an argument. Rakesh told me you initiate the violence many times. You need to examine your role in this!"*

I could not believe what I was hearing. I was infuriated, livid, outraged. How dare she tell me to look at my role? How dare she believe his lies I was the violent one? My head was spinning realizing he was twisting the facts to protect himself so I seemed abusive. How was this possible? The craziness of our situation hit me. Now he was lying to his sister as well as his mother. His violent behavior had been difficult for me to process, but I was clear lying was unacceptable. His blatant fabrications were another clue this was not a man I could trust. I hung up the phone and knew in my heart I would never call his sister or speak to her again. She had betrayed me after I had looked up to her, confided in her, and placed my trust in her as an elder sister all these years.

Even though his mother and sister were cognizant of the physical abuse for the past two years, had supposedly spoken to Rakesh privately and told him to treat me better, it had not been enough. Their lack of intervention and failure to take a stand against his behavior ultimately empowered him. Essentially, they had done nothing to stop him or protect me allowing the violence to escalate during that time period. Their tolerance of our situation should have been a sign abuse may run in the family. For the first time, I realized I was furious they had let me down after confiding in them instead of my own family. I understood their loyalty, but they had a responsibility to protect me from danger when my life was in jeopardy. Betrayal was the only fitting word to describe their unforgivable actions.

Confiding in My Best Friend

I longed to speak to my parents but they were still traveling in India and I had no way to reach them. Panicking, I decided to call my best friend who I had kept in the dark about my marriage not wanting to share this secret outside of the family. But I could no longer contain my emotion and the enormous well of anger I possessed terrified me. I needed someone who could help bring me back to my senses. After six years of silence, confessing about my fight with Rakesh was one of the most difficult things I ever had to do.

She responded, *"Oh, Anisha, Rakesh is just being Rakesh. You have to accept he is impatient and unreasonable and learn to live with it to a certain degree. You know he will never change."* I knew she would not say this if she knew the context of our fight and the history of the abuse. I could not tolerate hearing anyone be accepting of his behavior. I broke down and confessed Rakesh was physically abusive only to be greeted with dead silence on the other end. It took her a moment to process the shock and enormity of my words. She told me emphatically *"Anisha, you are not a woman who gets pushed around and beat up!"* I exclaimed, *"I'm not?"* Humiliated, I realized that was exactly who I was and who I had let myself become for the past six years. The insight was crushing. She told me urgently to get help and leave the home because I was not safe.

Before I had time to calm myself or leave, Rakesh returned from his jog. I bolted for my car but he chased me down before the garage door opened and I could escape. Begging me to come inside, he reassured me, *"Everything will be okay. I will move out of the house into a hotel for awhile and give us space. I know you are not safe here with me anymore."* Things had become critical and I was surprised and impressed at his radical suggestion, volunteering to leave, and his comprehension of the gravity of our situation. The "nice Rakesh" who I had not seen in ages was back, and I was falling for his trap. His kindness and sincerity touched me, and I realized how much power this man still held over my heart. With a single kind gesture I could be drawn to him again and my anger would dissipate.

My mental exhaustion overwhelmed me; I could not think straight. I no longer had the strength to resist or protest. All I knew was another day in his presence would make me go insane. I assisted him with gathering his belongings and ironically packed his bags like a dutiful Indian wife. The next day he moved into a hotel and we did relatively well with our separation. It was a desperately needed break from our daily, tense interactions. For the first time in years I felt my head was clearing a little although the heinousness of our predicament was sinking in.

Reaching Out

At the end of January, Rakesh moved back home after our trial separation of two weeks. We agreed to resume interacting slowly. It did not take long, however, for tension to escalate and the abusive atmosphere to seep into our life. One night after another explosion of his uncontrollable rage, I asked him to speak calmly. After he refused to listen to my request, he started taunting me over and over, *"Anisha, can you be calm?"* He kept mocking me, trying to push my buttons and trigger any sort of reaction.

Despite the challenge to remain composed, I refused to give him the satisfaction of reacting. Deciding it was best not to engage in any sort of dialogue with him since communication was futile, my only choice was to flee the scene. I grabbed my keys, purse, and phone and escaped. Not really knowing where to go, I drove through the streets aimlessly at night. This pattern had become all too familiar. I recognized it was not normal to flee my home because I felt unsafe.

While I waited for him to cool down, I called a friend from an empty parking lot. I confessed my marriage was a sham and a failure, but still noticed how I defended him in many ways and minimized the abuse. Listening to my voice, I asked her, *"I sound like one of those women, don't I? A terrified woman who is a victim and lives in fear of her husband?"* After so many years of silence I realized how crazy my story sounded. Not speaking about it had resigned me to my fate. As I shared the truth and the facts became more transparent, I began to appreciate my husband's true abusive nature emerging through the layers of confusion he had created to deceive me.

Radha Leads the Way

During this time period, my girlfriend Radha was emerging from her ten-year abusive marriage. I witnessed her growing stronger, having the courage to make such a monumental decision, and taking the necessary steps to break free. She planned her escape at nightfall with her four-year-old son to drive to another state and ultimately be free of her dangerous husband. After she reached a safe refuge, she joined support groups, visited domestic violence centers, and took advantage of receiving support she desperately needed.

She mentioned a great book that opened her eyes called: *Why Does He Do That? Inside the Minds of Angry and Controlling Men*. I still could not bring myself to tell Radha the truth about my own marriage, so I wrote down the title and told her I knew someone who might benefit from it. During the month of January when Rakesh and I were separated, I read that book from cover to cover several times. I can honestly say that book is what saved my life. After watching the web of confusion being spun thicker all around me for years and constantly being blamed for instigating his abusiveness, I had clarity and perspective about my predicament for the first time.

Bancroft's book offered remarkable insight and demonstrated how our marriage fit an exact pattern. It was as though the author had a video camera in my home that precisely described our interactions. I was awakening from a bad nightmare where I had been trapped for six long years. It was not until later that spring I finally admitted to Radha about suffering in silence with a terribly abusive husband. She was shocked just like everyone else with whom I would share my secret over time.

Marriage Counseling

In January, I told Rakesh firmly, *"The only way to save our marriage is to get outside help. There is no way for us to solve our problems on our own anymore. If you do not agree to marriage counseling, there is no way I will continue to stay in this marriage!"* After begging for two years I finally put my foot down and let him know I would not tolerate his excuses anymore. It had taken my complete breakdown and willingness to walk away for him to realize I was serious. I begged him, *"Please prove to me my patience and love for the past six years won't be in vain. Prove to me you love me the way I love you-completely, totally, and unconditionally."*

He had refused therapy before because of his apparent pride declaring I should only discuss my issues with him since he was my best friend, as well as claiming it was too expensive. He protested, *"A therapist will only convince you to leave me because that's what they all do. Is that what you want? We should only see one if divorce is what you seek."* But I held my ground and he reluctantly agreed after hearing me speak so affirmatively about walking out. I found a counselor who advertised she handled domestic violence issues. Over a two-month period we visited her for about ten sessions. I felt a mixture of hopefulness and doom as I saw how desperate we were. Our marriage was a sham and I was guilty of perpetuating the sham over the years by failing to be honest with myself.

In our counseling sessions, we spoke to Gina only about the verbal abuse and not the physical abuse for several reasons. After keeping my husband's secret for six years, it was a challenge to open up. I needed to feel comfortable with Gina, know I could trust her, feel safe discussing our issues, and build a solid relationship. It seemed easier to tackle the verbal abuse first and discuss the physical abuse in later sessions. Fearing she might be required to report to some agency was another reason not to mention the physical abuse right away. Rakesh offered no objections.

Despite everything that had happened, I still wanted to protect the man I loved and defend him so his career, medical license, or immigration status would not be jeopardized. Saving our marriage remained my number one priority. Compromising his status in any way was not in either of our best interests. My thoughts of protecting him were stronger than trying to protect myself. I also kept silent because I was nervous to openly discuss the abuse in front of Rakesh and was terrified how he could possibly react. The biggest reason, however, was I could not face my humiliation and admit I was a victim of physical abuse to anyone else when I still struggled to admit it to myself.

During our sessions, my husband painted a picture of himself as a victim to my mythical "controlling, demanding, manipulative, and obsessive-compulsive personality." Gina's perception was shaped by what he said; she erroneously assumed his description of me was accurate. He never admitted to the abuse but used words to express he was sorry I felt hurt without taking responsibility for my suffering. After being quiet for the first few sessions, Gina was impressed when Rakesh became more vocal and expressive about his feelings.

Gina felt he had made a breakthrough and this was progress. On several occasions when I tried to defend myself on some issue, she would interrupt and say, *"Let him speak. This is a guy who has a hard time opening up. Look at how much progress he has made."* The outcome of our therapy: I was continuously silenced by both my husband and therapist. I watched in disbelief as my husband was charming, convincing, dominated conversations as he usually did, and succeeded at subtly winning Gina over.

Gina's Analysis

Gina's analysis dumbfounded me even more. She said, *"Anisha, you are too controlling. You have taken away his power and his feeling of being a man. He needs to feel like a king in his own home."* Too shocked to respond, I listened to her solution. *"We need to find ways to make him feel more powerful and in control, to feel like the king of his castle. We will conduct an experiment for the next two weeks where he will have all the power and make all the decisions. You are allowed to express your opinion, but he will have the final, ultimate say."*

This thereby effectively empowered my husband to feel justified in doing whatever he desired and let him believe I should have no voice, which was exactly the wrong message an abuser needs to hear. I questioned this woman's professional background and training because she clearly did not seem to know anything about domestic violence. Her next solution was to help us divide the household chores so he would participate more in domestic life. I pointed out this was helpful but not our primary goal for therapy nor did it address our principal issue of abuse. She responded, *"One thing at a time,"* as if the abuse was less of a priority and we could wait to deal with it later. Her inability to understand the urgency of our situation amazed me.

I confided to Gina privately about the time he swung a broom at me when his mother was present and then lied to her about being abusive. She encouraged me to bring it up in our next session with Rakesh. When I did so, Gina responded irritably, *"Anisha, we've already discussed this. Why are you bringing it up again?"* Before Rakesh had a chance to respond, Gina zealously defended him. *"Don't you think he was ashamed and embarrassed? Don't you think it is hard for him to admit this and tell his own mother the truth?"*

As difficult as it may have been for him, she justified his abuse, protected his lies, and made it seem as if I was unreasonable for not understanding the situation. After that last session I left in tears and refused to ever see Gina again. I could not believe what was happening. Our last resort, professional counseling, had completely backfired. Gina's statements were appalling, unprofessional, and aggravated his abusive mentality. My husband felt more powerful and increasingly justified for using force against me knowing no one would hold him accountable for his actions and he could essentially get away with being abusive.

Confronting our Therapist

My husband moved out of the home and while we were separated continued to see Gina on his own several times. He had found a therapist essentially who did not hold him accountable for the abuse and made him feel powerful and justified. Believing every word he fed her, she harped on how I needed to work on my "controlling behavior." In March, I decided to call Gina and confess I was also a victim of physical abuse. Even though I had not shared this with her before, I thought it appropriate for her to know if Rakesh planned to continue therapy with her.

Gina's response was surprising. *"I am not responsible for my clients not being completely truthful with me. I can only work with the information you give me. You came here saying you wanted to fix your marriage so that is what I tried to do. I usually do take the side of the victim,"* implying in this case she was not. She showed no concern as a therapist for my well-being, the fact I was a victim, or how difficult it was for me to confess to her. Most therapists would assume there might be physical abuse if there was already verbal abuse or it might be difficult to open up and discuss if I felt unsafe.

I also recommended she read Bancroft's book: *Why Does He Do That? Inside the Minds of Angry and Controlling Men*. I told her it was an excellent resource on domestic violence and elucidated clearly why couples therapy is ineffective for abusive relationships. I hoped Gina would read it to prevent repeating her mistakes with future couples. Defensively she responded, "*I am a professional who attends conferences, reads books on abuse, and am very well aware of domestic violence issues.*" She seemed irritated and offended by my suggestion. If she had been knowledgeable on the topic she would have known her "therapy" had intensified the abuse, driven us further apart, and destroyed any chance of salvaging our marriage.

In mid-April, after one of his sessions with Gina, Rakesh sent me a shocking, emotionally-charged email. Despite the fact we barely communicated in March, he accused me of being verbally abusive and demanded I seek professional help. Gina encouraged him to avoid contact with me, declared I would never be satisfied with anything he said or did, and I was in effect still trying to control him. Here is a quote from his email:

"*You have an incredible amount of anger and for a long time you have been trying hard to verbally hurt me as much as you can-through face to face conversations and via emails. This anger has already hurt your health and it will only worsen your health and that of your parents'. Gina said you are in a retaliatory and punitive phase, which is obvious, and it is best not to even respond to this or stay in touch. Gina even said that whatever I do will never be enough for you and I have already told you that. Trying to monitor everything I do or say or don't say, trying to control what I am doing to work on myself, constantly verbally attacking me-all these actions are only going to create more obstacles to us getting back together. So please get counseling ASAP for your anger. While we are separate, focus on yourself and your issues instead of me. Stop spelling things out for me.*"

I was dumbfounded. Where were these accusations coming from? After insisting he would work on himself and stop blaming me for all his issues, ultimately nothing in his personality had changed and his behavior had only been exacerbated thanks to Gina. I found myself vulnerable to his attack; every word was a dagger impaled in my heart. I was still too weak and distraught to not feel completely defeated. He knew exactly how to penetrate my fragile armor.

Abuser's Accountability

I was appalled by Gina's advice that painted an inaccurate picture of me based on all Rakesh's lies. The first thing an abuser must do is take accountability for his actions and make amends. Gina's work with Rakesh unfortunately made him feel increasingly justified for treating me badly, confirmed to him I was the cause of all our problems, and strengthened his abusive tendencies. He never assumed accountability, believed he was at fault, and felt justified in lying to his mother about our situation. Gina convinced him I had stripped him of his power and the goal was to become increasingly powerful and more in control of me.

Enraged, I decided to write an official complaint to the Department of Health refusing to silence my voice any longer. I wanted Gina to be cognizant of all her mistakes as a marriage counselor. After educating myself, I asked her for a referral so Rakesh could enroll in a specialized batterers program. This was really the only solution according to Bancroft's book since I felt the marriage counseling sessions were rendered completely ineffective. Gina's response was to encourage us to continue with her methods and give it time.

It was my sincere wish Gina not advise other couples with domestic violence issues until she received proper training on how to effectively deal with abusers so violence does not escalate. I strongly believe any therapist who advertises herself as specializing in domestic violence receive special certification to be equipped to handle these problems effectively and prevent further damage. Unfortunately, after investigation, the Department of Health decided there was no disciplinary action they could take.

Processing Abuse

Processing the reality of my victimization at the hands of the man I loved was confounding, emotionally paralyzing, and took time to sink in. Over and over in my head I heard the same mantra: *"I feel sick. I feel sick. I feel sick."* My heart had been ripped out, wounded repeatedly, and was incapable of healing. Awakening from a nightmare lasting six long years was no easy undertaking.

After reading Bancroft's book, it was an astounding experience to make sense of and accept my victimization. Others may think it sounds crazy I could not comprehend what was happening to me all those years, recognize the pattern, or break free but the nature of abuse is so insidious and creeps up on you so slowly it is challenging to decipher. If a stranger is violent, it is easy to identify a crime. But when it is someone you love, trust, and want to protect, someone you have committed to spend the rest of your life with, it complicates the situation. Things are less clear.

Admitting my marriage was a failure seemed unbearable. More than that, I realized I would have to own up to the fact I had been lying to everyone, including myself. I had proven I was an exceptionally skilled actress over the years but now the act was over. Confronting my own deception and being honest with myself for the first time was a daunting process. I could not help but ask myself over and over, *"Why me? How in the world did this happen to me?"* Up until my marriage, I had a beautiful life others would find envious, a wonderful loving family, and so many dreams and goals ahead of me. Rakesh had taken all that away from me, crushed my spirit, broken my heart, and destroyed my will to live. It was difficult to accept I never really had any chance for happiness with him.

My love blinded me from accepting he never really loved me. I believe he was too selfish and self-absorbed to be capable of caring about anyone else. All these years of deception I had been a fool to not see the truth. Rakesh had never recognized my needs, my dreams, or really anything that was important to me. He could not acknowledge the love I showered on him, my patience, loyalty, or commitment to saving our marriage. He had been blind to my pain, my injuries, my wounds, and all his destructive violent actions. Amazingly, I never considered leaving him or divorcing him even at our darkest moments. My belief in marriage was too potent, my desire to honor a commitment too deep. But now I saw clearly the nightmare had to end. As my new self-awareness dawned, I recognized the futility of my desperate attempt all those years to try to make a blind man see.

Processing Betrayal of Love

The most confusing aspect for me all those years was accepting why someone who loved me would want to hurt me. I could not grasp that and it prevented me from admitting he did not really love me, was not even capable of love, and the "nice Rakesh" was an imposter. At some point I believed he would come to his senses, treat me better, respect me, love me, but he never ever cared. Apparently, he seemed to have used me for my citizenship, money, family connections, and generosity. I had to remind myself you do not treat someone you love this way, you do not resort to violence against someone you genuinely care for, and whatever he felt for me was not love. Naïve and idealistic about love, I had longed for a husband who would be my partner, best friend, and soul mate. I believed being married would be the best thing to ever happen to me, but that was the furthest thing from the truth.

How was it possible to love a man so completely despite all his flaws, and then have that love utterly disintegrate? How can you go from love to nothing? I grappled with these thoughts. I wished I had never met him and he had never come into my life. Yet, a part of me wished it did not have to be this way and we could have found a way to stay together and make it work. If only he had truly loved me the way I had loved him. Our life could have been wonderful if he had made different choices. I was no longer shocked he could walk away so easily from all the love I had showered on him. His inability to fight to save our marriage *finally* made sense.

Turning to Others for Intervention

A few months prior, out of desperation, we had turned to help from Mukesh, an elder Indian male friend we both respected and looked up to as a spiritual advisor. I felt it was critical to reach out to people Rakesh respected due to his complete lack of respect for me. Mukesh was kind and supportive. *"Rakesh must transform himself through sincere prayer and dedication. I recommend he takes the 'art of living course' with Sri Sri Ravi Shankar and learn specific breathing and cleansing yogic practices."* I fully supported this idea but knew this advice was not the only remedy but part of the overall solution. Conveniently, Rakesh used his lack of time, inability to take the course, and lack of flexibility in his schedule as an excuse for his continuing abusive behavior. *"True change will not be possible until I can take the course,"* he claimed.

No, I corrected him, *"True change will come only when you fully admit to the abuse and comprehend your actions are wrong!"* What he needed to hear from Mukesh and everyone else in the community was abuse was unacceptable and intolerable! When I told Mukesh his advice was not making a difference, he replied almost helplessly, *"What else can I do? What do you want me to do?"* An abuser needs pressure from the outside community, including his family and peers, to truly change. But he was not receiving this message from his mother, sister, therapist, or Mukesh. Why was everyone so afraid to confront him?

In the beginning of 2008, when I saw our therapy sessions were failing, reaching out to his family had been utterly ineffective and the spiritual advice from Mukesh was not useful, I became desperate to have anyone intervene at this point. I called Kiran, another one of our elder Indian male friends Rakesh respected. I begged him, *"Please speak to Rakesh. Tell him this is not okay!"* Didn't people realize my safety was at stake or care my life was in jeopardy? At first, Kiran was sincere, but the next day he told me, *"Anisha, I cannot be caught in between. There is nothing I can do."* I sat there, abandoned and betrayed... once again.

I asked my friend Rakhi who lived in India to speak to Rakesh's mother since they met often. At first, Rakhi assured me not to worry, she would help however she could. The next week when we spoke she said, *"Anisha, I cannot intervene. It puts me in an awkward position and I do not want to be forced to pick sides."* I was perplexed. Why did no one want to help? I realized I had to be careful whom I chose to confide in and stay away from those who supported Rakesh either purposefully or inadvertently by not taking a stand. With his skills of manipulation, persuasion, and deception, I was certain he would convince others to believe him, twist the facts to his advantage, and lie whenever necessary to protect himself and his ego.

Questioning Faith

Mukesh, our spiritual advisor so to speak, had encouraged me to pray more. After six long, miserable years of enduring the abuse and praying every day for the violence to end so there would be only love, compassion, and understanding between us, not a single god had listened to my invocations. I continued to pray for guidance, strength, and wisdom, for a better life where I could heal myself of this pain and survive my trauma but my pleas lacked earnestness since I questioned my faith completely. I was not sure who to pray to or if anyone was listening.

I felt betrayed by God, my faith, the arranged-marriage system, and the Indian community I had turned to for help. I wished to turn back time so it could have been only six weeks or six months instead of six years for me to see through his act and grasp I was a victim of deception. I wished so desperately for the magical time of my youth when I believed in destiny, a higher power, and stars aligning. I questioned whether I could ever believe or have faith again. I could no longer pray to the same gods and goddesses who had betrayed me.

Chapter 26 CALM BEFORE THE STORM

The future depends on what we do in the present. Mahatma Gandhi

The Fog Starts to Lift

Consumed by my frenzy to make sense of the past six years of my life, I hungered for any sort of knowledge, information, or insight into my predicament. The dense fog enveloping my mind throughout the marriage was lifting. I spent most of January and February researching domestic violence online, devouring books, speaking to hotlines, and educating myself about the gravity of our situation. Armed with the knowledge I gained, it was a weapon to see through all the layers of deception and what a coward my husband truly appeared to be.

My mind was reeling trying to process these revelations and how narrowly I had escaped with my life. The more I learned, the more terrified I became of Rakesh's potential for future violence. I recognized he was a criminal, a batterer, and domestic violence was punishable by law. If I had reported him to jail instead of protecting him all those times, his career, medical license, and immigration status would have been jeopardized. Life as he knew it would have been over. The enormity of what I had done to protect him began to hit me. This man owed me so much.

Saying Goodbye

On March 1, 2008, I asked Rakesh to move out of the house again. Even though he had moved back into our home in February, we lived in separate rooms, avoided all contact, and were not on speaking terms. It was essentially the calm before the storm. My little sister was to arrive the next day and stay with me for a month. Quite frankly, I did not feel safe with him at home. I could not afford to have him explode or threaten violence in front of Nandita as he had when his mother lived with us. He could not be trusted. Rakesh seemed surprised by my request, but agreed to it, perhaps because he wished to avoid my family.

That night, Rakesh spoke with genuine sincerity for the first time about saving our marriage. Maybe he finally accepted how serious I was. He pleaded, "*I am committed to the marriage. I will not stop fighting for your love. I will earn your trust back and prove I can become a good husband and treat you well.*" Since the marriage counseling with Gina had not worked, he promised he would get the necessary professional help with a batterers intervention program I had found.

Rakesh agreed to read Bancroft's book on abuse because I recommended it so highly. He exclaimed, "*I will do everything I can to make things right. I promise to make it up to you. Anisha, you are a saint for putting up with me all these years and being so patient. I admit I've been selfish and only thought of my own needs. I neglected your needs and never made them a priority. It is not right I have hurt you so much and always made you cry. You are my Lakshmi, you are my goddess."*

I had held my breath for years waiting for him to own up to his behavior, acknowledge his mistakes, and make amends. It was a monumental turning point for him. Part of my heart melted at the relief of finally hearing this admission. Although I appreciated his sincerity and genuine apology, I was wary. Too much damage had been done. I could not trust this man. My patience had been worn thin and in many ways his effort felt too late. I had desperately needed to hear these words years ago-the first time he broke my heart and every time after that.

My heart was heavy, exhaustion overwhelmed me, and I questioned my strength to continue fighting this uphill battle. I wondered whether our marriage was still worth fighting for. Despite these thoughts, I could not face the reality of divorce or the implications of such an enormous decision. When Rakesh begged me for one more chance, my heart caved in not because of blind hope anymore but out of sheer exhaustion. After giving him a million chances previously, I convinced myself to give him one more. It was my duty as an Indian wife to continue to try to make the marriage work after all, wasn't it?

The last statement he made the night before he left tore me apart inside. Quietly, he uttered, *"You seem stronger now."* The implications of this amazed me. What did he mean? Had he known all these years I was weak? Was he conscious of systematically wearing me down? Although this fit exactly with the abuser's strategy, a part of me had refused to believe it. I cannot describe the intense anguish I felt that moment. His betrayal was incomprehensible. I had made so many excuses for him. How had I not seen the truth? Crushed by his statement, how could I not blame myself for my inability to uncover his past deception or take action? Unsuspecting, I had no idea this would be our last night living together.

Changing His Tune

Encouraged by his confession and breakthrough the previous night, I was hopeful yet again maybe Rakesh really was capable of change. Alas, he dashed my hopes just as quickly. After moving out, he called the next day and said, *"Anisha, it is my home too and I want to move back April 1 after your family leaves. We should take turns living in the house."* I protested, *"Rakesh, there is no reason why I should be forced to leave my own home when I haven't done anything wrong."* He didn't care. On top of this new demand, he threatened to separate his income and have his paycheck from work directly deposited into his new private bank account.

Essentially, he would cut me off financially from access to his income. Supposedly he would transfer funds into our joint account for me to pay the bills, but how was I to trust him? Where had all these sudden decisions come from in a single day? Things were spinning out of control and I did not know what had come over him. I explained patiently,

"Rakesh, you should be doing things now while we are separated to build my trust and confidence, not the opposite." He did not see it that way. He was doing everything he could to protect himself under the guise of his financial adviser's recommendation. Our situation was rapidly taking a turn for the worse.

My Parents' Visit

My parents visited in mid-March. I had wished to confide in them back in January when they were in India but I did not want to break the news of our separation by phone. They were attending my cousin's wedding, and I did not wish to spoil everyone's happiness during the festivities with my depressing news. After returning to America in February, I thought it best to wait until I saw my parents in person. Partly I delayed speaking to them because after trying to protect them from the truth for so long I was scared how they would handle it. It was time though-I knew I could not hold anything back from them anymore.

The night my mother arrived I confessed every incident of abuse I had documented over the years in my journal. We called my father on the phone so he could also hear every detail. Their reaction was to be expected; they were devastated. After six years of believing I was happily married, it was hard for them to process how much I had to suffer at the hands of the man they had trusted as a son with my life. It was incomprehensible to them why I had kept this a secret for so long and why I had failed to confide in them. Their pain and anguish was palpable. I wish I could have protected them so they would not have had to face this but I needed their strength and comfort. I could not be the strong one anymore.

Two days later, my dad was on a plane to Atlanta. I expressed how touched I was he was coming to see me without a moment's hesitation. My mother replied, *"Anisha, your father would do anything for you."* Unexpectedly, hearing this brought tears to my eyes. In that moment it hit me, how much my parents had showered me with genuine love and affection my entire life. My suspicions were correct; Rakesh had never ever felt this true love for me. It was evident to me he never possessed the ability or the desire to go out of his way and do anything for me, think of my needs, respect me, or care for me. In those months when I drowned in my sorrow, my parents' infinite love and support was the lifeline that kept me going. Their love gave me a reason to live. They were the foundation for my existence, the pillars of my life; I owed them everything.

There was no way I could have survived that time period without their unwavering support and feeling them by my side every step of the way. Their love and encouragement allowed strength to gently flow back into me. For the women who break free without the encouragement of a loving family, I infinitely admire how much strength they must possess. I regretted keeping my secret for so long. My parents would never have tolerated the abuse and part of me always knew that. I believe that was the reason I kept the truth hidden from them. I needed to give my 110% to the marriage and know I had done everything possible to save it. I did not want anyone's pressure or influence to leave unless I felt ready to leave. It had to be my choice. My father said clearly, *"Anisha, it can only be your decision if you want to stay in this marriage. We will not make that decision for you."* It meant the world to me they would stand by me no matter what I decided.

Rakesh Faces My Parents

Several days later, my father confronted Rakesh on the phone who listed the existing problems in the marriage and emphasized we needed time to work through our "mutual" issues. He admitted to making mistakes but still never used the words "verbally and physically abusive." Rakesh promised to meet my parents in person to show them that respect and agreed he owed them an apology for everything that had happened.

A few days later, however, he changed his tune again. *"I don't think it is necessary or fair to meet your parents when my family is not present."* How could he keep going back on his word? Didn't he see how important this was to me? The logistics of his request were ridiculous: his mother was in India. Were we supposed to wait for her to fly to America before we could have a discussion? His sister insisted she must fly to Atlanta and be present in order for us to meet. This was ludicrous.

I begged Rakesh to reconsider and tried once again to explain to him why this meeting was crucial. Finally he relented, but only on his terms. He demanded to meet my parents alone. If my sisters and I were there, he vowed he would be forced to walk out. How did he have the nerve to deny my right to be there? How could he set the terms of the meeting or even be in a position to make demands?

The truth was, Rakesh seemed afraid to face my parents, be held accountable, and feel outnumbered. Apparently, he needed his family present to defend him, protect him, and stand by him. Dictating the terms of the meeting allowed him to demonstrate his authority, regain power and control, and dominate the conversation with his version of events. By denying my right to be there he showed, once again, my voice did not matter. Perhaps he assumed he could manipulate my parents to believe him.

When Sunday afternoon came, after much anticipation and debating, my sisters and I left the house. Parked on my street, I could not bring myself to drive away. How could we work on reconciling our marriage if I was not allowed to be there? I had every right to be present! I wanted to explain to Rakesh why he should not shut me out or silence me anymore. I needed to reclaim my voice; I had a right to speak, especially in front of my own family. I refused to allow him to keep wielding power and control over me. After not seeing my husband in a month, I also missed him and desperately wished to reason with him.

I could not break my habitual pattern of seeking reconciliation and attempted to break through one last time. My sisters and I turned the car around and returned to the house. We walked in with trepidation, fearful of a volatile situation but prepared to call 911 if Rakesh was violent. Thankfully, it did not come to that. Visibly surprised when we entered the home, he expressed his disapproval and attempted to leave. At my parents' request, he resigned himself to accepting our presence but made it clear he was upset.

Endless Excuses

My father continued the interrupted discussion by insisting Rakesh agree to not cut me off financially. Rakesh protested with a list of justifications for creating his own account based on the advice of his financial advisor. Reluctantly, he agreed when he saw my father would not waver on this issue. My father also requested he receive immediate professional help by joining a specialized program for batterers. Once again Rakesh's denial of the situation and resistance amazed all of us. Calmly, he declared, *"I do not believe I need professional help. With sincere prayer and religious rituals I will transform myself. I have everything under control. After a period of three months if that does not work, then I will consider joining a program but it is not located in a good part of town and I don't want to associate with men who are criminals. It is beneath me."*

I wanted to laugh. Is that all he cared about? His image? Enraged, my sister yelled, *"Rakesh, the time for prayer is long gone. A lifetime of prayer will not mitigate all the bad karma you have accrued from hurting Anisha. You need to do serious work to remedy this!"* My sister would be one of the *only* people bold enough to confront him and take a stand. I wish so many others I had confided in could have had her courage. My dad used the analogy of an alcoholic who refused to admit he had a problem and says he wants to continue drinking for another three months before getting help. Firmly he said, *"It is unacceptable to not receive professional help. If you wish to stay in this marriage, you do not have a choice about getting help."*

After sitting silently, Rakesh realized my family was serious and reluctantly agreed to therapy. He promised to email my parents after each session so they would be informed of his progress, a promise he failed to honor. We agreed to live separately for a three-month trial during which time he would find a short-term apartment to move into. My father insisted that under no circumstances was I to move out of the home. At the end of our trial we would reevaluate where things stood depending on his progress. In my heart, I really believed Rakesh would change with professional help and especially now that my parents were involved to hold him accountable for his actions. After all, I still believed he loved me and would do anything to make our marriage work. Unsure of how much time would be required, I was ready to be patient and wait for the man I loved to transform himself.

Even after seeing how upset my parents were, Rakesh never apologized to them. He spoke about "his mistakes," his struggles, his stress, but never came out and admitted to being abusive or violent. He seemed to be missing the point of the discussion completely. It was as if it was impossible for him to articulate that confession. I was amazed to see this side of him: his persistent denial and egoistic instinct to preserve his image and reputation at all costs. In front of his mother, there was no shortage of words to describe my faults and flaws, but he was at a loss when it came to himself. His apparent narcissistic sense of grandiosity prevented him from being honest with himself.

My parents also had to face the deception of my mother-in-law. In January, they had attended my cousin's wedding in India and unsuspectingly, had invited Rakesh's mother to the festivities. Even though I was no longer on speaking terms with her, this did not faze her. Despite knowing about all the struggles in our marriage, witnessing our fights, and being aware Rakesh and I were living separately, she had the nerve to attend the wedding. With a deceptive smile, she allowed my family to cater to her needs and mentioned nothing to them. How did she dare put up this charade! Did she not feel any shame? My parents were outraged and appalled by her betrayal.

Sherine to the Rescue

Frustrated by the marriage counseling sessions with Gina, I knew I still desperately needed professional help to start processing my trauma. Focusing on my own needs after neglecting them for so many years was a pivotal step. Jaded by my search for a new therapist, I did not want to waste my time with someone unqualified like Gina again. A friend referred her long-distance therapist who I started speaking to regularly over the phone in March.

In our first conversation I told Sherine, *"I want to stay in my marriage and find a way to make it work. I am determined and a hard worker."* I appreciated her honesty when she responded, *"Anisha, in my experience men like these don't change. It is very rare and would really take a miracle. I am biased because I am a survivor of abuse myself and have very little tolerance for men like Rakesh."*

When I persisted in declaring I wanted to make my marriage work, Sherine's response brought me to my knees. She questioned, *"Why do you believe after six years he is suddenly going to change now? What is your evidence?"* This was a turning point for me. Up until then, the only reason I believed he would change was blind hope. When I examined the facts, I realized Rakesh showed no signs of changing. He still exhibited no remorse, assumed no responsibility for his actions, and the abuse had steadily exacerbated every year.

Something in me shifted when I gained this clarity and looked at my predicament objectively. I could not let my blind hope and muddled emotions overpower me anymore. The harsh reality was staring at me in the face. I had to wake up and see the truth. Sherine was a spark of light in the darkness I was drowning in. She gave me clarity and courage to continue on my path towards liberation all the countless times when I felt like giving up the fight.

Domestic Violence Agency

Sherine encouraged me to visit a domestic violence agency, be familiar with my local options, attend a support group, and know where to turn to if I needed immediate help. While my family was still in town I went reluctantly one afternoon after putting it off for some time. As soon as I stepped in the door, I hung my head in shame knowing it had finally come to this. I really was a victim of domestic violence; I could not deny that official label any longer.

I filled out their paperwork and spoke to a counselor who assessed if I was in any immediate danger by asking me a series of questions. I felt humiliated. How did I let this happen to me? How could I not see what was happening? As quick as I was to blame myself, I grasped I could not mimic Rakesh by beating myself up for my predicament. I had to fully understand that part of my healing now was to accept and comprehend my victimization.

I took advantage of the shelter's weekly support groups and attended three sessions. It was an eye-opening experience listening to other women share their pain, knowing I was not alone. Compared to the other women in my support group, I knew I should count my blessings. I was lucky to at least still have a roof over my head, a car to drive, family and friends who supported me, a job to show up to every day and make me feel my life was still meaningful. So many of these women had run out of their homes with literally the clothing on their backs. They had nothing: no family, support, money, or job, often with many kids in tow. I could not even imagine their struggle for food and shelter to support their children.

Yet I found it difficult to relate to these victims in many ways because my issues and my struggle were so different from theirs. They could not comprehend my cultural bias, frustration with my in-laws, or my resistance to divorce. What I desperately needed was a support group of Indian women to whom I could relate, but no such group existed. Dejected, I chose to continue with my individual phone therapy sessions with Sherine to navigate through this challenging time period and not rely on support groups.

Legal Options

In March, my family joined me to consult an attorney and discuss my legal options. I was overwhelmed with gratitude by their support. For the first time I felt I was not alone facing my ordeal. I did not have to fight this battle by myself. The meeting was a formality to educate myself about my rights and understanding the legal process if need be. I still had not made the decision to divorce or even accepted that reality; every Indian fiber in my body resisted it. I was reluctant to consider it until the end of our three-month trial hopeful he would show some signs of transformation. The meeting was informative, and I was touched by my attorney's compassion.

She discussed ways to protect myself including obtaining a restraining order if necessary. The possibility of taking such a strong stand against Rakesh was alarming. Most likely she said I would be denied a restraining order since too much time had elapsed since our last incident in January when I had not taken action. I regretted once again my failure to protect myself. Neglecting my own needs and safety for so many years, I had always put my husband before me and could not afford to do that anymore. The thought of Rakesh returning home and retaliating against me physically was terrifying. I needed to put myself first.

Minimal Interactions

At the end of March, my parents flew back home and I was alone for the first time since our official separation a month earlier. It was one of the most exigent months knowing my marriage had come to this point but my family's presence made all the difference. Their continued love and support helped me hold on day by day. After they left, I felt an emptiness and sense of despair that felt as vast as a desert. My vulnerability was palpable. I began to process the reality divorce was a strong possibility. I needed time to make my decisions, process my layers of emotion, release my traumas. Each conversation with Sherine buoyed my confidence. It was amazing to discover I was capable of healing and my spirit was so resilient. I watched as awareness filled me and I slowly grew stronger each day.

Contact with Rakesh was minimal throughout March and April. Avoiding the phone and direct conversation, we only sent necessary emails about bills or issues related to maintaining the home. Whatever contact we had left me feeling disturbed and concerned about what was really going through his mind. He sent me emails about how distraught he was and as a consequence could not focus at work. He admitted to making mistakes on the job, and I worried for the sake of his patients and his medical license. To prove how distraught he was, he confessed to driving to my office at 10 p.m. many nights and sitting outside thinking of me. These worrisome confessions only revealed how troubled he really was. The idea of him brooding in an empty parking lot at night was disconcerting.

Mid-April I planned to attend a one-week workshop in California. My shuttle at 5 a.m. canceled on me at the last minute, so I panicked about missing my flight. I had no one to call at that early hour. Desperately, I contacted Rakesh and he agreed to drive me to the airport. Adrenaline flooded my system at the idea of seeing him again for the first time in a month and a half. I tried to sit in the backseat but he insisted I sit up front. Too emotional to protest, I avoided making any eye contact. He tried to hold my hand but that gesture of tenderness was too much for me to handle. Suddenly, I could not control my tears. I confessed how upset I was by his accusatory email from a few days prior where he outrageously claimed I was verbally abusive after his therapy session with Gina.

He professed he did not mean those hostile comments and admitted to lashing out at me because I called him an immature two-year-old. In his presence, I could not stop the flood of tears or calm down. Unable to tolerate my weeping, he started yelling, *"You need to urgently get professional help! Look at you; you are a mess. You are crazy and need to deal with your issues!"* I could not believe it. Didn't he see how much I had controlled and suppressed my emotions for six years and I was not capable of that anymore? Why couldn't he understand it was healthy for me to vent my feelings and allow me that freedom? He had expressed his anger and violence unchecked for years. We reached the airport and I left without saying goodbye or looking back. I needed to get as far away from him as quickly as possible. Even though it was our first encounter in a month and a half, I was exhausted from the interaction.

Deception

We had decided many weeks before he would move back into the house for the ten days I would be in California. Living in hotels for the past month, this would allow him to transition into a short-term apartment. I no longer felt I could trust him but chose to ignore my instincts so I would not go back on my word. There was no way I could have anticipated the events of that week or the deception my husband was capable of. I checked my voicemail every day while I was away and was surprised to hear a message from the phone company saying they had received an order to disconnect the phone service the next day. I called them immediately and insisted I never placed that order and did not want to have my phone service interrupted. The only other name on the account was Rakesh; no one else was authorized to have placed the order.

Alarm bells were ringing in my head with this news. Why would he deliberately tamper with our utilities? What was his underlying motivation? His unpredictability was increasingly frightening. Events were unfolding like drama scenes in a movie. Unfortunately, the representative had not documented his name on their records. I could not get any proof from them he had ultimately been the one to try to disconnect the phone service. This evidence would have been extremely useful down the road but luck was on Rakesh's side once again.

Insight of Jyotish

While I was in California, I met a *jyotishi* (Vedic astrologer) who hinted at issues in the marriage of physicality, secrets, and danger. My intention was to receive advice about salvaging our marriage, not necessarily confess about the abuse. The jyotishi warned me, *"There are dangerous times ahead. It is essential you do everything possible to protect yourself. Change the locks, install a security system, and avoid living home alone."* He told me to be wary of anything Rakesh said or did and mentioned the word deception numerous times. He reiterated, *"Things are not as they seem."* I did not know what to make of this phrase until much later when I learned of other events that took place that week and the extent of my husband's deception.

I tried to focus on my workshop but my mind was distracted as I contemplated the danger back home. If Rakesh had disconnected the phone lines because he was planning something for the weekend when I returned home, I was terrified. His obsessive mind, attention to detail, and penchant for strategizing raised red flags. After returning to Atlanta, I spent the weekend at my uncle's home to be safe at the insistence of my therapist, astrologer, parents, and friends. On Monday, I returned home and changed the locks on the doors. Rakesh's actions proved to me I was not safe and could not trust him any longer. I was rapidly losing hope there was any chance of saving our marriage.

Beneath the Disguise

After the events that transpired during those weeks, I was forced to scrutinize the facts and process Rakesh's duplicity over the years. The fact he could hide behind his lies, deceit, and fake persona because he was apparently not brave enough to face himself or his actions amazed me. What was once love that I felt in my heart for him was replaced with pity. I saw him transparently now for who he truly was: a scared little boy who had to be abusive to feel powerful. His outward confidence evidently was an act to not reveal the cowardice underneath. His opinionated, aggressive, dominating exterior stemmed from his need to prove others wrong to cover his insecurity. Denial seemed to be the only way he could live with himself. What was the purpose of living a dishonest life where he could not even face himself in the mirror?

With lucidity, I appreciated his "loving" gestures were merely acts to rope me in and deceive me; they were never genuine. There is no way violence is ever an option when you truly love someone. I gave myself permission to vent my intense emotions and hatred of this man. I despised him for everything he had done, turning my life upside down, treating me so horribly, and laughing at my dreams. I loathed him for not treating me with basic human dignity.

How did I put up with his domination over every aspect of my life, thwarting my attempts to succeed at my business, and crushing my aspirations? Battling my emotions, I could not forgive him for pushing me until my breaking point, not even caring how much he had hurt me, and for walking away all those times not even turning back to see if I was okay or conscious. I hated him with a passion I could not even begin to describe. Surprisingly, this emotion fueled my motivation to stop feeling worn down, depressed, and non-functional.

Chapter 27 EYES WIDE OPEN

Our lives teach us who we are. Salman Rushdie

Trial Separation

Living with Rakesh day in and day out was a whirlwind of chaos, torment, volatility, and unpredictability. It was not until our physical separation that I could disengage from this constant dynamic, remember what peace was like once again, and embrace the ease of living without the ever-present aggravations, tense interactions, and heated discussions. I did not miss the daily frustration of trying to be heard, our inability to communicate, or the crazy conversations where no amount of logic or rationality could get through to him. My never-ending struggle for sanity was replaced with a silent solitude that refreshed my soul and allowed me to gather my strength. I took pleasure in the quiet simplicity of each day knowing Rakesh could not disturb me, victimize me, subject me to his anger, or be hurtful and destructive.

During our trial separation for a few months, I finally had space to think. My mind vacillated: to divorce or not to divorce. The first time my husband threatened me at the beginning of our marriage, I was appalled he would consider using that word. At this point, I wondered whether divorce would be such a terrible thing after all. Despite my sheer persistence to make this marriage work all these years, I had to accept maybe divorce was not only necessary but would prove therapeutic. However, it was still daunting to face the divorce process. In many ways staying together seemed easier than dealing with the unknown. Not divorcing would mean keeping my beautiful new home, finishing all my decorating projects, having financial security, and not having to fight yet another battle.

After all the time invested in our relationship, I decided it was not worth it to rush my decision. I needed time to have absolute clarity. The best approach, and the only one I was emotionally capable of anyway, was to take it slowly each day. Looking ahead into the future was impossible when I could not even predict week by week where things would stand. I did know, however, I could not exist in a state of limbo forever. If we separated, I needed to move on with my life as soon as possible, but how to possess clarity or determine the best course to take evaded me.

Those months of our separation crept by and left ample time for contemplation. I would sit by the ocean often, the only place where I could clear my mind, empty my thoughts, and attempt to be still in the midst of the torrent of questions that plagued me. I could not help but wonder: Did he miss me at all? Did he ever think of me? Did he have any regrets? Did he want me back? I wish it did not have to be this way. I wish he had loved me enough to want to change and become the better person I knew he could have been.

Reasons to Stay Together

During this time, the reality of being on my own hit me. Being single and divorced in my thirties without a husband, children, a home, or financial security was too much to face. I pictured growing old without anyone by my side, grieving for the loss of the familiar Indian family structure I had always envisioned. My dreams of being a mother seemed further away than I could ever imagine, and I had no idea how to surrender the one dream I had longed for the most. I mourned the loss of all my aspirations, forfeiting my innocence and trust, and starting over again.

Compromising my financial stability, losing my home and my material possessions was scary. Where would I go? Trepidation of the future filled me. Moving forward, I had to force myself to contemplate the practical reality of my future, the financial mess I was in, the expenses of a complicated divorce, how to pay my bills, and how to survive in general. It would be a challenge to stay motivated to work, allow my business to flourish, and find the inspiration to keep serving my clients. There would be no shortage of struggles. How was I to find the strength to persevere?

My entire lifestyle would change from socializing with married couples to friendships that would be put to the test having to take sides. My relatives in India would be devastated hearing what I had to endure, that my marriage was over, and living without a man to provide for me in the traditional sense. I would have to face the stigma and shame in the Indian community, the hushed whispers about what had really happened in my marriage, the possibility of losing Indian friends who were not open to the idea of divorce. My parents would have to deal with reactions from their peers and potentially uncomfortable social situations, to which I hated to subject them. It was alarming how much there was to grieve and how much change there was to process.

After everything I had endured, I knew I could not give up hope now… I willed myself to take a deep breath. In my heart, I searched for the right answer. I did not want to stay married simply because of my fears or lack of funds to pay an attorney. I needed to face these hurdles and move past them. I decided to make a list of pros and cons about whether to stay together or divorce. Astonishingly, I came up with seven reasons to not divorce him: (1) to uphold my commitment to be with this man for life, (2) to keep my dream of being a mother and having children one day, (3) not compromise my financial stability and security, (4) not face my fear of being alone, (5) avoid the unknown prospects of divorce and what that entailed, and (6) avoid the intimidating legal process. The main reason to stay: (7) my heart was still connected to this man, a part of me still loved and cared for him despite everything and could not fully let him go. I could not deny my lingering, unhealthy attachment to Rakesh.

Wavering Mind

During those few months, my mind seemed to waver daily. I was conflicted by the mixed messages Rakesh sent and how strongly I was affected by everything he said and did. Encouraged he was supposedly seeing a therapist in a batterers intervention program after the talk with my parents, I felt with time maybe he really would be transformed into the better person I knew he could be. Or would he? I received his emails about his commitment to change, self-improve, treat me better, and I *so* desperately wanted to believe him. Rakesh declared he would take me to India to renew our vows, have the wedding of which I had dreamed, followed by a spectacular honeymoon in Bali. I remembered the life we had promised each other, all the dreams we had shared, and giving up on those possibilities was heartbreaking.

The real question that plagued me day and night-could he *really* change? I had to assess whether he was capable of transforming and admit I did not know the answer. Given our history of the past six years and the probability of a man at the age of forty-two undergoing a radical transformation, most likely not. It seemed there were too many variables, too many "what if's." Being forced to see a therapist against his will reluctantly, I had to admit he could just be learning the drill of saying *"I'm sorry,"* but apologizing without any sincerity was meaningless. A part of me did not want to give him any more chances, put myself in danger ever again, or be vulnerable to his volatile anger and unpredictable violence. I had to acknowledge a part of me wished to never see him again. I longed for space and silence, a life where I could make my own decisions and no longer live in fear.

My nervous system was in overdrive with an abundance of adrenaline surging through me. It was challenging not to be overwhelmed by the life-altering decisions I needed to make to end the marriage. Being separated from Rakesh was akin to extracting the poison that had entered my bloodstream and infiltrated my mind and heart. It was painful, slow, and tormenting, but I fought for a way to survive and choose freedom over the easier option of returning to him. It was crucial for me during this time to reclaim my voice, set my limits, find my power, and not be isolated. I had to work on finding a way to hold onto my integrity.

Seeking Support

When I felt utterly alone, it was a blessing at late hours of the night to rely on the National Hotline for Domestic Violence where staff was available twenty-four hours. I honestly do not know what I would have done without them. They were present when nobody else was during my toughest moments. The anonymous voices on the other end kept me holding on through my darkest and scariest periods. I was touched and amazed by how much support I could find from perfect strangers who could understand my predicament, be compassionate, and help me hold on another day.

Moments of courage surfaced after speaking to my therapist Sherine. A true role model, I admired her for transforming herself into a pillar of strength after her abusive marriage. She gave me hope I had a purpose, I would survive, and I could choose a beautiful future for myself. My friend Radha showed me it was possible to extricate oneself from a difficult marriage even after many years of bondage. She was my mirror as I saw her gather her strength day by day, break free, and mend from the trauma. Most of all, my incredible family meant the world to me. I do not know where I would have been without them. But my strength was still fleeting at times as my mind easily fluctuated and I immediately found myself questioning my decisions and my resolve.

More Reasons to Divorce

I needed to ponder the cons for staying together. I had to be absolutely honest with myself about dealing with a man I no longer trusted, did not want to be near, and to some extent not sure if I still loved. There were countless reasons to divorce, but I came up with an extensive list of the most compelling ones:

(1) I questioned how to mend my heart he had broken a thousand times. I simply could not keep putting all the pieces back together again.
(2) He still refused to take responsibility, own up to his mistreatment, blamed me, and continued to justify his actions.
(3) He had been consistently resistant to change, reluctant to do therapy, insincere when he occasionally apologized, and did not seem truly genuine about transforming himself.
(4) He had completely broken my trust and I had no idea how to repair that.
(5) He made no effort to see things from my perspective, empathize, or comprehend the psychological damage he inflicted. I could not picture him being respectful or treating me well.
(6) I had lost all respect for this man feeling he was a coward who could not face himself or his emotions and resorted to violence to feel powerful.
(7) I wondered how to keep finding the strength within me to forgive him time and time again. After giving him what seemed like a million chances already, I was weary. He had failed me every time he had the opportunity to make things right.
(8) The pain and suffering I felt in this relationship was all-consuming, it overpowered any remaining feelings of tenderness.
(9) When I comprehended he had consciously, willingly chosen to treat me so horribly, I literally felt sick to my stomach.
(10) I did not know how to let go of the past and my painful memories and even start to heal my wounds but I knew this was my priority. I could not survive another day of his abuse.
(11) He had shown my needs would never be his priority and he was not even capable of recognizing them. He made it clear his mother

would always come first and there was no room for anyone else in his life.
(12) I could not imagine him being a loving father and was certain I did not want to have children with him.
(13) I had lost the ability to feel safe and secure in my own home.
(14) He had destroyed any chance for happiness I had over the years.
(15) I could not think of his mother and sister as family again after their betrayal. They still skirted the issue of addressing his violence and harped instead on my "out of control" anger rather than label it as a healthy response of a victim.
(16) How could I stay married to a man whose face I could not even stand to look at?
(17) Given everything that had transpired, I could not see a future for us together. All of our dreams were shattered, all his promises mere illusions.
(18) Even though a part of me still loved him, a bigger part of me despised him for his betrayal, deception, breaking my heart, and for all the pain he had caused my family and me.

It was clear the reasons to separate outnumbered those to stay together. I knew it was better to be divorced and lonely than married and trapped in an abusive relationship but I remained paralyzed by my fears...

Desperate Plea for Intervention

In my desperation and last attempt to save my marriage, I wrote a final letter to his mother and sister begging them to reach out to my husband. It seemed he had instructed them to avoid all contact with me and of course, they had obliged. I wrote, *"Rakesh has minimized all his abusive actions to make it seem like I am exaggerating but I have only been truthful with you. Abuse is solvable. His behavior can change only with the encouragement and pressure of his family. He needs you now more than ever."*

Not surprisingly, there was no response. Even though his mother and sister had failed me, I decided to contact his other relatives. I truly believed any family member Rakesh respected could get through and talk some sense into him. Rakesh had many cousins I respected and admired and to whom I felt close. In my email I pleaded, *"Please-I am reaching out to anyone who truly cares about Rakesh to help him. His mind is too clouded with emotion to know what the right thing to do is. He needs professional help. Only a small percentage of abusers actually change and it is because they have a strong support network of family and friends who insist violence is not permissible under any circumstance."*

Disappointingly, most of them ignored my email. One couple forwarded my letter to Rakesh and wrote, *"Anisha, do not try to hurt him, seek revenge, or get back at him in any way. Domestic violence is a difficult issue and it is hard to know which side is telling the truth. We may never know the whole truth, but we will always support our cousin who is our family."* Their response was not what I had hoped for. Honestly, I had expected more from them, to side with truth, justice, and fairness and know this was not about taking sides.

This was not about family loyalty. This was about helping him and trying to save our marriage. Did they not see that? Revenge was the last thing on my mind, and I was shocked they questioned my sincerity and motives. Trying to salvage any sort of relationship with his family was pointless; I felt defeated and forlorn, betrayed yet again by people I trusted. I resigned myself to the fact that in the end I could not rely on anyone else. No one was willing to help or be involved.

Financial Abuse

Events in May unfolded rather rapidly. I discovered Rakesh had created his own separate bank account after promising my parents and me that he would not. Despite my father's insistence on this issue, he pretended the discussion never occurred and he was merely following his financial advisor's recommendations. I was enraged he was capable of going back on his word to my parents especially. His disrespectful actions revolved around his own selfish motives. Instead of his entire salary now being deposited into our joint account, the amount was reduced by 50%.

I struggled to pay the mortgage, utilities, and bills for our expensive home, make my car payment, and have much left over. Later, I would discover he would maliciously continue to reduce this amount as it apparently made him feel in control. I resented all the sacrifices I had made in my career to help him advance, always putting him first, and as a consequence becoming financially dependent on him.

I would never have anticipated the extent of his financial abuse-withholding money to which I was legally entitled, making me beg, reducing me to live off my credit cards. I started to panic questioning how I would pay the bills and manage my life. I genuinely wondered how it had come to this. He was a physician with a lucrative income, was he really going to be this petty? My attorney asked for temporary financial relief but Rakesh seemed to realize he had gained an advantage. It was evident to me he would use the tactic of financial abuse to threaten me and feel in control of the situation.

He seemed to assume that in my desperation, I would take any scraps he threw my way. These actions confirmed for me even more clearly this was not a man I could trust. He had lied to his own family and mine showing the deception of which he was capable. I had been patient, hopeful, given Rakesh a chance to build my trust, receive professional help, and make me feel financially secure, but he had consistently let me down. Actually, it was enlightening to see the extent of his cruelty and how far he would go to usurp power and control.

I was amazed he could treat me this way after everything I had done for him over the years. In many ways the financial abuse was an eye-opening experience to see what he was truly capable of and understand his complete lack of respect for me. His actions provided a glimpse of clarity when my mind was still clouded with feelings of love and tenderness for this man. In a way, I was thankful he was not being deceptive anymore and showing me his true nature that I had resisted seeing for so long. After years of living with his dual personality, I could identify the "nice Rakesh" as an imposter. It was refreshing to be free of my confusion and know only the "evil Rakesh" was real.

Decision to Divorce

As my mind wavered, I fought my demons, wrestled with decisions I needed to make, and trained myself to sit in the silence between my thoughts. I had to face my darkest moments, and I struggled to overcome the intensity of my pain no matter how unbearable. In the midst of that darkness I saw the light... life was so much more than the pain, suffering, and torture to which I had been subject. I accepted life was more beautiful than I could ever imagine. Instead of dwelling on the past, I had to learn to forgive and love myself for finally having the courage to wake up and confront reality.

I forced myself to step back, shift perspective, and envision my new life. No matter how frightening it was to consider divorce, the past two months had been transforming. I was able to feel safe in my own home, not live in constant fear every day of being a victim to Rakesh's anger and violence, and know I had the unconditional love and support of my family. Having a refuge from the abuse cleared my head. Something within me shifted and there was no going back. Now that my eyes were wide open, I could never be blind to my reality again or tolerate the abuse anymore. One of my girlfriends said it best, *"You are too conscious and awake now to let things continue in the same manner. You are too evolved to stay in that old, destructive pattern. Things will have to change to accommodate your new awareness."*

After much deliberation, I was clear about my decision. My heart was heavy but I felt certain divorce was the only option. Staying in this marriage that no longer served me would be a lie. I would be inauthentic to my true self, which had lain dormant and suppressed for far too long. It was one of the most challenging decisions I ever had to make. My freedom, sanity, and salvation were dependent on taking this difficult step but I took solace in knowing I would not have to walk the path alone. My family was with me; with their love and support anything was possible. I would never compromise my safety or risk my life again. Life was too beautiful and precious to waste another day of it being married to an abusive, violent man who did not love or respect me. This decision set me free and began my journey to liberation.

Preparing myself emotionally for the divorce process meant recognizing this would be the last and final battle concerning Rakesh. It was daunting to think of the path looming ahead and anticipate what was to come. I knew he would not make it easy. It would take everything I had and I could not afford to let my mind vacillate anymore. I drafted a concise record of forty-two abusive incidents over the years to inform my attorney of our history.

As I read through the material from my journal I observed what a brute Rakesh truly was and finally grasped the big picture. Reading about the abuse horrified me, how systematic it was, how it got worse, the excuses he made, how traumatized I became with each incident, and the extent of my victimization. I defended and protected him until the very end. Blinded by my hope for change, I believed him it would not happen again. Abuse was scary and ugly and crept over my life so subtly I was too blind to see it happen.

Filing for Divorce

On May 19, 2008, I filed for divorce. Consulting my attorney that morning I felt confident, clear, ready to take action. My parents accompanied me to the attorney's office as we drafted the necessary paperwork for the divorce petition. I felt guilty Rakesh had to find out about my decision this way. I would have preferred to say goodbye in person and spoken face-to-face one last time.

I had asked him to visit the home over the weekend while my parents were still present so I could return all his belongings, inform him of my intentions, and have a calm, realistic discussion about how to divide our possessions. I would not have dared to meet him alone or put myself in any position that compromised my safety. Of course, Rakesh replied he was busy and needed to be at his office on Sunday evening, no doubt a convenient excuse to not honor my request to meet in person. I did not, however, allow myself to be disappointed or attached to the outcome of his response.

Rakesh was served the papers at 3:15 p.m. that same afternoon while he was at work. The server told me he did not respond with anger like I expected, but then again he was an expert at concealing his emotions in public. When I found out he reacted with surprise, it made my heart break. I wish I could have been there to give him a hug, comfort him, let him know I was sorry this was the way things turned out. I wish I could have told him my decision in person and seen his expression. I realized those days we could turn to each other for comfort were over. The finality of it all inundated me.

Restraining Order

The same day I filed for divorce I contemplated whether I had the courage to file for a restraining order. A very small percentage of Indian women actually overcome the cultural impediments to take such a drastic action against their husbands. The majority of women are prevented by the apprehension of her husband's reputation, job, career, or immigration being on the line. The fear of the in-laws and the rest of the Indian community shunning such an action and bringing shame upon the family and community should not be underestimated. No matter how much I feared Rakesh before, I was terrified of how he would handle the news of the divorce. I was aware statistically the rate of violence increased after separation and a woman was in jeopardy of possible retaliatory acts. I anticipated Rakesh's anger would intensify a hundredfold but my thoughts still revolved more around him than myself.

I thought filing for divorce was hard, but this was much more difficult. Sitting outside of the courthouse deliberating for an hour, I felt I was unraveling. Finally, I mustered the courage to go inside, fill out the necessary paperwork, and wait with anticipation to see if it would be granted. I was terrified to obtain it and terrified not to. After protecting him for so many years, I deserved to protect myself and take a stand against the injustices I had faced. I needed to obtain the maximum protection possible and could not keep living in fear. To my surprise, the temporary restraining order was granted. I felt vindicated knowing officially there was proof I had been a victim of domestic violence. He could not deny or minimize what had happened; the U.S. justice system at least recognized I was in imminent danger and needed protection.

Closure

Later that afternoon, I emailed Rakesh a four-page letter to say goodbye since we had not had the opportunity in person. I had prepared the letter when I made the decision to divorce months before. I desperately required closure after months of living apart without contact. It may seem odd, but I needed to communicate without the risk of violence. I had to convey why I did what I did and express how much stronger I felt. I wish it had been easier to walk away but letting go of seven years of my life was an enormous undertaking.

Those next few days I lived in a daze, unable to process the shock over my actions. The fact I had filed for both a divorce and a restraining order on the same day seemed surreal. I would never have imagined this was the direction my life would have taken in a million years. I went through the motions day by day, feeling trapped in a dream, wondering when I would wake up, when it would be over. I was plagued with self-doubt and second-guessed my decisions.

Rakesh's email the following day said, *"Your petition is like a bullet that went through my chest. I can't imagine a life without you. I am devastated. Divorce is not what my family or I want."* Reading that broke my heart and I felt a strong desire to reach out to him. But then I reflected... Maybe he was confounded accepting the finality of divorce or being humiliated at work by being served a restraining order. Could he even begin to understand my devastation with every abusive incident over the years or grasp a fraction of the pain I had endured?

For the first time, his mother called from India to speak to my parents and reiterate the same message, *"We do not approve of the divorce. Please, we beg you to ask Anisha to reconsider."* Rakesh proposed another three-month trial for a second chance. I laughed at the idea of subjecting myself to more of his financial and emotional abuse. If it was not for the grim financial reality of the complete lack of funds in my bank account, I probably could have been swayed to give him another chance. But being forced to live off of my credit cards was a rude awakening making it quite clear this man did not care about my well-being.

His bizarre behavior was also a warning sign that his intentions could not be trusted. Rakesh sent me an email demanding he be able to visit the home alone to perform a *puja* (religious ceremony) for the safety and welfare of my parents and me, who he stated were in danger. His request that we vacate the home was so ludicrous, I was amazed he believed I was gullible enough to fall for his lies.

It was still challenging for me to emotionally detach from him during this time. I found myself frequently wondering what he was going through. Did I regret my decision? No, but I still wished he could have transformed himself into a better person, seen the error of his ways, and made amends for his mistakes. I had accepted he would rather end the marriage than do any sort of inner work on himself or face his flaws. He preferred to make excuses such as incompatibility or blame me for being over-controlling. To me, it was painfully obvious staying together, treating me well, loving me or respecting me was not what he wanted.

Rumors & Betrayal

Later that month, I heard stories Rakesh's mother was spreading rumors in India I was a schizophrenic. Simultaneously devastated and outraged, I questioned how she could do this. I had trusted her, confided in her, looked up to her. How could she resort to such lies and be capable of such cruelty? I felt betrayed by the person I had thought of as a second mother, whom I had cared for, respected, and loved. Even though I knew she was undoubtedly following her son's orders blindly, no mother would take such an action against her child. I realized *"like mother, like son"*; the pious veneer was a mere façade. I had genuinely loved these people and thought of them as family, but I had never dealt with anyone capable of such falsehoods and deception.

Wasn't it enough they had done nothing to protect me from the abuse in the first place? Now they wanted to blatantly lie and destroy my reputation? It was apparent they only cared about preserving their family reputation and covering up the scandal of abuse. If they could discredit me, make it appear I was crazy and out for revenge, no one would believe the abuse ever happened. Rakesh would remain in everyone's eyes the wonderful, compassionate, religious doctor incapable of ever committing such a crime.

My family warned me to be detached and not react to the gossip. They said it was common for rumors like this to occur and at least our family would know the truth. I tried to let that comfort me, but the pain and devastation of betrayal weighed on me. My trust and faith in the benevolence of others had been shattered. In addition to my husband's deception this was too much for me to process. I was incredulous to discover his mother also had the audacity to visit our family guru in India and lie to her saying Rakesh had never been violent and I was a liar. My guru did not believe her, but she also did nothing to intervene. Her failure to take any action was yet another betrayal.

Meanwhile, Chara Auntie, the same woman who had first introduced us, did nothing to intercede after I begged her to help. If she had spoken to Rakesh or his mother to let them know his violent behavior was absolutely unacceptable or expressed any outrage, it would have sent them the clear and strong message that society would condemn them for these actions. I can never forgive her for her silence and reluctance to be involved. At a dinner party several months later, Chara Auntie would say to my parents, *"Well, it is good that you are at least showing your face outside of the home."* Shocked by her inconsideration, I wondered how did she have the audacity to say this to my parents and assume they were ashamed by the fact their daughter was going through a divorce?

My Regrets

I had to come to terms with acknowledging my seven-year investment in this man and this marriage was over. Processing my heartbreak, anguish, and complete desolation of spirit, I wished I could have set myself free sooner. I could not go back in time but it was crippling to know I had endured this intense suffering unnecessarily. How could I not feel totally foolish for my blindness?

I wish there was a way to erase the pain, reclaim all those years of my life wasted pursuing a dream never meant to be. I wished for some way to make the anguish more bearable even though I longed for an escape. I accepted the healing process would take time. In the end, I would live through this, transform myself, and be a stronger person for surviving this. There must be a reason or purpose to my suffering, and I was determined to find it even if I could not see it from my current vantage point.

Chapter 28 AT WAR

Vitality shows not only in the ability to persist but in the ability to start over. F. Scott Fitzgerald

New Arena

There was no way I could have anticipated the direction our life would take once the legal battle commenced. I had not expected my soon-to-be ex to continue to be abusive but Rakesh took his animosity towards me to a heightened level. The legal process would now apparently be his arena to manipulate and intimidate me and continue the addictive dynamic on which he seemed to thrive. I had been hopeful for many months justice would be served and Rakesh would be fair and reasonable in splitting our assets to make up for what he had done to me, but he proved me wrong very quickly.

I told him, *"Rakesh, it is never too late to do the right thing; it is never too late to be a better person."* I reasoned after everything I had done to protect his career and reputation, it seemed only natural he would try to redeem himself and do that much for me. Yet it was foolish to think he would be different now since he had never showed me any fairness or kindness in all the years I had known him. It was ludicrous I still held onto some hope he would be fair during the divorce process. Alas, my naïveté persisted leading me to feel constantly let down and betrayed during our negotiations.

Initial Court Hearing

At the end of May, we had our initial courtroom drama where I would meet Rakesh for the first time since filing for divorce. Terrified of his anticipated hostility, I was surprised instead he was cold, indifferent, and acted as if I was a total stranger. Seeing him after our separation of a few months, I felt a surge of so many emotions-fear, panic, anger, hatred, rage, betrayal, frustration. I wanted to yell and scream at him, beg him not to keep treating me this way, and express all my pent-up emotion.

I hated myself for still longing to speak to him face-to-face and holding a glimmer of hope I could get through to him. Alas, there was no opportunity to speak to each other. The day was anticlimactic as his attorney asked for a continuance to postpone the hearing and it was granted. He also cleverly asked the restraining order go both ways, implying his client needed protection from me. I was shocked and upset that was the card they were going to play and was extremely disappointed my attorney was not sharp enough to object.

The next day, his attorney asked me to drop the restraining order on the grounds it was a "drastic and unnecessary measure" jeopardizing

Rakesh's job and immigration status. I wanted to laugh. Had Rakesh never realized before what was on the line? I decided to hold my ground. Several days later we received his counter-petition in which he denied all the allegations of abuse and my right for alimony; reading that was like a knife piercing my chest. After everything he had put me through, did he not even have the decency to provide some sort of temporary financial support? How was I supposed to survive? The following week, his attorney offered a mediocre temporary settlement on the grounds I willingly drop the restraining order. It was obvious to me they were desperate to save face.

Restraining Order Hearing

On June 18th 2008, we showed up to court for the second time. I was nervous but well prepared by my attorney and therapist. I walked into the courtroom feeling confident, knowing truth was on my side, and my focus was to stay calm. My attorney had warned the permanent restraining order could be denied on the grounds of my lack of evidence. I told myself to be detached from the outcome; the most important task was to not feel afraid of Rakesh. It was my chance to take a stand, be strong, and show him he could not get away with his crimes against me anymore.

Relieved Judge Sanchez was a female, I assumed she would be compassionate and understanding. I was grateful she permitted me to speak freely for an hour to tell my side of the story and review the extensive documentation I had provided with forty-two abusive incidents described in detail over the past six years. Calm and poised, I answered her questions honestly. After a lunch break she allowed Rakesh to also speak for an hour and describe his version of events. Dressed in an expensive suit, he was confident, collected, and listed his credentials and medical accomplishments to impress her. He denied all allegations of abuse and painted the picture I was a vindictive wife out for revenge and to ruin his reputation.

Up until this point, I had expected everything he said. I knew after being in denial for six years, he was not going to openly admit to the abuse now, especially when it jeopardized his career and immigration status. He would do everything possible to protect himself. What did surprise me was the extent to which he would go to accomplish this, including lying under oath.

His lawyer proceeded to quote a letter that said "*obtaining a restraining order would be an advantage in the divorce process.*" To my astonishment, he was reading the notes my sister had taken upon my request at our first meeting with an attorney earlier in March. With all the chaos of events that ensued in those next few months, I lost the notebook and never had a chance to read her notes. During the one week in April when I traveled to California and trusted Rakesh to live in the home, I realized he somehow went through all my personal belongings, photocopied the notebook, and allowed his lawyer to present the notes in court as evidence against me many months later.

MY FIGHT FOR FREEDOM 293

Now I understood the extent of his deception and how he was cleverly building his case against me just like the jyotishi had warned. Just as he had done with the marriage counselor, he would portray himself as a victim of a bad marriage in the courtroom. This fit with the common theme throughout our marriage where Rakesh always played the victim as misfortune "mysteriously" happened to him whether it was due to circumstance, bad luck, people's misunderstandings, or being in the wrong place at the wrong time.

My attorney asked me to describe one of the abusive incidents in detail so I chose the assault when my husband banged my head into the wooden floor repeatedly until I lost consciousness. After Rakesh carried me to my bed, I was desperate for any sort of relief from the excruciating pain and pleaded with him for some aspirin to dull my throbbing headache. Rakesh's lawyer replied incredulously, *"Do you really want the court to believe you asked for aspirin after such an incident?"* In disbelief of this reaction, I wanted to question him: *"Have you ever been beaten to the point of unconsciousness by someone before?"* If he had, he would know it was an amazing feat for me to make any request at all after the trauma I had endured.

Twist of Fate

I was flabbergasted when they proceeded to submit other evidence to the court, pictures of "his injuries." I had no idea at first what it could be. Then I realized on the fateful day of January 1st when he had provoked me and egged me on to hit him during our fight in the kitchen, I had finally pinched his cheeks when he came towards me aggressively. It was only because I had long nails that the impression of my nail marks were left. Ashamed of my actions, he had promised he would not tell anyone. When he had flown the next day to visit his sister and say goodbye to his mother who was leaving for India the following week, they had taken a picture.

The betrayal at the hands of my husband and his entire family was too much for me to process. He came home after that weekend and made me believe he was sincerely trying to work on saving our marriage but the deception had been there all along. I thought of all the times I could have collected evidence and never thought to do so. The second time I touched him in six years had left a mark and he instantly thought of documenting it to protect himself. I realized we were miles apart. All of his actions were based only on his self-interest and self-preservation.

Rakesh proceeded to tell the judge: *"Your honor, she is an angry, violent woman, who has always been the aggressor. She likes to kick me, hit me, punch me, and I have only acted in self-defense in our marriage."* How could he lie under oath so nonchalantly? It was a ridiculous claim to make when I was half his weight and clearly no match for his physical stature. I was appalled at the depth of his lies, fabricated stories, and constant betrayal. I could not believe it had come to this.

Maintaining my composure and fighting back my anger was one of the most difficult things I had to do. In my opinion, he was a coward who could not face the truth, take responsibility for his actions, or have the strength to stand up and be a man. Understanding his true nature was horrifying. Rakesh never followed through with his own request for a restraining order, which I see in hindsight was merely a strategy to unnerve me.

What many judges and attorneys may not be cognizant of is the secret inner battle every victim must go through in the courtroom to face her husband, take a stand, control her emotions, refrain from reacting to all his unjust accusations, and squelch her rage she might be experiencing for the first time. It is no easy undertaking. As if enduring the abuse was not challenging enough, her fear and intimidation of the legal process, placing her life in someone else's hands, watching events spin out of control, and believing she is at the mercy of an unsympathetic court system are overwhelming.

The Verdict

I was hopeful the judge would see through his act, recognize these men often play the role of the victim, and accept it is common for them to lie in self-defense. After spending half the day in the courtroom, I felt confident the judge had been patient and would grant the restraining order. What Judge Sanchez said next brought me to my knees. She declared, "*I do honestly believe you are a victim, but I cannot understand how in six years you have such extensive documentation but failed to call the police any of those times, have witnesses, or get any medical reports. I am truly baffled.*" She could not understand the cultural biases dictating my actions or the fact Indian women rarely take such a stand. She continued, "*I cannot grant the permanent restraining order on the grounds of your lack of evidence and the fact your husband denies all allegations.*"

I felt someone had just stabbed me in the gut. I could not move. Paralyzed by shock, I tried to comprehend how the justice system could fail me and defend and protect a criminal. How was it possible he could get away with this and always seem to win? Did the judge not realize how much strength I had to muster just to come into the courtroom that day, face him, and speak publicly about the abuse? How could these abusive men be so clever at manipulating the system, playing everything to their advantage, and getting away with their crimes?

I was gripped with fear knowing how victorious Rakesh felt and there was no protection granted to me even though the judge believed I was a victim. My attorney reassured me I could call 911 during an emergency situation, but that was no consolation. Physically overpowering me, Rakesh had always made it impossible to reach a phone. If he wanted to harm me, he would find a way to do so and there would be no way I could protect myself. I was utterly defeated.

I was disappointed my attorney had not been more aggressive to secure this victory for me. He was kind and compassionate but failed to explain to the judge my cultural impediments and that only a small percentage of Indian women actually file for restraining orders. He did not mention all the reasons I protected my husband and refused to report him. This was not an action an Indian wife would typically take, especially if living in a joint-family where in-laws would testify against me.

My attorney failed to tell her informing the police would jeopardize my husband's immigration status, a crucial reason to keep my silence. Unless I was prepared to have him be deported or be left without any way to support myself, in my mind, calling them was not an option. He omitted the fact I was afraid of requesting medical care since another Indian physician could easily discover my husband was an abuser and it would affect his employment. If I had acted to protect myself and sent my husband to jail, I would have had to face the fear of his retaliation, the disapproval and wrath of his family who would never have forgiven me, and ruining my relationship with them forever. There was no way the judge could have known these things.

If my attorney had persuasively made this case, she might have understood why I waited until filing for divorce to file for a restraining order. It was only when I was certain my marriage was over that I could take this stand. My attorney also commented my evidence was "stale," referring to our last incident occurring in January. I will never forgive him for using those words. Rakesh's pit bull lawyer immediately pounced on his word choice and used this to his advantage. I lost my case essentially because my attorney failed to make a convincing argument about the present fear of imminent danger.

After everything I did to protect this man, my actions had ultimately cost me and it finally came down to them being used against me. Judge Sanchez was now protecting Rakesh because of my silence and foolishness. Devastated, I regretted all my choices over the years to think of him first. If it had been granted, the restraining order would have ruined Rakesh's life, put his job in jeopardy, his citizenship would have been denied, and he would have faced deportation. He would have returned to India in shame and dealt with his family's humiliation.

I blamed myself for being ignorant, naïve, taken advantage of, and not savvy enough to defend myself or gather evidence. In some ways, I was an accomplice to his crime because I did nothing to stop it and that weighed on my conscience heavily. I saw Rakesh and his lawyer smiling, a wave of relief apparent on their faces, victory in their eyes. I was crushed. I understood the magnitude of his victory: he got away with perjury, painting the picture he was a victim of my aggression, and convincing the judge to take his side. He won the battle of protecting himself, walking away with a clean record, keeping his job, and staying in America. I knew now there was no justice; there was no god. I had been betrayed by my attorney, the justice system, and more importantly, my gods.

Pivotal Moment

If I had been granted a restraining order, the immense satisfaction justice had been served would have allowed me to move on from the past and rebuild my new life. But that pivotal instant shaped my battle in many ways. In that moment, time stopped for me. I wanted to get down on my knees and scream. It was the most raw, unprocessed emotion I have ever felt surging through me. At my core, I felt something much larger than myself; it was the collective cry and pain of all the women in history who have been unable to protect themselves and lived at the mercy of abusive men's violent and cruel nature. Something in me snapped! I knew deep down in my gut I would fight, if not for myself, then for the greater battle of all women who had suffered this injustice unnecessarily. That day in court was one of the most definitive days of my life.

I questioned this consistent theme of domination throughout the history of mankind. We all have the right to live our lives in peace and harmony without being hurt by another. It was unacceptable for perpetrators to get away with these crimes, walk away without any accountability, and for women to be left unprotected. Someone had to take a stand. I wanted to be the voice for all the women who had never had one. More than my private struggle, finding justice was about joining the collective fight to protect basic human rights and dignity for all abused women, assisting victims in extricating themselves from their situations and rebuilding their lives again, educating the public about the truth behind domestic violence, dispelling the myths, and teaching communities to stop inadvertently protecting the abuser.

If my suffering had no other purpose than to let me be a voice for these women, I accepted it. That day was my turning point to provide the determination and fuel I needed to fight the battle and persevere, to reclaim the suppressed voice within me and unleash it. Preventing other women, and young Indian girls especially, from my fate of enduring needless suffering in the name of being a dutiful wife was my mission. Dedicating myself to this cause was the only way I could derive any meaning from my pain. Without this fuel, the desire to write this book, bring to light the true nature of abuse, and highlight its nuances in the Indian community, would probably not have bloomed in my heart.

Revenge Versus Justice

I believe every victim fantasizes about revenge and wants her perpetrator to suffer the same way she has. A part of me wished to hurt him, not physically, but at a deeper level inside so he could experience a fraction of my pain. I thought of all the reasons I desired revenge and how much I hated this man for using me all these years. I now knew he was evil, cruel, heartless, someone who never deserved all the love I showered on him. How could I expect any less from a man who had battered me repeatedly? I felt an urgency to finish the legal process as quickly as possible; he was like a poison that needed to be extricated from my system.

I could not stand the sight of him. Most of all, I hated myself for falling in love with this man, giving him my heart, and trusting him with my life.

But I realized revenge was futile and at best would only bring temporary satisfaction. Besides, I did not want to be like the man I detested and stoop to his level. More than revenge I craved justice, which I knew was not in my hands. I lost my legal battle because I always put him first and protected him, losing my own voice and rights in the process. Even if the legal system failed me, I believed there was a higher force that would make him face what he had done and be held accountable for his actions. The law of karma could not be evaded. The best revenge was focusing on myself and my healing process, recovering from my trauma, and moving on with my life. I cherished a famous quote I repeated to myself often, *"The best revenge is living well."*

My Victory

In hindsight, my victory was larger than the courtroom. Rakesh may have won the legal battle, but mine was a spiritual victory in every sense. I believe our victories are shaped by the battles we choose to fight. I chose to stand up for myself and for every woman who has suffered an injustice similar to mine. I mustered the courage to face him in court, stand my ground, look at the judge and his lawyer in the eye, and discuss my intensely private victimization I had kept a secret for six long years.

I focused on staying calm and centered and speaking my truth. I reclaimed my voice and my power thereby sending Rakesh the message I was no longer scared of him. I gained tremendous clarity into his true nature hearing him lie, seeing the lengths to which he would go to defend himself, and observing that ultimately he only seemed to care about his pride and reputation. There was no way a coward who was so weak and petrified that he had to resort to violence to feel like a man could ever have power over me again. Any lingering sentiments of love I felt for him vanished that day.

Because he probably still thought of me as weak, vulnerable, scared, and easy to take advantage of, he felt confident in winning this battle like he had all others. But what he did not recognize was I was now awake, conscious, and resilient. I had support and was on my way to recovery. I took comfort in knowing at the end of this experience I would be transformed into someone who I could not even begin to fathom right now, a woman who was strong, had purpose, clarity, and a voice. No one would ever be able to steal that away from me again.

Legal Battle Continues

Drenched in the legal process, the next couple of months were intense. The reality of refinancing my home, selling my car, changing my name in numerous documents, and all the legal paperwork kept me too preoccupied to focus on self-care. I had no time to process my emotions, receive therapy, or get the help I desperately needed. Rakesh kept me on my toes week after week as new dramatic events unfolded. He seemed determined to continue the abuse through legal means by intimidating me in any way he could whether it was through financial tactics, depleting my energy, or weakening my resolve. He had found a lawyer who barked ferociously like a pit bull and could act as his bully.

I had to confront my emotions as we received a constant stream of nasty, scathing letters from Rakesh's attorney, whose apparent sole intention seemed to be to harass me. Each letter was devastating, emotionally crippling, a blow to my gut, evidently designed to erode my spirit. I understood it was a psychological mind game they were playing and the apparent strategy would be to prey upon my vulnerabilities the same way he had during the abusive marriage.

I would like to say I was strong, but there were countless times I wanted to give up my fight, feeling I could not recover from his onslaught of nastiness. I often regretted filing for divorce thinking it would have just been easier to stay married than to face his wrath or deal with the financial insecurity. I questioned whether it would have been easier to just be beaten up or killed by his hands than deal with the uncertainty and agony of the legal process and what I would have to face day after day. I wondered what was worse: dealing with the abuse every day or dealing with the legal battle where he now had many powerful partners in crime. I did not have an answer.

Chapter 29 MY INTERNAL BATTLE

Much of your pain is the bitter potion by which the physician within you heals your sick self. Kahlil Gibran

Fracturing

After filing for divorce in May, the summer and fall of 2008 was a tumultuous time period. I was on an emotional roller coaster during this volatile phase while I wrestled with my conflicting thoughts, battled my despair and self-doubt, and processed my anguish. I realize now waking up from the nightmare, having the courage to get out of my marriage, and initiating the legal battle were only the beginning of the process. It was daunting to know how much further I needed to go and the path ahead of me would not be easy. In the midst of processing my trauma and understanding my victimization, I still had to function on a daily basis and handle the twists and turns of the divorce process. As relentlessly as the merciless consuming legal battle continued on the exterior, my personal battle was being waged on the interior.

The cognitive dissonance pattern that had become my way of adapting throughout my marriage resulted in extreme fragmentation of my mind, heart, and spirit. I had increasingly relied on the part of me pretending to live an abuse-free life. No matter how scary it was I knew it was time to take an honest look at myself in the mirror and not hide anymore. I had to come to terms with what a sham my marriage was and do away with my dependence on my impeccable thespian skills all these years deceiving my family, my friends, and most importantly, myself. I could not even comprehend my self-betrayal. I faced the enormity of mending my broken heart, tending to my wounds that ran deep, and the dilemma of mastering wholeness again.

Throughout the years of my marriage and separation, having a career, running a business, and using my clinical skills were what gave my life meaning. Following my *dharma* (life's purpose) sustained and nourished my spirit and soul. I cherished the relationships I had with my clients and valued our interactions. I was grateful and humbled being able to serve them in their healing journeys. But now I found myself questioning how to motivate and inspire my patients when I could not do this for myself. At work I had to maintain appearances I was strong, still functioning, capable of working, and not share my personal life with anyone, despite the fact my inner struggle gnawed at me.

The fracturing created a rift in every area of my life, and as a result I lacked emotional cohesion. After finally creating the practice of my dreams, setting up a beautiful, inviting office space that everyone complimented me on for its healing ambience, and obtaining my lovely home, it was suddenly all devoid of meaning. I could not enjoy any of those things in my state of detachment where none of the parts of my life cohesively fit or made sense. Focusing on work, marketing my practice, or putting energy into running my business was a struggle when my priority was to just keep myself going from day to day. I forced myself to move through the motions mechanically of getting from place to place, trying desperately not to fall apart while continuing to smile to the outside world.

Many of my *sadhanas* (spiritual practices) that had been a way of life for me since I was a teenager, especially my daily disciplined yoga and meditation practice, had deteriorated. I gave up teaching yoga for the year since I could not practice myself. It was a challenge to concentrate and reach the same level of spiritual absorption that had been familiar to me over the years as I battled my PTSD symptoms: flashbacks and intrusive recall of abusive incidents and altercations. I struggled to reclaim this part of my life again by surrendering, gently allowing myself to be a beginner all over again, but painfully aware of how much I had lost.

Battling My Despair

After denying my emotions for so many years, I felt a dam ready to burst inside and recognized how unprepared I was to handle their sheer intensity. I could finally acknowledge these feelings were real; they did exist and possessed a life of their own. I marveled at how to face the competing sentiments inside of me: anger, grief, frustration, betrayal. Which one would I choose to pay attention to that day? I constantly fluctuated from periods of weakness to strength, never knowing when I woke up what reactions I would battle that day. I wanted to scream and cry, pound my fists against the wall, unleash the unbearable pain that finally penetrated my numbness like winter ice thawing under beams of sunlight. The anguish of my heart was unbearable. Drowning in the immense ocean of my pain, my invisible wounds were raw.

The fear of losing myself completely during this isolation overwhelmed me as I watched my disintegration. I did not know how to think straight after so much had been taken away from me. Not sure where to find the strength or the ability to heal myself, I sat in the silence of my fear feeling there was no escape from my heartbreak and desolation. Yet, I found there were no tears, no release, no outlet. This could not possibly be healthy. After crying my heart out for the six years Rakesh and I were together, I was no longer able to shed a single tear. My numbness had reached a pinnacle. Every night I dealt with the same questions: how will I sleep tonight, cope with my loneliness, endure the pain? The anticipation of tomorrow and what struggles it might invariably bring kept me awake.

The mornings were no easier. Finding it difficult to get out of bed, I wondered how to find the courage to face the day. How would I endure more of the litigation process whose uncertainty and drama eroded my strength? How would I hold my head up and keep going? Did I have the capacity to continue when I was hanging on by such a fine thread? This battle had already taken everything I had and there was so much further left to go... I found myself struggling to find meaning in my life, trying desperately to hold on to some purpose when I felt that meaningless violence had destroyed everything in my life I held dear.

I was a broken person. I had no strength left, no will to live, no joy or hope, no dreams left to pursue. I had withstood violence and torture I did not even imagine possible at the hands of the man I loved. I needed to find a way to thrive despite all the pain and destruction in my life. There were layers of emotions to peel through. Desperate for someone to throw me a lifeline, I had to accept facing this pain was my journey. I craved stillness and tranquility, yet the more I sought them the more unobtainable they became. I longed for simplicity, for a mended heart, for my life to make sense again. I yearned for clarity, direction, and to feel whole again. I prayed to find a way to release my pain and anger, be free of my past, and discover peace in the midst of all this chaos.

Survival

Those months were extraordinarily taxing while trying to function on a daily basis posed a challenge. Processing the abuse could not be prioritized, unfortunately, while I dealt with basic survival issues. Constant anxiety and adrenaline flooded my system. The pendulum was swinging after gaining weight steadily throughout my marriage to effectively provide a buffer against Rakesh. Since I no longer needed that protection or defense, the weight was melting away. I lost close to twenty pounds as my appetite disappeared completely. I consumed only one meal every two days. My attempts to feed myself were in vain. As my emotions ate away at me, I constantly felt sick to my stomach. Hoping soup would go down easier, I found the spoon frozen in midair, unable to bring it to my lips. Nourishing myself was a battle. My physical body was wasting away the same way my spirit had after enduring so much abuse.

My body had a difficult time functioning whether it was sleeping, waking, eating, or working. Everything was a monumental struggle. I faced the complete disintegration of my being and had no clue how to heal myself. In this weakened state, there were countless days I contemplated giving up the fight. Processing my hurt and devastation made me question my will to live. I listened to the steady barrage of negative thoughts that tried to dominate my mind. There were times over the years I had fantasized about death as the only escape from the abuse but now I simply longed for an end to my internal war.

I coached myself repeatedly: *"I will persevere. I will make it through this. I will survive. I will not give up or lose hope. I will cross to the other shore."* Somehow I persisted and kept myself going because giving up would only show Rakesh he had won. After everything I had endured, I could not concede now. In the midst of my pain, I pondered how to tap into my strength and find inspiration. *"Life was too beautiful and precious to waste another day"*-that became my mantra for survival to hold on. In the midst of the darkness of divorce, I was determined to remember the beauty of life and not let my spirit slip away any further.

My Inner Healer

As engulfed as I was by the immensity of my suffering, I consoled myself there was a higher purpose and I was determined to bring forth meaning. I took comfort in knowing my wounds would heal with time no matter how unbearable they felt. I had to accept pain as one of my most profound teachers; it would cleanse my soul, process my karma, and take me deeper on my journey. By allowing my pain to flow through me instead of resisting it, it felt inevitable I would find the emotional freedom I so desired. From the depth of my pain, was the seed to heal myself. I had to water and nourish this seed and restore my withered health patiently and with care.

I embraced the healer within me and felt hopeful for the first time in years. After dispensing tremendous effort into fighting a losing battle for six years, it was critical to redirect the same energy and intensity I had put into salvaging my marriage into saving myself. Preserving my life and maintaining my dignity was a battle I could not afford to lose. Every moment was an opportunity for healing. Even in my weakened state, the potential for change and transformation always existed. Nothing was static. As I did my spiritual work I became clear what I desired most from my life: to know joy, tap into a deep inner peace, discover beauty, find my purpose, and be prosperous doing the work I loved.

I knew I desperately needed therapy but I was out of money, living on credit cards, and financially struggling. Fortunately, my extraordinary therapist Sherine agreed to work with me through this difficult time period and eventually pay her when I had sufficient funds. If not for her generosity, I do not know how I would have survived. As a fellow survivor, she understood my pain in a way no one else could.

I admired Sherine tremendously for everything she had been through, was inspired by her remarkable strength and ability to guide so many victims across to the other shore. If she could undergo that profound transformation, I knew I could do it, too. Therapy assisted me in my journey through many layers of healing as I began to grasp the consequences of my victimization. I observed myself sincerely as I processed my emotions that were an offering at the altar of my new self-awareness.

The Victim Label

The more time I had to contemplate my situation and the mess my life had become, I realized in the end I was the one who let myself stay in my predicament. I recognize my paralysis and inability to act were part of the abuser's strategy and an inherent contributor to my victimization. If I had clarity, I could have left at any time. I did not in any way blame myself for the abuse; I was a victim or rather I was victimized. If this could happen to me, it could happen to anyone. Anyone can have her wallet stolen by a pickpocket, be deceived by a con artist, or be a victim of any other horrific crime. Abuse was no different except instead of a one-time incident, it was often a reoccurring phenomenon. It was similar to accusing a rape victim of asking for it. Nobody asks to be raped; nobody asks to be abused.

But I *did* blame myself for not seeing the signs, not facing reality, for choosing the path of denial because it was the easiest way to cope, for making the mistake of not getting out sooner. I blamed myself for keeping his secret, not speaking to anyone else, not confiding in my parents who would have done anything to help me, and working so diligently to protect my husband from going to jail, losing his license, or facing deportation. Unknowingly, I participated in co-creating the reality of abuse each time I made the unconscious or conscious decision to stay. I accept, however, that I was trapped by my cultural impediments, personal belief system, resistance to divorce, and his ruthless manipulation and deception.

There is another aspect to co-creating this reality of abuse that ensnared me. During each abusive dynamic, I struggled to change the ending because I desperately needed to have closure for my own healing. My logical, rational mind made me honestly believe each time a different outcome was possible. By bringing him clarity, I felt he would choose to act non-violently and do the right thing. Ultimately, it was my very strategy to end the cycle of violence that kept perpetuating it as I engaged in the dynamic he thrived on instead of walking away. Unable to admit my defeat or accept he was consciously choosing to use violence and force against me, the cycle continued.

I understand now what it means to take responsibility. Before, I would be angry when I heard comments like *"there is no such thing as a victim"* and completely reject this concept. I still do not agree with this statement fully because I think a woman needs to contend with her victimization first as part of her healing process. During the six years I was with my husband I never once identified with the term victim until the very end when I was ready to process my abuse. Using that label and calling myself a victim was an eye-opening realization and absolutely necessary for me to develop the clarity to escape.

Taking responsibility, however, meant comprehending more clearly the role I played in allowing the abuse to continue, how I co-created the reality by not leaving him and allowed the abusive dynamic to keep playing out. But I learned the most crucial part of my healing was to learn to forgive myself and be gentle with myself. With time, I would also learn to forgive others who were not supportive, who could not be there for me, or who judged me.

I hated admitting to others I was a victim because I knew it instantly conjured in their mind the impression I was weak, spineless, had low self-esteem and no self-worth if I would let a man treat me that way.

They made these assumptions in a split second and I could tell by the way they looked at me they had already passed judgment. Instead of compassion, they felt pity. Yes, abuse does undermine a woman's confidence but that does not mean all women start out this way or only weak, insecure women are subject to violence.

I truly believe abusive men are drawn to good-natured and strong-spirited women who pose more of a challenge to dominate, labeled in Part 1 as the "foxes." I had always been extremely confident, more so than anybody else I know. When I confessed to a close friend I was a victim, she replied in shock, *"Anisha, you are one of the strongest women that I know. How could this have possibly happened to you?"* That meant a lot to me, but after being victimized I felt anything but strong.

Emotional Isolation

My "disconnect" during these months was overwhelming as the legal process continued to isolate me further. I attempted to deal with the multiple layers of isolation among family and friends that created deeper fractures in my life. As supportive as my family was, I felt a strain in my individual relationships. My mother needed space to go through her own emotional process, accept the reality of her daughter divorcing, and face her fears for my future. It was not easy with her traditional upbringing to accept I would be the first person in her family to divorce. My father was clearly upset I had not confided in them sooner (as he had every right to be), and regretted his generosity in supporting Rakesh to advance his career at every step.

My sister Arya and I did not see eye to eye on everything. I felt pressure from her to handle situations a certain way and she was frustrated whenever I did not follow her advice exactly. This only made me more cognizant of why it is so critical for family to know how to be supportive of a victim as outlined in Part 1. Even with the best intentions, I knew it was a challenge for my family to be patient and watch me struggle. But I needed space to make my own decisions, sort out my thoughts, and figure out how to handle things my own way.

I was emotionally isolated by the separation from Rakesh himself, from his immediate and extended family to whom I had felt close, and living on my own again. As healthy and refreshing as it felt, I had to acknowledge a new internal void after losing my constant companion of six years. I attempted to keep myself as busy as possible throughout these months to free my mind from the stress of litigation whether it was socializing, traveling, playing tennis, or being occupied with work. But occasionally, without any warning, a sense of loneliness and emptiness would creep up on me. When I slowed down enough to observe myself from a quiet place within, I was surprised to find I missed him from time to time. In my weaker moments, I still felt the desire to address unresolved aspects of my relationship with Rakesh.

I reflected on the "good" times we shared when he seemed to care for me and we had fun and laughed together however fleeting that was. It sounds simplistic but I wished for a way to erase the bad memories and preserve the happy ones. I missed discussing my daily life and our engaging discussions about our acupuncture clients. I had to remind myself those times were sporadic and unpredictable with no guarantee to how long they would last. There was no telling when he would become upset over something trivial and fly into the next rage.

Whatever "happiness" existed in our marriage was overshadowed by Rakesh's violence, abusiveness, and mistreatment of me. I had to face it was not him I had been in love with-it was the illusion he created of the "nice Rakesh." In reality, he evidently was an imposter, a con artist, a mockery of a man. All these years... I was in love with an illusion. Yet, I forgave myself knowing it was not a crime to want to believe in the best of people.

Volatile Friendships

Even though I reached out to others, part of my emotional isolation stemmed from not being able to share my deepest feelings or my inner turmoil. Recently relocating to Atlanta, I did not feel close enough yet to any of my new friends to confide my intimately personal experience. As a result, I chose to keep up my acting skills with many, pretending to live a normal life or steer clear of certain people altogether. I could not bring myself to tell our married friends with whom I was used to socializing as a couple that we were separated. So I made up pretenses for showing up alone to social events such as Rakesh was working late or traveling to avoid telling the truth. I did not want to deal with the stigma of divorce so I avoided the Indian community completely.

Many of my relationships with people seemed to be in flux throughout this volatile time and were put to the test. It was difficult to relate to those who had no understanding of abuse. Surprised by the reaction of some who chose to remain neutral or did not take a stand against Rakesh's abusive behavior, I lost trust in them entirely. I had to deal with rejection and betrayal by those who did not want to believe the truth.

One loyal friend of Rakesh's said, "*Violence is never acceptable but there are always two sides to every story.*" No, I wanted to inform him, violence is the only time when there is one side to the story since the perpetrator's version is completely unreliable. I could not maintain a friendship or associate with anyone who was not totally supportive of me or did not reach out during this time to help me. As a result, I lost my best friend of twenty-five years and a number of other friends in the process. I had to come to terms with the fact that not everyone would be an ally or understand how to be supportive. During this transition, it felt like people were being weeded out of my circle who could not grow into this new phase of my life with me.

After my years of isolation, however, socializing was a much-needed, healthy outlet. I watched myself grow from an isolated victim to someone who yearned to connect with others and saw that my relationships, old and new, helped me heal. Synchronicity graced my path as I met amazing individuals and cherished new friendships with people who did not know my past, where I did not have to act, and could start afresh with them. It frequently surprised me others enjoyed my company after Rakesh made it seem I was unbearable. I received compliments from strangers who appreciated my sense of humor or acknowledged other traits they admired. The stark contrast with Rakesh was apparent who only saw faults and weaknesses and never once complimented me in the six years we were together.

I was deeply touched by every act of kindness, whether it was strangers or dear friends. I reconnected with many old friends who I had lost touch with over the years, grasping how much the abuse had alienated me from everything I held dear. Reuniting so many years later, many friends came to visit throughout the summer and reminded me how to have fun again, something I had not done in six years. I found solace and comfort in my strong female friends whose presence carried me through my darkest time period. It was the reassuring voices of my family, friends, and therapist that allowed me to endure.

My Self-Care

I do not want to make this time period seem completely dark and bleak because it was a mixture of so many fluctuating emotions and experiences. It was also an uplifting time when I felt I was being reborn and anything could be possible after this ordeal. I felt this amazing sense of freedom the longer Rakesh and I were separated knowing I could reclaim my own life again, live without fear and abuse, and pursue my dreams and ambitions. I ascertained a prisoner of war must feel this way after being in captivity for so long. There was a sense of liberation after being imprisoned for six years. I felt like I could fly, the sky was the limit. I look back and wonder how I ever let myself fall under his dark spell; it was only because my love was truly blinding.

Strength flowed into me with my family's love and acknowledging how many people stood behind me and supported me. Talking to my best friend Radha on the phone daily as we went through our divorce process simultaneously was the best support system I had. I continued to rely on resources like speaking with the hotline staff at a South Asian women's organization to gain clarity and confidence. I witnessed my strength growing daily and weekly. Surprisingly, I was progressing swiftly.

I look back at where I was a month ago or a year ago and acknowledged I was not the same person. I had made tremendous progress and I was encouraged I would emerge on the other side. I felt an intense awakening, a pivotal transformation taking place, and my deeper purpose unfolding. I recognized my struggle was a spiritual battle to reclaim my personal power I had surrendered to Rakesh and had lain dormant in me for what felt like an eternity. I needed to tap into my inner strength, let it awaken, and allow it to fuel my battle.

Physically I needed to stay active and reconnect with my physical body that had withstood so much neglect and abuse over the years. Ungrounded, out of touch with myself, I needed to feel centered again. I had wanted to take a self-defense training course but with my limited financial resources did not have sufficient funds to pay for anything besides groceries, household bills, basic survival needs, and exorbitant legal expenses. Battling my intense emotional process required an outlet of some sort so I turned to tennis, a sport I had not played in years to vent some of my anger and aggression. It helped me get in shape, make new friends, and feel good about myself again. I started to cook for myself and eat nourishing foods as I watched my appetite gradually start to come back. I was healing slowly but surely.

Healing Modalities

I found my own personal acupuncturist, so I did not have to rely on treating or diagnosing myself. Specializing in treating PTSD, the irony was not lost on me I had failed to recognize these same symptoms in myself early on. Filled with adrenaline from the stress of trauma and litigation, I knew I was in dire need of treatment. Observing many of my clients over the years resolve their PTSD symptoms and recover from their trauma gracefully, I knew I would immensely benefit from treatment. Visiting a traditional Chinese medicine clinic, I instructed my practitioner in clinical protocols I had developed to treat trauma. I told her exactly which acupoints to stimulate to facilitate adrenaline release, calm my nervous system that was in overdrive, release my fear and anger, increase my strength and energy, and induce mental clarity and peace. The effects were profound. Within weeks, I felt like a new person.

My friend Aruna flew in for a weekend and walked me through a few somatic trauma resolution exercises to re-establish my boundaries. She explained how any assault or trauma ruptures the energetic field and creates an energy leak or weakness. She made me relive specific abusive incidents, track the sensations in my physical body as my nervous system was rewired to experience the trauma, and release the impulses trapped in my nervous system. She instructed me to rewrite those scenes so instead of being a victim I took charge, felt empowered, and changed the ending.

As I imagined saying no, taking a stand, and felt what it was like to defend and protect myself, the fear and panic began to melt away. I was given permission to do anything I wanted, be physical with my aggressor, walk away, say anything my heart desired. It was a liberating experience and I felt stronger and more powerful after that. I sensed the release of negative toxic emotions trapped in my system. Aruna said something that resonated with me deeply, *"You have been given this experience to find your light in the midst of all this darkness, and to hold onto that light."*

SAWO Meetings

During the summer months as I researched domestic violence online and looked into South Asian Women's Organizations (SAWO) specifically, I attended two pivotal meetings. The first one was four hours away but I felt compelled to go. They had invited the South Asian Bar Association (SABA) to partner with them for this program so the speakers included a judge, attorneys, and other members to provide different legal perspectives on DV, share their insight, and speak frankly on matters such as restraining orders.

An immigration attorney discussed legal issues for women who were not citizens. I had never contemplated the struggles immigrants would have to deal with such as language barriers, visa issues, and an inability to work or have a career. I was starting to grasp the complexities within the field of DV and appreciate how each woman's struggle was unique. The meeting was incredibly informative and began to open my eyes.

That night was another turning point for me. I was overwhelmed being in a room filled with Indian people who were supportive of the cause, open to discussing a topic still considered taboo by many members of the community, and who sincerely wanted to help. After feeling betrayed by so many people I had turned to, especially in the Indian community, it brought tears to my eyes to know even a group of strangers I had never met before felt compassion for my struggle.

I spoke to a therapist in the audience who brought to my attention there was another young Indian woman close to my area she could put me in touch with. We exchanged phone numbers and I spoke to Devi, one of my first Indian girlfriends going through the same experience I was. After feeling alone in our respective cities without any contacts or resources in the Indian community, it was amazing to connect and share our experiences. Comparing notes we realized how similar our stories were, the identical patterns playing out, the familiarity of our struggles. We bonded and laughed over the fact both our in-laws had spread rumors we were schizophrenic. It was a relief to know I was not the only Indian girl who was an accused schizophrenic!

I was infected with Devi's enthusiasm and encouragement, her same passion to reach out and educate others, her desire to be involved, and that she was not afraid to share her story. After feeling alone for so long, it was amazing to be supported and know I had company on this journey. I recognized our meeting as the beginning of a great friendship. We discussed creating our own regular local support group in our area and meeting other Indian women who wanted to open up and be involved. It would be a wonderful opportunity to make new friendships.

The very next week, I attended another meeting for a relatively new SAWO and felt inspired and empowered, once again, to be in a room filled with people who supported this cause. Devi also joined me at this meeting and we both had a chance to briefly share our stories. We were the only two survivors in the entire room and everyone complimented us on our courage for opening up. It was extremely disappointing, however, that the organization did not have any resources available for us. Even though we desperately needed immediate assistance during our struggles to break free, there was no support group created yet and they did not think it would be feasible for quite some time.

I felt a sense of exhilaration opening up after years of silence, speaking with participants, admitting I was a survivor, and understanding the relevant issues and concerns to tackle this problem. Knowing so many people championed this cause, I felt validated not having to fight this on my own as the DV movement grew within the South Asian community. After all my years of isolation, feeling confident I could reach out to others made a world of difference in shaping my battle.

Chapter 30 MY LIBERATION

You have within you the strength, the patience, and the passion to reach for the stars and change the world. Harriet Tubman

Mediation

September 4, 2008 was the day of mediation. It would be the first time I would see Rakesh in months since our courtroom drama in May. Before we began our proceedings, I asked him to speak with me. I sought some connection in the midst of our cold, unforgiving legal battle. Talking to him after so many months, sitting so close to him, looking into those eyes I had peered into countless times, I had to ask: *"Rakesh, did you ever truly love me?"* After a long pause with his head hung down, he replied quietly, *"Yes, Anisha... I did."* Hearing him say yes after all this, my heart exploded with a pain and intensity I had not known before. I felt the deceptive tenderness and love I used to believe he had for me. The sheer complexity of my emotions overwhelmed me.

I inquired, *"Rakesh, would you ever beat your mother the way you assaulted me, or be okay watching someone else attack me up the way you have?"* Vehemently he said no. My attorney walked in at that moment, visibly surprised to see us speaking, and immediately pulled me into a separate room for our negotiations. That was the last time we ever spoke, our final interaction. I believe he might have thought he loved me in his own way, as much as he was capable, but it was not true love. His apparent narcissistic personality prevented him from genuinely caring about anyone besides himself. I had to face once again that I was a deluded victim, prey to his manipulation and deception, with an unhealthy attachment from my traumatic bonding I mistook as love all those years.

Signing Divorce Papers

After endless months of the legal process involving hearings, mediation, and countless letters from our attorneys back and forth, we were nearing the grand finale. On October 23, 2008, Rakesh signed the divorce papers after much anticipation. I saw his signature and was curious-what went through his mind at those last moments? Did he hesitate at all? Did he have any regrets? Did he feel sadness or remorse? But in my heart I knew the answer: he was a man with a cold heart of steel who did not possess the courage to face himself or be honest regarding his emotions. The realization he was not capable of feeling anything hit me hard.

Before I was to sign the papers, I read through all seventeen pages of our marital settlement agreement after numerous drafts between our attorneys. I had requested two years of alimony to get me on my feet after all the sacrifices I made with my career and always putting his professional goals first. Of course, Rakesh refused to be understanding, and I ended up with less than two years. I could expect no better of him knowing it was not in his nature to be generous. As I read through the agreement my repulsion for this man and his behavior spewed to the surface. Once again I had to process Rakesh's betrayal, how much he had used me, detested me, and all the ways in which I had been a victim of his manipulation.

On October 27, 2008, I sat in my attorney's office overwhelmed by the finality of it all. I was not pleased with our agreement; there were many things I wanted to change and had settled for because Rakesh refused to compromise. I was emotionally exhausted and defeated. Rakesh may have assumed if he dragged out the legal proceedings he would wear me down psychologically so I would accept anything at the end just to resolve this quickly. I was aware there was nothing that could be changed now.

Under duress, with a heavy heart and a clouded mind, I signed the papers just to end this battle and move on with my life. I felt let down by the heartless and cruel legal process, my unsympathetic and unmotivated attorney, my withering spirit, and my inability to continue fighting. I had lost yet another battle. Even though the anticipation had built for months to officially sign the divorce agreement, my reaction was not what I expected. I thought I would feel relief, elation, jubilation, or excitement. But I felt none of those things. Instead, I felt empty inside, numb, devoid of all feeling. It was a strange sensation that took me by surprise.

Day of Liberation

Our final court hearing was on October 28, 2008. I stood before Judge Mendell as he looked deeply into my eyes and asked me, *"Why do you believe your marriage is irretrievably broken?"* Surprised by this human touch in the midst of the coldness of all our legal proceedings, I was dumbfounded how to answer him. A myriad of reasons ran through my mind for why our marriage was a sham, which one to pick was the dilemma. After some deliberation, I responded quietly, *"Because he never truly loved me and he did not treat me well."*

With one swift pounding of his gavel, the judge declared us officially divorced, almost seven years from our wedding day. I like to think of that moment as the day of my liberation, my emancipation from the prison of abuse where I had been trapped. I felt an enormous weight lift off me knowing I would not be subject to this man's violence any longer and could reclaim my own life. I was free at last. Anything was possible.

I assumed when my divorce was finalized I would want to celebrate and share my excitement with others. But instead, I felt a profound quietness and a yearning for stillness deep within. I sat in my backyard watching the trees sway rhythmically in the wind, seeing their suppleness, resiliency, and grace. Who knows what they had witnessed in their lifetime? Yet they stood tall, and I knew in that moment I would, too. Just as they were firmly rooted to the earth with their branches reaching for the heavens, I would find a way to let my spirit soar. Nature always found a way to persevere and so would I.

I lit some candles, put on soothing music, and went deep into meditation, entering a place within me transcending space and time, beyond pain or pleasure. I felt a sense of freedom that was infinitely light, expansive, and exhilarating. I stepped outside of all my pain and suffering and identified with my soaring spirit that could not be touched by anything. I felt the life force moving through me with exquisite grace, listened to the miracle of my heart still beating after everything I had been through, and watched my breath flowing smoothly with ease. In that moment, I knew my pain had a purpose, and gently, I allowed myself to fall deeply in love with myself once again…

Rebuilding

The arduous journey to break free was in some ways just as challenging as living with the abuse, yet each had its own veritable struggles. Reflecting on the stages I had traversed to break free, I identified four phases a victim must pass through even though there was a great degree of overlap between them: (1) the Crisis Phase (2) the Legal Phase (3) the Healing Phase and (4) the Rebuilding Phase. There was no doubt that the crisis phase was the most intensely critical period where finding ways to be safe, getting out of immediate danger, and strategizing how to escape while I was still so weak dominated my life. The most crucial element was the ongoing unwavering support I had from family, friends, and my therapist.

Overlapping with the crisis phase, the legal phase took over without much warning, leaving no time to think, recover, or gather my wits. I had no chance to mentally prepare myself for the major legal battle that ensued. It was consuming, messy, complicated, and unjust, exacting its own emotional toll on top of recovering from the abuse. Rakesh had succeeded in making extricating myself from the marriage as difficult as possible. Others underestimate how difficult this stage can be and how much support a victim requires to continue her fight and take a stand against the one person she has been afraid of standing up to throughout her relationship.

When I had an opportunity to come up for air, I entered the third phase of healing. Although this occurred simultaneously with the other phases, it was also a separate time of reflection, gaining clarity and perspective on my situation, prioritizing my health, and strengthening my resolve. Only after the crisis and legal phases were over could a substantial amount of healing take place. Subsequent to my official divorce was when I could finally enter the rebuilding phase where I contemplated restructuring my life, adjusting to my situation, trying to stabilize my career situation and finances, building trust, and entering new relationships. This last stage was also a time of deeper reflection and introspection.

I wish I could say rebuilding was quick and easy but that was hardly the case. I struggled with maintaining my career, my instability of income, and not having health insurance for the first time in my life. Having alimony temporarily helped, but I had lost my dream practice and beautiful office space since I could not afford to stay in my lease. As a consequence, I entered into a legal battle with my landlord that would continue to drain me. For a period, I juggled two to three jobs in my attempt to find stability.

While in the crisis phase, I lived my life one day at a time. In the rebuilding stage, I lived from month to month, never knowing what unexpected twists and turns would come my way. I fought to keep my life in Atlanta, my independence, my business, my friends, and finally put down roots in one city after all the moves Rakesh had subjected me to for his career advancements. It was a constant struggle to survive financially, but I relished my freedom and never took it for granted.

My Healing

Reflecting on my onerous journey this past year, I was exhausted. It had taken so much out of me and there were so many times when I could have easily given up, but that would have only proved to Rakesh he had won. His destructive, abusive patterns had taken a toll on so many levels: mentally, emotionally, physically, and spiritually. I contemplated everything I had steadily lost.

The image of the Hindu goddess Kali in all her might and splendor came to mind. She represented death and destruction, necessary forces ultimately responsible for growth and renewing life. Creation can only come from destruction and even though my abusive marriage had destroyed my spirit and shattered my heart, I inherently trusted the healing process. I embraced the idea of being reborn and that from the ashes of my pain something new would surface and be created.

Staring at my full-length mirror I realized my flashbacks were not as frequent as they were. I could glance at my reflection now without the fear of being hurled into a mirror with glass shattering around me. Memories that would flood my day of the trauma still came and went but not as often. My mind gracefully let go of select recollections so I did not have to keep reliving the fear and panic that used to be my daily reality. Time was assisting in feeling safe and protected, re-establishing my boundaries, and learning to trust again. Amazed at my resiliency and how forgiving my mind and body were, I grasped I was healing.

Observing myself in the mirror, I gazed at the innocence in my face. Despite withstanding intense pain, I saw eyes that had a quality of softness and gentleness that spoke to me. I glimpsed a woman who was strong, who loved life, whose face was not hardened by suffering. I smiled at my reflection and surprisingly she smiled back. In that moment, I knew divine grace guided my path and life would blossom with abundance and sweetness. I accepted healing was an incessant journey from birth to death, a continuous process of enfoldment, a constant search for truth and meaning. I embraced the many opportunities for growth and self-awareness I would encounter. I had never been this inspired to fulfill my dreams, embrace joy, or be as in love with life as I was now.

My Transformation & Spiritual Battle

As time passed, I marveled at witnessing my transformation, the sense of freedom and elation I could feel after too many years of repression and confusion. It was truly remarkable how the human spirit could be so resilient after enduring such intense trauma. I felt a new chapter of my life waiting to be revealed, a new destiny awaiting me, a future where there would be no looking back. I was older, wiser, stronger. Over the years I had lost myself to this man and the evilness that lived inside of him, but I would never make the mistake of surrendering my power, identity, or self-expression again.

After my liberation, I knew life would never be the same. I was given a second chance to live, a privilege I would never take for granted. I was eternally grateful to be alive, to have this physical body, and cherished my right to simply be and exist. From my perspective I could look back at this experience as a gift; a gift to know myself, find my power, discover my voice, and unleash my strength. Each day was an offering; I had to make the most of it and not waste the precious gift of being alive. No matter how much pain I had experienced, there was so much beauty to absorb around me, so much joy to be discovered within, so many reasons to enjoy life *especially* after surviving the horrors of abuse.

For so long I had focused on the practical and superficial levels such as the legal battle, finances, and everyday, mundane struggles, because that was required. It had taken a toll, draining me mentally and physically. But now I saw with lucidity this conflict was so much deeper. Sherine, my therapist, had told me early on: *"This is very much a spiritual battle."* At first I did not know what she meant, but after contemplating it awhile I had an epiphany. The line resonated deeply and I realized, *"How could the fight for life, freedom, and the right to stay alive be anything but a spiritual battle?"*

Breaking free from an abusive relationship forced me to tap into the indestructible force within me that Rakesh could never touch. After struggling to find meaning in this experience and know what my destiny truly was, I saw breaking free was my chance to reclaim my power and search for freedom on so many levels. Everything in my life had led me up to this moment. The yearning for truth and liberation made this a spiritual battle. Freedom was the destiny of every soul.

My Mission

There were countless times during my struggle when I felt utterly alone, betrayed by life. I longed to reach out to other survivors who could be beacons of light as I swam through the darkness of the divorce process.

But where were they? Who else could understand my pain the way another fellow survivor could? My loneliness fueled my desire to connect with the greater community, be guided by the wisdom of other women, and seek their encouragement. For my own healing, I desperately needed to discover how they recovered from their trauma and moved on with their lives.

To heal I immersed myself in my work, doing what I loved, and feeling my life was meaningful again. As I developed myself professionally I trained in community acupuncture to treat trauma with an organization named "Acupuncturists Without Borders." In March 2010, I traveled to Ecuador for two weeks with an amazing team of acupuncturists. We treated close to nine hundred patients in that time who had little or no access to health care, and I saw the benefits of community healing. This inspired me to delve deeper in my specialty of treating PTSD.

In the fall of 2010, I launched a trauma clinic for DV victims at a local nonprofit center. Using the community model, a room filled with victims/survivors experienced the tranquil harmonizing effects of acupuncture together in a supportive atmosphere. The women I met were incredibly grateful and generously shared their stories of pain and healing with me. My mission was to train other acupuncturists in specific trauma protocols for DV victims, assist in their healing and recovery time, and create a sense of community healing within the domestic violence world.

Writing with Purpose

As I reclaimed my voice after seven years of silence and suppression, I discovered how deeply my heart ached to express itself. I found solace in writing, which brought me to the present moment in a way nothing else could. The pen became my savior to strip away layers of secrets, lift me out of the darkness where I had been trapped, and open the floodgates of repressed emotions. Every word made me stronger, and slowly, I started to remember who I was, who I used to be, and who I dreamed of being in the future. I felt a force growing within me that was both profound and powerful. Its intensity amazed me and I knew I did not suffer in vain.

Writing became my vehicle to allow strength and purpose to flow and to find meaning in my life again. I surrendered to the process cognizant that creating this book would be an extraordinary way to heal. It was a privilege to have a voice again. I could not give up the fight now simply because the crisis in my own life was over. I had to reach out and assist as many women as I could to find the power within themselves to cross to the other shore and break free.

AFTERWORD

Many people falsely believe that after leaving an abuser or divorcing, a victim's life suddenly transforms for the better, yet the aftermath of my turbulent divorce continued to haunt me more than two years later. I would like to say life became easier, but I still struggled with the detrimental impact on my career and precarious financial instability. I did not have the funds to maintain my own private practice and was dependent on the mercy of various employers during an economically unstable time for work. I considered my colleagues who had been practicing acupuncture for the past decade and how I was leagues away from their financial success. I had to contend with moving out of Atlanta after desperately fighting for so long to preserve my life there. More than two years after my divorce, I would uproot myself once again, longing for stability that seemed way beyond my reach.

Another legal battle with the ex-husband was re-opened in 2011 when Rakesh failed to uphold one of his financial promises. It would seem that he had fraudulently entered our divorce agreement without any intention of keeping his word. I had to face his betrayal yet again and knew I was mentally too exhausted to fight him anymore. He had the upper hand because I lacked the financial resources for adequate legal representation and good attorneys were difficult to come by.

The lawyer I hired made the mistake of taking me to the wrong court where the judge lacked jurisdiction to enforce the matter of collecting this debt. As a result, our case was dismissed but as the prevailing party Rakesh was granted the cost of attorney's fees. Rather than collect the debt he owed, with a sudden twist of fate, I would ironically end up being liable for an exorbitant legal bill that was beyond my means to pay because of my attorney's unbelievable incompetence. Realizing his mistake, my lawyer withdrew from the case leaving me unprepared to represent myself at subsequent hearings.

On June 8, 2011, I would see Rakesh in court after believing our paths would never have to cross again. Realizing I was representing myself, it appeared he wished to make an appearance to attempt to daunt me. Refusing to be intimidated by the legal system, I stood my ground and recounted my side of the story confidently to Judge Brown. Rakesh's pit bull lawyer would once again zealously defend his client. I tried to remain detached and unaffected by the lies and distortions they spewed about me aware this was the only behavior I could expect from them.

Infuriated by the judge's verdict and without an attorney to defend me, I felt betrayed by the justice system once again. Afterward, I asked a police escort to walk me to my car to avoid any attempts Rakesh might make to approach me. The escort told me this was a daily occurrence in his job as he had witnessed many women truly be in danger when their abusers try to retaliate with violence after leaving the courtroom.

Regardless of the outcome of the hearing, I focused on how every experience is meant to teach us a spiritual lesson. I may have lost this final legal showdown, but I found solace in knowing that this battle was so much larger than the legal system. I was able to witness how much stronger I was nearly three years later after my divorce and gain tremendous perspective about how far I had come.

Seeing Rakesh that day, he was a shadow of his former self. He appeared to hide behind his lawyer for protection and seemed intimidated by the fact I was taking a stand against him. Unbelievably, I detected fear in his eyes. I could only assume he was consumed with the internal war he would always wage, tormented by his denial and deception. Living with the truth of his actions and his brutality, mental peace would always allude him. I could only feel pity for him.

I walked away from the courtroom that day knowing I had won my freedom and nothing this man said or did could affect me anymore. To the best of my knowledge, Rakesh continued to practice medicine as a partner at his medical firm, did not have his license revoked, and suffered no legal or financial consequences. I heard rumors he was searching for a new, unsuspecting Indian wife and I prayed for her safety and that she would possess the clarity to not suffer the same fate as me.

❖

My healing continued with every passing year as I focused on my spiritual growth and freed myself from the shadows of abuse. After celebrating three years of freedom post-divorce, I finally completed this manuscript and had the opportunity to treat myself to a women's healing retreat with Lundy Bancroft, the insightful author who had started my journey towards breaking free.

I was privileged to meet twenty-five bold, admirable women who were anything but "battered." Despite their wounds, these were some of the strongest, most resilient, courageous women I have ever met. I would always treasure our bond from sharing our stories of suffering and redemption with each other. Seeing women still in crisis whose wounds were fresh and raw, I realized how far I had truly come. After surviving the darkness of abuse, I could confidently say the path ahead was brightly illuminated.

My healing would continue to be a lifelong process, but I opened my arms to the adventure of life, braced myself for the twists and turns, and looked forward to the many surprises on this journey. There was power in knowing my destiny and freedom were in my hands as I started a new chapter of my life…

PART 3

VOICES OF INDIAN WOMEN

Chapter 31 DEVI'S DEVASTATION

Staring at her computer screen vacantly, Devi could not recollect what she was writing. The bellowing of her father-in-law yanked her back to reality. It was time to cook dinner, and she was already exhausted from preparing an elaborate breakfast and lunch for her in-laws, but this was the daily ritual she had become accustomed to since moving into their miserable home. She knew if the meal was not prepared exactly as her father-in-law wished, she would be forced to begin from scratch all over again. Devi felt more like a servant than a wife. No, she reasoned, even servants were treated better than this. Before rushing to the kitchen, she finished the one-line email to send to her girlfriend. *"Every day I am dying a little death..."* That summed up her life in a nutshell ever since her dreadful marriage.

Born and raised in Bangalore, Devi immigrated to the U.S. when she was twenty-five to earn her master's degree and to work with a reputable company as an engineer. It had taken two years to become accustomed to life in a new country and being independent for the first time. Every month, she diligently sent a portion of her income back to India to support her retired parents and younger sister. At the age of twenty-seven, Devi was well settled in her job but felt the pressure from her parents to marry before she turned "too old" at thirty.

Devi had been hopeful joining an Indian matrimony website she would find a suitable match. It was a challenge to meet reliable men online, but she felt a comfortable connection with Samir. Five years older, he seemed mature and stable. As they spoke daily on the phone, he steadily gained her trust. There was no instant attraction or magnetism that defined the relationship but that was not her primary motivation. She sought someone dependable and trustworthy who would prove to be a proper candidate for marriage. After two months, the mutual decision was made to meet in person.

Samir flew to Dallas to visit her and was on his best behavior. Devi was impressed; he was calm, sweet, peaceful, and well mannered. After an enjoyable and mostly uneventful day together, Samir asked, *"Do you wish to proceed?"* Confident of her decision, Devi said yes, wondering how she became so lucky. Originally, she wanted to take things slowly, be sure of herself, and not rush into a marriage proposal. But Samir made it clear his parents would not approve of any delays and pressured her into a quick decision. He indirectly threatened to break off their relationship if she postponed agreeing to get married.

Once Devi shared the news of her engagement with her parents, they were thrilled she was fortunate enough to meet an eligible Indian husband while living abroad. Soon after, wedding plans were underway to prepare for a big celebration in Bangalore where both of their families were from. For those next six months during their engagement, there were red flags but Devi was busy with work and wedding plans and conveniently ignored them. Each time Samir displayed a bit of his temper, his outburst took her by surprise, but she reasoned he was a good man who just needed to address his anger management issues.

One day Samir inquired casually, *"Are all your student loans paid off?"* Without much contemplation, Devi replied, *"No."* Fervently, Samir insisted, *"You must pay off your student loans before the wedding! Make whatever concessions you need to. Do not eat out if necessary so you can save money."* Surprised by this demand, Devi found it incredulous she was supposed to feel guilty for having loans. She tried to oblige his request, but sometimes when he called to inquire if she had dined out, Devi felt forced to lie so he would not yell at her about spending money. His threats worked and she scrambled to pay off as much of her loans as she could to pacify him. At the time, she did not realize this was the beginning of his financial abuse tactics.

As the wedding day approached, Devi did not feel excited or lovestruck as she had expected. Even her friends commented on changes in her personality, mood, and appearance during the past few months. There were subtle differences that only those close to her noticed. She admitted she was not in love with Samir, but many Indian marriages began this way. Devi reasoned she would adjust to her new life. Her mother expressed some doubts after seeing her daughter's lack of enthusiasm, but she reluctantly trusted Devi's judgment when she heard her resolute decision to go forward with the alliance.

Samir's parents demanded a lavish wedding in India, requiring a certain amount of funds be spent for the wedding itself. They also insisted Devi's parents host all the guests in a luxurious five-star hotel along with providing a specific weight of gold for the dowry. Although the ancient Indian practice of dowry was outlawed in the 1990s, many in-laws regrettably continue to make these excessive demands. Traditionally, this practice was to ensure a daughter was given certain goods to commence her new life at her husband's home, a form of insurance and security for the marriage.

As the practice of dowry was abused, in-laws started to make unreasonable requests from the daughter-in-law's family and threatened to break off the wedding at the last minute if their demands were unsatisfied. Without a sufficient dowry, many girls remained unwed. In-laws would competitively select only the bride who could provide the highest material value of dowry. Because Devi was the eldest daughter and they were happy she had found a compatible suitor, her parents complied with the requests of her future in-laws despite the financial strain.

On the wedding day, everything that could go wrong went wrong, an ominous sign of what was to come in the marriage. The groom arrived early, and as a result, Devi's in-laws insisted she rush to get ready and not make him wait. Frustrated she had not finished applying her makeup before the ceremony, she scrambled to please them. Her mother-in-law glanced at Devi and retorted, *"Why have you become so thin? You do not look like a beautiful healthy bride at all!"* Although discouraged, Devi tried to ignore her mother-in-law's insults and focus on enjoying her wedding day.

Last minute, both families clashed over which traditional practices should be included as part of the elaborate Hindu wedding ceremony. Samir's parents insisted on changing all the details, disrespecting Devi's parents' wishes. Despite every attempt to accommodate Samir's family, Devi's parents were surprised by their unwillingness to compromise. Somehow they persisted, but it was not the wedding Devi had dreamed of and she was distressed by how much her parents had to suffer at the hands of her in-laws.

The next day, Devi and Samir had their first official fight over applying *sindhoor* (vermillion powder traditionally applied by married women to the forehead), of all things. Samir was shocked she was only wearing a small *bindi* and vehemently accused her of not taking the marriage seriously. He exclaimed, *"You are mocking me! I knew you were not keen on marrying me and forced into the alliance by your father! How dare you disrespect me this way!"* In dramatic fashion, he removed his wedding ring and insisted on calling a taxi to leave. Devi's parents tried to calm him after hearing the commotion. Samir apologized profusely for his conduct, and everyone mutually decided to overlook this one outburst.

During their two-day honeymoon in Goa the fights continued. He accused her of staring at a gentleman at the table next to theirs in a restaurant. Samir brazenly pronounced, *"I never knew you could be like this. You were stealing glances at him all night long."* Unaware of to whom he was referring, Devi was shocked by his baseless accusations. He had not displayed any jealous or possessive behavior before so this caught her by surprise. Upon returning from the honeymoon, Samir's parents accused Devi of not providing real gold for the dowry. With a heavy heart, Devi ran to the bathroom and cried. How dare they insult her parents this way! This was not how she imagined her new married life would be.

Hopeful life would improve after leaving India, she tried to be optimistic. These disputes were probably normal for any newlyweds and she reasoned it would take time for them to get to know each other. Saying goodbye to her family and friends, Devi left for the U.S. a few days later to begin their new life as husband and wife. The first month of marriage they would be forced to live apart as she would continue to work in Dallas and commute to Seattle to visit Samir on the weekends. Devi's roommate was the first to comment on Samir's controlling personality as she heard them fight over the phone repeatedly. She questioned Devi, *"Why are you letting him treat you like this?"* Devi was unable to respond.

One weekend, Samir informed Devi he was ready to buy a new home for them. When she objected to the price he quoted, he hollered, "*It is none of your business and does not concern you what I decide to spend!*" She noticed any time her opinion differed from his, he would yell, "*Stop disrespecting me! You should listen to me now. I am your husband!*" He claimed total authority and she was not to resist or question him in any way. Every detail of her life was consumed by Samir's mandates. When she was busy at work, he would call multiple times throughout the day demanding her attention. When Devi was sick and unable to fly due to a fever, Samir retorted, "*That only proves you are not interested in the marriage if you do not want to see me. I insist you fly here this weekend and stop making ridiculous excuses!*"

Samir's next demand caught her by surprise. He stipulated she no longer send money to her parents in India. Essentially, he wanted to control their finances and regulate Devi's spending. She held her ground, "*My parents need the financial support and I cannot abandon them now after sending them my income for the past two years!*" Apparently threatened by her decision to stand up for herself, Samir became physically aggressive. Maybe the strain of living apart was the issue, she reasoned, and once they were together it would be better. After that first month, Devi's boss gave her permission to move to Seattle and work from home. Ignoring her doubts and fears, she packed her belongings, determined to give the marriage her best try.

Moving into her marital home where Samir lived with his parents and younger sister, life did not get any easier. The in-laws soon joined in the abuse as well. Devi's younger sister-in-law screamed profanities at her and accused her of being mentally unstable. Never having experienced anything like this before, Devi was appalled by her behavior but Samir remained silent. Next, he demanded she relinquish her passport and important documents to him to keep safely. He insisted, "*The neighborhood we live in is not safe, and it is best that I keep everything with me so you do not lose it.*" Without questioning him, she handed over her documents, never suspecting he would withhold them later.

Samir lashed out at her from time to time, but it was his father who was the most severe abuser. Besides physically pushing and shoving her, he was strict and controlling. He demanded Devi behave submissively and learn from his exemplary wife who was tolerant and forgiving. He boasted, "*I hit Samir's mother at the beginning of our thirty-year marriage but deferentially she did not leave me because she respects me.*" He chided Devi, "*You must have this same respect for your husband's authority and look up to your mother-in-law as your role model.*" Meanwhile, her mother-in-law passively witnessed Devi's mistreatment at the hands of her husband, son, and daughter, but she never interfered.

When her father-in-law was in a particularly nasty mood he would degrade Devi's parents proclaiming, "*They knew you were crazy but married you to our son before we could find out and cheated us. They are frauds for not telling us you were mentally unstable."* Stunned, Devi did not know how to respond to these ludicrous accusations. Paralyzed, unable to stand up to them and risk being blamed for being disrespectful, she maintained her silence. Why would her husband not side with her at these critical times?

Devi wondered how had she landed in this difficult marriage. There was no way to predict her husband's family would mistreat her like this. She longed to call her parents in India and confide about the horrors of her marriage. It would be so comforting to hear their voices, but not surprisingly, her in-laws restricted her phone use. They forbid her from calling them frequently and restricted her privacy when she did speak to them along with regulating many of her other activities.

Nor was Devi permitted to speak freely to her friends on the phone, as they would be a "distraction" from Devi's duties. Even a brief phone conversation was interrupted by demands for Devi to cook for her in-laws. In a desperate attempt for freedom, she decided to search for a new job in Seattle instead of working at home, but this proved more difficult than she imagined. Her father-in-law thwarted her attempts to show up for job interviews or disconnected the line when potential employers called. He vehemently protested, *"Your place is in the home now and you must realize that taking care of us is your first priority!"*

Adding to the verbal assault, both Samir and his father became physically abusive, hitting, slapping, and pushing Devi. The more aggressive they became, the more paralyzed she was. All of these incidences occurred in the privacy of their own home without other witnesses to the cruelty Devi experienced firsthand. In the company of others, Samir lavishly praised her until people exclaimed, *"You are so lucky to have such a wonderful husband."* His deception haunted her. How could he be so loving in public and so cruel in private? She had been so hopeful before the wedding, convincing herself that this marriage was for the best, but she could not believe how wrong she was.

Devi noticed Samir's cyclic behavior pattern being abusive one day and showering her with gifts the next. Believing his temper could be abated, she endured it. Once she boldly suggested Samir attend anger management classes but he retorted, *"You must be totally crazy. You are the one who needs to go! Don't you realize your anger is out of control?"* Devi's thoughts were spinning as Samir fired his accusations, leaving her bewildered. At the end of the conversation she wondered if he was right and she was the one who needed help. Conversations with Samir always left her feeling she was to blame somehow.

Samir threatened her, *"If you ever try to leave me, I will hire hit men to come after you and kill you. Don't think you can get away so easily!"* During their fights, Samir deliberately ensured she had no way to call for help and quickly snatched away her phone. When she was raging with a fever one evening, Samir denied her medication. Their abuse grew progressively worse until they locked her in a bedroom for an entire day without any food, water, or a cell phone. Sobbing uncontrollably, Devi felt helplessly trapped in her own private hell, reduced to being a defenseless servant with people she thought would be her family.

One uneventful evening at home, Samir picked a fight with Devi. There was no trigger to ignite his hostility, but suddenly her in-laws ganged up on her. Shouting baseless accusations, they yelled, "*You are psychotic and out of control. We know you are a schizophrenic. You need medication!*" Samir forced some unidentified pills down her throat, holding her firmly so she could not physically resist. Alarmed, Devi wondered if they were poisoning her. At her wit's end, she knew this could not go on much longer. Her life and safety were on the line. No marriage was worth this!

Without warning after this altercation, Samir kicked her out of the house. "*You do not belong here! You do not deserve to live with us! You are not my wife!*" After being shoved out the door, Devi stood at her doorstep helplessly, wondering what to do. She knocked on the door repeatedly, but they ignored her. Surely they would not leave her outside in the cold and dark of the night alone? After awhile, it was clear they had no intention of letting her back in. Where would she go without shoes? Who could she ask for help? If only it had occurred to her to call the cops, but even then, she did not have her phone, purse, or money. Panic seized her. Her family was on the other side of the world, and she had no way to contact them.

Realizing she really knew no one in America, not even her own neighbors, Devi felt utterly alone and vulnerable. It had been less than a month she had been living in this new home with her in-laws and she was not even familiar with her surroundings since they never let her venture past the doorstep. A chill went down her back as she crouched behind the bushes near the house. There was nothing else she could do but wait. Surely they would let her back in soon? This was only their attempt to teach her a lesson, right? Unable to sleep, Devi stared at the hands on her watch that refused to move. Embarrassed, she thought of what the neighbors would think if they saw her hiding in the bushes. What would her parents think? How had it come to this?

As morning arrived, Devi finally heard Samir open the door. It was not to let her back in as she would have hoped but because he was rushing to work. He did not even acknowledge Devi's presence. Slipping in the door quietly, she was greeted by her in-laws who scolded her, "*You must leave today and never come back. Your presence here is not welcome. Get out immediately!*" Devi knew them too well by now not to expect kind words or an apology, but she had not imagined this. Quickly, she grabbed her purse, phone, two outfits, and headed out the door silently not wishing to speak to them. Was this what Samir wanted, too? Was her marriage really over? Betrayal and rage consumed her.

That day, Devi contacted a South Asian women's organization based in her city. She spoke to a hotline staff member who counseled her about the necessary steps she needed to take. Their periodic calls to follow up and check on her were reassuring. At least someone cared. It was comforting to feel she had some support system since her family was so far away in India. For three months Devi utilized their services. Luckily, Devi was able to return to her former job in Dallas, grateful to have employment and a way to survive financially.

She immersed herself with being productive at work and putting the past behind her. A co-worker provided her with reading material on domestic violence, and she realized for the first time that she was a victim and that abuse was not simply physical violence. Reflecting on the chaos she endured at her husband's home, she wondered how she tolerated their torture. Her official marriage had lasted two months and the first month they had not even been living together. She had never heard of such a short union. What would the Indian community say?

Once in Dallas, she purchased new clothing since her entire wardrobe was left behind at Samir's home. She wished they had at least given her some time to pack. Devi was desperate to retrieve her belongings. Almost two months after separation, she hired a police escort to accompany her to her marital home and request Samir return her passport, immigration papers, and the rest of her belongings. Calmly, Samir told the officers Devi was lying. Refusing to be defeated, Devi was determined to somehow recover her valuable possessions.

After six months of separation, Devi hired an attorney in Seattle who encouraged her to obtain a temporary order of protection for two months. When the court hearing was scheduled to obtain a permanent restraining order, Devi was unable to travel to Seattle. Her boss would not permit her any additional time off work and she could not afford airfare. Reluctantly, she withdrew her motion while Samir walked away feeling victorious.

Devi realized it was time to file for divorce. Grateful for her family's encouragement even though they were a million miles away, she was happy they completely supported her decision. If only she could afford to visit them in India. She felt so alone in this foreign country before marriage, but now with her divorce, she felt ostracized by the Indian community. Would she ever find happiness or remarry? No Indian man would look at her now. The stigma of being "damaged goods" would haunt her forever.

At her parents' suggestion, Devi contacted a divorce attorney in India to fight using dowry laws to claim damages for Samir stealing her possessions, clothing, and expensive wedding jewelry that had sentimental value. Finances were tight and Devi struggled to send funds to her parents and pay her divorce attorney that cost her an entire month's salary. Months went by while she anxiously waited for the proceedings in India to bring some resolution. One afternoon, her mother called, *"Devi, beta, I have bad news. Samir has paid off the judge, the attorney, and the police station, and your divorce case is officially closed."*

Unfortunately, accepting a bribe in Indian bureaucracy was routine and Samir had unlimited funds to do so. Crushed, Devi realized she would have to obtain a divorce in America where there would be no consideration or understanding of dowry laws. At their first court hearing Samir adamantly denied they were ever married and claimed Devi was fabricating this story. After she submitted wedding pictures as proof of the marriage to the court, Samir insisted they were photographs of a party and nothing more. The battle between attorneys would ensue for a few years.

During this time, Devi struggled emotionally, battling her loneliness and desperately missing her family. It was challenging to make new friends and not be judged by her past. She was cautious, reluctant to be as trusting and naïve again, and afraid of repeating her past mistakes. Alienated by the Indian community for revealing her separation, it was not what they said that affected her; it was what they did not say and the look of pity in their eyes that troubled Devi the most. She needed their compassion, not their pity. Her marriage was an honest mistake, a brief period in her life from which she simply wished to move on.

Even if she said she was single, the typical Indian reaction was, *"Why is an Indian girl of your age not married yet? You know you are running out of time, don't you?"* There was no escape from the condemnation of being unmarried. Sometimes it was easier to avoid the Indian community all together, but amongst Americans, Devi had a different set of issues. They could not understand arranged marriages, the concept of a dowry, or living in a joint family household. They questioned how she could marry someone she barely knew. Exasperated, Devi did not wish to keep explaining herself to them either.

Along with the emotional drama of the divorce process, Devi had to deal with practical issues such as finances and her immigration status. She hired a well-known attorney who assisted Indian women in obtaining citizenship. VAWA, the Violence Against Women's Act, offered permanent resident status to immigrant women in abusive marriages with a U.S. citizen or green card holder, so that she could build her own life without the support of her abuser. It took her a year and half to receive her green card, but Devi felt one step closer to finding her freedom.

Confiding in a therapist allowed her to voice her pain and realize she was not alone. Over a two-year time period she felt herself growing more confident about beginning a new life. Desperate to derive some meaning from her experience, Devi committed to volunteering at a local women's shelter for three months. Connecting with the community and feeling she could do something meaningful for other victims gave her a sense of purpose. She found herself deeply soul searching, contemplating her life, and finding solace to heal her aching heart. Receiving unconditional love from her family and finding new supportive friends also facilitated her recovery.

More than a year into their sluggish divorce proceedings, Devi did a background check on Samir and stumbled upon a public record from a woman who had filed suit against him. Digging a little deeper, Devi was shocked to discover she was Samir's previous wife. He had never mentioned this. How had she known so little about this man before deciding to spend the rest of her life with him? Allegedly, this first wife left Samir shortly after marriage and accused him of domestic violence. Attempting to contact her and garner some support, the first wife blatantly refused to speak to Devi and instructed her to never contact her again.

It has now been three years since their official separation and Devi and Samir are still not divorced. The painfully slow litigation process continues because of Samir's resolute decision to make this as difficult for Devi as possible. One afternoon an old friend of Samir's called. Devi had been too embarrassed to speak to anyone in Seattle since their separation. Her in-laws had spread horrible rumors declaring she was schizophrenic. Meena stated matter-of-factly, *"Devi, Samir is remarried. I am close friends with his new wife, Kavita. She has a one-year-old daughter with Samir."* Devi was shocked. How could he marry someone else before he was officially divorced?

Meena confided, *"Kavita told me Samir has been beating her. She is ready to seek a divorce and was hoping you could give her some advice."* Incredulous that Devi was not officially divorced yet, she replied, *"Samir told Kavita and the entire Indian community here that your marriage was annulled!"* Samir had shown consistently throughout his history he would mistreat his wives regardless of who they were. He believed women were his property to do with as he wished and his parents had only empowered him.

Soon after hearing this news, Samir's attorney called requesting they speed up the divorce process. It was apparent the divorce with the third wife was complicating Samir's legal situation, and he was afraid of being accused of polygamy. Devi did not know whether to laugh or cry at the irony of it all. Men like Samir would never change, but she had faith his karma would eventually bring justice.

Reflecting on the past few years, Devi wished she had paid attention to the red flags, taken more time to get to know Samir, or postponed the wedding until she was sure of her decision and resisted his family's pressure. By succumbing to his demands, she let him believe she was controllable, without a mind of her own, and could be subjugated to his brutality. Devi would never make the same mistake again of not listening to her instincts.

Time healed her emotional wounds and the lingering doubts that plagued her mind. She had faced loneliness, uncertainty, and anguish, but never for a moment did she regret her decision. Recuperating from the financial damages, litigation costs, and material loss of her personal possessions over the past three years of her life was the greatest toll, but Devi was hopeful her future was promising and she could create a new life of her choosing. Despite her suffering, she was still optimistic and resilient, confident that nothing could hold her back from achieving her dreams.

Chapter 32 RADHA'S REDEMPTION

It was approaching midnight. Radha stared at the hands on the clock that barely seemed to move all evening, waiting for her husband Roy to leave her apartment. Two weeks of planning her escape would be jeopardized and all her effort go to waste if he decided to spend the night or did not leave soon. They had been separated for two years since she had moved out of their home to be far away from Roy's crazy, unpredictable behavior. After six years of marriage, she discovered his affair and confronted him. Rather than deny it, Roy claimed, "*I am a king who has the right to have multiple queens.*" His sense of entitlement did not surprise her at this point.

Heartbroken, Radha could no longer live with this man who had repeatedly betrayed her on multiple levels. She had asked for a divorce at that time, but Roy flew into a rage over her request. While driving, he became a mad man behind the wheel, swerving the car dangerously, unconcerned about anyone's welfare. She begged him to pull the car over, but he refused. "*I don't care if we all die tonight. If you do not want to be with me you cannot be with any other man. If we die, then it will be all three of us at the same time. This is the end.*" Fearing for her life, Radha tried desperately to appease him.

Defeated, she knew she had to pick her battles carefully. Moving into her own studio apartment with her six-month-old son gave her a slight sense of independence she cherished after all the years in her oppressive marriage. Without any invitation or warning, Roy still made it a point to drop by daily to check up on her. His unannounced visits were a reminder she could never be free of this man who refused to leave her alone and insisted on being able to visit his son whenever he pleased. His controlling personality still dominated every aspect of her life and she learned not to protest. Even if he did not always treat her well, he still showered their son Ram with affection and Radha did not feel she could sever their bond.

During that time, Roy pleaded with her to assist in obtaining his green card since he was an illegal alien. Radha agreed simply because she was still his wife after all, she had loved this man dearly, and in some sense she felt obligated to help him. Two years had dragged on as she waited for Roy's green card process to be completed. In the meantime, she watched her son grow while continuing to work a full-time job to support them both. Radha had always been the breadwinner supporting Roy during their marriage as well. Now that Ram was two-years-old, it was imperative they live in a safe home away from Roy's instability.

When Roy visited her two weeks prior, Radha finally worked up the courage to confront him about his multiple affairs. "*This is not my idea of marriage! I need to be free of this relationship and start my own life. I insist we file for divorce."* It had been two years since she last requested this. Roy's responsive anger was a force to be reckoned with. He ransacked her belongings, slammed his fist against the wall, and within minutes simultaneously turned their apartment and their world upside down.

Radha clenched Ram who stood paralyzed in front of her, both of them terrified of what he would do next. It broke her heart to see the petrified look in Ram's eyes. How could she let her child live like this? She thought moving out of their home would bring some security, but Roy had only brought his reign of terror into their apartment. Radha knew in that instant she would leave him for good but how and when still needed to be determined. As long as he left without touching either of them, it would be okay, Radha reasoned. He could do whatever he wanted to her belongings, but she prayed he would not lay a finger on her, especially in front of their son.

Before his rage escalated, she had to pacify him. Reassuringly she said, *"Fine, Roy, I didn't mean it. I don't want a divorce."* Unsure if it was her words that got through to him, the rage he unleashed on all her material possessions abated. Radha had no idea what switch made him turn his emotions on and off at will. Decoding his behavior remained a mystery. Glancing around the room, Roy seemed satisfied her place was sufficiently destroyed. Radha remained silent to avoid triggering him further. Her mind was reeling absorbing the realization that this man she had known and loved for ten years was never going to change. Why had it taken her so long to see that?

After he left abruptly, Radha sorted through Roy's mess, a familiar routine by now. She was always left trying to salvage her sanity and clean up the damage after the wake of his unrelenting emotional outbursts. How long had she been doing this? They had been married for eight years and dated for two years before eloping against her parents' wishes. Nobody in her family had approved of the match. It was not because they were upset Roy was not Indian, or moreover, Maharashtran like herself. In that way, her parents had always been open-minded and never expected Radha to have an arranged marriage after growing up in the U.S. They knew she was a free spirit who would always follow her heart.

Radha's parents objected simply because they deemed Roy untrustworthy. His previous marriage, sons from another woman, illegal alien status, and lack of a decent job did not make him a promising catch. Radha hated the idea of displeasing them but despite their protests she held her ground. After falling head-over-heels in love with this man, she announced, *"It is my destiny to be with him!"* How could she deny the instant, compelling attraction she had to Roy? She had never felt this way before in any of her previous relationships and simply could not imagine a life with anyone else. Roy showered her with affection proclaiming, *"I am helplessly in love with you. We were meant to be together. I cannot even dream of being with another woman."*

Soon after eloping the abuse occurred with regularity, but Radha had no way to label it as such at the time. There had been warning signs: witnessing his short temper countless times, his lack of respect for others, his indomitable ego and sense of entitlement. In his tirades, he insulted everyone, listed their faults, and stated why he was superior to everyone. Being estranged from his mother or sister should have been a red flag he did not respect women. One time he had even pushed Radha up against the wall during a fight but he apologized profusely, *"This will never happen again."* Of course, she had not only believed him but forgave him since his sincerity was so touching. Confident they would move past this incident, she reasoned every relationship had its struggles.

Radha became accustomed to reading Roy's moods every morning to ascertain his emotional build-ups and detect undercurrents of tension to predict how the day would go. Sometimes his transient pleasant mood surprised her, but within the hour he would switch into his temperamental self. Without any trigger or provocation, the troubled Roy emerged when she least expected it. It seemed they were constantly bickering over trivial matters and the bitterness between them overshadowed fleeting moments of happiness. When they did truly enjoy each other's company, it was short-lived but deceptively fooled Radha into hoping he would change. At times, his dependence on marijuana seemed to keep him mellow but there was no way to tell when his rage would emerge. She had spent years trying to diagnose his erratic-ness and apparent bipolar personality. She encouraged him to receive treatment but he persistently refused.

He seemed to possess endless justifications for his behavior whether it was his never-ending hardships and struggles or being abused by his father. Everyone appeared to be against Roy or out to get him, whether it was family or friends did not matter. Listening to his excuses, she had been compassionate and patient, believing Roy would be transformed by her love for him. Underneath the layers of his short-fused temper and hostility, the man she fell in love with remained trapped. She had to allow time for the real Roy to emerge and the angry Roy to fade away. He would learn to trust her at least if no one else. Her blind hope persisted preventing her from acknowledging his mistreatment of her had only exacerbated.

When their relationship reached a heightened level of tension, Radha considered confiding in her parents. But what would she tell them now? How could she admit they had been right all along and she had not heeded their warnings? How could she acknowledge following her heart and marrying the man of her dreams had been a mistake? Rather than tell them the truth and confess to the disappointments in her marriage, it seemed easier to maintain her silence. Why create more complications and worry them unnecessarily? She landed herself in this mess and she was determined to get herself out.

Despite disapproving of the marriage, they had come to accept Roy as their son-in-law with time even though they still did not trust him. Unintentionally, Radha grew distant, calling her parents less frequently since Roy discouraged contact. At family gatherings he quarreled frequently with everyone, making Radha wish she had come alone. When she suggested this once, Roy pronounced, "*I will not let you travel without me.*" Suddenly, she needed his permission to work, travel, talk to family, or spend time with friends. Forced to cut off ties with those friends of whom Roy disapproved made it increasingly difficult to maintain her friendships and support network.

Some of her colleagues had sensed her unease and questioned if everything was okay at home. Since Roy insisted on dropping her off so he could use her car, she was always at his mercy to be on time. When her boss confronted her after hearing her countless excuses about being late, she was defenseless. One day she showed up to work with a scratch on her cheek. Roy had kicked her in the face but Radha covered up the injury claiming her dog jumped on the bed suddenly. These instances when she was forced to lie made her feel sick to her stomach. The physical abuse had crept slowly into their lives when he realized it would take more to control her. How could she tell anyone else the truth about her deepest darkest secrets that haunted her?

After Ram was born, Roy hit her head once while she was nursing, not caring if he hurt the baby. Apparently, the close bond between mother and son threatened him. Immediately, she moved Ram out of his reach to protect him. Attempting to establish some boundaries so he would not jeopardize the baby's safety had only led to bickering. As expected, Roy refused to listen and dominated the conversation instead. He screamed, "*Radha, you have the wrong priorities and should be making time for me!*" Discussing anything with him when he was in this mood was useless.

No matter how damaging the physical incidents were, they were nothing compared to the scars from Roy's verbal assaults. His long tirades denouncing her friends and family drained her. She had listened to countless monologues where he listed Radha's endless flaws. "*You fail to appreciate me and don't know how lucky you are! I think you take me for granted. You must learn to be more submissive and treat me like a king.*" Life with Roy was suffocating and left her paralyzed, numb, and unable to act. Each incident plunged her into deeper depression. In the evenings, Radha had started drinking an occasional glass of wine to take the edge off but it had become almost a nightly ritual now.

Radha glanced at the clock. It was almost 11:45 and Roy was still in her apartment. Ram was fast asleep. Why wasn't he leaving? He usually never stayed this late. Yawning, Radha said, "*Roy, I am tired. I cannot keep my eyes open much longer.*" Taking the bait, he finally took off. "*Fine, I'll see you in the morning.*" As the door closed behind him, Radha felt her heart thumping wildly in her chest. She did not have much time to execute the radical plan she had conceived only two weeks prior. Committing the meticulously planned details to memory, her hands shook as she quickly dialed a girlfriend's number. "*He just left!*" she said simply giving the signal.

Within ten minutes the doorbell rang and a crew of close friends who had been waiting for her signal arrived. They descended like angels. Knowing time was limited, they efficiently loaded their cars with all her belongings. Radha had packed some things before but had purposefully left some items scattered around the apartment to not alert Roy's suspicions. Her plan had worked thus far, but what if he turned the car around and came back to her place? The only thing she could do was pray he would not. After staring at the hands on the clock all evening thinking they were moving too slowly, now they seemed to move too fast. Her heart was beating loudly in her chest while sweat dripped down her brow.

Her younger brother Raj had flown in that night and been picked up at the airport by one of Radha's friends. She had called him two weeks earlier when she concocted her escape plan to ask if he would accompany her on the drive. Without hesitating, Raj agreed. God knows his family had been waiting for Radha to leave her husband for years. He would do anything possible to help her, take her to safety, and find her freedom. They had witnessed Radha deteriorating over time, overcome with depression and grief, becoming just a shadow of her former glowing, happy self. Raj knew they longed to see the old Radha they had once known again.

Raj hugged her briefly and then assisted her friends in transferring her belongings to the storage unit nearby that Radha had reserved. Within an hour, the apartment was empty and they were ready to go. Tearfully, Radha hugged her friends. At a loss for words, she knew she could not have had the courage to take this bold step without them. Their blessings and prayers felt like a wave of support carrying her forward, giving her the momentum she needed to make this great escape. Knowing so many people wished her well was encouraging and gave her the strength she needed.

Raj lifted Ram gingerly in his arms and carried him to the backseat of the car so as to not wake him. By nightfall, they drove in silence. Radha had plenty of time to listen to the turbulent thoughts raging in her mind. Had she made the right decision? Was it too late to go back? What if Roy turned around and discovered the empty apartment? He could be following them right now. She was banking on the few hours until morning for them to be far enough away, out of Roy's restricting reach.

What would he do in the morning when he discovered they were gone? Radha could not even begin to imagine the rage he would feel. She had spent her entire marriage trying to avoid his fury and now her actions would only provoke him. The undeniable panic she felt consumed every minute of the drive. It was only a matter of time before he would try to find her. Radha left her cell phone behind so he would not reach her. She had acquired a new secret cell phone last month whose number she only disclosed to her immediate family members hoping that would keep her safe for awhile.

Looking out the window as they traveled from city to city, the growing distance from Roy brought a modicum of comfort. Radha tried to relax, letting her mind drift to pleasant memories. She reminisced about Jeremy, a man she had clandestinely dated for a few months without Roy's knowledge. In Jeremy's company she remembered how it felt to be appreciated by a man and to feel good about herself again. She had not felt that way with Roy except for their initial dating period. It was a new experience to feel safe with a man and trust him to not hurt her. Radha cherished her time with him and felt hopeful of finding happiness in her life again.

Roy had systematically conditioned her to accept his mistreatment. In that weakened state, Radha had surrendered countless dreams feeling any sort of peace and contentment in her life would always be beyond her reach. In contrast, Jeremy showed her she deserved to be treated well. That was when she pressured Roy for a divorce again knowing she could never be free to be with someone else.

Describing her predicament to Jeremy had also proven challenging. How could she explain she was married but separated and her husband refused to give her a divorce? Radha also feared for Jeremy's safety hearing Roy's threats. *"You know I will never allow you to be with another man except me. I will kill any man who even tries to lay a finger on you! I will hire a hit man if I need to take him out."* His jealousy and possessiveness was ironic when he felt entitled to be with as many women as he chose, but Radha did not take his threats lightly.

Light emerged on the horizon. It would soon be dawn. Radha glanced at Raj who was still driving. How many hours had it been? Crossing the state line gave her a sense of peace. Gratitude filled her heart for her younger brother who had come to her rescue when she most needed him. Unsure if her family would be supportive after becoming so estranged from them over the years, they had definitely come through for her. Raj drove them to safety until they reached their destination by morning.

Ram woke up and asked, *"Mama, where are we?"* Radha replied, *"Just going on a road trip, honey, a little vacation."* What would she tell him if he asked her the same question tomorrow, and the next day? When would she tell Ram they were never going home again, they would never be safe if his father knew where they were? Radha did not have the answers to these inevitable questions. Adrenaline still filled her from the escape and she knew she had to take it one day at a time. Ten years of living with this abusive man, a man she had loved and given her heart to completely, left her weakened and weary. She had seen herself growing stronger the past two years with their separation, but she could not deny she was still under his subtle control, never able to evade his constant manipulation.

In those next few weeks, Radha moved from place to place, never staying in one city long enough in case Roy attempted to find her. Feeling like hunted prey, she was certain he was searching for her. It was unsafe to stay with Radha's parents since Roy knew where they lived. She knew he could follow through with his previous threats to hurt them. Using his resources and connections, Roy asked his friend who worked for the cell phone company to track Raj's phone number and check all his incoming calls. From the list, Roy cleverly picked out Radha's new number. She knew it was only a matter of time before he would find her. She hoped changing her number and blocking it would keep him from tracking her down again. Meanwhile, Ram accepted they were on a fun vacation not realizing their life had been turned upside down.

Radha found an attorney who handled domestic violence cases and agreed to represent her pro bono since she desperately lacked financial resources. Roy had been served the divorce papers on the same day she had fled the state. Now the legal battle would ensue for the next year as they went back and forth between lawyers. Roy's attorney would prove to be just as ruthless as his client as he successfully dragged out the legal process to antagonize Radha.

The biggest dilemma they faced was custody. Radha knew Roy would not make it easy. But how could he prove he would be a good father under the circumstances? He was an illegal alien, with a warrant out for his arrest in the state, unemployed, and addicted to marijuana. He had already declared he would not pay for child support. Serving Roy with a restraining order had slightly eased her worries and empowered her. It affirmed she was sending him the clear and strong message she would not tolerate his behavior any longer and she wanted him out of her life for good. She knew deep down the restraining order did not guarantee her safety and Roy would never feel threatened or intimidated by her actions.

As the legal process consumed her days, Radha sought the care she desperately needed. Visiting various domestic violence centers, she met therapists, attended empowering classes to learn the subtleties of abuse, and read as many books as she could on the topic. In the ten years she had been with Roy she never once labeled herself a victim or even thought of the term domestic violence. His manipulation, brainwashing, and reign of control had dominated her. Educating herself facilitated breaking through all the layers of confusion Roy had steadily woven around her mind. Slowly, Radha remembered memories of her old life when she was happy and carefree. Could she be that person again?

Therapy forced her to reexamine her life with Roy, the unhealthy attachment between them, and how she had denied his abuse. Uncovering his deception, processing his betrayal, and tackling her pain was monumental. Each therapy session made her feel brave enough to face her trauma but Radha knew she was in a safe environment and she needed to understand exactly how she had let herself be victimized. She recounted incidents of physical abuse: being slapped, kicked, shoved, pushed. As the therapist patiently listened, Radha's emotions flooded to the surface and she felt new waves of pain, disgust, rage, and grief.

Sharing these horror stories helped her appreciate how crazy her situation truly was. No matter how much she had accepted Roy's domination and been conditioned to his violence, the guns had always scared her. She recounted how Roy often went to the shooting range for sport but she never imagined he would use a gun against her. One morning Roy stood in the front door and blew out all her tires when she was leaving for work. Another day she was greeted with a fully loaded gun staring at her in the face when she stepped out of the bedroom. The terror she felt in that instant was an understatement. Dismissing these incidents as Roy's erratic mood being off those days and living in deep denial was the only way she could cope with his insanity.

Radha recounted the car accident they had a few years into their marriage. Driving on a cold winter night through snow-laden mountains, their car had toppled off the icy bridge. Radha had been five months pregnant at the time. She had waited for hours before an ambulance came to the rescue and rushed her to the hospital. Her baby had died instantly in the crash but the doctors induced her into labor to deliver the placenta with the dead fetus attached.

Roy's guilt for being the driver devoured him and the incident drove a deeper wedge between them. In hindsight, Radha understood how the depression from the trauma consumed her. Healing from her injuries had taken time and energy to recover from. A metallic rod was inserted to support her femur bone that had been fractured in the accident. It was almost a year before she emerged out of that fog and started to receive physical therapy.

Her physical therapist was the first one to detect the signs of abuse. Questioning Radha gently, she probed into her past history to uncover whether her suspicions were correct. After a few sessions, Radha felt too threatened to return. She was not equipped to confess her secrets to anyone, let alone a stranger. How could she adequately describe the pain and emptiness she felt inside? Even though she had confided in a few close friends about Roy's mistreatment, she purposefully avoided mentioning the physical incidents. Somehow she still found herself protecting Roy. It was ingrained in her to avoid his wrath.

Ram, who was now four, also visited a counselor to ascertain how the abuse had affected him. In his sessions, Ram confessed that he loved his dad and missed him dearly. He did not know where he was or why he could not see him. "*I have nightmares,*" he said softly, "*where daddy is coming after us. I am so scared he is going to hurt mommy again. I don't want him to do that. I love mommy too much.*"

In another session Ram recounted, "*Daddy came once before we left and was throwing things all around the apartment. I didn't know what he was going to do to us. It is scary seeing him like that. I wish he would not be that way.*" The therapist reassured Ram he was safe now and there was nothing his daddy could do to him or his mommy. It took time to recover but being around family and friends who loved and supported them during this time was instrumental.

Roy's attorney insisted on visitation rights for his client. Radha protested that she could not risk her son's safety or trust Roy around Ram. What if he attempted to kidnap him? Her attorney intervened with, *"The courts will not look favorably upon you if you deny the father visitation rights."* How could they insist Roy visit his son when he had put their lives in jeopardy countless times with his dangerous behavior? It hardly seemed fair.

Her attorney told her frankly, *"Radha, nothing about the legal process will be fair and easy. The courts always try to make sure a child has both parents involved in his life."* Reluctantly, against all of her instincts for self-preservation and protecting her child, she agreed to supervised visitation. Each time, Radha waited anxiously for Ram to return while her stomach churned with fear, but it never became easier.

After almost a year of litigation, Radha's divorce was finalized. The judge granted a permanent restraining order in her divorce decree forbidding Roy to be within three hundred yards of her. Would she truly be safe? No, Roy's armed and dangerous cadre of friends would have no hesitations tracking her down if necessary but at least Radha had done everything she could to protect her and her son.

She knew the separation would not be easy for Ram, but she could not risk Roy endangering them again. Occasionally, Ram asked, *"Mama, where is he? Is he going to come visit us?"* But as eager as he was to see him, he also expressed his concern. *"Mama, is he going to hurt us again? Will he come after you?"* It broke her heart to hear these questions. Radha never knew how to answer. What was she supposed to say to comfort him?

The aftermath of the divorce haunted her as she continued to clean up Roy's mess. Because he was an illegal alien, Roy strategically placed all the mortgage, car, and expensive credit card bills he had racked up in Radha's name. Forced to confront her husband's reckless spending during their marriage, she eventually declared bankruptcy to start over with a clean slate. Returning to school part-time to obtain a degree was empowering and part of her recovery plan. It was not easy working odd jobs during the day, attending school at night, and still finding time to spend with her son, but she knew this was the plight of many single mothers. After two years, Radha received her accounting degree, found a promising job, and had a steady income again.

Living in a safe home where they could fill their lives with laughter instead of violence, Radha would never look back or regret leaving. It had taken three years since her divorce to feel she had rebuilt herself, created financial stability, and life could be predictable again. The journey to escape had been fraught with difficulties but it was worth every second of it to get her to where she was now: a free woman who had infinite possibilities before her.

Chapter 33 SITA'S SHACKLES

Sita felt like a caged bird, trapped in her own home with no way out. Unlike the heroine from the famous Indian epic the *Ramayana*, her husband was the one who had held her prisoner and there was no one to rescue her no matter how much she prayed to Hanumanji. The past five years of marriage had been nothing like what she had imagined. Sita once had high hopes and ambitions to succeed in her career as a software engineer. She had dreamed of obtaining a reliable job with a decent income before marriage to avoid being a housewife. Her parents arranged the alliance through an Indian matrimonial website and found the groom-to-be who was also from Punjab. At the age of twenty-seven, they met and soon after were officially engaged. Sita agreed to the match telling her parents, "*I trust your judgment and feel confident he is a promising suitor.*"

Before the wedding, Lankesh's parents made numerous demands that Sita's parents did their best to accommodate. After all, this had been the custom for centuries that the bride's family must please the groom's family. Even when his parents conveyed their displeasure that the dowry was insufficient, Sita acknowledged this was typical in many Indian weddings and dismissed it. Throughout the engagement, Sita and Lankesh spoke over the phone often and he was always pleasant. They met several times but it was always in the company of others at social settings. Never alone, there was no opportunity to truly get to know each other and there certainly were no red flags of which Sita was aware.

Due to family circumstances, the wedding was postponed for more than a year. At the late age of twenty-nine, they were finally married and Sita moved into her marital home where Lankesh lived with his parents. She had always observed how her husband was charming and entertaining in front of others. Erroneously believing in this false image he projected, she did not discover his true colors until the day after the wedding when she saw the fire in his eye that hinted of some deeper disturbance. There is no way she could have predicted he would erupt into an infantile temper tantrum without any provocation. Suddenly, he was arrogant, entitled, and insulted her for no apparent reason.

Sita glimpsed the beginning of his dual personality and how easily he slipped into various modes depending on the company he kept. How could he turn his charm on and off at will? Lankesh had created a great impression on Sita's parents and they had been quite taken by him. Sita had also felt she was fortunate to have found such a wonderful husband. It was almost as if he was a talented actor, adapting to every situation and wearing the appropriate mask and costume for that particular role. She realized how little she really knew of this man.

Trying to be optimistic, she reasoned that she would get to know her husband better with time, understand his moods, and learn how to avoid provoking his temper. Meanwhile, Sita worked diligently to please her in-laws as is expected of every obedient Indian wife. It was challenging adjusting to a new home where so much was expected of her. Her in-laws demanded, *"You must stay at home now and take care of us. We do not want you to work."* Surprised by this request, she sought advice from her own parents who told her simply, *"It is best to take your new in-laws' wishes into consideration. Do not do anything of which they would disapprove."* She reasoned since her husband traveled for work, his parents must feel lonely in his absence.

A few days after the wedding, Lankesh brought her a resignation letter to sign insisting she quit her job right away. Sita protested, *"But it is a new job. I just recently commenced there and I worked so hard to secure this promising position. Please, I do not want to leave!"* Forcing her signature, he made it clear her wishes did not matter. Regretfully, Sita was not given a chance to leave her job properly or stay on good terms with her employer. Lankesh purposefully ruined any opportunity she had to be rehired. Despite the distressing turn of events, Sita consoled herself that she would find a new job in the future. This positive attitude would sustain her throughout the turbulent marriage.

A mere ten days after the wedding, Lankesh announced he had to travel for work. She soon became accustomed to his unpredictable schedule never knowing when he would be home. With his long absences, they barely had time to get to know each other. Trying to make the best of every situation, Sita told herself, *"I should be grateful my husband has a reliable job and works so hard. We are still newlyweds. I am sure when our life stabilizes things will improve."* Immersed in his career, Lankesh was reserved and secretive. She questioned why he never disclosed his salary or discussed any of their finances with her. But she learned early on not to ask too many questions. Anything could trigger Lankesh's hostility, so she needed to do everything she could to keep him calm.

It had not taken long for both her husband and in-laws to start being verbally abusive. They seemed to have no respect and value for her as a human being and constantly degraded and humiliated her. Never having dated anyone or been in a relationship before, Sita had no basis for comparison. She reasoned every couple has some sort of struggle, no marriage is easy; maybe they just needed time to work things out. Months passed and Sita's family grew suspicious something was wrong especially when they witnessed how Lankesh subtly looked at his wife. It was apparent Sita did not seem like her usual self and the newlyweds were not totally at ease with each other.

Sita's parents questioned her frankly one day: *"Is everything okay at home with Lankesh? Are you happy?"* Holding back her tears, Sita softly replied, *"Yes."* No matter how close she was to them, she could not bring herself to confide what a disappointment her marriage was. They had wanted only the best for her and worked steadfastly to select the groom they thought was worthy of their daughter. How could she let them down? Praying her marriage would improve over time, she could not share her misery with them. Sita's parents decided it was best not to interfere and that the couple needed space to work out their relationship on their own, never suspecting Lankesh was abusive.

Day by day in that toxic environment, Sita's spirit withered. Lankesh had never treated her with any kindness and she had no idea what it meant to be treated well. His behavior cycled between indifference to her existence and raging hostility. After lashing out at her, whether it was physically or verbally, he never apologized. More than two years into the marriage, Sita's mind was rapidly deteriorating living at home. Determined to start working again and have some mental stimulation, she desperately needed an escape from her miserable living conditions.

Searching for employment was not easy. Living in a remote village in Punjab, her access to travel for interviews was restricted. Getting back into the I.T. field was more challenging than she expected. She was told to take a training course to update her skills. Without any income of her own, she begged Lankesh, *"I am at your mercy to pay for the course. Please let me go! I have been a dutiful wife for more than two years living at home with your parents."* Not surprisingly, Lankesh denied her request. Refusing to be disheartened, she turned to her brother who offered to pay for the course. Amazingly, Sita found a promising job soon after and could not believe her luck.

Within two months of starting her new job, Sita discovered Lankesh's boss was transferring him to a position in the U.S. unexpectedly. After living in India for three years, the idea of moving to a different country took her by surprise. She felt encouraged when Lankesh gave her a work permit form to fill out. But just as suddenly, he decided he would not let her apply and forbid her to interview by phone. Any time Sita tried to assert her independence, Lankesh responded with heightened aggressiveness to keep her in place.

Resignation set in but Sita convinced herself their lives would hopefully be better when they moved to America. They arrived in Buffalo, New York in the cold of winter. Unprepared, Sita had only a shawl to keep her warm. Realizing her clothing was insufficient, she asked Lankesh, *"May I please buy a proper winter coat?"* He flatly refused. They moved into a brand new five-bedroom home his company had found and tried to get settled. During their first week they shopped at an Indian grocery store where Lankesh selected some rice and dal, staples for any Indian kitchen. Sita asked, *"May I please buy a few vegetables and some soap and toothpaste?"* Without any explanation, he adamantly refused to buy anything else. Tersely, he insisted she remain silent. Wishing to avoid making a scene, Sita said nothing.

Shortly thereafter, Lankesh confiscated her passport and other important documents declaring, *"You do not need these anymore."* She had no idea where he hid them or if he had destroyed them altogether. Within a few days, he packed his bags and left town for a three-month business trip without any warning, giving her no indication when he would return. Sita was left home alone in a brand new country where she did not know anyone. Without a telephone, there was no way to even call home, speak to her parents, or tell them how she was. Scared to leave her home and walk around the subdivision, Sita was afraid she would not find her way back. How could she venture out into the unknown?

The idea of being in America by herself was intimidating. The isolation those first few months was unbearable. Without even a television, she realized how much she longed to hear another human voice. The silence was deafening. In India when she felt trapped in her in-laws' home at least there were still the sounds of people coming and going, the television, or her parents visiting occasionally. She longed to have children, be a mother, and raise a family, all dreams she had thought would be fulfilled when she had looked forward to her wedding. But Sita had decided there was no way she would have children in the toxic environment Lankesh had created. She could never have foreshadowed this would be her fate.

Sita had no idea how to even reach out for help. Lankesh kept no cash at home and she was penniless. There was no way out and nowhere to even go. Living without soap or toothpaste, Sita felt worse than an animal. How could he not even have the decency to treat her like a human being? How was she supposed to live like this? It was degrading, humiliating, and stripped her of any remaining dignity she possessed.

One summer day when Sita felt brave enough, she opened her front door and timidly sat on her porch. How much longer could she endure living trapped indoors for months at a time? Inhaling deeply, her lungs breathed in fresh air. Gently, the rays of the sun caressed her skin and she felt their welcomed warmth. It was a strange and unusual feeling. How long had it been that she was cooped up inside? She had lost all sense of time. When would she venture beyond her porch, out of this subdivision, into any sort of civilization? Sita missed her family, her friends, and longed for human company again.

Neighbors who were casually walking by looked visibly shocked to see someone living in the house they believed was vacant. One neighbor approached her but instead of a friendly greeting she rudely commented on the unkempt appearance of Sita's lawn. *"What a disgrace. How can you leave your yard looking like that? It looks terrible and reflects on the whole neighborhood. You need to take care of it right away!"* This was one of the first Americans Sita had ever encountered. She did not know what to say. How was she to respond to this or hire a landscaper?

Her husband had left her no money, no phone, and no way to run the household in his absence. She did not even have any cleaning supplies since Lankesh refused to buy them. She gulped and replied in a timid voice, *"Do not worry, I will take care of it."* Forlorn, Sita's helplessness was only compounded by this small interaction with her neighbor. Anxiously, she awaited her husband's return. When Lankesh did eventually arrive back in town, Sita greeted him with warmth and affection. The long months apart made the memories of his abusive nature start to fade. After every absence she felt hopeful their relationship would be better. She had longed for his company, but truthfully, craved any company at all.

When Lankesh returned, life was not easier. He had started drinking, albeit inconsistently, but Sita knew when his eyes became bloodshot, his short-fused temper would ignite and she was in danger. Lankesh had started to blatantly lie to her as well. Once he told her, *"I am leaving for a few weeks on a business trip to Germany."* Later, Sita would discover he had fabricated that story and traveled to India instead. It would have meant the world to her to see her family, but Lankesh had never thought of her needs. He chose to leave her isolated at home rather than accompany him on a free, expense-paid trip from his company. Shocked by his maliciousness, she felt even more hopeless. How could she expect anything less from him?

One evening around six, Lankesh told her casually, *"Some colleagues from work may come over. You should prepare something for them to eat."* Timidly she asked, *"Who did you invite Lankesh?"* Sita received no response. Ignoring her when she spoke had become common so Sita proceeded to rush to the kitchen not waiting for an answer. She looked at her empty refrigerator, rummaged through the cupboards salvaging a few potatoes, some rice, and flour that she immediately kneaded to make pooris. Who were these guests? How would she feed them? Why hadn't Lankesh given her any advanced warning? Her extreme isolation made her crave human interaction and she reasoned that it would be nice to have some company after all. Maybe Lankesh had invited them for her sake.

By 7:00 p.m., guests started arriving. This included Lankesh's boss and his wife. They saw her struggling in the kitchen to prepare a few Indian dishes and asked her, *"Didn't Lankesh tell you we were coming?"* It was apparent to everyone he had not. As the doorbell kept ringing incessantly, people trickled in pairs. At least twenty people were now sitting in their living room. Sita stood there unsure of herself. Lankesh asked her to prepare masala chai, but she realized she did not even have a tea strainer. What was she supposed to do?

Remembering Draupadi from the famous epic *Mahabharata* who had lived in the forest during their thirteen-year exile, she found herself in the same dilemma. An army of men had arrived at Draupadi's cottage expecting to be fed. Praying to Lord Krishna, he miraculously heard her prayers and appeared just then. Gifting her with a magic vessel, Krishna ate the single grain of rice he found at the bottom. After commenting how full his belly was, the men who were waiting told Drapaudi they were suddenly satiated and did not need her to prepare an elaborate meal for them anymore. It was one of Krishna's tricks but Draupadi was grateful for his intervention. Alas, Sita realized she would not be so fortunate. Despite her earnest prayers, there was no Krishna to come running and save her from this predicament. There was no magic vessel that would help her feed all these people.

Standing at the stove frying pooris, beads of sweat trickled down her forehead. As more and more people started to fill their home, Sita realized Lankesh had invited fifty colleagues from work and never bothered to inform her. Some of the guests were chuckling as they realized the predicament Sita was in. There would simply not be enough food to feed everyone. Looking around, one gentlemen laughingly asked her, *"How do you survive here without a phone or Internet connection? How do you contact your husband when he is traveling for so many months?"* Embarrassed, Sita was unable to reply.

Instead of dwelling on the impossible situation Lankesh had put her in, Sita's thoughts revolved only around her husband. Used to always putting him first, she wondered, *"What will his boss think of him? How will this affect his career?"* On the verge of tears, Sita kept her chin up and finished frying all the pooris and making potato subji and rice. That night was a disaster but somehow she made it through. For some inexplicable reason, Lankesh avoided her and refused to speak to her or make eye contact. What had she possibly done wrong? Was he not even grateful for how hard she had worked that evening to make him look good in front of his colleagues? Didn't he realize what he had put her through?

After that nightmare, Sita was overwhelmed by the opinions their guests must have made about her. What would they think if they realized she had never ventured outside of the home, had not spoken to her own family in ages, and was treated like a slave by her husband? They would certainly not believe she was well educated with an engineering degree and had a promising career at one time. If they only knew the harsh conditions she lived in, they would probably blame her for being weak, enduring the abuse, and living like this. Who would show her compassion? Who could she approach for help in her isolated state?

Lankesh warned her, *"If you ever try to leave me, make no mistake, I will harm your family!"* Hearing his intimidating threats, Sita worried how her actions would endanger her loved ones. There was no telling of what her husband was capable. How could she trust him? How would he retaliate against her? Once he put that fear in her mind, Sita felt more trapped. She could not let any harm come to her family or live with herself if she was to blame. His maliciousness had taken a new turn and he had successfully found another way to instill terror and have control over her mind. Living at his mercy, day in and day out, was taking its toll.

During their fifth year of marriage, Sita had adapted to her lifestyle somewhat but started to take her first steps towards getting back on her feet. Finding employment at a doctor's office that was a mile walk from her home, she was happy to leave her home for a few hours daily. Doing some menial secretarial work was no comparison to her engineering jobs but engaging herself in something meaningful was refreshing. At her new boss' insistence, she received her first cell phone. Feeling slightly more empowered and independent, Sita felt a brief respite from Lankesh's suffocating domination.

One evening as Lankesh hastily packed his belongings, he declared, "*I am leaving tomorrow for a business trip.*" Unable to hold herself back, Sita asked him directly, "*Lankesh, where are you going? Why won't you tell me? I appreciate how hard you work and how much you do for us but how am I supposed to survive here by myself without food or basic essentials? I need groceries. I have survived on just rice and dal for so many months. Why don't you at least let me buy some vegetables?*"

After five years of living with this man and being treated so inhumanely, she demanded answers. "*You are not giving me the basic respect that a wife deserves. You treat me like a prisoner who you can just feed whenever you wish! My basic living needs have to be met!*" Immediately, Sita regretted her actions. How had she been so bold? This would only trigger Lankesh's fury and she did everything she could to avoid him lashing out at her.

"*I will hurt your family, Sita, if you continue to be so disrespectful to me. You better watch what you say!*" Sita fell silent after hearing this threat, the words she wished to say stuck in her throat. All her courage from mere minutes ago had vanished. Before this day she had never confronted Lankesh but after her small taste of freedom outside of the home she wanted more and knew she deserved it.

Suddenly, Lankesh lunged towards her, grabbed her hair and yanked it out. The pain was excruciating. He dragged her by the ear, up the stairs, into the bathroom. Lankesh seemed deaf to Sita's screams. He pulled out huge tufts of her long beautiful black hair and flushed it down the toilet. She begged him, "*Lankesh, please stop! I beg you. I did not mean to upset you!*" In a world of his own, consumed by his insurmountable rage, there was nothing Sita could say to get through to him. He ignored her like he always had.

Repeatedly, he hit her with his slipper. Sita struggled to escape but found herself trapped in the bathroom. He punched her face, beat her until her nose was broken, and pummeled her left eye until it was swollen shut. What if she would never see out of that eye again because he had permanently damaged it? Feeling dizzy, she glanced at the floor with her blurry vision out of one eye and saw drops of blood staining the rug. Where was it coming from? She discovered her ear was bloody. Lankesh bent her finger backwards and she cried out in agonizing pain. Unable to get her bearings, Sita's mind was in a fog. She was beginning to lose consciousness.

There was no telling how long he raged war against her. Sita had lost all sense of time. She kept praying her husband would stop and show her some mercy. Krishna, Ganesh, Hanumanji... where were these deities when she needed them the most? In his rage, Lankesh ripped off her jewelry, including her *mangalsutra*, the sacred necklace he had given her on their wedding day that signified their union. Horrified of this symbolic gesture, it was clear he did not value her life, her body, or their marriage. After all the years of confusion, clarity was finally surfacing.

Storming off, Lankesh left the room when he was done unleashing his fury. Sita scrambled to find her cell phone. Her time was limited and she knew he could return at any moment. Dialing 911, her fingers trembled. What would she tell them? When the police and ambulance arrived she begged them, *"Please do not take me to the hospital. I have no medical insurance."* But Sita's injuries were too severe. From the hospital she was immediately transferred to a women's shelter. Coming from India, she had not even imagined that such places existed and there were resources available to help victims.

A counselor at the shelter told Sita, *"It is not safe for you to go home. You must stay here for awhile to rest and recover. We must go to the courthouse and file for a restraining order."* Sita had no idea what that meant but was grateful the counselor accompanied her to the courthouse. She did yet know her rights or the laws in this strange new country. She felt she was in a dream where things were happening to someone else. The counselor informed her, *"Your husband has been arrested. He was released shortly after on a misdemeanor since some of his well connected attorney friends got him out of jail fairly quickly."* Sita was still too in a daze to process what was really happening.

"Please let me go home now!" she told the staff at the women's shelter. Sita was desperate to return to her home and what was familiar. Everyone meant well but she had never lived with strangers or Americans or in such an unfamiliar environment. But the staff insisted she was not safe and they could not allow her to return. So Sita focused on recovering from her injuries during what ended up being a three-month stay at the shelter. It gave her time to deeply reflect on her situation. Looking down at her bent finger, this was one injury her doctor said would not heal. Sita realized all these years living as a prisoner, Lankesh had never cared when she was sick, never permitted her the right to visit a doctor, and denied her medication.

Being hospitalized forced Sita to clearly examine all the physical and emotional abuse she had endured over the years at the hands of the man she loved. Despite how much she had cared for him, her sentiments had not been reciprocated. Sita thought of her parents and how much they loved her. Comparing the affection they had showered on her with Lankesh's mistreatment, the stark contrast was apparent. Her parents would help her no matter what. Whether it was a bloody ear or a swollen eye, they would be concerned for her well-being. Feeling she had almost permanently lost her vision in one eye after he punched her was the biggest wake-up call. If she went blind, her husband would not have even cared.

For the first time, she comprehended all of Lankesh's inconsistencies and mistreatment in a glaring new light. She had been deluded by her hope and optimism, but it was evident he was never going to change. He had never loved or cared for her. Meanwhile, he lavishly spent money on himself for expensive collections of fancy watches or other trivial possessions. Looking at the pile of mail on their kitchen table one afternoon, Sita glanced at a $2,000 bill for a cosmetic dentist appointment. Whether it was for cosmetic reasons or material possessions, Lankesh maintained his high standard of living while she lived like a neglected captive.

No doubt, the stay at the hospital and women's shelter was definitely a turning point. Sita knew returning to her home meant living with Lankesh's hostility and endangering herself further. She was terrified of what he was capable of and understood now he was dangerous. Tension had escalated to the point of no return. The shelter contacted a South Asian woman's organization (SAWO) in the neighborhood who intervened on Sita's behalf. The Indian counselors understood the cultural issues she grappled with and were incredibly supportive.

The SAWO assisted her with moving into an apartment she could share with another Indian woman who was also a survivor. Speaking to another fellow victim who had suffered the way she had, Sita did not feel so alone. Maneuvering her way through the legal system, finding an attorney, and educating herself on the laws was a challenge. Sita felt at a disadvantage in this new country, but the SAWO aided Sita throughout the legal process and eventually to get her divorce.

Now almost two years after her divorce, she recognizes that time has helped her heal her wounds, feel confident again, and create an independent life without Lankesh. Prayer, the support of her family in India, and the social support from the SAWO assisted her in making new friends. It took almost a year and a half after her divorce to obtain new employment within the engineering field since her skills were not up-to-date but she was determined to never be unemployed again, at the mercy of someone else's oppression, or prevented from having a career. Looking at her colleagues, Sita observed how well settled they were, advanced, and financially stable. In hindsight, she wished she had focused on building her career instead of saving her marriage.

Does she blame herself for her predicament? No, she says defiantly, *"There is nothing wrong with trying to save one's family life and marriage. I did everything possible to find happiness but sometimes circumstances are out of one's control."* Sita endured his mistreatment because of her cultural values, upbringing, and social fears that prevented her from considering divorce an option. Lankesh's threats to harm her family paralyzed her. Being at the hospital was the wake-up call that made her realize she could never return to her husband. Sita would advise other victims, *"Be strong for yourself and your children. If you are in a bad situation, know that nobody will ever be happy."*

Chapter 34 LAKSHMI'S LOSS

Lakshmi stared in horror at the bank statement in her hands. Where had all her hard-earned money gone? As she scrambled to look at her financial portfolio she had spent her career building up, she noticed that none of her assets, including her retirement accounts, were in her name anymore. Somehow after marriage, her husband Chandru had steadily changed everything over into his name. How had this happened? She was the breadwinner in the family, working more than fifty hours a week as a physician with a lucrative income while he chose to sit at home. He had quit his only job claiming, *"I was too good for them. I am not going to insult my intelligence by working for morons who do not know how to respect me."* His sense of entitlement had only progressively worsened throughout the years.

With time, Lakshmi had grown accustomed to the arrangement of supporting him since he refused to work. Meanwhile, Chandru boasted to others of being financially savvy, trading stocks aggressively, and making more money than his wife. The truth was, he lounged at home all day long watching television and surfing the 'Net, demanding Lakshmi work harder to generate more income. When she had medical conferences, he would select which ones she was allowed to attend and always accompanied her insisting she could not travel alone. Only once had she protested, and Chandru had made her pay for her rebellion by yelling at her relentlessly.

His foul, derogatory language shocked her at first. Every insult depleted her strength but she fought back and defended herself vigorously each time. Over time though, his verbal attacks left her paralyzed. Why was he treating her this way? What had she done to deserve this? His accusations left her feeling perplexed and questioning her role in their arguments. Was it true she was purposefully provoking him and instigating his anger as he claimed? Chandru bellowed, *"You are the abusive one! Look at the way you disrespect me! Look at how much anger you have against me when I have not done anything wrong."* His relentless mind games left her questioning her sanity daily.

Willing herself back to the present moment, Lakshmi carefully put all the financial statements away. Chandru had hid them from her. If he discovered she had found his hiding place, he would be livid. How had all the craziness surreptitiously seeped into her life? Their relationship had started on such a promising note. Well set in her career as a physician, Lakshmi was completing her medical fellowship at Harvard. Turning thirty-three, she decided she had waited long enough and it was time to get married. Her friends had encouraged her to give online dating a try.

She and Chandru clicked right away and spoke regularly over the phone for a few weeks before meeting in person. She was impressed by his charming persona, seemingly romantic nature, and how he spoke highly of all the women in his family. He was an only child but he mentioned how much he would have loved to have a sister. He was from the city of Delhi, a Rajasthani, but she knew her parents were open-minded if she did not meet someone who was Bengali like herself. Three years younger than her, Lakshmi accepted their age difference as well.

Chandru genuinely complimented and appreciated Lakshmi. She truly believed she was falling in love with a wonderful man. Soon after, she met his parents who were kind and welcoming. They spent the weekends together and Lakshmi slowly felt confident he was the one for her. After a whirlwind dating experience of only a few months, they were soon engaged. Lakshmi's mom had disliked Chandru instinctively and said, *"Beta, there is something odd about him."* But Lakshmi dismissed her concerns thinking her mother was always skeptical of everyone.

There had been no red flags while they were dating, but after becoming engaged Chandru's personality suddenly changed. One weekend after her parents visited, Chandru berated her: *"How dare you spend the weekend without me! What were you thinking? Why didn't you invite me? You cannot go anywhere without me now that I am your fiancé!"* Shocked that she was "in trouble" for spending time with her family, Lakshmi had no idea how to respond. No one had ever tried to control her this way and monitor her every move.

On another occasion, Lakshmi missed a dinner party her mother-in-law was hosting because of work obligations. She had asked her boss permission to take the evening off but he had refused. Instead of understanding, Chandru had yelled, *"How dare you be disrespectful to my mother! How could you not attend? We should be your first priority now! Don't ever treat my family like that again!"* Once again, Lakshmi did not know how to react to this outburst or rationalize his behavior.

Throughout the engagement, she had kept her doubts to herself wondering if she was making the right choice. Each time a red flag surfaced, she made excuses to dismiss it. Her own family pleaded with her, *"Please wait and postpone the wedding a little bit longer. We feel you are rushing it. Why don't you take some time to get to know him better?"* They never directly expressed their dislike, but Lakshmi ignored their subtle hints. Remembering her broken engagement from the previous year, she wondered how the Indian community would react if she repeated that pattern again. Always full of judgment, the community would surely hold that against her, possibly ruining her chances of marrying in the future.

As if sensing her doubts, Chandru insisted they have a rushed legal ceremony in the summer before their public Indian wedding later that fall with all their family and friends. Even though Lakshmi's family protested, they reluctantly had the civil ceremony when Chandru refused to back down. Shortly after they moved in together, it did not take long for the daily tension and hostility to become suffocating. Overwhelmed, Lakshmi had finally admitted, *"Chandru, I cannot marry you. I don't think we should go ahead with the Indian ceremony."* Outraged, he protested, *"My parents told me you would do something underhanded like this to me!"*

After his rage abated, they mutually decided the best solution was to attend couples counseling sessions. In each session, Lakshmi watched as her fiancé was charming, attentive, and acted completely devoted to her. Their therapist stated, *"He is such a wonderful guy. It is obvious how much he loves you. You should marry him."* Because her therapist was so convincing, Lakshmi dispelled her doubts once again and reluctantly agreed to proceed with the wedding. They had an elaborate Indian ceremony according to custom and invited 500 guests to commemorate their special day. Caught up in the excitement, Lakshmi tried to convince herself she had made the right choice and they would find a way to reconcile their differences. She was determined to be optimistic and put their past behind them.

The following month, Lakshmi surprisingly discovered she was pregnant. She had wanted to take her time to finish her fellowship and establish her career but Chandru insisted that they needed to start a family right away. It was almost as if he seemed worried she would leave him. She had been on birth control pills but discovered her husband had somehow tampered with them. Lakshmi tried to be positive convincing herself that maybe starting a family right now was for the best. She was excited to be a mother but had just not expected this development so soon.

Throughout the pregnancy, Lakshmi was amazed by how unsupportive Chandru was when she was forced to attend all her doctor's appointments by herself. Somehow, she convinced herself to ignore her growing sense of unease. His parents had insisted on moving in with them to help with their growing family. Lakshmi wished they had given them a little more space as newlyweds but knew she could not stand up to her in-laws. After living an independent lifestyle for many years, Lakshmi forced herself to adjust to the temporary arrangement but she hated the lack of privacy. It was awkward every time her parents called as she felt her in-laws were listening to her conversations. It was clear her in-laws would not be her allies; they constantly complained about her behind her back and declared her parents were not welcome to visit.

As her isolation grew, Lakshmi was only permitted to visit her family once a year. Chandru refused to accompany her the first year, but after that he cried, *"Please don't ever leave me again! I love you. From now on we should only travel together. Promise me you won't leave me like that again!"* Lakshmi noticed his increasing emotional dependence on her, but she was unsure what to make of it. Month by month, she felt herself growing steadily weaker, losing her confidence, her mind slipping into confusion. That was the pattern throughout their eleven-year marriage; Chandru's subtle manipulation had slowly taken hold of her mind and she felt trapped in a world where he had complete domination over her. She quickly learned that giving in many times just to appease him would sometimes stop his barrage of insults.

Systematically, Chandru cut off ties with her family to destroy her support system by offending and antagonizing them. Her husband declared, *"Can't you see your elder brother is trying to destroy our marriage? He hates seeing our happiness. He brainwashed you while you were growing up and now you don't know how to think straight when it comes to him."* At first, Lakshmi protested against Chandru's outrageous claims that had no basis in reality and tried to patiently correct him. But after awhile, she grew tired of constantly defending herself and realized there was no point trying to rationalize with someone who was delusional. Choosing to remain silent and be passive was so much easier than fighting. For now, she told herself, she would choose the easier path.

Chandru had lashed out at her brother a few months after the wedding. After the incident her brother declared, *"I am sorry, Lakshmi, I know you are my sister but I cannot have anything more to do with you or your wretched husband. His behavior is appalling. I do not wish to be a party to this."* It had been years since they last spoke and Lakshmi missed him terribly. They had been so close growing up, she had not imagined this estrangement was possible. Their parents had attempted to have them reconcile but her brother had stood his ground and said staunchly, *"I will never speak to Lakshmi again and she is not welcome in my home."*

Ten months after the wedding, their beautiful daughter Anamika was born. Lakshmi requested her mother visit for a few weeks to assist her but Chandru had insisted their home was not big enough and she would have to rely solely on his mother for help. She was amazed Chandru did not care what was important to her, but she had learned it was easier to surrender some battles. Trying to adjust, she wanted to make the best of her situation and focus on the baby but life with Chandru continued to be a series of disappointments. Not only was he aloof and unconcerned during her pregnancy, he showed little interest in the baby and was unwilling to participate in her care. Lakshmi was forced to push aside her concerns to focus on adjusting to her new role feeling like a single mother.

After Anamika turned one, Lakshmi discovered she was pregnant again. She was exhausted and did not know how to handle another pregnancy. Chandru insisted it was a blessing from God and they needed to grow their family. Juggling her second pregnancy with taking care of her daughter and her demanding work schedule posed a challenge. She simply had no time to think about her failing marriage. Her in-laws still insisted on living with them but her mother-in-law refused to cook. She declared, *"Lakshmi, you must show me that respect as a mother-in-law and cook for us every day. I am not here to be your servant and take care of you. It is the other way around. Don't think just because you have a baby or you are pregnant you can escape your responsibilities to us."*

After the second pregnancy, their son Akshay was born. Rather than take responsibility for being a father, Chandru seemed to grow even more detached expecting Lakshmi to handle everything on her own. He took the backseat and insisted she run the errands on weekends as well as handle all the parenting. When Lakshmi pleaded for help, he seemed to grow more erratic. He screamed in her face and blocked doorways when she attempted to escape his verbal assaults. To her amazement, her in-laws who lived with them never commented or intervened.

After living with her in-laws for more than two miserable years, Lakshmi could not handle the daily stress anymore. Their subtle manipulation of Chandru led her to believe he could transform himself with a change of environment. She believed the source of their marital misery was his family's meddling. Separation from their toxic influence was the only way for Chandru to overcome his emotional issues. Maybe his anger, frustration, and lashing out at her would subside once he stopped always being confrontational with his parents. Determined to save their marriage, she decided it was time to take a stand.

One day Lakshmi told her husband frankly, *"I cannot live with your parents any longer. I tolerated it up until now, but I cannot stand the constant bickering. We need to get our own place as quickly as possible."* Surprisingly, Chandru permitted her to research new jobs around the country since her fellowship was ending. Lakshmi's career was on a promising path and there appeared to be abundant job opportunities available, but deciding which one to pick turned out to be more difficult than she imagined. Chandru immediately rejected any offers in cities where her family members lived. *"We cannot live in the same city with their dominating influence. They will just try to control and manipulate you."* Disappointed, Lakshmi kept searching.

Finally, she received a promising offer in Nebraska. The income, position, and benefits were impressive and Chandru seemed to advocate for this job strongly even though it was far away from all of their family, isolated, and in the middle of nowhere. Instinctively, she questioned whether it was the best opportunity, but she was tired of fighting her husband. Resigning herself to accepting the position, she wished to move forward with their lives and quickly move out of their living situation with the in-laws. She had hope that their attempt to build a life in Nebraska would change the dynamics of their marriage.

Convincing herself this move would be for the best, she took her two-year-old daughter and newborn son to Nebraska but could not deny their life steadily worsened. Dependent on having a constant sense of chaos in his life, Chandru maintained tension and conflict even in their new abode together. Whether he was lashing out at her or antagonizing his parents, his mental instability proved to be worsening. His anti-depressive medication seemed to have no effect. Lakshmi reasoned that acclimating to a new city, environment, and job took time. But were these just excuses to cover up the underlying reason for the chaos in their home?

At work, Chandru called repeatedly to ask her to come home earlier. He protested her long work hours failing to understand these were the regular duties of any physician. Lashing out, he yelled, "*Lakshmi, you have the wrong priorities. I think you are just working overtime to avoid me!*" When Lakshmi's demanding work hours increased, she was forced to rely on her husband to be the primary caretaker of the children.

Anamika was still too young to attend daycare. Chandru still fed her out of a bottle at the age of two and made her sit in front of the television all day. In front of others, he always acted like a doting father but at home he neglected the children, and Lakshmi had to beg him to look after them. She tried to hire a nanny but Chandru refused saying, "*I am a great caretaker. No one can look after our children better than I can. I will not let a stranger come into our home and take over my role.*" Defeated, Lakshmi did not know what else to do.

Believing some time away might be refreshing, they went on a luxurious vacation but the getaway proved to be a disaster. Not only was Chandru demanding, he was jealous whenever she spent more time with the children. Lakshmi found his immaturity astounding. He complained constantly about their accommodations shouting, "*I could have obviously planned this better. You put no thought into my needs for this vacation. You are too distracted by your job to know how to do anything for your family.*"

A few months later, Lakshmi decided she would take Anamika and Akshay with her to visit her parents after Chandru refused to join. But then he exclaimed, "*How dare you try to leave without me! You know you cannot travel alone!*" Since when did Lakshmi have to ask his permission for everything she did? How could he dictate whom she saw and try to dissuade her from seeing her own parents? Reluctantly, Chandru joined her but she wished he had not. His charming act was a thing of the past and he made no pretenses of being respectful to her parents.

At their home, he threw a temper tantrum. "*You are both so controlling! You have interfered and meddled in our life too much!*" Lakshmi wanted to retort how unfair it was that Chandru had barely ever let her parents come visit while his parents had lived with them off and on for years. If anyone had meddled, it was his parents. He continued his rant, "*You are the reason my wife is becoming so independent and making decisions without consulting me. I know everyone in your family hates me! You cannot get my wife to leave me!*"

Venomous, Chandru continued, "*Get out of our life and leave my wife alone! I don't want her to be brainwashed by you anymore!*" His behavior was appalling. Would he not stop until he had driven her parents completely out of her life? The next day her mother quietly confessed, "*Lakshmi, your husband is obviously mentally unstable and we do not trust him. It is best that we do not visit you and stay out of your lives.*" It seemed as if Chandru had successfully alienated her family. First her sibling, and now her parents wanted nothing to do with him.

Opening up to her parents, they reaffirmed how abnormal her situation was, but she remained numb and paralyzed. Wasn't she supposed to save her marriage? How could she walk away from the commitment she had made? How could she separate her children from their father? Those grueling years in Nebraska made Lakshmi question everything. With her loved ones so far away and forbidden from contacting her, her long, demanding hours at work, and so little time to spend at home with her children, she wondered if this was really the way life was supposed to be.

Seeking to understand her predicament, she read books on verbally abusive relationships. Chandru's behavior had perplexed her for years. Was she truly a victim if he had never laid a finger on her? At her breaking point she would announce, "*I cannot deal with this anymore. You have to change!*" Seeing she meant it, Chandru promised to transform himself. Every time she threatened to walk away, he attempted to pacify her. During the honeymoon stage, he displayed his charming side so she erroneously believed his apologies were genuine. Because she wanted her marriage to work, she chose to believe him even though there was no evidence to support this rationale.

Tension continued to escalate as Chandru's insults became more degrading with time. He screamed disgusting, filthy names whether in public or in private that left her utterly humiliated. He shouted, "*If you dare try to leave me, I will just get a younger, prettier wife and make sure that our children call her mom and not you!*" Once he spat, "*You are stupid and a terrible mother! Look at yourself! You are disgusting!*" How could he treat her this way? She had wept uncontrollably that day. He seemed to thrive on these confrontations and feel powerful afterwards.

Blinded by hope and Chandru's empty promises, it took her months to realize the pattern was not changing. Just when she thought there was a brief respite from the abuse and let her guard down, he would lash out at her mercilessly and intensify his verbal assaults. The idea of leaving her husband had fleeted in and out of her mind for years and there was always some excuse not to: her fear of being a single mother, how it would affect the kids, his retaliation, not having the support of her family that he had alienated. Once, he had even threatened to commit suicide and begged her to stay with him. At her wit's end, Lakshmi could not live with his daily drama and mental instability any longer. They had been married now for four years. She desperately needed to find a way out.

Discouraged by a reputable attorney who informed her she would have to wait a year to divorce otherwise Chandru would get full custody of the children, she decided to take small steps towards reclaiming her independence. Opening a separate bank account, she put some money aside for what she anticipated would become an expensive legal process. However, Chandru soon discovered what she had done and reprimanded her. "*Don't ever go behind my back again!*" Threatened by her growing independence, Chandru responded by becoming more controlling. He monitored her phone calls and her odometer on her car to make sure she was not going anywhere after work.

Lakshmi soon discovered she was pregnant again. Once again, he had tampered with her birth control medication. She had decided two children were enough for her to juggle with her career, but Chandru had once again shown he was in control and she could not defy him or make her own decisions. During her third pregnancy, Lakshmi felt her depression worsening. Trapped and hopeless, she wondered how it had come to this point. Wishing to end her marriage, she had only been ensnared deeper. Confiding in her parents, she desperately needed their support. She told them her plans to seek a divorce after the third baby was born.

That spring, Lakshmi gave birth to a healthy baby boy, Arun. Anamika was now four and Akshay two-years-old. Exhausted, Lakshmi struggled once again to balance the demands of three children and her career. She wondered if this had been Chandru's plan all along to keep making her pregnant so she would not have the opportunity to leave. Secretly, she had her tubes tied so that her husband could not impregnate her again. She started sleeping in the children's bedroom to avoid him all together and not be physically intimate. In her own way, she was taking small steps to reclaim her independence.

Overwhelmed with all her responsibilities, Lakshmi had to deal with her exhaustion and depression. Not surprisingly, Chandru refused to allow her parents to move in with them temporarily to help out at home. How was she supposed to pursue her divorce plans? She simply did not have any extra time after work when she rushed to be home with the children. The idea of separation was daunting and she knew she would have to take her time to plan this carefully.

When it was time to enroll Anamika in kindergarten, Chandru insisted on home schooling her. Taking a stand, Lakshmi said, *"She needs to interact with other children and learn how to communicate and play. You cannot keep her cooped up in our home all day!"* She could not trust Chandru to be a fit parent any longer. His signs of neglect were growing more obvious. Defiantly, Lakshmi enrolled Anamika in a school nearby. Her passivity had persisted for far too long, but when it came to her children, Chandru could not hold her back any longer from taking action.

Throughout that year she witnessed Anamika bloom in kindergarten and felt reassured that taking measures into her own hands had proved successful. Maybe she did have the strength within her all this time despite Chandru's attempts to make her believe she was too weak. Maybe she could turn her life around and not have to live with his abusiveness. Lakshmi could not even begin to imagine what freedom would be like. She dreamt of a quiet, simple life away from his rage, somewhere where he could never find her, surrounded by close family and friends who loved and appreciated her. A new sense of hope filled her; it was a strange sensation she had not felt in years.

Lakshmi pulled herself back to reality. Anamika was now seven, Akshay was five and had just begun kindergarten, and baby Arun was three. They were growing so quickly before her eyes. She thought of their futures. How could she let them continue to live in this home with an abusive father? She was forty-one-years-old herself. How much longer was she going to wait to start the rest of her life? What exactly was she waiting for... for things to get worse? She saw how Chandru's verbal assaults affected the children. The older two would grow quiet and stare at them with solemn eyes. The baby would start crying adding to the chaos. All of Lakshmi's attention would be deferred to trying to keep the baby calm, but Chandru would only become more outraged if she ignored him.

Sensing Lakshmi's growing strength when she stood up to him more frequently, Chandru unleashed his fury one evening. Screaming at her at the top of his lungs, he was a force to be reckoned with. Swinging his hand in the air he almost slapped her across the face but then restrained himself at the last minute. Knowing that it had come down to almost using physical violence, Lakshmi knew this was unacceptable. Anamika had burst into tears watching them. Lakshmi tried to pretend nothing had happened to calm the children but she was terrified he could hurt them. It was time for drastic action.

Without hesitating, Lakshmi called the police. When they arrived, Chandru completely lost it, hollering at the officers, "*My wife is just being vindictive and trying to get back at me! I have not done anything wrong!*" Seeing his instability, the cops instructed her, "*Miss, you need to leave your apartment with your children to be safe. Drop them off at daycare or with a friend. Here is the address of a domestic violence center you can visit.*" Weeping and trembling in the car, Lakshmi followed their instructions and dropped the children off at a friend's place.

At the center, she was grateful an advocate patiently and compassionately listened to her story. When was the last time Lakshmi had unburdened herself and spoke so freely? How many stories and secrets were bottled up inside her over the years. It was time to let them out and not hold anything back anymore. Chandru had made sure to ruin their social life so they had no real friends she could confide in over the years.

Having an advocate validate her experience and help her understand how she was victimized allowed clarity to surface. She said, "*I cannot tell you what to do but I can tell you your options. You can obtain a restraining order to protect you so you will feel safer in your home. I can accompany you to court if you are too scared to go alone.*" Lakshmi filed for a restraining order that same afternoon and Chandru was served that day. Returning home in the evening she discovered he had taken all of their valuables. Without a phone or a computer, he had ensured she would be unable to communicate with the outside world.

To her amazement, Chandru served her with a restraining order the next day supposedly to protect himself. It was evident he would not make this easy. She had falsely believed that separation would make things tolerable, but Chandru proved he would keep fighting her in any way he could. Before she could alert her credit card companies, he obtained the maximum amount from all her credit lines and depleted her bank accounts leaving her penniless. Despite changing her phone number multiple times, he monitored her phone logs until she uncovered the tracking device he had secretly placed on her phone.

The advocate explained that without any evidence of physical abuse, the courts did not have much sympathy for verbal abuse. After their first hearing in court, the judge proceeded to grant Lakshmi a permanent restraining order and denied the one Chandru requested. During the next few weeks, her husband violated the order multiple times. Without hesitation, Lakshmi called the cops each time he threatened her. She felt stronger day by day and was not afraid to take action despite his new methods to harass her.

Living in constant fear of his retaliation, his unpredictability and erraticism left her questioning if she was safer living separated. Had she made a mistake? Had she taken the best action for her children? She was tired of constantly having to look over her shoulder. During their separation they shared joint custody of the children every other week. When the children were with their father, Lakshmi felt her stomach churn wondering if he was neglecting them.

The slow legal battle would unfortunately drag on for the next three years of their lives. Chandru was determined to make her regret leaving him. Every penny she had was spent on paying her attorney and fighting for her children. Determined to win, Chandru did not really care about the kids but wanted to pounce on her weakness. At the end of an emotionally exhaustive battle, he won full custody of the children. He played taped conversations of Lakshmi yelling at him to prove Lakshmi was a hysterical, unfit mother. He used her busy work schedule to support his case that the children were not her priority. The fact that he was a stay-at-home father who spent the majority of time with them ultimately persuaded the judge to take his side. Chandru's behavior and the judge's verdict had only added insult to her injury of victimization.

Devastated, Lakshmi realized that at the age of forty-four she would have to start over, but she was nothing without her children. Despite having to pay alimony and child support, she could rebuild her financial prosperity but that was meaningless now. Her ex-husband had succeeded in destroying any chance she had for happiness. How could she live with herself knowing that all of her children were with that wretched man and there was nothing she could do about it?

After much soul searching, Lakshmi decided to devote herself to fighting for domestic violence causes. She was determined to fight for other mothers in custody battles with their abusers and help them escape the nightmare she had lived through. It was the only way to find some meaning in her life again. Someone needed to raise society's awareness of children's rights to be safe in their own homes. When would the justice system realize that abusive husbands would never be reliable fathers? Years later, when the children were old enough, they returned to visit Lakshmi and embraced their mother into their life again, but she had missed out on so many precious years of their childhood.

Chapter 35 GAYATRI'S GLORY

Gayatri glanced at her reflection in the mirror. Before her stood a beautiful bride dressed in a vibrant yellow sari, inlaid with rich, gold embroidery and a peacock green border. Admiring her elegant mehndi designs covering her hands and arms, the dark burgundy patterns came alive. The wedding day she anticipated for months had finally arrived. Accompanied by Gita, her older sister, and the other women in her family, she waited patiently in the dressing room. After spending a lifetime waiting for this man to come into her life, she could wait a few more minutes. At the auspicious time, her uncle would walk her towards the wedding hall where the groom and guests waited her arrival.

This time was different, Gayatri noticed. She was joyous and knew in her heart she had met a wonderful man, someone who deeply loved her and would care for her. This was nothing like her first marriage when she had questioned whether she was making the right decision until the very last moment. Despite her reservations, she had proceeded with the wedding. Gayatri was only eighteen when she had met Babu in college. He was five years older than her, intelligent, and seemed mature. During the two years they dated, Gayatri witnessed Babu's temper but she brushed it aside reasoning, *"Men can be difficult."*

When she finally informed her parents about their relationship, they reacted as most Indian parents would. *"How could you date him behind our back? What were you thinking? You are Gujrati and he is South Indian. He is not even of the same caste as us! You know we would not approve of a love marriage. What kind of a future could you possibly have with him?"* Gayatri met their relentless questioning with her own fierce stubbornness. *"Mom and Dad, Babu and I are right for each other. I would like your blessings to be with him."* As progressive as Mumbai was, dating was still considered taboo in many Indian communities. Her father insisted she marry Babu exclaiming, *"Who else would look at you now?"*

Feeling their pressure, she and Babu were engaged shortly thereafter. For the next year leading up to the wedding, Gayatri witnessed his true personality emerge. He had cleverly concealed most of his temperament until now. He hurled insults, uttering disgusting, profane words to degrade her, tease her, and diminish her self-esteem. Unaccustomed to this kind of language, Gayatri had grown up in a loving, safe environment where nobody swore or yelled. Each time he behaved this way, Gayatri was at a loss for words. She made excuses such as he did not mean it or was merely carried away by his temper. How else was she supposed to make sense of his actions? Ignoring her instincts and slipping into denial became routine.

It was not solely his temper that alarmed her, it was the degree of control he insisted on having over her life. He dictated whom she was permitted to socialize with and where she was allowed to go. Too young and naive to know any better, Gayatri had no prior dating experience. Moreover, how could she discuss her troubled relationship with her parents when they had already made it clear they did not approve of Babu or the marriage? Even Babu's mother had strict expectations demanding Gayatri assist her with cooking preparations for various festivities even though she was not yet her daughter-in-law. Trying to be polite and respectful, Gayatri felt forced to oblige her.

It was during this engagement period when Gayatri graduated from school and told Babu, *"I want to work in America and be financially independent first before marriage."* The timing was perfect and she was convinced this was the path she wanted to take. Nothing had prepared her for Babu's reaction. In a fit of intense rage, he slapped her hard across the face. Reeling back, Gayatri could not believe he was hitting her and that too in a public place. Too shocked to respond, she had done nothing. After declaring the job was unacceptable, he forced Gayatri to acquiesce to stay in India. Their parents also pressured her to arrange a rushed court wedding and not leave the country.

At that pivotal moment in time, if Gayatri had left and had some distance in the relationship, she would have gained greater insight, been more sure of herself, and had a taste of independence. In retrospect, she would have easily broken off the engagement if she had been in her right frame of mind and been able to make her own decisions without family or cultural pressure. Against her will, she had been forced to go through with the court wedding and turn down the promising job offer in the U.S. For immigration purposes, her in-laws insisted Gayatri adopt Babu's last name so it would be easier for him to get a visa down the road. It seemed everyone was making decisions on her behalf without her consent.

That spring, at the young ages of twenty-one and twenty-six, they were officially married even though neither family had been happy about the union. Returning from their brief honeymoon in Goa where Babu had lashed out at her physically, Gayatri moved into her in-laws' home as was the custom for a new bride. She had expected to live in a joint home but had not realized it would be a nightmare from the first day. Besides the lack of privacy, Babu insisted on his parents accompanying them everywhere, even if it was a trip to the movies. Gayatri questioned why they could not spend some time alone even as newlyweds.

Her mother-in-law's demands were relentless. As a new bride she was expected to wake up at 5 a.m. and prepare breakfast and lunch for Babu's parents, older brother, and her sister-in-law. She thought maybe her sister-in-law would become her ally but she was just as manipulative and demanding as the rest of them. Babu professed, *"Just because you are entering the house I do not want my mother to be bothered with extra work. You should be lightening her work load and not adding to it."* Gayatri had responded icily, "*I did not go to school and have a great education to learn how to become a maid.*"

Gayatri's older sister Gita was also recently married but her living situation was vastly different. Gita's new in-laws were supportive and encouraged her to return to school to finish her medical training. They allowed her to come and go as she pleased and visit her parents any time she wished. Gayatri's parents commented, "*Why can Gita visit us so often and you need to ask for permission all the time? You have hardly been to visit us since your marriage!*" Unable to explain her situation, the tension always mounted during these conversations. She could not account for why Gita lived a life of freedom while she lived like a slave.

In her new marital home, Babu always seemed poised for battle. When he returned home in the evenings, his mother greeted him outside to list her daily grievances against Gayatri. Babu would enter the home already furious and lash out at Gayatri. Never having any privacy, it was inevitable that his mother also ganged up on her. The cycle of violence repeated itself daily as the tension became insurmountable. To add to her misery, her in-laws took it upon themselves to degrade her parents with swear words and demeaning comments. When they lashed out at her, Babu remained silent. In his eyes, his parents could do no wrong. Jumping in to defend his wife was not an option when he believed she was to blame for upsetting his parents.

One night during a particularly intense fight, Babu hit her on the chest repeatedly. The severe pounding left her sore and bruised. The in-laws must have heard the commotion because the next day, Babu's father said, "*Beta, it is okay if you slap your wife once in awhile but you cannot beat her relentlessly.*" Gayatri did not know what to think. Should she be shocked he was giving his son permission to beat her or grateful that he was telling him to control himself?

After six months of enduring the abuse, Gayatri found a low-paying job just to escape from the house for a few hours a day. The income was only enough to pay her bus fare but she relished having some time to herself. From a payphone she called her parents to hear their comforting voices even though she was not yet ready to confide in them. At home, her in-laws listened to all her conversations without any regard for her privacy.

A year in that tormented house passed by until Gayatri received her visa to work in the U.S. This had been her suppressed dream that had been sidetracked by the rushed marriage but she refused to be derailed again. That spring, she journeyed to the U.S. alone, hopeful of pursuing her dreams and starting a new life of opportunity. Those first few months she veritably struggled to adapt to a new culture, commence a new job, and manage life on her own.

Later that fall, Babu joined her but made it clear he was anxious to return to India. Unable to work because of his restricted visa, Babu spent most of his days in the apartment waiting for Gayatri to return home in the evenings. During those months, Gayatri observed how his domination over her seemed to worsen in direct proportion to his restlessness and insecurity.

Gayatri remained the sole breadwinner in the family, providing for all of Babu's travel expenses. She longed to visit her parents in India but there simply were insufficient funds to do so. Meanwhile, Babu's parents insisted on traveling to the U.S. for several months and staying with them. Of course, Gayatri footed the bill, unable to say no to her in-laws' demands. They took her income for granted and insisted her hard-earned U.S. dollars belonged to the entire family.

Babu's financial demands became increasingly manipulative. After his parents purchased a new residence in Mumbai, he declared, *"We must contribute to my parents' household since we have been living with them since the wedding. Let us pay for all the furnishings and decorations."* Since Babu had no income, their only source of funds was Gayatri's savings account. Almost half of her savings were depleted by Babu's lavish spending spree. At the time, Gayatri had no idea this was financial abuse. She had become a puppet at this point, brainwashed into listening to her husband's wishes so as not to upset him.

For the next two years, Babu traveled back and forth to the U.S. leaving Gayatri to live alone for long stretches of time. During these periods, she learned to be independent and discovered she was quite content on her own. Without Babu's constant demands of her, there was ample time for reflection. She questioned why she tolerated his abhorrent behavior. The strain on their relationship was apparent from living apart for such long periods, and that too, in separate countries. Clarity was starting to dawn that her marriage was not what she dreamed it would be and brought her no joy. In comparison, she saw her sister Gita flourish in her marriage and observed how her husband treated her lovingly.

At the four-year mark of their union, Babu returned to India and finally found employment. They decided Gayatri would continue working to save some money and then join him. Living their separate lives had become routine at this point as she felt she was more single these days than married. One evening she headed out with her friends, unsuspecting that her entire life would be turned upside down within a few hours.

Later that night she received a phone call from India, *"Your mother has passed."* Shock, confusion, anger, and a host of other emotions flowed through her. How could this be? Four years had passed while she lived in America and been unable to return and visit her parents even once. If she had not been struggling financially to establish her career, she would have flown back every year to see them. There had been no warning or indication something like this would happen so soon. Her mom was still so young but she had died suddenly of a heart attack.

Consumed with grief, Gayatri rushed to be by her father's side. Gita, who also lived abroad, could not travel back to India because she was too far along in her pregnancy. Gayatri decided it was best to move back to India to be close to her grieving father, and of course, to try to mend her tenuous marriage. She was not thrilled about leaving the U.S. and the independent life she had created for herself but family had to come first. Guilt consumed her for not being present beside her mother during her last years, but Gayatri owed it to her father to be there for him now.

Moving back into her in-laws' home, she was amazed their demands and expectations of her had only intensified and it was apparent they felt no compassion about her mother's passing. Forbidden to visit her father, even though that was why Gayatri had chosen to uproot her life in America, she pleaded, *"At least can my father come here to visit me once in awhile?"* She could not understand their unreasonableness. *"No, of course he cannot,"* her mother-in-law retorted, *"His feet are always dirty and he will sully our white marble floor."* How dare they speak about her own father this way! A sense of helplessness and resignation set in at that point as she felt her spirit erode steadily.

Unable to work in India due to job restrictions, she felt trapped in the home all day long, confined and restricted like a hostage. Babu left for work early in the morning and returned home late at night, immersed in his own activities and ambivalent to her plight. He seemed apathetic to her needs and did not even care whether she ate or not. He made it clear he would not be her ally in the battle against his parents. Somehow, Gayatri found she had become the domesticated housewife, a role she had always dreaded. The isolation she felt now was particularly heightened after experiencing the freedom of living on her own in the U.S.

Months passed living in this unbearable environment until Gayatri knew she could not take it anymore. She had to do something drastic. Unable to see her own family or reach out to anyone she knew, she was utterly miserable. Resolute, the next day she took a lethal dose of sleeping pills when no one was home. Never had Gayatri imagined she would be this desperate or do something so uncharacteristic. Apparently, Babu found her when he came home and rushed her to the hospital where they pumped her stomach. Gayatri could not remember the events that transpired in those few days and was only told the details after her recovery.

Somehow life went on. Battling her intense nausea after the incident, Gayatri found it difficult to eat. Babu retorted, *"Can you not eat any faster? You are making it difficult for my mother to finish her work in the kitchen."* Gayatri ignored her husband's inhumane comments and the looks of disgust from his parents. Only a few days after her return from the hospital, another particularly nasty fight ensued. Her in-laws telephoned Gayatri's father in the middle of the night demanding he take her away. Unsuspecting, her father rushed to her home at 3 a.m. after receiving the disturbing phone call. He wondered what the ruckus was all about since his daughter had never hinted of any unhappiness in her marriage nor commented on her in-laws' mistreatment of her.

Even after moving into her father's home briefly for five days, Gayatri could not burden him with her problems. They had just lost her mother earlier that year and the wounds were too fresh while they were still grieving. How could she break her father's heart further? Even after always confiding in Gita, how could she tell her sister the profanities Babu uttered about them? Her father called her in-laws daily to ask, *"What is your decision?"* Her mother-in-law would reply with contempt, *"We have not yet determined if we will allow her back in our home!"*

A few days later, Gayatri returned to her marital home, numb and detached, a shadow of her former self. The sleeping pill incident and being kicked out of her own home left her defeated. How was she to recover? How was she supposed to continue living her meaningless life that brought her no joy? The heartache of losing her loving mother left her drifting without an anchor. She could not help but feel more estranged from everything she held dear. Her isolation now only seemed to deepen with each incident. She had never felt so alone in her entire life. There was no one she could speak to who would understand the anguish she endured.

To her horror, Gayatri discovered she was pregnant a few weeks later and made it clear she wished to terminate the pregnancy. Despite her in-laws' tremendous pressure to keep the baby, the implications of having a child in this family terrified her. This was not a loving, safe home. Babu watched unperturbed as his parents yelled at her daily. How could they be caring grandparents? Would they yell and hurl insults at her child, too? Every fiber in her body resisted motherhood. As luck would have it, Gayatri was diagnosed with rubella during her first trimester. The doctor told her matter-of-factly, *"I am sorry to say that you will have to abort this fetus."* Relieved, Gayatri felt she had been saved. Maybe there was a god after all looking over her. She felt a glimmer of hope again.

After reaching her lowest point, Gayatri knew she had to find a way to improve her situation. In the spring, she discussed her plan to move back to the U.S. with Babu. He responded, *"I am happy here in India, working at my new job where I am a big shot. People look up to me and respect me. I am perfectly content living with my parents. You just need to adjust to be an accommodating wife and a better daughter-in-law."* But Gayatri was determined to work in the U.S. and fulfill herself professionally. Sitting at home and serving her in-laws constantly as per their demands was not the life of which she had dreamed. Needless to say, Babu was not pleased with her decision stating, *"If you want to leave, then go on your own. I will not join you any time soon."*

Gayatri left without looking back. Living on her own that year was a transformational period. Her independence taught her for the first time she had choices about how she wanted to live and what she wanted to deal with. Life was so much easier when she did not have to answer to Babu or his parents, follow their rules, or let them dictate her life. After living with their oppression for so many years, a strange sense of elation filled her. She had never felt this free or been this happy in a long time.

The next spring, Babu returned to America to visit her. It had been almost a year since they had seen each other. Driving to the airport, Gayatri felt an icy hand grip her heart instead of being enthusiastic to see him. This was not what marriage was supposed to be. She wondered if he would be different after this long absence. Hesitant, Gayatri felt the flood of emotions that used to paralyze her when they lived together. In his absence, she had grown so much stronger and sure of herself. She had to let Babu know he could not dictate the show any longer and their relationship would now have to be on her terms. Upon his arrival, she told him firmly, *"Don't you dare lay a hand on me or I will kick you out of my home."* Giving him that ultimatum and being firm about her boundaries, Babu acknowledged his wife had changed.

As the months dragged on, Gayatri sensed this change as well. Unable to be physically intimate with her husband, she felt the distance between them growing at an alarming rate. Their marriage was rapidly disintegrating. Even though the physical abuse had ended, she observed Babu was still the same manipulative, controlling, arrogant man he had always been. He was never going to change. She detested his presence in her home and felt she was losing her sanity. Desperate for intervention, Gayatri visited a therapist weekly for six months but was disappointed she could not understand her cultural issues and resistance to divorce. Finally, Gayatri made the tough decision she must take the initiative and end her marriage. Confronting Babu she informed him, *"I cannot live with you any longer in this unhealthy relationship. I am much happier on my own."*

At first, Babu resisted wholeheartedly. Divorce was not acceptable in India. He threatened her. *"How dare you try to leave me? You cannot humiliate me like this! If you try to divorce me, I will drag you through a legal mess in India and confiscate your passport so you will never be able to return to the U.S. You will regret trying to take a stand against me!"* After his initial hysteria passed, Gayatri reasoned, *"Let's face it, Babu, this is never going to work and neither of us are happy."* He finally accepted that her home was now in America and she would never return to India to be his parents' "servant." Of course, Babu would not make it easy for her as his spite and underhandedness would soon take a new turn.

After Babu packed his bags and left, Gayatri felt an enormous wave of relief. The next day when she checked her bank account, her heart sank looking at the balance. There was less than $1,000 remaining. What happened to her savings? She had spent the past year working a second job to save money and now it was all gone. With one click, Babu had withdrawn $20,000, all of her hard-earned income, and left her without even enough to pay the rent next month. Throughout their marriage she had been the primary breadwinner and supported them both, flown her husband back and forth to India countless times, and supported her in-laws. How could he do this to her and be so vindictive? She had not expected he would be this malicious. Panic and trepidation consumed her. She detested him with every fiber of her being.

After confronting Babu about stealing her money, he refused to pay her back and said simply, *"I clearly deserve the money and you are not entitled to it. You have wasted six years of my life. I have calculated that* *you owe me a total of $100,000. Right now, I will accept this advance of $20,000 but you must pay me monthly as you earn money towards that debt."* Gayatri reeled with the disgust and rage she felt towards this man. How dare he talk to her this way and keep making demands! He had treated her like an indentured servant their entire marriage and now still wanted to hold her in bondage. This was ridiculous. A speedy divorce was the only option to be rid of this man from her life forever.

That spring, they filed for divorce in India by mutual consent. The legal process went fairly smoothly and was finalized by autumn. It still took her time after she initiated the divorce process to confide in her family. Not wishing to burden her father or sister for so many years with the struggles of her marriage, losing her mother had only complicated the matter and strengthened her desire to protect them. When she finally spoke to her sister, the betrayal in Gita's voice spoke volumes. *"Why didn't you tell us? How could you have kept this secret for so long? Why would you not trust me and be honest about your suffering?"* Beneath her anger, she felt Gita's underlying guilt for not protecting her younger sister. Gayatri realized it was time to mend all of her relationships, be honest, and not have any more secrets.

The stigma of divorce weighed heavily on her. Subject to social pressure, her dad resented her choices and disapproved of the divorce. There was no precedent for his daughter's behavior. All of his friends had children who were happily married, and if not, they did not get divorced. Not only had Gayatri gone against his wishes dating someone of a lower caste and then having a love marriage, she had kept so many secrets from him. He truly believed Gayatri had landed herself in this mess. His denial kept him from admitting his daughter had been abused.

Gayatri realized with a heavy heart that her father may never fully understand why she divorced Babu. He was a traditionalist, stuck in his old-fashioned ways, unable to accept that she had gone against cultural beliefs to end her unhealthy, violent marriage. She would have to live with her father's blame and accept he would never support her decisions. After everything she had been through, she desperately wished for her father's blessings but he made it clear where he stood. Gayatri had to find a way to move on with her life and rebuild her future. She needed to put the past behind her and not let her horrible marriage haunt her any longer.

Her father was not the only one battling the stigma of divorce. Whenever Gayatri met Indians in the community, she felt forced to hang her head in shame and reluctantly admit to being divorced. In their eyes, she would always be blamed for failing to be a good wife. It was so much easier to speak about her divorce with Americans who took the news in stride and offered no judgment. If only the Indian community would accept that it was better to leave a doomed relationship than to endure simply because that was the cultural norm. Afraid of breaking too many taboos, Gayatri kept her secret that she was a victim of domestic violence from both Indians and Americans. She did not want to add to the already unpleasant, awkward conversations she was forced to have with a disapproving society.

Gayatri reflected on the past decade of her life, meeting Babu at eighteen, marrying at twenty-one, and now divorcing at twenty-eight. Her gravest mistake was not having a career first and being financially independent. If only she had realized during those hellish years that she had options instead of feeling trapped and helpless. She remained enslaved to his family for years while she became financially responsible for supporting them. Ultimately, it was establishing herself professionally and being successful that was the biggest factor in her recovery.

Haunted by her mistakes, Gayatri wished for a way to go back in time. If only she had confided in her family instead of believing she was protecting them. They should have been the first ones to know about her abusive marriage and not the last. In the end, she was dishonest with them and most importantly, dishonest with herself. During those dark years she had not only lost her mother, but the sense of how to care for and nurture herself. Struggling with the physical and verbal abuse, she had questioned her life and purpose. She sank into a deep depression after Babu sabotaged her personal savings, but she was determined to find a way to save again and refused to be defeated.

She could not dwell on the past any longer and had to learn from her mistakes. Gayatri focused on rebuilding her life and immersed herself in her career. Being on her own again in the U.S., Gayatri discovered her strengths, relied on her innate abilities, and regained her confidence. Enjoying her freedom and relishing her independence, she found the sweet satisfaction of living her own life without anyone dictating it. Time was the best salve for her wounds. It allowed her to heal from her past slowly, take time to build her trust in others, and feel safe in new relationships. Within a short period of time, Gayatri was able to invest in her own business. Economic independence and success was an achievement she could be proud of and prove to her father she could make it on her own.

Almost five years after her divorce, Gayatri found herself amongst friends at an Indian cultural event. She had clicked with Vivek almost instantly. Being around him was comfortable, easy, and she felt she could be herself. Vivek appreciated her and listened to her in a way Babu never had. Realizing the social stigma was an integral part of her, Gayatri confessed on their first date, "*I want to be completely honest with you. I am ashamed to say I am divorced.*" Surprised Vivek did not seem bothered by her admission, she discovered how open-minded and atypical he was from the Indian guys she usually met.

Witnessing the contrast between a healthy and unhealthy relationship was overwhelming at first. How had she lived with so much oppression and abuse over the years? But she reasoned how young, naïve, and inexperienced she was at twenty when she was pressured to marry early before being emotionally ready or mentally prepared. Now she was older, wiser, and knew what she would tolerate or find acceptable in a relationship. Over the course of two years, they dated long-distance and took it slowly so as to not rush the relationship. Gayatri wanted to get to know Vivek well and not have any surprises in the future. She found herself questioning, *"How can I really trust this guy? What if he changes down the road? What if I grow to really like him and then he turns out to be like Babu?"*

Listening to her instincts this time, Gayatri realized there were no red flags. She observed his personality and behavior in various scenarios, how he handled disagreements, or reacted to unexpected situations. His expectations of her were totally different than Babu's. He encouraged her to be her own person, speak her mind openly, and disagree with him when her opinion differed and not feel threatened by it. He never degraded her, but on the contrary, always treated her with respect. It was refreshing to have this level of freedom in their interactions. Finding herself always at ease around him, she slowly realized she could trust him.

As their relationship deepened, Vivek confessed he was ready for marriage. Hesitant, Gayatri had given up on the idea of remarrying. She treasured her freedom and independence and never wished to sacrifice that again even if it meant staying single for the rest of her life. Facing her fears, she was terrified of repeating past mistakes. Vivek entered her life when she least expected it and somehow found a way to open her heart. Could she trust herself to make the right decision this time? It was not him she doubted now, but herself. Was she ready to have in-laws who might expect her to move back to India or live in a joint household with them? What would they think of her divorced status?

Reassuringly, Vivek addressed her worries and told her she had nothing to fear. *"Gayatri, my family and I don't care about your past or the fact you are divorced. My parents are just happy I have met someone I love and want to spend my life with. Not all Indians are traditionalists. You'll find my parents are quite open-minded and progressive."* When Gayatri met his parents, she was pleasantly surprised by how they embraced her into the family without any reservations. Every word Vivek spoke was true. If they could look at her this way, then maybe others would too and she did not have to be ashamed anymore.

With their blessings and her family being overjoyed by the match, she felt a new sense of peace about remarriage. This time, Gayatri knew the marriage was on her terms. Bringing herself back to the present moment, tears filled her eyes. Today was her wedding day and she was about to marry the man of her dreams. Looking at her reflection in the mirror, Gayatri saw a new woman. She was thirty-five, mature, independent, confident, and not the naïve young girl she once was. She saw someone who was not haunted by her past or repressed by cultural taboos, and who had found a way to triumph despite all her suffering. It had taken a long time but now Gayatri was free. Her redemption had not only brought her financial success and a prosperous career, it had brought her a wonderful man to share that with.

Chapter 36 THE INDIAN VICTIM & KARMA

Cultural Struggles

Every victim's struggle is unique, as is her individual journey towards freedom. The heroic stories of Devi, Radha, Sita, Lakshmi, and Gayatri reveal the remarkable ability of these women to break free from their abusive marriages despite the monumental cultural, societal, and personal obstacles they each faced. After enduring unimaginable suffering at the hands of the men they married, and in some cases genuinely loved, they knew at their breaking points that no marriage was worth their pain. All of their accounts demonstrate the inherent oppressive themes of abuse and the resilience that characterizes so many victims.

Throughout this book, the minority issues of the South Asian/Indian Hindu victim have been highlighted: emphasis on the survival of the family unit over the individual, the joint family structure with its inherent potential for abuse by in-laws, theme of self-sacrifice and surrender expected of all wives, and the cultural taboo of divorce. In my process of interviewing Indian women for this book, however, there was a particular cultural theme of self-blame I felt the need to address and elaborate on here.

Cultural Self-Blame

Many of these women had a tendency to blame the *type* of marriage they chose for making them susceptible to the abusive relationship. Indian victims in love marriages often regretted marrying someone not of their parents' choosing or foregoing their approval. Victims from introduced marriages lamented not allowing significant time to get to know their spouses or date them before exchanging vows. Those in arranged marriages wished they had been as fortunate as those they observed in happy, successful arranged relationships or selected a spouse of their own choosing. As we observed in the stories of all these women, however, abuse can occur in *any* type of marriage, whether one's family supported the alliance or not. Most Indian victims interviewed expressed grief over the stark contrast between their lives before marriage and after the wedding. It was customary to hear "*I wish I had just remained single and never decided to marry.*"

Yet, despite the type of marriage, the most common reaction I heard from these women was, "*This must have been my karma to endure this abusive marriage. I must have done something really terrible in my past life to deserve this.*" It is heart-wrenching to hear a victim blame herself for her abusive predicament when she absolutely cannot hold herself responsible for her batterer's actions. There is nothing she has done to deserve this. Although there is a certain element of self-blame all domestic violence victims experience, the notion of karma further complicates this issue for the Hindu victim. The idea she has committed "horrible" deeds in her past to bring this upon herself is a fallacy that only perpetuates her self-blame and victimization and must be corrected here. Injustice does exist in the world and cannot always be explained through the lens of karma.

Introducing Karma

As the term has become popularized and frequently misused in the West, karma is often inaccurately translated as "fate" or "destiny". Karma simply means "action." Every action produces a reaction, thus creating a karmic cycle of action and reaction. Hence, religious and spiritual teachings throughout the ages have expressed *"As you sow, you shall reap,"* implying that one benefits from performing good deeds or inevitably has to face the consequences of one's malicious actions. Hinduism explains this as accruing karmic merit from virtuous deeds versus "negative" karma from deliberately hurtful actions.

Thus, every individual faces a choice in each moment about *how* to act. Self-awareness allows one to evaluate one's intentions, act with deliberation, and contemplate the short- and long-term consequences of how an action might benefit or harm others. The dictionary defines karma as *"the force generated by a person's actions held in Hinduism and Buddhism to perpetuate transmigration and in its ethical consequences to determine the nature of the person's next existence."*

Karma encompasses *both* a mixture of fate and free will and varies according to individual circumstance at various points in one's lifetime. Only jyotish, or Vedic astrology, is a science that can predict karmic patterns. Hence, many Hindus have frequently relied upon this ancient system of reading an individual's horoscope to provide direction and insight for managing all aspects of one's life. Explaining the profound science of karma beyond this simple overview, however, surpasses the scope of this book.

Hinduism

According to Hinduism, this cycle of action and reaction generates karmic momentum that propels the soul to reincarnate over numerous lifetimes until one faces the total summation of results from one's previous actions, whether they are desirable or undesirable. Moksha, defined as spiritual freedom from the bondage of the cycle of birth and rebirth, is only achieved by completely surrendering the ego, acting selflessly, and embracing oneness with divinity.

There are various paths to find liberation such as: jnana yoga (path of knowledge), bhakti yoga (path of devotion), raja yoga (path of meditation), and karma yoga (path of action). Karma yoga emphasizes self-awareness of one's actions by taming the mind so one does not act while blinded by emotion, but from a mental state of peace and balance. Performing good deeds in the service of others and the greater community creates a positive momentum of karmic merit and acting selflessly that benefits all. Volunteer work and philanthropy are examples of karma yoga.

Ahimsa or Non-Violence

Ashtanga yoga, or the eight-limbed path, is an aspect of raja yoga that has become popular not only in the West, but globally. It also delineates a systematic progression towards self-development and accruing karmic merit with sequential steps to tame the mind, transcend one's emotions, create purity, and establish spiritual discipline. Following these eight limbs leads to spiritual mastery, self-realization, and achieving moksha. A detailed discussion of ashtanga yoga is also beyond the scope of this book, but briefly these eight limbs are:

(1) *Yamas*-Ethical Disciplines
(2) *Niyamas*-Observances
(3) *Asanas*-Physical Postures
(4) *Pranayma*-Regulating the Breath
(5) *Pratyahara*-Withdrawal of the Senses
(6) *Dharana*-Concentration
(7) *Dhyana*-Meditation
(8) *Samadhi*-Spiritual Absorption

Yamas, the first limb, are the ethical disciplines that should be observed that include abstaining from violence, from stealing, from coveting, practicing truthfulness, and celibacy. Of these five practices, the principle of ahimsa, or nonviolence, is critical to the discussion on domestic violence. This tenet is the foundation for pursuing a spiritual path that must be adhered to before any of the subsequent principles can be practiced. Ahimsa does not merely mean refraining from violent actions such as assault or battering that physically hurts another.

Ahimsa also includes nonviolent speech that does not emotionally wound others and communication that is respectful. It embraces the idea of non-violent thoughts where the idea of physically or verbally attacking another does not even enter one's mind. To act nonviolently is to act peacefully, consciously, compassionately, and respectfully. Ideally, all of one's actions become based on this principle of integrity to create a harmonious peaceful life. Even following a vegetarian diet where the life of an animal is not taken for sustenance or being environmentally conscious becomes an inherent part of this yogic practice. This concept of nonviolence is not limited to Hinduism of course, but embraced by many of the world's religions.

For a Hindu victim who is first assaulted or verbally attacked by her partner, not only has she been violated, but so have her religious principles. Any man who chooses to use violence against a woman has dishonored a basic spiritual code to respect life and the sanctity of her right to exist unharmed. Beyond religion, respect for life and for others is the true essence of spirituality. This intrinsic virtue is reflected in the customary Hindu greeting of pressing the palms together in front of the heart and saying *"Namaste: I salute the divinity and light within you which is also in me."* This is a profound way to acknowledge another being, show respect, and express the oneness between all people.

Abuser's Karma

As a batterer creates and perpetuates the cycle of violence, he generates negative karma from his lack of self-awareness, failing to observe the detrimental effect his actions have on his victim. The end result is prolonging the tormented life he leads as he is destined to experience the inevitable effects of his wrath. Eventually, he must face his actions one day and atone for the damage he has caused, if not in this lifetime, then definitely in the next. There is no escape from this, although a victim may find it hard to believe when she witnesses the depths of her batterer's denial as well as that of his family. Her only consolation is to sincerely trust in the science of karma, diminishing her desire for revenge. She should find satisfaction in knowing there will be a higher justice for the suffering she has endured that is not in her hands to deliver.

A victim must also see a batterer's choices about how to behave or act destructively in the moment as "new" karma he is creating based on free will that has nothing to do with her past karma. She cannot ascribe this to being her "fate" because karma inherently implies action and also free will and her perpetrator could choose to not use violence against her. She also can *choose* a different life for herself. Her conscious actions to extricate herself from her abusive environment, gain support, and take necessary steps to liberate herself from her suffering, is the true destiny of every victim to find freedom. She has the power with this new cultivated self-awareness to fashion her own destiny.

Collective Karma

There may also be a higher purpose to her suffering. Along with individual karma, there is the collective karma of families, countries, or nations. The overall worldwide oppression of women for centuries has generated a global karma that at least one-third of the world's female population will statistically experience some form of this violence. It does not mean that all these women "deserve" it because of their past actions.

Removing the illusion of separation, a victim realizes something much larger is at stake than just her individual struggle. Her personal fight is on behalf of the emancipation of women everywhere who suffer in silence and are subject to this senseless violence. When she takes a stand, she becomes a role model encouraging all oppressed women to break free. This awareness fuels her with new passion and vigor. The option to forfeit her voice and not fight simply does not exist as she joins the collective voice for freedom with all survivors.

This perspective views the suffering these souls experience as both the individual and group imperative to shift this karma, overcome the injustice, and change this dynamic of global anguish. It is very clear with the growing awareness of domestic violence and the explosion of women's advocacy groups that the tide is turning, women *and* men are demanding change, and this widespread repression of the female race will no longer be tolerated. The time is optimal for a worldwide transformation of consciousness, a major shift where the voices of women everywhere will be heard, respected, embraced.

As each individual woman grows stronger, declares her opposition to this tyranny, and demands the rebalance of power between the genders, her voice is being heard. As each survivor of abuse takes a stand to fight for her freedom, her cries inspire others. Every individual fight for emancipation is part of the collective shift that must occur to end abuse on a global scale. It can be done; it is within our reach in this lifetime. We must sincerely believe this and know freedom is possible for every oppressed woman if we join our hands and act on behalf of the global family.

Finding Freedom

For any survivor who feels weak, trust in the fact that power will come, strength will flow, and guidance will emerge. After everything you have endured, know that life *can* still be glorious, beautiful, and benevolent. Marvel at the beauty in breaking free; see the kindness and grace in your redemption. Honor your feelings, listen to the deepest voice within, and be authentic to fully embrace the power of who you are. Rejoice in what you have overcome and celebrate your journey from surviving to thriving. Cherish being alive and the second chance you have been given.

Life is about gracefully opening to the endless possibilities that exist within, experiencing the beauty of your breath moving through you, and treasuring every precious moment as a wonderful gift. You possess the power to break free from anyone or anything that holds you back and radically heal from your past. *There are moments in your life that define you: choosing your freedom is one of them.*

NOW AVAILABLE:

The Power to Break Free Workbook
For Victims & Survivors of Domestic Violence

The workbook is designed to facilitate healing, process the deep-seated trauma of abuse, and find the necessary steps to recovery. For victims currently still in an abusive relationship, these exercises will help to evaluate your relationship, the effect of the abuse, how safe you are, and provide clarity about your situation. Exercises to examine yourself, your partner, types of abuse, and power and control tactics will prove instrumental. How you can get help, enlist the aid of the community, deal with the difficulties of separation, and evaluate true change are mentioned here.

For survivors who have left their abusive partners, this workbook will build your strength and self-awareness and provide necessary tools to find closure. Healing exercises will increase your confidence in your ability to move forward and embrace a new abuse-free future. The last section contains inspirational quotes and space to write your reflections and insights. This is an excellent resource to use during healing retreats and workshops for victims.

REFERENCES 379

APPENDIX 1 STATISTICS ON DOMESTIC VIOLENCE

VICTIMS: WHO IS AFFECTED
Global
- Domestic violence is both a national and a worldwide crisis. According to a 2000 UNICEF study, 20-50% of the female population of the world will become victims of domestic violence.[461]
- The United Nations Development Fund for Women estimates that at least 1 of every 3 women globally will be beaten, raped or otherwise abused during her lifetime. In most cases, the abuser is a member of her own family.[462]
- A 2005 World Health Organization study found that of 15 sites in 10 countries-representing diverse cultural settings-the proportion of ever-partnered women who had experienced physical or sexual IPV in their lifetimes ranged from 15% in Japan to 71% in Ethiopia.[463]

U.S. Population
- Nearly 1 in 4 (25%) women report experiencing violence by a current or former spouse or boyfriend at some point in her life.[464]
- In the U.S. 2 million women are battered by their partners each year.[465]
- Nearly 3 out of 4 (74%) of Americans personally know someone who is or has been a victim of IPV. 30% of Americans say they know a woman who has been physically abused by her husband/boyfriend in the past year.[466]

Gender
- Women are much more likely than men to be victimized by a current or former intimate partner.[467]
- Women account for 85% of victims while men account for 15%.[468] In other words, women are *5 to 8 times more likely* than men to be victimized by an intimate partner.[469]
- Women are 84% of spouse abuse victims and 86% of victims of abuse at the hands of a boyfriend or girlfriend and about 75% of the persons who commit family violence are male.[470]
- The vast majority of domestic assaults are committed by men. Even when men are victimized, 10% are assaulted by another man. In contrast, only 2% of women who are victimized are assaulted by another woman.[471]

Age
- Women of all ages are at risk for domestic and sexual violence, and those age 20 to 24 are at the greatest risk.[472]
- Young women age 20 to 24 also experience the highest rates of rape and sexual assault, followed by those 16 to 19.[473] /Women age 18 and 19 experience the highest rates of stalking.[474]
- Younger victims of IPV were least likely to report the violence to the police.[475]

Income
- IPV affects people regardless of income. However, people with lower annual income (below $25K) are at a 3-times higher risk than people with higher annual income (over $50K).[476] *Please note that those with less resources are more likely to report incidents of violence and this statistic does not reflect upscale abuse.
- On average between 1993 and 2004, residents of urban areas experienced highest level of nonfatal IPV. Residents in suburban and

rural areas were equally likely to experience such violence, about 20% less than those in urban areas.[477]

Race
- Women of all races are about equally vulnerable to violence by an intimate partner.[478]
- Black and white women experienced IPV at similar rates for every age group except age 20 to 24. Among that group, there were 29 violent victimizations per 1,000 black women compared to 20 per 1,000 white women.[479]
- Between 1993 and 2005, rates of nonfatal IPV decreased for white females, white males, and black females. Between 2004 and 2005, rates of IPV remained stable for white females at 3.1 per 1,000 persons age 12 or older; black females at 4.6 per 1,000 persons age 12 or older; white males at .7 per 1,000 persons age 12 or older.[480]
- Average annual rates of IPV between 1994 and 2004 are approximately the same for non-Hispanic and Hispanic females and males.[481]

Immigrant Women*
- Abusers often use their partners' immigration status as a tool of control.[482] In such situations, it is common for a batterer to exert control over his partner's immigration status in order to force her to remain in the relationship.[483]
- Immigrant women often suffer higher rates of battering than U.S. citizens because they may come from cultures that accept domestic violence or because they have less access to legal and social services than U.S. citizens. Additionally, immigrant batterers and victims may believe that the penalties and protections of the U.S. legal system do not apply to them.[484]
- Battered immigrant women who attempt to flee may not have access to bilingual shelters, financial assistance, or food. It is also unlikely that they will have the assistance of a certified interpreter in court, when reporting complaints to the police or a 911 operator, or even in acquiring information about their rights and the legal system.[485]
- Married immigrant women experience higher levels of physical and sexual abuse than unmarried immigrant women, 59.5% compared to 49.8%, respectively.[486]
- A recent study in New York City found that 51% of intimate partner homicide victims were foreign-born, while 45% were born in the U.S.[487]
- 48% of Latinas in one study reported that their partner's violence against them had increased since they immigrated to the U.S.[488]
- A survey of immigrant Korean women found that 60% had been battered by their husbands.[489]

DOMESTIC VIOLENCE INCIDENTS
- Every 9 seconds in the U.S. a woman is assaulted or beaten.[490]
- The majority of nonfatal intimate partner victimizations of women (2/3) in the U.S. occur at home.[491]
- In this country, a man beats up a woman every 12 seconds. That's 7,200 outbursts of violence every day, 50,400 every week, 2,620,800 every year.[492]
- According to a national crime victimization survey, 6 times as many women are hurt by their husbands and lovers as are hurt by strangers.[493]
- Estimates range from 960,000 incidents of violence against a current or former spouse, boyfriend, or girlfriend to 3 million women who are physically abused by their husband or boyfriend per year.[494]

REFERENCES 381

- On average between 2001 and 2005, nonfatal intimate partner victimizations accounted for 22% of the violent crimes against females age 12 or older compared to 4% of nonfatal violent crimes against males age 12 or older.[495]
- Battering increases during (1) Pregnancy (2) Infant children who demand mother's time (3) Adolescence. Adolescents either became supportive of their mother and attempted to stop the batterer from harming her, or they identified with the batterer and began to abuse their mother themselves.[496]
- Several studies show a correlation between lethality and animal abuse where women report a pet had been threatened, injured, or killed by their abuser.[497] In another survey, 20% of women delayed leaving the abusive situation out of fear their pet would be harmed.[498]

SEPARATION VIOLENCE
- Separated and divorced individuals are at a greater risk of nonfatal IPV.[499]
- Women separated from their husbands were victimized by an intimate at rates higher than married, divorced, widowed or never married women.[500]
- In 1995 the Bureau of Justice Statistics found that women separated from their husband were 3 times more likely to be victimized by their spouse than divorced women, and 25 times more likely to be victimized by their spouse than married woman.[501]
- Although divorced and separated women compose only 7% of the population in U.S., they account for 75% of all battered women. They report being battered 14 times as often as women still living with their partners.[502]
- 75% of domestic assaults reported to law enforcement agencies were inflicted after separation of the couples.[503]
- Nearly 75% of battered women seeking emergency medical services sustained injuries after leaving the batterer.[504]
- A 1997 report from the Florida Governor's Task Force on Domestic and Sexual Violence found that 65% of intimate homicide victims physically separated from the perpetrator prior to their death.[505]

DOMESTIC VIOLENCE HOMICIDES
- On average more than 4 women a day are murdered by their husbands or boyfriends in the U.S.[506]
- Other studies have found that women are most likely to be murdered when attempting to report abuse or to leave an abusive relationship.[507]
- Government statistics indicate that 1,500 to 2,000 women are murdered by partners and ex-partners per year, comprising more than 33% of all female homicide victims, and that these homicides almost always follow a history of violence, threats, or stalking.[508]
- Only 20% of all homicides are committed by strangers, even though this is the violence that captures our fear and attention. The other 80% are committed by people we know.[509]
- Most intimate partner homicides occur between spouses, though boyfriends/girlfriends have committed about the same number of homicides in recent years.[510]
- Between 1993 and 2004, IPV on average made up 22% of nonfatal intimate partner victimizations against women. The same year, intimate partners committed 3% of all violent crime against men.[511]

- Homicide is the second leading cause of traumatic death for pregnant and recently pregnant women in the U.S., accounting for 31% of maternal injury deaths.[512]
- About 15% of serious assaults are reported to the police... Only 78% of these reports lead to police action, this means that police come into contact with approximately 12% of all severely violent acts. But only half of these contacts lead to the criminal justice system. So, now ...only 6% of severely violent episodes lead to the batterer entering criminal justice system... In about 94% of the cases of severe assault, there are no legal consequences at all for the batterer... About 2/3 of cases that enter the criminal justice system end up in court. When cases do go to court, a conviction occurs 50% of the time. But quite often the conviction involves either a suspended sentence or probation. When all these factors are taken into account only about 1 out of every 10,000 acts of battering result in a fine or a jail sentence.[513]

DOMESTIC VIOLENCE & HEALTH CARE
Injuries:
- About 50% of all female victims of IPV report an injury of some type, and about 20% of them seek medical assistance.[514]
- In 2008, the Centers for Disease Control and Prevention published data collected in 2005 that finds that women experience 2 million injuries from IPV each year.[515]
- A 2002 study by the U.S. Department of Justice found that most victims injured by IPV did not report seeking professional medical treatment for their injuries.[516]
- 1 out of 4 (25%) women's visits to emergency rooms are due to DV.[517]
- 37% of women who sought treatment in emergency rooms for violence-related injuries in 1994 were injured by a current or former spouse, boyfriend or girlfriend.[518]
- Nearly 75% of the battered women seeking emergency medical services sustained injuries after leaving the batterer.[519]
- Among 218 women presenting in a metropolitan emergency department with injuries due to violence, 28% required hospital admission and 13% required major medical treatment.[520]
- A 2005 study using data from a national telephone survey of 8,000 women about their experiences with violence, found that on average, women who reported injuries as a consequence of their most recent incident of physical IPV visited the emergency room twice, a physician more than 3 times (3.5), a dentist more than 5 times (5.2) and made nearly 20 visits (19.7) to physical therapy.[521]

Mental Health Care:
- IPV results in more than 18.5 mental health care visits each year.[522]
- 37% of battered women have symptoms of depression,[523] 46% have symptoms of anxiety disorder,[524] and 45% experience PTSD.[525]
- A study of 84 women diagnosed with depression who disclosed IPV revealed that 18.6% of abused women reported Post Traumatic Stress Disorder (PTSD), compared to 6.7% of non-abused women. The same study found that 53.5% of abused women reported sleeping problems/nightmares, compared to 23.3% of non-abused women.[526]

- 56% of women who experience IPV are diagnosed with a psychiatric disorder.[527] 29% of all women who attempt suicide were battered.[528]
- The emotional effects of partner violence are a factor in more than 25% of female suicide attempts and are a leading cause of substance abuse in adult women.[529]

FAMILY VIOLENCE & CHILDREN
Who is Affected:
- 15.5 million children in the U.S. live in families in which IPV occurred at least once in the past year, and 7 million children live in families in which severe partner violence occurred.[530]
- The UN Secretary-General's Study on Violence Against Children conservatively estimates that 275 million children worldwide are exposed to violence in the home.[531]
- Children under age 12 are residents of the households experiencing IPV in 38% of incidents involving female victims.[532]
- On average between 2001 and 2005, 38% of children witnessing IPV were young girls and 21% were young boys.[533]
- The National Woman Abuse Prevention Project reports that children are present in 41 to 55% of homes where police intervene in DV calls.[534]
- In a single day in 2008, 16,458 children were living in a DV shelter or transitional housing facility. Another 6,430 children sought services at a non-residential program.[535]
- By the age of 18, children in America will have witnessed 200,000 acts of violence in the media.[536]

Injuries:
- More than 90% of battered women said that their children have witnessed their battering.[537]
- The U.S. Advisory Board on Child Abuse and Neglect suggests that DV may be the single major precursor to child abuse and neglect fatalities in this country.[538]
- Approximately 1 in 4 incidents (25%) of relationship abuse involves injury to children.[539]
- Children may indirectly receive injuries. They may be hurt when household items or weapons are thrown or used, when their mothers who are being attacked by the batterer are holding them.[540]
- In homes where partner abuse occurs, children are 1,500 times more likely to be abused.[541]

VICTIMS SEEKING ASSISTANCE
- Domestic violence is one of the most chronically underreported crimes.[542]
- Most do not report the violence to police, largely because they fear reprisals from their abuser.[543]
- 50% of battered women never tell anyone about it, according to a poll by Louis Harris & Associates.[544]
- Based on reports from 10 countries, between 55 to 95% of women who had been physically abused by their partners had never contacted non-governmental organizations, shelters, or the police for help.[545]
- At least 1 in 5 women reporting physical abuse had never told anyone about it.[546]
- Victims may wait to contact counselors or seek nonemergency care after an

initial delay period of several days.[547]
- On average, 21% of female victims and 10% of male victims of nonfatal IPV contact an outside agency for assistance. Of those females and males contacting an outside agency, 45% contact a private agency.[548]
- Nearly 2.2 million people called a DV crisis or hot line in 2004 to escape crisis situations, seek advice, or assist someone they thought might be victims.[549]
- Reporting domestic violence to police appears to reduce the risk of a husband attacking his wife again by as much as 62%.[550]
- A recent study found that 44% of victims of DV talked to someone about the abuse; 37% of those women talked to their health care provider.[551] Additionally, in 4 different studies of survivors of abuse, 70 to 81% of the patients studied reported that they would like their healthcare providers to ask them privately about IPV.[552]

LAW ENFORCEMENT
- Statistically, only 10% of victims call the police for help. Of these, most stated that the police were ineffective: when the police left, the assault was renewed with added vigor.[553]
- Only approximately 25% of all physical assaults, 20% of all rapes, and 50% of all stalkings perpetuated against females by intimate partners are reported to the police.[554]
- On average, only 70% of nonfatal IPV is reported to law enforcement. Of those not reporting, 41% of male and 27% of female victims (34% average) stated victimization being a private/personal matter as reason for not reporting, 15% of women feared reprisal, 12% of all victims wished to protect the offender, and 6% of all victims believed police would do nothing.[555]
- 80% of batterers were violent only in their domestic relations. 80% of them had never been brought before the criminal justice system prior to the battering incident.[556]
- 1/3 of all police time is spent responding to IPV disturbance calls.[557]

Restraining Orders
- TROs are issued in America at the rate of more than 1,000 every day.[558]
- Approximately 20% of the 1.5 million people who experience IPV annually obtain civil protection orders.[559]
- Approximately 50% of the orders obtained by women against intimate partners who physically assaulted them were violated. More than 2/3 (66%) of the restraining orders against intimate partners who raped or stalked the victim were violated.[560]
- More than 17% of homicide victims had filed for a protection order against the perpetrator at the time of the murder.[561]
- 50% of women in one study said the TRO worsened their case.[562]
- In a U.S. Department of Justice study, 1/3 (33%) women had continuing problems after getting restraining orders.[563]
- In one study nearly 50% of the victims who obtained a protection order were re-abused within 2 years.[564]

APPENDIX 2 Timeline & History of Domestic Violence Movement

- **753 B.C.E.** During the reign of Romulus in Rome, wife beating is accepted and condoned under The Laws of Chastisement that permit a husband to beat his wife with a rod as long as its circumference is no greater than the girth of the base of his right thumb, hence "The Rule of Thumb." This notion is perpetuated throughout most of Europe.[565]
- **1866** American Society for the Prevention of Cruelty to Animals is formed. It predates the founding of the Society for the Prevention of Cruelty to Children, established in 1875. Both predate any organization aimed at preventing cruelty to women.[566]
- **1871** Alabama is the first state to rescind the legal right of men to beat their wives. Massachusetts also declares wife beating illegal.[567]
- **1882** Maryland is the first state to pass a law that makes wife-beating a crime, punishable by 40 lashes, or a year in jail.[568]
- **1960's** Beginning of feminist movement in America.
- **1964** Haven house in Pasadena, California treats battered women married to alcoholic men. Between 1964-1972 it shelters over 1000 women and children.[569]
- **1967** Maine is one of the first states to create domestic violence shelter as the grass-roots movement begins.[570]
- **1971** Grass-roots organization in London opens first women's shelter in Europe. "Erin Pizzey founded the first known refuge in England in 1971. The house was donated by the local housing council and became known as Chiswick Women's Aid. Originally it served as a meeting place for women who wanted to talk. Almost immediately, however, women who were being beaten and did not want to return home came for safety and refuge, not just to talk."[571]
- **1972** July issue of Ms. Magazine reports in the "No Comment" section an ad for a bowling alley in Michigan which reads "Have some fun. Beat your wife tonight. Then celebrate with some good food and drink with your friends."[572]
- up until **1974** people were still questioning whether significant numbers of battered women really existed.[573]
- **1975** Most states permitted wife to file criminal charges against husband who inflicted injury or abuse.
- **Late 1970's** The term domestic violence was coined after these crimes began to receive more attention in the community.[574]
- **1976** The Domestic Violence Act allows for temporary exclusion from the house of the violent partner using a civil injunction with the possibility of attaching powers of arrest for subsequent violation.[575]
- **1978** National Coalition Against Domestic Violence (NCADV) is born after extensive organizing efforts by feminists nationwide.[576] Initial goals emphasize gaining financial aid for shelters and grassroots services, sharing information, and supporting research beneficial to the movement.[577]
- **1979** More than 250 battered women's shelters established in the U.S.[578]

- **1981** October established as National Domestic Violence Awareness month. National Coalition Against Domestic Violence (NCADV) declares Oct 17th national day of unity for battered women across country.[579]
- **1981** There are nearly 500 established battered women's shelters in U.S.[580]
- **1981** Restraining orders are granted only for divorce, separation, or custody proceedings in 12 states.[581]
- **1981** Nilda Rimonte, Filipino victim, creates 'Every Women's Shelter' in Los Angeles, the first shelter in U.S. for Asian women.[582]
- **1983** Over 700 shelters in operation nationwide serving 91,000 women and 131,000 children per year.[583]
- **1985** New York Asian Women's Center is formed. It sponsors programs to combat violence against Asian women.[584]
- **1987** National Coalition Against Domestic Violence (NCADV) created nationwide effort to educate and promote understanding of IPV to help victims.[585]
- **1989** U.S. has 1,200 battered women programs which shelter 300,000 women and children per year.[586]
- **1990** A survey of several hundred therapists regarding DV cases reveals that 41% failed to identify obvious evidence of violence. None of the therapists identified the lethality of the situation. Those who did identify conflict minimized the severity and 55% said they would not intervene. 14% said they would work on the couples 'communications style.'[587]
- **1992** U.S. surgeon general ranks abuse by husbands as leading cause of injuries to women aged 15 to 44.[588] AMA releases guidelines for doctors to screen women for signs of domestic violence.[589]
- **1994** Congress passes the Violence Against Women Act (VAWA), part of the federal Crime Victims Act, which funds services for victims of rape and DV, allows women to seek civil rights remedies for gender related crimes, and provides training to increase police and court officials' sensitivity.[590] It creates for the first time a federal right to sue the assailant for gender-based violence and provides that states and American Indian nations give full faith and credit to each other's restraining orders.[591]
- **1996** National DV hotline launched to address the growing need of victims needing to reach out for help.[592]
- **1996** Over 1,200 battered women's shelters in U.S. sponsored by approximately 1800 IPV agencies.[593]
- **1997** National DV summit said DIMA will clarify legal and privacy issues associated with domestic violence.[594]
- **1997** More than 2,000 shelters and safe-house networks across the U.S., and still there are not enough. Animal shelters outnumber DV centers by approximately 10 to 1 in Florida.[595]
- **2005** AMA developed guidelines on appropriate clinical responses to domestic violence outlined in *Diagnostic and Treatment Guidelines on Domestic Violence.*[596]

APPENDIX 3 TIMELINE for South Asian Women's Organizations

1983 Sneha established in Hartford, Connecticut.

1985 Manavi established in New Brunswick, New Jersey.

1987 Michigan Asian Indian Family Services (MAIFS) established in Livonia, Michigan.

1989 Sakhi established in New York, New York.

1989 Apna Ghar established in Chicago, Illinois.

1989 Asha established in Rockville, Maryland.

1990 South Asian Network (SAN) established in Los Angeles, California.

1991 Sahara established in Artesia, California.

1991 Maitri established in San Jose, California.

1992 Narika established in Berkely, California.

1993 Sakhi and Manavi co-organize "South Asian Immigrant Women: Our Social Realities," the first South Asian women's conference in the U.S. hosted at Columbia University.

1994 Violence Against Women's Act (VAWA) passed by Congress as a United States federal law. Protects the rights of DV victims and ensures immigrant women are able to self-petition for green cards so they are not dependent on their abusers.

1995 Raksha established in Atlanta, Georgia.

1996 Daya established in Houston, Texas.

1996 Saheli established in Boston, Massachusetts.

1996 Chaya established in Seattle, Washington.

1997 South Asian Women's Empowerment and Resources Alliance (SAWERA) established in Portland, Oregon.

1998 Kiran established in Raleigh, North Carolina, and then restarted in 2008.

2000 Dr. Margaret Abraham, former board member of Sakhi, publishes *Speaking the Unspeakable: Marital Violence among South Asian Immigrants in the United States.*

2000 Sandhya Nankani publishes anthology *Breaking the Silence: Domestic Violence in the South Asian American Community.*

2002 Asha Ray of Hope established in Columbus, Ohio.

2004 Sahara established in Miami, Florida.

2004 Arizona South Asians for Safe Families (ASAFSF) established in Scottsdale, Arizona.

2004 Saathi established in Rochester, New York.

2005 Chetna established in Dallas Fort Worth, Texas.

2006 Asha Kiran "ray of hope" established in Huntsville, Alabama.

2006 Peechan established in Tampa, Florida.

2007 Shamita Das Dasgupta, founder of Manavi, publishes *Body Evidence: Intimate Violence Against South Asian Women in America.*

2008 Breakthrough nonprofit organization launches the award-winning Bell Bajao "ring the bell" campaign. Recognized in 2010 by the Clinton Global Initiative. Encourages men and boys to participate in ending domestic violence by ringing the bell and getting involved.

2012 The Power to Break Free Foundation established to promote domestic violence education and create a national voice for South Asian victims and SAWO's.

Note: This timeline highlights the establishment of many of these SAWO's which are 501(c)(3) nonprofits. It does not include their milestones such as the creation of helplines, safe-houses, support groups, etc. Please see the resource list on our website at **www.power2breakfree.com** for contact information on these groups.

Please refer to our website at **www.Power2BreakFree.com**
for a more extensive list of statistics.

Bibliography

Domestic Violence Resources

1. Nankani, Sandhya. *Breaking the Silence: Domestic Violence in the South Asian- American Community.* Xlibris Corporation, 2000.
2. Abraham, Margaret. *Speaking the Unspeakable: Marital Violence among South Asian Immigrants in the United States.* Rutgers University Press, New Brunswick, NJ. 2000.
3. Shamita Das Dasgupta. *Body Evidence: Intimate Violence Against South Asian Women in America.* Rutgers University Press, New Brunswick, NJ. 2007.
4. Bancroft, Lundy. *Why Does He Do That? Inside the Minds of Angry and Controlling Men.* Berkely Books: New York. 2002.
5. Weitzman, Susan, Ph.D. *Not to People Like Us: Hidden Abuse in Upscale Marriages.* Basic Books: New York. 2000.
6. Gavin de Becker. *The Gift of Fear: and Other Survival Signals that Protect Us from Violence.* Dell Publishing, New York. 1997.
7. Walker, Lenore E. *The Battered Woman.* Harper & Row Publishers, New York. 1979.
8. Herman, Judith M.D. *Trauma & Recovery: The Aftermath of Violence- From Domestic Abuse to Political Terror.* Basic Books, New York, NY. 1992.
9. Jacobson, Neil and Gottmann, John. *When Men Batter Women: New Insights into Ending Abusive Relationships.* Simon & Schuster, New York. 1998.
10. Jayne, Pamela. *Ditch that Jerk: Dealing with Men who Control and Hurt Women.* Hunter House, Alameda, CA. 2000.
11. Dugan, Meg Kennedy and Hock, Roger R. *It's My Life Now: Starting Over After an Abusive Relationship or Domestic Violence.* Routledge, New York. 2006.
12. Evans, Patricia. *The Verbally Abusive Relationship: How to Recognize It and How to Respond.* Media, Avon, MA. 1992.
13. Lissette, Andrea & Kraus, Richard. *Free Yourself from an Abusive Relationship: Seven Steps to Taking Back your Life.* Hunter House Publishers, Alameda, CA. 2000.
14. Betancourt, Marian. *What to Do When Love Turns Violent: A Practical Resource for Women in Abusive Relationships.* Harper Collins, New York. 1997.
15. Forward, Susan Ph.D. with Donna Frazier. *Emotional Blackmail: When the People in Your Life Use Fear, Obligation and Guilt to Manipulate You.* Harper Collins Publishers, New York, NY. 1997.

Bibliography

Other Resources

16. Ford, Debbie. *Spiritual Divorce- Divorce as a Catalyst for an Extraordinary Life.* Harper Collins, New York, NY. 2001.
17. Lesser, Elizabeth. *Broken Open: How Difficult Times Can Help Us Grow.* Villard Books, New York, NY. 2005.
18. Wilson, Karen Kahn. *Transformational Divorce: Discover Yourself, Reclaim your Dreams, and Embrace Life's Unlimited Possibilities.* New Harbinger Publications, Oakland, CA. 2003.
19. Hotchkiss, Sandy. *Why is it Always About You? The Seven Deadly Sins of Narcissism.* Free Press, New York, NY. 2002.
20. Wilson, James L. *Adrenal Fatigue: the Twenty-First Century Stress Syndrome.* Smart Publications, Petaluma, CA. 2001.
21. *The Merck Manual of Medical Information.* Pocket Books, New York, NY. 1997.

References

CHAPTER 1

[1] Erasmus-in-india.blogspot.com/2005/09/arranged-marriages.html
[2] Ghosh, Uttam. "Once upon an arranged marriage..." India Abroad Magazine. September 23, 2011.
[3] http://nitawriter.worldpress.com/2007/04/04/divorce-rates-of-the-world/
[4] Abraham, Margaret. *Speaking the Unspeakable: Marital Violence Among South Asian Immigrants in the United States.* Rutgers University Press, New Brunswick, NJ, 2000. p.25.
[5] *IBID* p.27.
[6] *IBID* p.31.
[7] Walker, Lenore E. *The Battered Woman.* Harper & Row Publishers, New York, 1979. p.52.
[8] Dasgupta, Shamita Das. *Body Evidence: Intimate Violence Against South Asian Women in America.* Rutgers University Press, New Brunswick, NJ, 2007. p.59-60.
[9] adapted from Evans, Patricia. *The Verbally Abusive Relationship: How to Recognize It and How to Respond.* Media, Avon, MA 1992. p.118. and Lissette, Andrea & Kraus, Richard. *Free Yourself from an Abusive Relationship: 7 Steps to Taking Back your Life.* Hunter House Publishers, Alameda, CA 2000 p.188.
[10] Dasgupta, Shamita Das. *Body Evidence: Intimate Violence Against South Asian Women in America.* Rutgers University Press, New Brunswick, NJ, 2007. p.25.
[11] Partially adapted from Dasgupta, Shamita Das. *Body Evidence: Intimate Violence Against South Asian Women in America.* Rutgers University Press, New Brunswick, NJ, 2007. p.32.
[12] *IBID* p.57.
[13] Abraham, Margaret. *Speaking the Unspeakable: Marital Violence Among South Asian Immigrants in the United States.* Rutgers University Press, New Brunswick, NJ, 2000. p.120.
[14] Bancroft, Lundy. *Why Does He Do That? Inside The Minds of Angry And Controlling Men.* Berkely Books: New York, 2002. p.115.
[15] *IBID* p.65.

CHAPTER 2

[16] http://en.wikipedia.org/wiki/Sati_(practice)
[17] Nankani, Sandhya. *Breaking the Silence: Domestic Violence in the South Asian- American Community.* Xlibris Corporation, 2000. p.90.
[18] Dasgupta, Shamita Das. *Body Evidence: Intimate Violence Against South Asian Women in America.* Rutgers University Press, New Brunswick, NJ, 2007. p.56.
[19] Rampell, Catherine. *"Women Earn Less Than Men, Especially At The Top."* Economix magazine, November 16, 2009.
[20] Abraham, Margaret. *Speaking the Unspeakable: Marital Violence among South Asian Immigrants in the United States.* Rutgers University Press, New Brunswick, NJ, 2000. p.3.
[21] Bureau of Justice Statistics Crime Data Brief, Intimate Partner Violence, 1993-2001, February 2003.
[22] Dasgupta, Shamita Das. *Body Evidence: Intimate Violence Against South Asian Women in America.* Rutgers University Press, New Brunswick, NJ, 2007. p.16.
[23] Abraham, Margaret. *Speaking the Unspeakable: Marital Violence among South Asian Immigrants in the United States.* Rutgers University Press, New Brunswick, NJ, 2000. p.3.
[24] Dasgupta, Shamita Das. *Body Evidence: Intimate Violence Against South Asian Women in America.* Rutgers University Press, New Brunswick, NJ, 2007. p.4.
[25] *www.Dictionary.com*
[26] All terms defined on www.nolo.com/dictionary/assault-term.html
[27] *www.Dictionary.com*
[28] McGee, Susan G.S. *"20 Reasons Why She Stays: A Guide For Those Who Want to Help Battered Women."* 1995-2009. p.13.
[29] *IBID* p.13.
[30] Dugan, Meg Kennedy and Hock, Roger R. *It's My Life Now: Starting Over After an Abusive Relationship or Domestic Violence.* Routledge, New York, 2006. p.127.
[31] Kapoor, Sushma. *Domestic Violence Against Women and Girls.* UNICEF: Innocenti Research Centre. June, 2000.
[32] United Nations Development Fund for Women. 2003. *Not A Minute More: Ending Violence Against Women.* Available at http://www.unifem.org/resources/item_detail.php?ProductID=7.
[33] *Adverse Health Conditions and Health Risk Behaviors Associated with Intimate Partner Violence, Morbidity and Mortality Weekly Report.* February 2008. Centers for Disease Control and Prevention. Available at www.cdc.gov/mmwr/preview/mmwrhtml/mm5705a1.htm.
[34] Murray Straus, Richard J. Gelles, and Suzanne K. Steinmetz's. *Behind Closed Doors: Violence in the American Family.* (From Family Justice Center Domestic Violence Training Notes 2010.)

REFERENCES 393

[35] Abraham, Margaret. *Speaking the Unspeakable: Marital Violence among South Asian Immigrants in the United States.* Rutgers University Press, New Brunswick, NJ, 2000. p.9.

[36] Nankani, Sandhya. *Breaking the Silence: Domestic Violence in the South Asian- American Community.* Xlibris Corporation, 2000. p.91.

[37] Dasgupta, Shamita Das. *Body Evidence: Intimate Violence Against South Asian Women in America.* Rutgers University Press, New Brunswick, NJ, 2007. p.142.

[38] *IBID* p.82.

[39] Abraham, Margaret. *Speaking the Unspeakable: Marital Violence among South Asian Immigrants in the United States.* Rutgers University Press, New Brunswick, NJ, 2000. p.10.

[40] Dasgupta, Shamita Das. *Body Evidence: Intimate Violence Against South Asian Women in America.* Rutgers University Press, New Brunswick, NJ, 2007. p.142.

[41] Weitzman, Susan, Ph.D. *Not To People Like Us: Hidden Abuse in Upscale Marriages.* Basic books: New York, 2000. p.19.

[42] *IBID* p.19.

[43] *IBID* p.25.

[44] *IBID.* p.18.

[45] *IBID* p.23.

[46] de Becker, Gavin. *The Gift of Fear: and Other Survival Signals that Protect us from Violence.* Dell Publishing, New York, 1997. p.62.

[47] *IBID* p.261.

[48] Jayne, Pamela. *Ditch That Jerk: Dealing with Men Who Control and Hurt Women.* Hunter House, Alameda, CA, 2000. p.34.

[49] Abraham, Margaret. *Speaking the Unspeakable: Marital Violence among South Asian Immigrants in the United States.* Rutgers University Press, New Brunswick, NJ, 2000. p.5.

CHAPTER 3

[50] de Becker, Gavin. *The Gift of Fear: and Other Survival Signals that Protect us from Violence.* Dell Publishing, New York, 1997. p.277.

[51] Jayne, Pamela. *Ditch That Jerk: Dealing with Men Who Control and Hurt Women.* Hunter House, Alameda, CA, 2000. p.3.

[52] Bancroft, Lundy. *Why Does He Do That? Inside the Minds of Angry and Controlling Men.* Berkely Books: New York, 2002. p.64.

[53] *IBID* p.64.

[54] *IBID* p.63.

[55] de Becker, Gavin. *The Gift of Fear: and Other Survival Signals that Protect us from Violence.* Dell Publishing, New York, 1997. p.122.

[56] *IBID* p.180.

[57] *IBID* p.129.

[58] Bancroft, Lundy. *Why Does He Do That? Inside the Minds of Angry and Controlling Men.* Berkely Books: New York, 2002. p.145.

[59] Evans, Patricia. *The Verbally Abusive Relationship: How to Recognize It and How to Respond.* Media, Avon, MA 1992. p.46.

[60] *IBID* p.60.

[61] *IBID* p.115.

[62] *IBID* p.142.

[63] *IBID* p.144.

[64] Bancroft, Lundy. *Why Does He Do That? Inside the Minds of Angry and Controlling Men* Berkely Books: New York, 2002. p.26.

[65] Evans, Patricia. *The Verbally Abusive Relationship: How to Recognize It and How to Respond.* Media, Avon, MA 1992. p.98.

[66] Bancroft, Lundy. *Why Does He Do That? Inside the Minds of Angry and Controlling Men* Berkely Books: New York, 2002. p.159.

[67] *IBID* p.162.

[68] Abraham, Margaret. *Speaking the Unspeakable: Marital Violence among South Asian Immigrants in the United States.* Rutgers University Press, New Brunswick, NJ, 2000. p.63.

[69] Tifft, Larry. *Battering of Women: The Failure of Intervention and the Case for Prevention.* 1993. (From Family Justice Center Domestic Violence Training Notes 2010.)

[70] National Crime Victimization Survey: Criminal Victimization, 2005. U.S. Department of Justice, Bureau of Justice Statistics. Retrieved September 2006. *Available at http://www.ojp.usdoj.gov/bjs/pub/pdf/cv05.pdf*

[71] Campbell, et al. (2003). *Assessing Risk Factors for Intimate Partner Homicide*. Intimate Partner Homicide, NIJ Journal, 250, 14-19. Washington, D.C.: National Institute of Justice, U.S. Department of Justice.
[72] Jacobson, Neil and Gottmann, John. *When Men Batter Women: New Insights into Ending Abusive Relationships*. Simon & Schuster, New York, 1998. p.150-151.
[73] Bancroft, Lundy. *Why Does He Do That? Inside the Minds of Angry and Controlling Men* Berkely Books: New York, 2002. p.177.
[74] *IBID* p.63.
[75] Abraham, Margaret. *Speaking the Unspeakable: Marital Violence among South Asian Immigrants in the United States*. Rutgers University Press, New Brunswick, NJ, 2000. p.97.
[76] National Crime Victimization Survey, 1992-96; *Study of Injured Victims of Violence*, 1994.
[77] *Adverse Health Conditions and Health Risk Behaviors Associated with Intimate Partner Violence, Morbidity and Mortality Weekly Report*. February 2008. Centers for Disease Control and Prevention. Available at www.cdc.gov/mmwr/preview/mmwrhtml/mm5705a1.htm.
[78] Lissette, Andrea & Kraus, Richard. *Free yourself From an Abusive Relationship: 7 Steps to Taking Back Your Life*. Hunter House Publishers, Alameda, CA 2000. p.33.
[79] National Coalition Against Domestic Violence
[80] Walker, Lenore E. *The Battered Woman*. Harper & Row Publishers, New York, 1979. p.223,106,79.
[81] *No Safe Haven: Male Violence Against Women at Home, at Work, and in the Community*. (From Family Justice Center Domestic Violence Training Notes 2010.)
[82] Jacobson, Neil and Gottmann, John. *When Men Batter Women: New Insights into Ending Abusive Relationships*. Simon & Schuster, New York, 1998. p.50.
[83] Lissette, Andrea & Kraus, Richard. *Free yourself From an Abusive Relationship: 7 Steps to Taking Back Your Life*. Hunter House Publishers, Alameda, CA 2000. p.45-46.
[84] Dugan, Meg Kennedy and Hock, Roger R. *It's My Life Now: Starting Over After an Abusive Relationship or Domestic Violence*. Routledge, New York, 2006. p.11.
[85] Jayne, Pamela. *Ditch That Jerk: Dealing with Men Who Control and Hurt Women*. Hunter House, Alameda, CA, 2000. p.20-27.

CHAPTER 4
[86] de Becker, Gavin. *The Gift of Fear: and Other Survival Signals that Protect us from Violence*. Dell Publishing, New York, 1997. p.210-212.
[87] Bancroft, Lundy. *Why Does He Do That? Inside the Minds of Angry and Controlling Men*. Berkely Books: New York, 2002. p.19.
[88] Walker, Lenore E. *The Battered Woman*. Harper & Row Publishers, New York, 1979. p.32.
[89] Dugan, Meg Kennedy and Hock, Roger R. *It's My Life Now: Starting Over After an Abusive Relationship or Domestic Violence*. Routledge, New York, 2006. p.65.
[90] Lissette, Andrea & Kraus, Richard. *Free Yourself From an Abusive Relationship: 7 Steps to Taking Back Your Life*. Hunter House Publishers, Alameda, CA 2000. p.9.
[91] Walker, Lenore E. *The Battered Woman*. Harper & Row Publishers, New York, 1979. p.79.
[92] Weitzman, Susan, Ph.D. *Not to People Like Us: Hidden Abuse in Upscale Marriages*. Basic books: New York, 2000. p.87.
[93] Walker, Lenore E. *The Battered Woman*. Harper & Row Publishers, New York, 1979. p.58.
[94] Bancroft, Lundy. *Why Does He Do That? Inside the Minds of Angry and Controlling Men*. Berkely Books: New York, 2002. p.140.
[95] Jacobson, Neil and Gottmann, John. *When Men Batter Women: New Insights into Ending Abusive Relationships*. Simon & Schuster, New York, 1998. p.58, 63-67, 80.
[96] *IBID* p.81.
[97] *IBID* p.65-66.
[98] Walker, Lenore E. *The Battered Woman*. Harper & Row Publishers, New York, 1979. p.62.
[99] Dugan, Meg Kennedy and Hock, Roger R. *It's My Life Now: Starting Over After an Abusive Relationship or Domestic Violence*. Routledge, New York, 2006. p.6.
[100] Walker, Lenore E. *The Battered Woman*. Harper & Row Publishers, New York, 1979. p.62.
[101] *IBID* p.63.
[102] de Becker, Gavin. *The Gift of Fear: and Other Survival Signals that Protect us from Violence*. Dell Publishing, New York, 1997. p.214.
[103] *IBID* p.217.
[104] Bancroft, Lundy. *Why Does He Do That? Inside the Minds of Angry and Controlling Men*. Berkely Books: New York, 2002. p.32.
[105] Evans, Patricia. *The Verbally Abusive Relationship: How to Recognize It and How to Respond*. Media, Avon, MA 1992. p.53.
[106] *IBID* p.45.

[107] Walker, Lenore E. *The Battered Woman*. Harper & Row Publishers, New York, 1979. p.68.
[108] Bancroft, Lundy. *Why Does He Do That? Inside the Minds of Angry and Controlling Men*. Berkely Books: New York, 2002. p.137.
[109] *IBID* p.194.
[110] *IBID* p.226.
[111] Walker, Lenore E. *The Battered Woman*. Harper & Row Publishers, New York, 1979. p.108-109.

CHAPTER 5
[112] Bancroft, Lundy. *Why Does He Do That? Inside the Minds of Angry and Controlling Men*. Berkely Books: New York, 2002. p.18
[113] *IBID* p.43
[114] *IBID* p.23-25
[115] *IBID* p.329
[116] *IBID* p.325
[117] Source: Mid-Peninsula Support Network for Battered Women National Woman Abuse Prevention Project Hershey, Report to Eastern Psychological Association San Francisco Family Violence Project Dr. Richard Gelles California Alliance Against Domestic Violence
[118] Strauss, Gelles, and Smith. "*Physical Violence in American Families: Risk Factors and Adaptations to Violence*" Transaction Publishers,1990. (From Family Justice Center Domestic Violence Training Notes 2010.)
[119] http://domesticviolencestatistics.org/domestic-violence-statistics/
[120] de Becker, Gavin. *The Gift of Fear: and Other Survival Signals that Protect us from Violence*. Dell Publishing, New York, 1997. p.189.
[121] http://www.health.am/psy/narcissistic-personality-disorder/ Armenian Medical Network. 2006 p.3.
[122] Weitzman, Susan, Ph.D. *Not to People Like Us: Hidden Abuse in Upscale Marriages*. Basic books: New York, 2000. p.135.
[123] Bancroft, Lundy. *Why Does He Do That? Inside the Minds of Angry and Controlling Men*. Berkely Books: New York, 2002. *p.*91-94.
[124] *IBID p.*80-83.
[125] *IBID p.*96-99.
[126] *IBID p.*88-91.
[127] *IBID p.*83-85.
[128] Jacobson, Neil and Gottmann, John. *When Men Batter Women: New Insights into Ending Abusive Relationships*. Simon & Schuster, New York, 1998. p.29.
[129] *IBID* p.42.
[130] de Becker, Gavin. *The Gift of Fear: and Other Survival Signals that Protect us from Violence*. Dell Publishing, New York, 1997. p.344.
[131] Masterson, James F. *The Emerging Self: A Developmental Self & Object Relations Approach to the Treatment of the Closet Narcissistic Disorder of the Self,* 1993./ http://en.wikipedia.org/wiki/Narcissism p.4.
[132] Diagnostic and Statistical Manual of Mental Disorders Fourth edition Text Revision (DSM-IV-TR) American Psychiatric Association (2000). / http://en.wikipedia.org/wiki/Narcissistic_personality_disorder p.2.
[133] *IBID* p.2.
[134] http://en.wikipedia.org/wiki/Narcissistic_personality_disorder p.4.
[135] de Becker, Gavin. *The Gift of Fear: and Other Survival Signals that Protect us from Violence*. Dell Publishing, New York, 1997. p.275.

CHAPTER 6
[136] *IBID* p.17.
[137] Bancroft, Lundy. *Why Does He Do That? Inside the Minds of Angry and Controlling Men*. Berkely Books: New York, 2002. p.332, 386.
[138] Jayne, Pamela. *Ditch That Jerk: Dealing with Men Who Control and Hurt Women*. Hunter House, Alameda, CA, 2000. p.160.
[139] Jacobson, Neil and Gottmann, John. *When Men Batter Women: New Insights into Ending Abusive Relationships* Simon & Schuster, New York, 1998. p.88-89.
[140] Herman, Judith M.D. *Trauma & Recovery: The aftermath of violence- from domestic abuse to political terror.* Basic Books, New York, NY. 1992. p.75.
[141] Evans, Patricia. *The Verbally Abusive Relationship: How to Recognize It and How to Respond.* Media, Avon, MA 1992. p.167-168.
[142] Bancroft, Lundy. *Why Does He Do That? Inside the Minds of Angry and Controlling Men*. Berkely Books: New York, 2002. p.111.

[143] *IBID* p.31.
[144] Weitzman, Susan, Ph.D. *Not to People Like Us: Hidden Abuse in Upscale Marriages*. Basic books: New York, 2000. p.142.
[145] Jayne, Pamela. *Ditch That Jerk: Dealing with Men Who Control and Hurt Women*. Hunter House, Alameda, CA, 2000. p.109.
[146] Jacobson, Neil and Gottmann, John. *When Men Batter Women: New Insights into Ending Abusive Relationships.* Simon & Schuster, New York, 1998. p.87.
[147] *IBID* p.68.
[148] Weitzman, Susan, Ph.D. *Not to People Like Us: Hidden Abuse in Upscale Marriages*. Basic books: New York, 2000. p.142.
[149] *IBID* p.142.
[150] Bancroft, Lundy. *Why Does He Do That? Inside the Minds of Angry and Controlling Men*. Berkely Books: New York, 2002. p.330.
[151] *IBID* p.123.
[152] *IBID* p.113
[153] Jayne, Pamela. *Ditch That Jerk: Dealing with Men Who Control and Hurt Women*. Hunter House, Alameda, CA, 2000. p.151.
[154] Weitzman, Susan, Ph.D. *Not to People Like Us: Hidden Abuse in Upscale Marriages*. Basic books: New York, 2000. p.140.
[155] Jayne, Pamela. *Ditch That Jerk: Dealing with Men Who Control and Hurt Women*. Hunter House, Alameda, CA, 2000. p.167.
[156] Bancroft, Lundy. *Why Does He Do That? Inside the Minds of Angry and Controlling Men*. Berkely Books: New York, 2002. p.31.
[157] Evans, Patricia. *The Verbally Abusive Relationship: How to Recognize It and How to Respond*. Media, Avon, MA 1992. p.104.
[158] Jayne, Pamela. *Ditch That Jerk: Dealing with Men Who Control and Hurt Women*. Hunter House, Alameda, CA, 2000. p.111.
[159] Bancroft, Lundy. *Why Does He Do That? Inside the Minds of Angry and Controlling Men*. Berkely Books: New York, 2002. p.31.
[160] Evans, Patricia. *The Verbally Abusive Relationship: How to Recognize It and How to Respond*. Media, Avon, MA 1992. p.169.

CHAPTER 7
[161] Bancroft, Lundy. *Why Does He Do That? Inside the Minds of Angry and Controlling Men*. Berkely Books: New York, 2002. p.44-45.
[162] *IBID* p.48.
[163] *IBID* p.67.
[164] *IBID* p.48.
[165] IBID p.28.
[166] Jayne, Pamela. *Ditch That Jerk: Dealing with Men Who Control and Hurt Women*. Hunter House, Alameda, CA, 2000. p.80.
[167] Bancroft, Lundy. *Why Does He Do That? Inside the Minds of Angry and Controlling Men*. Berkely Books: New York, 2002. p.72.
[168] *IBID* p.58.
[169] Jayne, Pamela. *Ditch That Jerk: Dealing with Men Who Control and Hurt Women*. Hunter House, Alameda, CA, 2000. p.60-66.
[170] Evans, Patricia. *The Verbally Abusive Relationship: How to Recognize It and How to Respond*. Media, Avon, MA 1992. p.169.
[171] *IBID* p.169.
[172] Jayne, Pamela. *Ditch That Jerk: Dealing with Men Who Control and Hurt Women*. Hunter House, Alameda, CA, 2000. p.88.
[173] *IBID* p.113.
[174] Bancroft, Lundy. *Why Does He Do That? Inside the Minds of Angry and Controlling Men*. Berkely Books: New York, 2002. p.43.
[175] Jayne, Pamela. *Ditch That Jerk: Dealing with Men Who Control and Hurt Women*. Hunter House, Alameda, CA, 2000. p.90.
[176] Bancroft, Lundy. *Why Does He Do That? Inside the Minds of Angry and Controlling Men*. Berkely Books: New York, 2002. p.131.
[177] Weitzman, Susan, Ph.D. *Not to People Like Us: Hidden Abuse in Upscale Marriages*. Basic books: New York, 2000. p.15.
[178] *IBID* p.152.

REFERENCES

[179] de Becker, Gavin. *The Gift of Fear: and Other Survival Signals that Protect us from Violence.* Dell Publishing, New York, 1997. P.66-67.

[180] Weitzman, Susan, Ph.D. *Not to People Like Us: Hidden Abuse in Upscale Marriages.* Basic books: New York, 2000. p.67.

[181] Bancroft, Lundy. *Why Does He Do That? Inside the Minds of Angry and Controlling Men.* Berkely Books: New York, 2002. p.8.

[182] *IBID* p.8.

[183] *IBID* p.40.

[184] Jayne, Pamela. *Ditch That Jerk: Dealing with Men Who Control and Hurt Women.* Hunter House, Alameda, CA, 2000. p.1.

[185] Evans, Patricia. *The Verbally Abusive Relationship: How to Recognize It and How to Respond.* Media, Avon, MA 1992. p.169.

[186] Jacobson, Neil and Gottmann, John. *When Men Batter Women: New Insights into Ending Abusive Relationships* Simon & Schuster, New York, 1998. p.92.

[187] Dugan, Meg Kennedy and Hock, Roger R. *It's My Life Now: Starting Over After an Abusive Relationship or Domestic Violence.* Routledge, New York, 2006. p.215.

[188] Bancroft, Lundy. *Why Does He Do That? Inside the Minds of Angry and Controlling Men.* Berkely Books: New York, 2002. p.8.

[189] Herman, Judith M.D. *Trauma & Recovery: The Aftermath of Violence- From Domestic Abuse to Political Terror.* Basic Books, New York, NY. 1992. p.75.

[190] Bancroft, Lundy. *Why Does He Do That? Inside the Minds of Angry and Controlling Men.* Berkely Books: New York, 2002. p.251.

[191] Walker, Lenore E. *The Battered Woman.* Harper & Row Publishers, New York, 1979. p.39.

[192] *IBID* p.24.

[193] Weitzman, Susan, Ph.D. *Not to People Like Us: Hidden Abuse in Upscale Marriages.* Basic books: New York, 2000. p.137.

[194] Bancroft, Lundy. *Why Does He Do That? Inside the Minds of Angry and Controlling Men.* Berkely Books: New York, 2002. p.68.

[195] *IBID* p.9.

[196] *IBID* p.157.

[197] *IBID* p.152-157.

[198] Evans, Patricia. *The Verbally Abusive Relationship: How to Recognize It and How to Respond.* Media, Avon, MA 1992. p.120.

[199] Jayne, Pamela. *Ditch That Jerk: Dealing with Men Who Control and Hurt Women.* Hunter House, Alameda, CA, 2000. p.193.

[200] *IBID* p.185.

[201] Bancroft, Lundy. *Why Does He Do That? Inside the Minds of Angry and Controlling Men.* Berkely Books: New York, 2002. p.378.

[202] *IBID* p.335.

[203] *IBID* p.75.

[204] *IBID* p.18.

[205] Jayne, Pamela. *Ditch That Jerk: Dealing with Men Who Control and Hurt Women.* Hunter House, Alameda, CA, 2000. p.6.

[206] Bancroft, Lundy. *Why Does He Do That? Inside the Minds of Angry and Controlling Men.* Berkely Books: New York, 2002. p.25.

[207] Jayne, Pamela. *Ditch That Jerk: Dealing with Men Who Control and Hurt Women.* Hunter House, Alameda, CA, 2000. p.42.

[208] Bancroft, Lundy. *Why Does He Do That? Inside the Minds of Angry and Controlling Men.* Berkely Books: New York, 2002. p.366.

[209] Jayne, Pamela. *Ditch That Jerk: Dealing with Men Who Control and Hurt Women.* Hunter House, Alameda, CA, 2000. p.124.

[210] Bancroft, Lundy. *Why Does He Do That? Inside the Minds of Angry and Controlling Men.* Berkely Books: New York, 2002. p.341.

CHAPTER 8

[211] Weitzman, Susan, Ph.D. *Not to People Like Us: Hidden Abuse in Upscale Marriages.* Basic books: New York, 2000. p.74.

[212] *IBID* p.17.

[213] Noland, VJ, Liller, KD, McDermott, RJ, Coulter, ML, and Seraphine, A E. 2004. Is Adolescent Sibling Violence a Precursor to College Dating Violence? American Journal of Health and Behavior. 28: 813-823

[214] Whitfield, CL, Anda RF, Dube SR, Felitte VJ. *"Violent Childhood Experiences and the Risk of Intimate Partner Violence in Adults: Assessment in a Large Health Maintenance Organization."* Journal of Interpersonal Violence. 18(2): 166-185. 2003.

[215] Weitzman, Susan, Ph.D. *Not to People Like Us: Hidden Abuse in Upscale Marriages*. Basic books: New York, 2000. p.61.

[216] de Becker, Gavin. *The Gift of Fear: and Other Survival Signals that Protect us from Violence*. Dell Publishing, New York, 1997. p.74.

[217] *IBID* p.69.

[218] Dugan, Meg Kennedy and Hock, Roger R. *It's My Life Now: Starting Over After an Abusive Relationship or Domestic Violence*. Routledge, New York, 2006. p.40.

[219] Weitzman, Susan, Ph.D. *Not to People Like Us: Hidden Abuse in Upscale Marriages*. Basic books: New York, 2000. p.55.

[220] *IBID* p.55.

[221] de Becker, Gavin. *The Gift of Fear: and Other Survival Signals that Protect us from Violence*. Dell Publishing, New York, 1997. P.210-212.

[222] Hotchkiss, Sandy. *Why Is It Always About You? Saving Yourself From the Narcissists in Your Life*. Free Press, New York, NY. 2002. p.72

[223] Weitzman, Susan, Ph.D. *Not to People Like Us: Hidden Abuse in Upscale Marriages*. Basic books: New York, 2000. p.72.

[224] *IBID* p.31.

[225] Evans, Patricia. *The Verbally Abusive Relationship: How to Recognize It and How to Respond*. Media, Avon, MA 1992. p.109.

[226] Weitzman, Susan, Ph.D. *Not to People Like Us: Hidden Abuse in Upscale Marriages*. Basic books: New York, 2000. p.75.

[227] *IBID* p.56.

[228] Jayne, Pamela. *Ditch That Jerk: Dealing with Men Who Control and Hurt Women*. Hunter House, Alameda, CA, 2000. p.146.

[229] Evans, Patricia. *The Verbally Abusive Relationship: How to Recognize It and How to Respond*. Media, Avon, MA 1992. p.164-165.

[230] Weitzman, Susan, Ph.D. *Not to People Like Us: Hidden Abuse in Upscale Marriages*. Basic books: New York, 2000. p.139.

[231] Bancroft, Lundy. *Why Does He Do That? Inside the Minds of Angry and Controlling Men*. Berkely Books: New York, 2002. p.196.

[232] Weitzman, Susan, Ph.D. *Not to People Like Us: Hidden Abuse in Upscale Marriages*. Basic books: New York, 2000. p.104.

[233] *IBID* p.23.

[234] *IBID* p.181.

[235] *IBID* p.12.

[236] *IBID* p.60.

[237] Evans, Patricia. *The Verbally Abusive Relationship: How to Recognize It and How to Respond*. Media, Avon, MA 1992. p.226.

[238] Bancroft, Lundy. *Why Does He Do That? Inside the Minds of Angry and Controlling Men*. Berkely Books: New York, 2002. p.11.

[239] *IBID* p.153.

[240] Dugan, Meg Kennedy and Hock, Roger R. *It's My Life Now: Starting Over After an Abusive Relationship or Domestic Violence*. Routledge, New York, 2006. p.15.

[241] Bancroft, Lundy. *Why Does He Do That? Inside the Minds of Angry and Controlling Men*. Berkely Books: New York, 2002. p.221.

[242] Herman, Judith M.D. *Trauma & Recovery: The Aftermath of Violence- From Domestic Abuse to Political Terror*. Basic Books, New York, NY. 1992. p.78.

[243] *IBID* p.92.

[244] Dugan, Meg Kennedy and Hock, Roger R. *It's My Life Now: Starting Over After an Abusive Relationship or Domestic Violence*. Routledge, New York, 2006. p.15.

[245] Walker, Lenore E. *The Battered Woman*. Harper & Row Publishers, New York, 1979. p.43.

[246] *IBID* p.52.

[247] Weitzman, Susan, Ph.D. *Not to People Like Us: Hidden Abuse in Upscale Marriages*. Basic books: New York, 2000. p.15.

CHAPTER 9

[248] Dugan, Meg Kennedy and Hock, Roger R. *It's My Life Now: Starting Over After an Abusive Relationship or Domestic Violence*. Routledge, New York, 2006. p.14.

REFERENCES

[249] De Becker, Gavin. *The Gift of Fear: and Other Survival Signals that Protect us from Violence.* Dell Publishing, New York, 1997. P.46.
[250] Evans, Patricia. *The Verbally Abusive Relationship: How to Recognize It and How to Respond.* Media, Avon, MA 1992. p.48.
[251] *IBID* p.153.
[252] Bancroft, Lundy. *Why Does He Do That? Inside the Minds of Angry and Controlling Men.* Berkely Books: New York, 2002. p.59-60.
[253] *IBID* p.60.
[254] Evans, Patricia. *The Verbally Abusive Relationship: How to Recognize It and How to Respond.* Media, Avon, MA 1992. p.133.
[255] Weitzman, Susan, Ph.D. *Not to People Like Us: Hidden Abuse in Upscale Marriages.* Basic books: New York, 2000. p.118.
[256] Lissette, Andrea & Kraus, Richard. *Free Yourself From an Abusive Relationship: 7 Steps to Taking Back Your Life.* Hunter House Publishers, Alameda, CA 2000. p.209.
[257] Dugan, Meg Kennedy and Hock, Roger R. *It's My Life Now: Starting Over After an Abusive Relationship or Domestic Violence.* Routledge, New York, 2006. p.53.
[258] Wilson, James L. *Adrenal Fatigue: the Twenty-First Century Stress Syndrome.* Smart Publications, Petaluma, CA 2001. P.27-44
[259] Dugan, Meg Kennedy and Hock, Roger R. *It's My Life Now: Starting Over After an Abusive Relationship or Domestic Violence.* Routledge, New York, 2006. p.32-33.
[260] Walker, Lenore E. *The Battered Woman.* Harper & Row Publishers, New York, 1979. p.106.
[261] http://en.wikipedia.org/wiki/PTSD
[262] Bancroft, Lundy. *Why Does He Do That? Inside the Minds of Angry and Controlling Men.* Berkely Books: New York, 2002. p.296
[263] Walker, Lenore E. *The Battered Woman.* Harper & Row Publishers, New York, 1979. p.74.
[264] *The Merck Manual of Medical Information.* Pocket Books, New York, New York, 1997. p.430.
[265] http://en.wikipedia.org/wiki/PTSD
[266] *The Merck Manual of Medical Information.* Pocket Books, New York, New York, 1997. p.438.
[267] *IBID* p.432-433.
[268] *IBID* p.447.
[269] Patricia Tjaden and Nancy Thoennes, *Costs of Intimate Partner Violence Against Women in the U.S.* 2003. Centers for Disease Control and Prevention, National Centers for Injury Prevention and Control, Atlanta, Ga.
[270] Housekamp, B.M., Foy, D. *The Assessment of Posttraumatic Stress Disorder in Battered Women.* Journal of Interpersonal Violence. 1991; 6(3).
[271] Gelles, R.J., Harrop, J.W. *Violence, Battering, and Psychological Distress Among Women.* Journal of Interpersonal Violence. 1989; 4(1).
[272] Housekamp, B.M., Foy, D,. The Assessment of Posttraumatic Stress Disorder in Battered Women. Journal of Interpersonal Violence. 1991; 6(3).
[273] Bancroft, Lundy. *Why Does He Do That? Inside the Minds of Angry and Controlling Men.* Berkely Books: New York, 2002. p.7.
[274] Herman, Judith M.D. *Trauma & Recovery: The Aftermath of Violence- From Domestic Abuse to Political Terror.* Basic Books, New York, NY. 1992. p.86.
[275] *IBID* p.49.
[276] Bancroft, Lundy. *Why Does He Do That? Inside the Minds of Angry and Controlling Men.* Berkely Books: New York, 2002. p.46.
[277] Dugan, Meg Kennedy and Hock, Roger R. *It's My Life Now: Starting Over After an Abusive Relationship or Domestic Violence.* Routledge, New York, 2006. p.54.

CHAPTER 10
[278] Weitzman, Susan, Ph.D. *Not to People Like Us: Hidden Abuse in Upscale Marriages.* Basic books: New York, 2000. p.101.
[279] *IBID* p.47.
[280] *IBID* p.18.
[281] Dugan, Meg Kennedy and Hock, Roger R. *It's My Life Now: Starting Over After an Abusive Relationship or Domestic Violence.* Routledge, New York, 2006. p.14.
[282] Weitzman, Susan, Ph.D. *Not to People Like Us: Hidden Abuse in Upscale Marriages.* Basic books: New York, 2000. p.193.
[283] Bancroft, Lundy. *Why Does He Do That? Inside the Minds of Angry and Controlling Men* Berkely Books: New York, 2002. p.9.
[284] Weitzman, Susan, Ph.D. *Not to People Like Us: Hidden Abuse in Upscale Marriages.* Basic books: New York, 2000. p.60.

285 *IBID* p.96.
286 Walker, Lenore E. *The Battered Woman*. Harper & Row Publishers, New York, 1979. p.33.
287 Jayne, Pamela. *Ditch That Jerk: Dealing with Men Who Control and Hurt Women*. Hunter House, Alameda, CA, 2000. p.193.
288 Dugan, Meg Kennedy and Hock, Roger R. *It's My Life Now: Starting Over After an Abusive Relationship or Domestic Violence*. Routledge, New York, 2006. p.67.
289 Weitzman, Susan, Ph.D. *Not to People Like Us: Hidden Abuse in Upscale Marriages*. Basic books: New York, 2000. p.101.
290 *IBID* p.15.
291 *IBID* p.27.
292 *IBID* p.154.
293 *IBID* p.27.
294 *IBID* p.99.
295 *IBID* p.27.
296 *IBID* p.30.
297 Bancroft, Lundy. *Why Does He Do That? Inside the Minds of Angry and Controlling Men*. Berkely Books: New York, 2002. p.161.
298 Weitzman, Susan, Ph.D. *Not to People Like Us: Hidden Abuse in Upscale Marriages*. Basic books: New York, 2000. p.26.
299 Jayne, Pamela. *Ditch That Jerk: Dealing with Men Who Control and Hurt Women*. Hunter House, Alameda, CA, 2000. P.96.
300 Dugan, Meg Kennedy and Hock, Roger R. *It's My Life Now: Starting Over After an Abusive Relationship or Domestic Violence*. Routledge, New York, 2006. p. 3, 63, 21, 193, 157, 97, 203, 85, 213.

CHAPTER 11
301 Weitzman, Susan, Ph.D. *Not to People Like Us: Hidden Abuse in Upscale Marriages*. Basic books: New York, 2000. p.19.
302 *IBID* p.95.
303 Walker, Lenore E. *The Battered Woman*. Harper & Row Publishers, New York, 1979. p.43.
304 McGee, Susan. "20 Reasons Why She Stays: A Guide for Those Who Want to Help Battered Women." 1995-2009. p.16.
305 de Becker, Gavin. *The Gift of Fear: and Other Survival Signals that Protect us from Violence*. Dell Publishing, New York, 1997. p.214.
306 *IBID* p.216.
307 Weitzman, Susan, Ph.D. *Not to People Like Us: Hidden Abuse in Upscale Marriages*. Basic books: New York, 2000. p.79.
308 Bancroft, Lundy. *Why Does He Do That? Inside the Minds of Angry and Controlling Men*. Berkely Books: New York, 2002. p.272.
309 Dugan, Meg Kennedy and Hock, Roger R. *It's My Life Now: Starting Over After an Abusive Relationship or Domestic Violence*. Routledge, New York, 2006. p.161-162.
310 Betancourt, Marian. *What to Do When Love Turns Violent: A Practical Resource for Women in Abusive Relationships*. Harper Collins, New York, 1997. P.211.
311 Walker, Lenore E. *The Battered Woman*. Harper & Row Publishers, New York, 1979. p.182.
312 Evans, Patricia. *The Verbally Abusive Relationship: How to Recognize It and How to Respond*. Media, Avon, MA 1992. p.110-112.   verified
313 Bancroft, Lundy. *Why Does He Do That? Inside the Minds of Angry and Controlling Men*. Berkely Books: New York, 2002. p.219.
314 Klaus, Patsy and Michael Rand, "Special Report: Family Violence,: Bureau of Justice Report 1992.
315 Dugan, Meg Kennedy and Hock, Roger R. *It's My Life Now: Starting Over After an Abusive Relationship or Domestic Violence*. Routledge, New York, 2006. p.22.
316 *IBID* p.22.
317 Weitzman, Susan, Ph.D. *Not to People Like Us: Hidden Abuse in Upscale Marriages*. Basic books: New York, 2000. p.111.

CHAPTER 12
318 Jayne, Pamela. *Ditch that Jerk: Dealing with Men Who Control and Hurt Women*. Hunter House, Alameda, CA, 2000. p.156.
319 *IBID* p.155.
320 http://en.wikipedia.org/wiki/Divorce_demography and also http://nitawriter.worldpress.com/2007/04/04/divorce-rates-of-the-world/

REFERENCES 401

[321] Jayne, Pamela. *Ditch that Jerk: dealing with men who control and hurt women.* Hunter House, Alameda, CA, 2000. P.96.

[322] Daswani, Kavita. T*he Village Bride of Beverly Hills.* G.P. Putnam Sons, New York, New York, 2004. p,246.

[323] *IBID* p174.

[324] Herman, Judith M.D. *Trauma & Recovery: The Aftermath of Violence- From Domestic Abuse to Political Terror.* Basic Books, New York, NY. 1992. p.8.

[325] Walker, Lenore E. *The Battered Woman.* Harper & Row Publishers, New York, 1979. p.15-16.

[326] Bancroft, Lundy. *Why Does He Do That? Inside the Minds of Angry and Controlling Men.* Berkely Books: New York, 2002. p.290.

[327] IBID p.287.

[328] Walker, Lenore E. *The Battered Woman.* Harper & Row Publishers, New York, 1979. p.53.

[329] Weitzman, Susan, Ph.D. *Not to People Like Us: Hidden Abuse in Upscale Marriages.* Basic books: New York, 2000. p.100.

[330] Walker, Lenore E. *The Battered Woman.* Harper & Row Publishers, New York, 1979. p.146.

[331] Lissette, Andrea & Kraus, Richard. *Free Yourself From an Abusive Relationship: 7 Steps to Taking Back Your Life.* Hunter House Publishers, Alameda, CA 2000. p.156.

[332] Bancroft, Lundy. *Why Does He Do That? Inside the Minds of Angry and Controlling Men.* Berkely Books: New York, 2002. p.289.

[333] *IBID* p.297.

[334] Weitzman, Susan, Ph.D. *Not to People Like Us: Hidden Abuse in Upscale Marriages.* Basic books: New York, 2000. p.144.

[335] Bancroft, Lundy. *Why Does He Do That? Inside the Minds of Angry and Controlling Men.* Berkely Books: New York, 2002. p.372.

[336] Walker, Lenore E. *The Battered Woman.* Harper & Row Publishers, New York, 1979. p.242.

[337] Weitzman, Susan, Ph.D. *Not to People Like Us: Hidden Abuse in Upscale Marriages.* Basic books: New York, 2000. p.215.

[338] Bancroft, Lundy. *Why Does He Do That? Inside the Minds of Angry and Controlling Men.* Berkely Books: New York, 2002. p.355.

[339] Jayne, Pamela. *Ditch that Jerk: Dealing with Men Who Control and Hurt Women.* Hunter House, Alameda, CA, 2000. p.154.

[340] Bancroft, Lundy. *Why Does He Do That? Inside the Minds of Angry and Controlling Men.* Berkely Books: New York, 2002. p.333.

[341] *IBID* p.388-389.

CHAPTER 13

[342] Jayne, Pamela. *Ditch that Jerk: Dealing with Men Who Control and Hurt Women.* Hunter House, Alameda, CA, 2000. p.128.

[343] Weitzman, Susan, Ph.D. *Not to People Like Us: Hidden Abuse in Upscale Marriages.* Basic books: New York, 2000. p.180.

[344] *IBID* p.199.

[345] *IBID* p.186.

[346] Walker, Lenore E. *The Battered Woman.* Harper & Row Publishers, New York, 1979. p.230.

[347] Bancroft, Lundy. *Why Does He Do That? Inside the Minds of Angry and Controlling Men.* Berkely Books: New York, 2002. p.353.

[348] Evans, Patricia. *The Verbally Abusive Relationship: How to Recognize It and How to Respond.* Media, Avon, MA 1992. p.209.

[349] Bancroft, Lundy. *Why Does He Do That? Inside the Minds of Angry and Controlling Men.* Berkely Books: New York, 2002. p.352.

[350] Walker, Lenore E. *The Battered Woman.* Harper & Row Publishers, New York, 1979. p.227.

[351] Jacobson, Neil and Gottmann, John. *When Men Batter Women: New Insights into Ending Abusive Relationships.* Simon & Schuster, New York, 1998. p.227.

[352] Lissette, Andrea & Kraus, Richard. *Free Yourself From an Abusive Relationship: 7 Steps to Taking Back Your Life.* Hunter House Publishers, Alameda, CA 2000. p.225.

[353] *IBID* p.226.

[354] Weitzman, Susan, Ph.D. *Not to People Like Us: Hidden Abuse in Upscale Marriages.* Basic books: New York, 2000. p.207.

[355] Rodriguez, M., Bauer, H., McLoughlin, E., Grumbach, K. 1999. "Screening and Intervention for Intimate Partner Abuse: Practices and Attitudes of Primary Care Physicians." *The Journal of the American Medical Association.* 282(5).

[356] Dasgupta, Shamita Das. *Body Evidence: Intimate Violence Against South Asian Women in America.* Rutgers University Press, New Brunswick, NJ, 2007. p.146.

[357] Walker, Lenore E. *The Battered Woman.* Harper & Row Publishers, New York, 1979. p.212.
[358] *IBID* p.212.
[359] *IBID* p.26.
[360] Weitzman, Susan, Ph.D. *Not to People Like Us: Hidden Abuse in Upscale Marriages.* Basic books: New York, 2000. p.208.
[361] *IBID* p.8.
[362] Walker, Lenore E. *The Battered Woman.* Harper & Row Publishers, New York, 1979. p.208.
[363] National Center on Women & Family Law, Battered Women: The Facts, 1996.
[364] Walker, Lenore E. *The Battered Woman.* Harper & Row Publishers, New York, 1979. p.209.
[365] Betancourt, Marian. *What to Do When Love Turns Violent: A Practical Resource for Women in Abusive Relationships.* Harper Collins, New York, 1997. p.38.
[366] Bancroft, Lundy. *Why Does He Do That? Inside the Minds of Angry and Controlling Men.* Berkely Books: New York, 2002. p.311.
[367] *IBID* p.313.
[368] Tjaden, Patricia & Thoennes, Nancy. National Institute of Justice and the Centers of Disease Control and Prevention, *Extent, Nature and Consequences of Intimate Partner Violence*: Findings from the National Violence Against Women Survey. 2000.
[369] de Becker, Gavin. *The Gift of Fear: and Other Survival Signals that Protect us from Violence.* Dell Publishing, New York, 1997. p.231.
[370] Bancroft, Lundy. *Why Does He Do That? Inside the Minds of Angry and Controlling Men.* Berkely Books: New York, 2002. p.310.
[371] de Becker, Gavin. *The Gift of Fear: and Other Survival Signals that Protect us from Violence.* Dell Publishing, New York, 1997. p.227.
[372] *IBID* p.229.
[373] *IBID* p.226.
[374] *IBID* p.229.
[375] Bancroft, Lundy. *Why Does He Do That? Inside the Minds of Angry and Controlling Men.* Berkely Books: New York, 2002. p.303.
[376] Tjaden, Patricia & Thoennes, Nancy. National Institute of Justice and the Centers of Disease Control and Prevention, *Extent, Nature and Consequences of Intimate Partner Violence*: Findings from the National Violence Against Women Survey. 2000.
[377] Bancroft, Lundy. *Why Does He Do That? Inside the Minds of Angry and Controlling Men.* Berkely Books: New York, 2002. p.295-296.
[378] Walker, Lenore E. *The Battered Woman.* Harper & Row Publishers, New York, 1979. p.216.
[379] Bancroft, Lundy. *Why Does He Do That? Inside the Minds of Angry and Controlling Men.* Berkely Books: New York, 2002. p.313.
[380] Walker, Lenore E. *The Battered Woman.* Harper & Row Publishers, New York, 1979. p.206.
[381] Jacobson, Neil and Gottmann, John. *When Men Batter Women: New Insights into Ending Abusive Relationships.* Simon & Schuster, New York, 1998. p.215-216.
[382] McGee, Susan. *20 Reasons Why She Stays: A Guide for Those Who Want to Help Battered Women.* 1995-2007. p.17. found on www.ncadv.org
[383] http://shop.ncadv.org/inc/sdetail/119
[384] de Becker, Gavin. *The Gift of Fear: and Other Survival Signals that Protect us from Violence.* Dell Publishing, New York, 1997. p.217-219.
[385] Betancourt, Marian. *What to Do When Love Turns Violent: A Practical Resource for Women in Abusive Relationships.* Harper Collins, New York, 1997. p.126.
[386] Walker, Lenore E. *The Battered Woman.* Harper & Row Publishers, New York, 1979. p.199.
[387] *IBID* p.189.
[388] Campbell, JC, PhD, RN, FAAN. Anna D. Wolf, Johns Hopkins University School of Nursing, *Protective Action and Re-assaul*t: Findings from the RAVE study.

CHAPTER 14
[389] Goodman, Lisa & Epstein, Deborah. *Listening to Battered Woman: A Survivor-Centered Approach to Advocacy, Mental Health, and Justice.* American Psychology Association, 2008 (From Family Justice Center Domestic Violence Training Notes 2010.)
[390] www.*harborhousefl.com* (From Family Justice Center Domestic Violence Training Notes 2010.)
[391] de Becker, Gavin. *The Gift of Fear: and Other Survival Signals that Protect us from Violence.* Dell Publishing, New York, 1997. p.231.
[392] Catalano, S., Smith, E., Snyder, H., Rand, M. 2009. Female Victims of Violence. U.S. Department of Justice.
[393] Bancroft, Lundy. *Why Does He Do That? Inside the Minds of Angry and Controlling Men.* Berkely Books: New York, 2002. p.7.

[394] (From Family Justice Center Domestic Violence Training Notes 2010.)
[395] Bancroft, Lundy. *Why Does He Do That? Inside the Minds of Angry and Controlling Men.* Berkely Books: New York, 2002. p.158.
[396] de Becker, Gavin. *The Gift of Fear: and Other Survival Signals that Protect us from Violence.* Dell Publishing, New York, 1997. p.30.
[397] www.dangerassessment.org (From Family Justice Center Domestic Violence Training Notes 2010.)
[398] Dugan, Meg Kennedy and Hock, Roger R. *It's My Life Now: Starting Over After an Abusive Relationship or Domestic Violence.* Routledge, New York, 2006. p.22.
[399] Bancroft, Lundy. *Why Does He Do That? Inside the Minds of Angry and Controlling Men.* Berkely Books: New York, 2002. p.228-229./ Weitzman, Susan, Ph.D. *Not to People Like Us: Hidden Abuse in Upscale Marriages.* Basic books: New York, 2000. p.125.
[400] Herman, Judith M.D. *Trauma & Recovery: The Aftermath of Violence- From Domestic Abuse to Political Terror.* Basic Books, city, year. p.160.
[401] Whitfield, CL, Anda RF, Dube SR, Felitte VJ. 2003. *Violent Childhood Experiences and the Risk of Intimate Partner Violence in Adults: Assessment in a Large Health Maintenance Organization.* Journal of Interpersonal Violence. 18(2): 166-185.
[402] *Behind Closed Doors: The Impact of Domestic Violence on Children.* 2006. The United Nations Children's Fund (UNICEF), Available at http://www.unicef.org.nz/advocacy/publications/UNICEF_Body_Shop_Behind_Closed_Doors.pdf
[403] http://bjs.ojp.usdoj.gov/index.cfm?ty=tp&tid=315
[404] Betancourt, Marian. *What to Do When Love Turns Violent: A Practical Resource for Women in Abusive Relationships.* Harper Collins, New York, 1997. p.171.
[405] Source: Mid-Peninsula Support Network for Battered Women National Woman Abuse Prevention Project Hershey, Report to Eastern Psychological Association San Francisco Family Violence Project Dr. Richard Gelles California Alliance Against Domestic Violence
[406] Dugan, Meg Kennedy and Hock, Roger R. *It's My Life Now: Starting Over After an Abusive Relationship or Domestic Violence.* Routledge, New York, 2006. p.128.
[407] www.safefromthestart.org (From Family Justice Center Domestic Violence Training Notes 2010.)
[408] Straus, M., Gelles, R., and Smith, C. *Physical Violence in American Families; Risk Factors and Adaptations to Violence* in 8,145 Families. New Brunswick: Transaction Publishers. 1990. (From Family Justice Center Domestic Violence Training Notes 2010.)
[409] American Psychological Association, *Violence and the Family*: Report of the American Psychological Association Presidential Task Force on Violence and the Family (Washington D.C.: American Psychological Association, 1996), p.80.
[410] Weitzman, Susan, Ph.D. *Not to People Like Us: Hidden Abuse in Upscale Marriages.* Basic books: New York, 2000. p.173.

CHAPTER 15
[411] *Addressing Domestic Violence: A Corporate Response.* Roper Starch Worldwide. New York, NY. 1994.
[412] *Costs of Intimate Partner Violence Against Women in the United States.* 2003. Centers for Disease Control and Prevention, National Center for Injury Prevention and Control. Retrieved January 9, 2004 from http://www.cdc.gov/ncipc/pub-res/ipv_cost/IPVBook-Final-Feb18.pdf.
[413] Max, W, Rice, DP, Finkelstein, E, Bardwell, R, Leadbetter, S. 2004. *The Economic Toll of Intimate Partner Violence Against Women in the United States.* Violence and Victims, 19(3) 259-272.
[414] Governor's Task Force on Family Violence, 1991.
[415] *Costs of Intimate Partner Violence Against Women in the U.S.* 2003. Centers for Disease Control and Prevention, National Centers for Injury Prevention and Control, Atlanta, GA.
[416] Betancourt, Marian. *What to Do When Love Turns Violent: A Practical Resource for Women in Abusive Relationships.* Harper Collins, New York, 1997. p.154.
[417] Bancroft, Lundy. *Why Does He Do That? Inside the Minds of Angry and Controlling Men.* Berkely Books: New York, 2002. p.295.
[418] Evans, Patricia. *The Verbally Abusive Relationship: How to Recognize It and How to Respond.* Media, Avon, MA 1992. p.120.
[419] *IBID* p.60.
[420] *IBID* p.16.
[421] Jayne, Pamela. *Ditch that Jerk: Dealing with Men Who Control and Hurt Women.* Hunter House, Alameda, CA, 2000. p.75.
[422] *IBID*. p.198.
[423] Weitzman, Susan, Ph.D. *Not to People Like Us: Hidden Abuse in Upscale Marriages.* Basic books: New York, 2000. p.186.

[424] Hotchkiss, Sandy. *Why Is It Always About You? Saving Yourself from the Narcissists in your Life.* Free Press, New York, NY. 2002. p.78, 100, 143

[425] Bancroft, Lundy. *Why Does He Do That? Inside the Minds of Angry and Controlling Men.* Berkely Books: New York, 2002. p.151.

[426] Dugan, Meg Kennedy and Hock, Roger R. *It's My Life Now: Starting Over After an Abusive Relationship or Domestic Violence.* Routledge, New York, 2006. p.199.

[427] *IBID* p.196.

[428] Evans, Patricia. *The Verbally Abusive Relationship: How to Recognize It and How to Respond.* Media, Avon, MA 1992. p.132.

[429] Dugan, Meg Kennedy and Hock, Roger R. *It's My Life Now: Starting Over After an Abusive Relationship or Domestic Violence.* Routledge, New York, 2006. p.198.

[430] Bancroft, Lundy. *Why Does He Do That? Inside the Minds of Angry and Controlling Men.* Berkely Books: New York, 2002. p.279.

[431] Weitzman, Susan, Ph.D. *Not to People Like Us: Hidden Abuse in Upscale Marriages.* Basic books: New York, 2000. p.187.

[432] de Becker, Gavin. *The Gift of Fear: and Other Survival Signals that Protect us from Violence.* Dell Publishing, New York, 1997. p.216.

[433] Weitzman, Susan, Ph.D. *Not to People Like Us: Hidden Abuse in Upscale Marriages.* Basic books: New York, 2000. p.35.

[434] *IBID* p.114.

[435] *IBID* p.113.

[436] de Becker, Gavin. *The Gift of Fear: and Other Survival Signals that Protect us from Violence.* Dell Publishing, New York, 1997. p.147.

[437] Lissette, Andrea & Kraus, Richard. *Free Yourself From an Abusive Relationship: 7 Steps to Taking Back Your Life.* Hunter House Publishers, Alameda, CA 2000. p.63.

[438] Walker, Lenore E. *The Battered Woman.* Harper & Row Publishers, New York, 1979. p.56.

[439] de Becker, Gavin. *The Gift of Fear: and Other Survival Signals that Protect us from Violence.* Dell Publishing, New York, 1997. p.246.

[440] Bancroft, Lundy. *Why Does He Do That? Inside the Minds of Angry and Controlling Men.* Berkely Books: New York, 2002. p.223.

[441] Dugan, Meg Kennedy and Hock, Roger R. *It's My Life Now: Starting Over After an Abusive Relationship or Domestic Violence.*, New York, 2006. p.92.

[442] Jayne, Pamela. *Ditch that Jerk: Dealing with Men Who Control and Hurt Women.* Hunter House, Alameda, CA, 2000. p.56.

[443] de Becker, Gavin. *The Gift of Fear: and Other Survival Signals that Protect us from Violence.* Dell Publishing, New York, 1997. p.196.

[444] *IBID* p.230.

[445] Weitzman, Susan, Ph.D. *Not to People Like Us: Hidden Abuse in Upscale Marriages.* Basic books: New York, 2000. p.103.

[446] Evans, Patricia. *The Verbally Abusive Relationship: How to Recognize It and How to Respond.* Media, Avon, MA 1992. p.120.

[447] Weitzman, Susan, Ph.D. *Not to People Like Us: Hidden Abuse in Upscale Marriages.* Basic books: New York, 2000. p.197-198.

[448] Evans, Patricia. *The Verbally Abusive Relationship: How to Recognize It and How to Respond.* Media, Avon, MA 1992. p.134.

[449] Forward, Susan Ph.D. with Donna Frazier. *Emotional Blackmail: When the People in Your Life Use Fear, Obligation and Guilt to Manipulate You.* Harper Collins Publishers, New York, NY, 1997. p.128.

[450] Bancroft, Lundy. *Why Does He Do That? Inside the Minds of Angry and Controlling Men.* Berkely Books: New York, 2002. p.215.

[451] Hotchkiss, Sandy. *Why Is It Always About You? Saving Yourself from the Narcissists in your Life.* Free Press, New York, NY. 2002. *p.*78.

CHAPTER 16

[452] Dugan, Meg Kennedy and Hock, Roger R. *It's My Life Now: Starting Over After an Abusive Relationship or Domestic Violence.* Routledge, New York, 2006. p.68.

[453] Weitzman, Susan, Ph.D. *Not to People Like Us: Hidden Abuse in Upscale Marriages.* Basic books: New York, 2000. p.13.

[454] Evans, Patricia. *The Verbally Abusive Relationship: How to Recognize It and How to Respond.* Media, Avon, MA 1992. p.149.

[455] *IBID* p.127.

REFERENCES

[456] Dugan, Meg Kennedy and Hock, Roger R. *It's My Life Now: Starting Over After an Abusive Relationship or Domestic Violence.* Routledge, New York, 2006. p.149.
[457] Herman, Judith M.D. *Trauma & Recovery: The Aftermath of Violence- From Domestic Abuse to Political Terror.* Basic Books, New York, NY. 1992. p.197.
[458] *IBID* p.133.
[459] *IBID* p.73.
[460] *IBID* p.209.

APPENDIX 1

[461] Kapoor, Sushma. Domestic Violence Against Women and Girls. UNICEF: Innocenti Research Centre. June, 2000.
[462] *United Nations Development Fund for Women. 2003. Not A Minute More: Ending Violence Against Women.* Available at http://www.unifem.org/resources/item_detail.php?ProductID=7.
[463] García-Moreno et al. 2005. *WHO Multi-country Study on Women's Health and Domestic Violence Against Women.* World Health Organization. Available at http://www.who.int/gender/violence/who_multicountry_study/en
[464] *Adverse Health Conditions and Health Risk Behaviors Associated with Intimate Partner Violence, Morbidity and Mortality Weekly Report.* February 2008. Centers for Disease Control and Prevention. Available at http://www.cdc.gov/mmwr/preview/mmwrhtml/mm5705a1.htm.
[465] Murray Straus, Richard J. Gelles, and Suzanne K. Steinmetz's. Behind Closed Doors: Violence in the American Family. (From Family Justice Center Domestic Violence Training Notes 2010.)
[466] Allstate Foundation National Poll on Domestic Violence, 2006. Lieberman Research Inc., Tracking Survey conducted for The Advertising Council and the Family Violence Prevention Fund, July–October 1996.
[467] *National Crime Victimization Survey: Criminal Victimization, 2007. 2008.* U.S. Department of Justice, Bureau of Justice Statistics. Available at http://www.ojp.usdoj.gov/bjs/pub/pdf/cv07.pdf.
[468] Bureau of Justice Statistics Crime Data Brief, Intimate Partner Violence, 1993-2001, February 2003.
[469] Lawrence A. Greenfeld et al. (1998). Violence by Intimates: Analysis of Data on Crimes by Current or Former Spouses, Boyfriends, and Girlfriends. Bureau of Justice Statistics Factbook. Washington DC: U.S. Department of Justice. NCJ #167237. Available from National Criminal Justice Reference Service.
[470] *Family Violence Statistics: Including Statistics on Strangers and Acquaintances. 2005.* U.S. Department of Justice, Bureau of Justice Statistics. Available at http://www.ojp.usdoj.gov/bjs/pub/pdf/fvs.pdf.
[471] Callie Marie Rennison (2001*). Intimate Partner Violence and Age of Victim, 1993-1999.* Bureau of Justice Statistics Special Report. Washington DC: U.S. Department of Justice. NCJ #187635.
[472] Catalano, Shannan. 2007. *Intimate Partner Violence in the United States.* U.S. Department of Justice, Bureau of Justice Statistics. Available at http://www.ojp.usdoj.gov/bjs/intimate/ipv.htm.
[473] *National Crime Victimization Survey: Criminal Victimization, 2007. 2008.* U.S. Department of Justice, Bureau of Justice Statistics. Available at http://www.ojp.usdoj.gov/bjs/pub/pdf/cv07.pdf.
[474] Baum, Katrina, Catalano, Shannan, Rand, Michael and Rose, Kristina. 2009. *Stalking Victimization in the United States.* U.S. Department of Justice Bureau of Justice Statistics Available at http://www.ojp.usdoj.gov/bjs/pub/pdf/svus.pdf.
[475] Department of Justice. *Intimate Partner Violence and Age of Victim*, 1993-99.
[476] Bureau of Justice Statistics, *Intimate Partner Violence in the U.S.* 1993-2004, 2006.
[477] Bureau of Justice Statistics, *Intimate Partner Violence in the U.S.* 1993-2004, 2006.
[478] Bureau of Justice Statistics, *Violence Against Women: Estimates from the Redesigned Survey*, August 1995.
[479] Department of Justice. *Intimate Partner Violence and Age of Victim*, 1993-99.
[480] http://bjs.ojp.usdoj.gov/index
[481] Bureau of Justice Statistics, *Intimate Partner Violence in the U.S.* 1993-2004, 2006.
[482] Dutton, Mary; Leslye Orloff, and Giselle Aguilar Hass. "Characteristics of Help-Seeking Behaviors, Resources, and Services Needs of Battered Immigrant Latinas: Legal and Policy Implications." *Georgetown Journal on Poverty Law and Policy.* 2000: 7(2).
[483] Orloff, Leslye and Janice V. Kaguyutan. "Offering a Helping Hand: Legal Protections for Battered Immigrant Women: A History of Legislative Responses." *Journal of Gender, Social Policy, and the Law.* 2002. 10(1): 95-183.
[484] Orloff et al., 1995. "With No Place to Turn: Improving Advocacy for Battered Immigrant Women." *Family Law Quarterly.* 29(2):313.
[485] Orloff et al., 1995. "With No Place to Turn: Improving Advocacy for Battered Immigrant Women." *Family Law Quarterly.* 29(2):313.

[486] Dutton, Mary; Leslye Orloff, and Giselle Aguilar Hass. "Characteristics of Help-Seeking Behaviors, Resources, and Services Needs of Battered Immigrant Latinas: Legal and Policy Implications." *Georgetown Journal on Poverty Law and Policy*. 2000: 7(2).

[487] Femicide in New York City: 1995-2002. New York City Department of Health and Mental Hygeine, October 2004. http://www.ci.nyc.ny.us/html/doh/html/public/press04/pr145-1022.html

[488] Dutton, Mary; Leslye Orloff, and Giselle Aguilar Hass. "Characteristics of Help-Seeking Behaviors, Resources, and Services Needs of Battered Immigrant Latinas: Legal and Policy Implications." *Georgetown Journal on Poverty Law and Policy*. 2000: 7(2).

[489] Tjaden, Patricia and Nancy Thoennes. 2000. *Extent, Nature and Consequences of Violence Against Women: Findings from the National Violence Against Women Survey*. The National Institute of Justice and the Centers for Disease Control and Prevention. Retrieved January 9, 2004. http://www.ncjrs.org/pdffiles1/nij/183781.pdf.

[490] http://domesticviolencestatistics.org/domestic-violence-statistics/ from the Commonwealth Fund in July, 1993.

[491] Catalano, Shannan. 2007. *Intimate Partner Violence in the United States*. U.S. Department of Justice, Bureau of Justice Statistics. Available at http://www.ojp.usdoj.gov/bjs/intimate/ipv.htm.

[492] Lissette, Andrea & Kraus, Richard. *Free yourself from an abusive relationship: 7 steps to taking back your life*. Hunter House Publishers, Alameda, CA 2000. p.65.

[493] Betancourt, Marian. *What to do when love turns violent: a practical resource for women in abusive relationships*. Harper Collins, New York, 1997. p.19.

[494] U.S. Department of Justice, *Violence by Intimates: Analysis of Data on Crimes by Current or Former Spouses, Boyfriends, and Girlfriends*, March 1998. The Commonwealth Fund, Health Concerns Across a Woman's Lifespan: 1998 Survey of Women's Health, 1999.

[495] U. S. Department of Justice, Bureau of Justice Statistics, *Violence by Intimates*. Available at http://bjs.ojp.usdoj.gov/index.com

[496] Walker, Lenore E. *The Battered Woman*. Harper & Row Publishers, New York, 1979. P.151

[497] From Family Justice Center Domestic Violence Training Notes 2010.

[498] From Family Justice Center Domestic Violence Training Notes 2010.

[499] Bureau of Justice Statistics, *Intimate Partner Violence in the U.S.* 1993-2004, 2006.

[500] Department of Justice. *Intimate Partner Violence and Age of Victim Report*. 1993-99.

[501] Weitzman, Susan, Ph.D. *Not to people like us: Hidden abuse in upscale marriages*. Basic books: New York, 2000. p.111.

[502] Lissette, Andrea & Kraus, Richard. *Free yourself from an abusive relationship: 7 steps to taking back your life*. Hunter House Publishers, Alameda, CA 2000. p.72.

[503] Dugan, Meg Kennedy and Hock, Roger R. *It's my life now: Starting over after an abusive relationship or domestic violence*. Routledge, New York, 2006. p.22.

[504] Dugan, Meg Kennedy and Hock, Roger R. *It's my life now: Starting over after an abusive relationship or domestic violence*. Routledge, New York, 2006. p.22.

[505] Weitzman, Susan, Ph.D. *Not to people like us: Hidden abuse in upscale marriages*. Basic books: New York, 2000. p.111.

[506] Catalano, S., Smith, E., Snyder, H., Rand, M. 2009. Female Victims of Violence. U.S. Department of Justice.

[507] Weitzman, Susan, Ph.D. *Not to people like us: Hidden abuse in upscale marriages*. Basic books: New York, 2000. p.111.

[508] Bancroft, Lundy. *Why does he do that? Inside the minds of angry and controlling men*. Berkely Books: New York, 2002. p.7.

[509] Gavin de Becker. *The Gift of Fear: and Other Survival Signals that Protect us from Violence*. Dell Publishing, New York, 1997. P.26.

[510] Bureau of Justice Statistics, *Intimate Partner Violence in the U.S.* 1993-2004, 2006.

[511] Bureau of Justice Statistics, *Intimate Partner Violence in the U.S.* 1993-2004, 2006.

[512] Chang J, Berg C, Saltzman L, Herndon J. 2005. Homicide: A Leading Cause of Injury Deaths Among Pregnant and Postpartum Women in the United States, 1991-1999. *American Journal of Public Health*. 95(3): 471-477.

[513] Jacobson, Neil and Gottmann, John. *When men batter women: New insights into ending abusive relationships*. Simon & Schuster, New York, 1998. p.215-216.

[514] National Crime Victimization Survey, 1992-96; *Study of Injured Victims of Violence*, 1994.

[515] *Adverse Health Conditions and Health Risk Behaviors Associated with Intimate Partner Violence, Morbidity and Mortality Weekly Report*. February 2008. Centers for Disease Control and Prevention. Available at www.cdc.gov/mmwr/preview/mmwrhtml/mm5705a1.htm.

[516] Rennison, CM, Welchans, S., Intimate Partner Violence. Bureau of Justice Statistics. 2002.

[517] Lissette, Andrea & Kraus, Richard. *Free yourself from an abusive relationship: 7 steps to taking back your life*. Hunter House Publishers, Alameda, CA 2000. p.33.

REFERENCES 407

[518] Rand, Michael R. 1997. *Violence-related Injuries Treated in Hospital Emergency Departments*. U.S. Department of Justice, Bureau of Justice Statistics. Washington, DC.

[519] National Coalition Against Domestic Violence

[520] Berios, D.C. and Grady, D. Domestic Violence: Risk Factors and Outcome. The Western Journal of Medicine. 1991; 155(2): August 1991.

[521] Arias I, Corso P. 2005. Average Cost Per Person Victimized by an Intimate Partner of the Opposite Gender: a Comparison of Men and Women. *Violence and Victims*, 20(4):379-91.

[522] Patricia Tjaden and Nancy Thoennes, *Costs of Intimate Partner Violence Against Women in the U.S.* 2003. Centers for Disease Control and Prevention, National Centers for Injury Prevention and Control, Atlanta. Ga.

[523] Housekamp, B.M., Foy, D,. The Assessment of Posttraumatic Stress Disorder in Battered Women. Journal of Interpersonal Violence. 1991; 6(3).

[524] Gelles, R.J., Harrop, J.W., "Violence, Battering, and Psychological Distress Among Women. Journal of Interpersonal Violence. 1989; 4(1).

[525] Housekamp, B.M., Foy, D,. The Assessment of Posttraumatic Stress Disorder in Battered Women. Journal of Interpersonal Violence. 1991; 6(3).

[526] Dienemann J. Boyle E, Baker D, Resnick W, Wiederhorn N, Campbell J. Intimate Partner Abuse Among Women Diagnosed with Depression. Issues in Mental Health Nursing. 2000; 21(5):499-513.

[527] Danielson, K., Moffit, T., Capsi, A., and Silva, P. Comorbidity Between Abuse of an Adult and DSM-III-R Mental Disorders: Evidence From an Epidemiological Study. American Journal of Psychiatry. January 1998; 155(1).

[528] Stark, E. Flitcraft, A. Killing the Beast Within: Woman Battering and Female Suicidality. International Journal of Health Sciences. 1995; 25(1).

[529] Bancroft, Lundy. *Why does he do that? Inside the minds of angry and controlling men*. Berkely Books: New York, 2002. p.7.

[530] Whitfield, CL, Anda RF, Dube SR, Felittle VJ. 2003. *Violent Childhood Experiences and the Risk of Intimate Partner Violence in Adults: Assessment in a Large Health Maintenance Organization*. Journal of Interpersonal Violence. 18(2): 166-185.

[531] Behind Closed Doors: The Impact of Domestic Violence on Children. 2006. The United Nations Children's Fund (UNICEF), Available at http://www.unicef.org.nz/advocacy/publications/UNICEF_Body_Shop_Behind_Closed_Doors.pdf

[532] Catalano, Shannan. 2007. *Intimate Partner Violence in the United States*. U.S. Department of Justice, Bureau of Justice Statistics. Available at http://www.ojp.usdoj.gov/bjs/intimate/ipv.htm.

[533] http://bjs.ojp.usdoj.gov/index.cfm?ty=tp&tid=315

[534] Betancourt, Marian. *What to do when love turns violent: a practical resource for women in abusive relationships*. Harper Collins, New York, 1997. p.171.

[535] The National Network to End Domestic Violence. 2009. *Domestic Violence Counts 2008: A 24-hour Census of Domestic Violence Shelters and Services*. Available at >http://www.nnedv.org/resources/census/67-census-domestic-violence-counts/232-census2008.html.

[536] Gavin de Becker. *The Gift of Fear: and Other Survival Signals that Protect us from Violence*. Dell Publishing, New York, 1997 p.261.

[537] Source: Mid-Peninsula Support Network for Battered Women National Woman Abuse Prevention Project Hershey, Report to Eastern Psychological Association San Francisco Family Violence Project Dr. Richard Gelles California Alliance Against Domestic Violence

[538] *A Nation's Shame: Fatal Child Abuse and Neglect in the United States: Fifth Report*. 1995. U.S. Advisory Board on Child Abuse and Neglect. Department of Health and Human Services, Administration for Children and Families. Washington, DC.

[539] Dugan, Meg Kennedy and Hock, Roger R. *It's my life now: Starting over after an abusive relationship or domestic violence*. Routledge, New York, 2006. p.128.

[540] Source: Mid-Peninsula Support Network for Battered Women National Woman Abuse Prevention Project Hershey, Report to Eastern Psychological Association San Francisco Family Violence Project Dr. Richard Gelles California Alliance Against Domestic Violence

[541] Weitzman, Susan, Ph.D. *Not to people like us: Hidden abuse in upscale marriages*. Basic books: New York, 2000. p.167.

[542] U.S. Department of Justice, Bureau of Justice Statistics, *Criminal Victimization*, 2003.

[543] Betancourt, Marian. *What to do when love turns violent: a practical resource for women in abusive relationships*. Harper Collins, New York, 1997. p.19.

[544] Betancourt, Marian. *What to do when love turns violent: a practical resource for women in abusive relationships*. Harper Collins, New York, 1997. p.224.

[545] http://domesticviolencestatistics.org/domestic-violence-statistics/

[546] García-Moreno et al. 2005. *WHO Multi-country Study on Women's Health and Domestic Violence Against Women*. World Health Organization. Available at http://www.who.int/gender/violence/who_multicountry_study/en

[547] Walker, Lenore E. *The Battered Woman*. Harper & Row Publishers, New York, 1979. p.63.

[548] Bureau of Justice Statistics, *Intimate Partner Violence in the U.S.* 1993-2004, 2006.

[549] National Network to End Domestic Violence

[550] Betancourt, Marian. *What to do when love turns violent: a practical resource for women in abusive relationships*. Harper Collins, New York, 1997. From National Crime Victimization Survey.

[551] The Dorchester Community Roundtable Coordinated Community Response to Prevent Intimate Partner Violence. 2003. RMC Research Corporation. Portsmouth, New Hampshire.

[552] Caralis P, Musialowski R. 1997. "Women's Experiences with Domestic Violence and Their Attitudes and Expectations Regarding Medical Care of Abuse Victims." *South Medical Journal*. 90:1075-1080.
McCauley J, Yurk R, Jenckes M, Ford D. 1998. "Inside 'Pandora's Box': Abused Women's Experiences with Clinicians and Health Services." *Archives of Internal Medicine*. 13:549-555. Friedman L, Samet J, Roberts M, Hudlin M, Hans P. 1992. "Inquiry About Victimization Experiences: A Survey of Patient Preferences and Physician Practices." *Archives of Internal Medicine*. 152:1186-1190. Rodriguez M, Quiroga SS, Bauer H. 1996. "Breaking the Silence: Battered Women's Perspectives on Medical Care." *Archives of Family Medicine*. 5:153-158.

[553] Walker, Lenore E. *The Battered Woman*. Harper & Row Publishers, New York, 1979. p.26.

[554] Tjaden, Patricia & Thoennes, Nancy. National Institute of Justice and the Centers of Disease Control and Prevention, *Extent, Nature and Consequences of Intimate Partner Violence*: Findings from the National Violence Against Women Survey. 2000.

[555] Bureau of Justice Statistics, *Intimate Partner Violence in the U.S.* 1993-2004, 2006.

[556] Walker, Lenore E. *The Battered Woman*. Harper & Row Publishers, New York, 1979. p.212.

[557] National Center on Women & Family Law, Battered Women: The Facts, 1996.

[558] de Becker, Gavin. *The Gift of Fear: and Other Survival Signals that Protect us from Violence*. Dell Publishing, New York, 1997. p.231.

[559] Tjaden, Patricia & Thoennes, Nancy. National Institute of Justice and the Centers of Disease Control and Prevention, *Extent, Nature and Consequences of Intimate Partner Violence*: Findings from the National Violence Against Women Survey. 2000.

[560] Tjaden, Patricia & Thoennes, Nancy. National Institute of Justice and the Centers of Disease Control and Prevention, *Extent, Nature and Consequences of Intimate Partner Violence*: Findings from the National Violence Against Women Survey. 2000.

[561] Florida Governor's Task Force on Domestic and Sexual Violence, Florida Mortality Review Project, 1997.

[562] de Becker, Gavin. *The Gift of Fear: and Other Survival Signals that Protect us from Violence*. Dell Publishing, New York, 1997. p.226.

[563] de Becker, Gavin. *The Gift of Fear: and Other Survival Signals that Protect us from Violence*. Dell Publishing, New York, 1997. p.227.

[564] Weitzman, Susan, Ph.D. *Not to people like us: Hidden abuse in upscale marriages*. Basic books: New York, 2000. p.213.

APPENDIX 2

[565] Mincava electronic clearinghouse. Minnesota Center Against Violence and Abuse. "*Herstory of Domestic Violence: A Timeline of the Battered Woman's Movement*." SafeNetwork: California's Domestic Violence Resource. September 1999.

[566] *IBID*

[567] *IBID*

[568] *IBID*

[569] *IBID*

[570] *IBID*

[571] Walker, Lenore E. *The Battered Woman*. Harper & Row Publishers, New York, 1979. p.192.

[572] Mincava electronic clearinghouse. Minnesota Center Against Violence and Abuse. "*Herstory of Domestic Violence: A Timeline of the Battered Woman's Movement*." SafeNetwork: California's Domestic Violence Resource. September 1999.

[573] Walker, Lenore E. *The Battered Woman*. Harper & Row Publishers, New York, 1979. p.185.

[574] Wikipedia- 'domestic violence'

[575] Mincava electronic clearinghouse. Minnesota Center Against Violence and Abuse. "*Herstory of Domestic Violence: A Timeline of the Battered Woman's Movement*." SafeNetwork: California's Domestic Violence Resource. September 1999.

[576] *IBID*

[577] *IBID*
[578] *IBID*
[579] *IBID*
[580] *IBID*
[581] *IBID*
[582] *IBID*
[583] *IBID*
[584] *IBID*
[585] Google search 'national domestic violence history'
[586] Mincava electronic clearinghouse. Minnesota Center Against Violence and Abuse. "*Herstory of Domestic Violence: A Timeline of the Battered Woman's Movement.*" SafeNetwork: California's Domestic Violence Resource. September 1999.
[587] *IBID*
[588] *IBID*
[589] *IBID*
[590] *IBID*
[591] *IBID*
[592] Betancourt, Marian. *What to do when love turns violent: a practical resource for women in abusive relationships.* Harper Collins, New York, 1997. p.5.
[593] Mincava electronic clearinghouse. Minnesota Center Against Violence and Abuse. "*Herstory of Domestic Violence: A Timeline of the Battered Woman's Movement.*" SafeNetwork: California's Domestic Violence Resource. September 1999.
[594] Google search 'national domestic violence history'
[595] Betancourt, Marian. *What to do when love turns violent: a practical resource for women in abusive relationships.* Harper Collins, New York, 1997. p.118.
[596] Dasgupta, Shamita Das. *Body Evidence: Intimate Violence Against South Asian Women in America.* Rutgers University Press, New Brunswick, NJ, 2007. p.145.

Made in the USA
Charleston, SC
05 March 2012